The German Poetry of Paul Fleming

UNC | COLLEGE OF ARTS AND SCIENCES
Germanic and Slavic Languages and Literatures

From 1949 to 2004, UNC Press and the UNC Department of Germanic & Slavic Languages and Literatures published the UNC Studies in the Germanic Languages and Literatures series. Monographs, anthologies, and critical editions in the series covered an array of topics including medieval and modern literature, theater, linguistics, philology, onomastics, and the history of ideas. Through the generous support of the National Endowment for the Humanities and the Andrew W. Mellon Foundation, books in the series have been reissued in new paperback and open access digital editions. For a complete list of books visit www.uncpress.org.

The German Poetry of Paul Fleming
Studies in Genre and History

MARIAN R. SPERBERG-MCQUEEN

UNC Studies in the Germanic Languages and Literatures
Number 110

Copyright © 1990

This work is licensed under a Creative Commons CC BY-NC-ND license. To view a copy of the license, visit http://creativecommons.org/licenses.

Suggested citation: Sperberg-McQueen, Marian R. *The German Poetry of Paul Fleming: Studies in Genre and History.* Chapel Hill: University of North Carolina Press, 1990. DOI: https://doi.org/10.5149/9781469656830_Sperberg-McQueen

Library of Congress Cataloging-in-Publication Data
Names: Sperberg-McQueen, Marian R.
Title: The German poetry of Paul Fleming : Studies in genre and history / by Marian R. Sperberg-McQueen.
Other titles: University of North Carolina Studies in the Germanic Languages and Literatures ; no. 110.
Description: Chapel Hill : University of North Carolina Press, [1990] Series: University of North Carolina Studies in the Germanic Languages and Literatures. | Includes bibliographical references and index.
Identifiers: LCCN 89016499 | ISBN 978-1-4696-5682-3 (pbk: alk. paper) | ISBN 978-1-4696-5683-0 (ebook)
Subjects: Fleming, Paul, 1609-1640 — Criticism and interpretation.
Classification: LCC PT1726.Z5 S64 1990 | DCC 831/ .5

Marley
In memoriam

Contents

Acknowledgments — xi

Orthography and Citation Practices — xiii

Introduction — 1

1. Roots and New Beginnings: The *Arae Schönburgicae* and Fleming's Earliest Surviving German Poems (1629–1630) — 10
   - The Fleming Family and the House of Schönburg — 11
   - Fleming's Strategic Use of Models for the *Arae Schönburgicae* Cycle — 12
   - Formal Characteristics of the German Poems — 21
   - *Sonnet* and *Elegie* — 24
   - *Epigramma* and *Der klagende Bräutigam. I* — 31
   - *Der klagende Bräutigam. II* — 33
   - The *Arae Schönburgicae*, Epicedia, and the Beginnings of Fleming's Neo-Stoicism — 40
   - The Fleming Family and the House of Schönburg Again — 50

2. Politics and Poetry in Saxony: The Policies of Elector Johann Georg of Saxony and the *Schreiben vertriebener Frau Germanien* (1631) — 53
   - The Iconography of Fleming's Frau Germania and Connections to Other Irenicist Works — 64
   - Means of Persuasion Employed by Frau Germania — 67
   - Fleming's Politics, His Search for Patronage, and His Decision to Leave Germany — 72

3. Baltic Pastoral: Fleming's *Schäferei* for Reiner Brokmann (1635) — 78
   - Fleming's Journey to Reval, His Contacts There, and His Friendship with Reiner Brokmann — 80
   - Structural Correspondences between P.W.III.6 and Opitz's *Hercinie* — 83
   - The Panegyrical Poems in Fleming's and Opitz's *Schäfereien* and Fleming's Focus on Friendship — 87
   - Fleming's Realism — 92
   - Fleming's Epithalamium as a Critique of Opitz's Depiction of Love — 96

Sources and Development of Fleming's Concept
of *Treue* 109
4. Epistolae ex Persia: The Poetic Epistles Written during
the Persian Journey (1636–1638) 133
    History and Theory of the Poetic Epistle 135
    The Poetic Epistles of Martin Opitz 139
    Fleming's Poetic Epistles 141
    Nach seinem Traume an seinen vertrautesten Freund
        (P.W.IV.50) 143
    An Herrn Olearien vor Astrachan der Reußen in Nagaien
        (P.W.IV.44) 150
    An einen seiner vertrautesten Freunde auf dessen seiner
        Buhlschaft ihren Namenstag (P.W.IV.49) 158
    An Herrn Hansen Arpenbeken, vertrauten Bruders, auf
        dessen seiner Liebsten ihren Namenstag in Gilan
        begangen (P.W.IV.51) 166
    Characteristics of Fleming's Poetic Epistles 172

Epilogue 179

Notes 181

Works Cited 211

Index 229

Acknowledgments

Material from "Martin Opitz and the Tradition of the Renaissance Poetic Epistle," published in 1982 in *Daphnis*, has been revised and incorporated into two sections of chapter 4, "History and Theory of the Poetic Epistle" and "The Poetic Epistles of Martin Opitz"; it is used with the permission of the publisher. I have also drawn upon my dissertation, "Opitz, Fleming, and the German Poetic Epistle," for that chapter. Chapter 2 is a translation, revised and expanded, of "Ein Vorspiel zum Westfälischen Frieden: Paul Flemings 'Schreiben vertriebener Frau Germanien' und sein politischer Hintergrund," published in *Simpliciana* in 1985; it is used here with the kind permission of the editors and publishers.

Had I not met with the generous advice and assistance of colleagues and library staff that I did, this work would be much the poorer. A number of people have helped me in this endeavor: Diskin Clay, Lowell Edmunds, Georg Luck, and David Price advised me in the translation and interpretation of Latin and Greek texts; Joseph Dallett read and commented on the manuscript with an attentiveness to detail and to cogency of argumentation for which I am most grateful; Heinz Entner, Klaus Garber, and Anthony Harper shared with me the fruits of their own research into Leipzig poetry; Kerry Cochrane, Annette Fern, Lynn Hattendorf, Peggy Warren, and E. Paige Weston of the Reference Department and Kathy Killian of the Interlibrary Loan Department of the Library of the University of Illinois at Chicago were most helpful in answering bibliographic queries.

Especial thanks are due to three institutions: the Alexander von Humboldt Foundation, whose fellowship grant made possible a year of uninterrupted research in Germany; the Herzog August Bibliothek in Wolfenbüttel, where I worked during that year; and the University of Illinois at Chicago, whose Campus Research Board helped defray publication costs.

Lastly, I thank my parents for helping me enter the electronic age, Paul T. Roberge for his generous support, and C. M. Sperberg-McQueen, whose assistance and encouragement have been invaluable at all stages of this project.

Oak Park, March 1989

Orthography and Citation Practices

The titles Fleming gave to his books of poems are abbreviated as follows:

P.W. — *Poetische Wälder*
Ü. — *Überschriften*
O. — *Oden*
So. — *Sonnetten*
Sy. — *Sylvae*
M. — *Manes Glogeriani*
E. — *Epigrammata*

Individual poems are referred to by book title, book number, and poem number, as numbered by J. M. Lappenberg in his editions of Fleming's poems; thus, P.W.IV.1 is the first poem of the fourth book of the *Poetische Wälder*. "B." (*Beilage*) designates the sections of additional materials that Lappenberg appended to his edition of the German poems.

In spelling names of Fleming's contemporaries, I have generally used the form that appears in Lappenberg's index to his edition of Fleming. In transcribing poems from this edition, I have not taken over Lappenberg's use of spaced type, which is not textually significant but appears to have arisen in connection with the creation of his indices; I have also not reproduced spaced type or different typefaces in other sources. When citing Fleming's odes, I have restored the blank lines between the strophes that Lappenberg economically deleted. I have attempted to retain the orthography of the texts I cite, not normalizing, for example, *v* to *u* or *j* to *i*. Vowels (*ae*, *oe*) written with ligatures have, however, been resolved into their two components, and I have not distinguished between long and short *s*. I have not indicated typefaces, full caps, or line breaks in titles.

The German Poetry
of Paul Fleming

Introduction

My purpose in the following studies is to offer a picture of Paul Fleming's German poetry and, to a lesser extent, of his life, that is historically more accurate than has heretofore been available, while simultaneously drawing attention to poems and genres in his *oeuvre* that have received unduly little notice. These objectives find a twofold justification in the history of Fleming's poetic and personal reputation and in the effect that reputation has had on Fleming scholarship.

Fleming's reputation certainly needs no rescuing, for almost alone among the poets of the seventeenth century he has consistently been held in high esteem. Within a few years of his death, other poets began mentioning his name in the same breath with that of Martin Opitz, sometimes to Fleming's advantage,[1] and in 1682 Daniel Georg Morhof places him above "der Vater der deutschen Dichtung."[2] Fleming's slightly muted, but no less favorable renown during the next century or so suffered little from Goethe's dismissive remarks ("ein recht hübsches Talent, ein wenig prosaisch, bürgerlich; er kann jetzt nichts mehr helfen"),[3] and when Opitz's stock started to slip badly after Georg Gottfried Gervinus and August Heinrich Hoffmann von Fallersleben attacked his politics and patronage seeking, Fleming's rose by contrast (Gervinus: "Er ist der schönste Charakter unter all den weltlicheren Dichtern des Jahrhunderts") and has remained high to this day.[4] Fleming has appealed to a variety of interests: almost immediately following his death, composers began setting his odes to music, and several of his poems became part of the Protestant hymnal and attracted the exegetic skills of theologians; German Protestants, Saxons, and Reval Germans alike have felt him to be particularly their own.

About Martin Opitz we have few illusions; we know almost more than we care to about his politics and his love life. Fleming, by contrast, has shared with Johann Christian Günther the fortune, or misfortune, of being, in Richard Alewyn's phrase, a "Lieblingskind der Legende."[5] The legend draws upon the adventurous and romantic features of Fleming's life. The son of a Lutheran minister, he lived in Leipzig during some of the fierce battles between Protestants and Catholic Imperials in the Thirty Years' War; he participated in an extraordinarily perilous and exotic trip to Russia and Persia, was engaged successively to two sisters of a Reval family, was jilted by one, and died at the age of thirty before he could claim the other.

Despite being so well liked, Fleming and his poetry have remained imperfectly known. Of his approximately five hundred German poems, a canon of perhaps thirty at most consistently forms the basis of his representation in anthologies and provides the texts for study. A scarcity, extreme even by seventeenth-century standards, of primary documentation (correspondence to or from Fleming, records of professional life, information about his financial situation) has discouraged objective examination of his politics and his relationship to his patrons while, on the other hand, doing nothing to hinder romantic speculation about his character and affairs of the heart. Fleming's life, the subject of numerous biographies, which shade off almost imperceptibly into works of fiction, is a life known in its broad outlines, but not in detail. It has been used to illuminate his poetry which, also known but partially, has in turn been called upon to illustrate his life.[6] Part of Fleming's appeal, sometimes explicitly acknowledged, has been that he could be regarded as less a child of the seventeenth century than many other poets. He belonged to none of the poetic societies and held no positions in the bureaucracies of German princes, and, most importantly, he spent much of his productive life away from Europe and, so the theory goes, away from the pernicious influence of baroque poetic practices. Speaking of Fleming's journey to Persia, Harry Maync remarked: "So ward er, der zum Glück auch keiner der großen Literaturgesellschaften angehörte, von der unerfreulichen Dichtung seiner Zeit so gut wie völlig abgeschnitten und auf seine Individualität angewiesen"; his words echo Gervinus and Karl Goedeke and anticipate Hans Pyritz.[7]

Even the two painstaking and astute modern scholars to whom we owe the greatest debt for our knowledge and understanding of Fleming, Johannes Martin Lappenberg, editor of Fleming's poems, and Hans Pyritz, author of the most influential modern study of Fleming, have not been free of a tendency to use or, indeed, contribute to a legend of Fleming and his poetry, and have at times failed to ask whether some of their claims could be historically attested. Lappenberg perhaps unwittingly fostered the notion that Fleming gradually developed a unique personal voice that transcended his own age, under the influence of deeply felt experiences, when he chose chronology as a central organizing principle for his edition. His elucidation of Fleming's relationship to Elsabe and Anna Niehus (for our knowledge of whom Fleming's poetry is almost the sole source) similarly, and more deliberately, contributed to the image of Fleming's poetry leading up to and culminating at the end of his short life in the odes and sonnets written under the influence of two poignant love affairs.

Lappenberg's uncritical view of Fleming's character accords with Gervinus's, and the juxtaposition of unequalled *Akribie* with deep reverence for "der herrliche Paul" is at times both touching and comic, as when Lappenberg explicates Fleming's references in his poems to women encountered during the journey and insists "Der Verdacht der Hingebung an Sinnengenüsse sollte hier nicht geweckt werden."[8]

Pyritz made explicit that which was suggested by Lappenberg's chronological arrangement of the poems, that is, he explicated a development in Fleming's poetic style and voice that paralleled his life story and that culminated in poems for the Niehus sisters.[9] These late poems are beautiful, according to Pyritz, precisely because in them Fleming, influenced by the intensity of his emotional life, triumphed over and discarded the generic and stylistic shackles of Petrarchism, the pervasive Renaissance love poetry tradition. To Lappenberg's romantic version of the legend Pyritz added something approaching a heroic dimension, as he traced Fleming's breaking through to areas of poetic intensity and expression otherwise unknown in his age.

Richard Alewyn, in his generally and justly positive review of Pyritz's work—the description of European Petrarchism draws on a wide range of not easily accessible material and is extraordinarily perceptive and precise—pointed to the problematic nature of Pyritz's results. Although he had, indeed, succeeded in locating passages in Fleming's poetry that showed little or no trace of Petrarchism, Pyritz overlooked the possibility that such passages might betray not the glimmerings of a new sensibility, but rather other generic and stylistic traditions just as deeply rooted in the Renaissance as Petrarchism. Alewyn respectfully argues at the end of the review that it is only in examining the development of entire suprapersonal motif complexes and traditions of thought, such as Petrarchism or Stoicism, that the attempt to discover traces of the beginnings of *Erlebnisdichtung* might bear fruit. Seeking these traces within the works of an individual poet of the seventeenth century, whose creativity always worked within the bounds of such complexes and traditions, is doomed to failure.

Alewyn's caveat is no longer news to the present-day scholar of seventeenth-century literature. Major studies by Karl Otto Conrady, Joachim Dyck, Wilfried Barner, Wulf Segebrecht, and others have elucidated the roles of tradition and rhetoric in seventeenth-century German literature and have shown that much of interest is to be discovered when that literature is studied for its own sake and understood to the extent possible on its own terms rather than on the terms of a later epoch.[10] This historical approach has, however, made little impression on Fleming scholarship. The two German dissertations that treat a substantial part of Fleming's *oeuvre* and that are most often cited, Liselotte Supersaxo's *Die Sonette Paul Flemings: Chronologie und Entwicklung* and Eva Dürrenfeld's "Paul Fleming und Johann Christian Günther: Motive, Themen, Formen," betray in their very titles their debt to problematic notions of Lappenberg and Pyritz, and a standard, oft-reprinted literary history such as Richard Newald's *Die deutsche Literatur vom Späthumanismus zur Empfindsamkeit* bases its account of Fleming's development upon Pyritz. There have been other dissertations and a number of articles in the half century since Pyritz wrote (though by no means as many as one might expect, given Fleming's stature), but, with the exception of an all too brief study by Jörg-Ulrich Fechner, nothing approaching a general reevaluation of Fleming and his poetry in the light of Alewyn's remarks and modern scholarship on seventeenth-century literature has appeared.[11] Pyritz's study, with all its virtues and flaws, remains the standard work. Wiedemann's characterization was apt when, reviewing the reprint of Lappenberg's edition of Fleming's German poems, he referred to the "nach Pyritz ziemlich eingeschlafene Beschäftigung mit Fleming."[12]

In attempting to offer an initial corrective to the view of Fleming particularly associated with Pyritz, I chose four very different groups of works by Fleming from different periods of his life and asked what could be learned about them by investigating their genre and the historical situation in which they were written. I found that there is considerably more continuity linking Fleming's poetry to that which had been written before him than one would suspect from the many studies that seek in Fleming a premonition of the poetry of a later era. Far from struggling to overcome tradition (Pyritz's central chapter is entitled "Überwindung der Tradition"), Fleming worked within and deliberately exploited traditional genres, both German and Latin. Some of what has been heralded as thematically new and innovative actually has long roots reaching down to early phases of Fleming's own poetic activity and to the poetry of earlier ages.

The earliest of the works chosen and the subject of the first chapter is the *Arae Schönburgicae*, a bilingual cycle of funerary poems printed in 1630. The cycle exhibits a complex and rich relationship to generic models, both Latin and vernacular. Fleming imitates his central neo-Latin model for the cycle while simultaneously modifying its structure in a way that helps him legitimate including in his own cycle several German poems—the first, or very nearly the first by him that are preserved. The German poems themselves, particularly given that they were written so early in the history of the Opitzian movement, are quite remarkable for being technically nearly flawless. The praise of one in particular requires no qualification. Based upon another poet's halting attempt at the new style, Fleming's poem brilliantly surpasses the model while, again, deliberately pointing to the rise of the vernacular; the analysis of *Der klagende Bräutigam. II* indicates that there is no need to locate all of Fleming's best poetry at the end of his career.

The examination of this cycle of funerary poems leads to more general considerations of Fleming's epicedia and their themes, particularly to the appearance of neo-Stoic thought in them. Fleming's early funerary poems prove not to exhibit the neo-Stoic philosophy generally assumed to pervade his work, and point to the end of his Leipzig period (i.e., autumn 1633) as the probable beginning date of his significant adoption of neo-Stoic ideas.

The focus of the second chapter is a long heroic epistle Fleming wrote in the spring of 1631, *Schreiben vertriebener Frau Germanien an ihre Söhne oder die Churfürsten, Fürsten und Stände in Deutschlande*. It has been used as a witness to Fleming's unalloyed and partisan allegiance to the Lutheran cause in the Thirty Years' War and to his welcoming the intervention of the Swedish king Gustav Adolf into the war from the very beginning. Careful dating of the *Schreiben*, however, and an examination of the historical and political situation surrounding its composition, show that it actually documents something more complex, the Saxon attitude to the combined Protestant cause and the emperor just before hopes for concord and peace were dashed—and before Gustav Adolf came to be regarded as the savior of the Protestant cause. Fleming's sense of religious allegiance resembles Opitz's insofar as the politics of a *Landesherr* and potential patron had a tangible effect upon it.

Fleming's pastoral work based on Martin Opitz's *Schäfferey von der Nimfen Hercinie* and conceived as a wedding gift to a friend in Reval in 1635 is the subject of chapter 3. Most likely because it appears to be merely an imitation of Opitz's influential work, Fleming's has received little attention. As with the *Arae Schönburgicae*, however, the imitation is rich and dynamic, and Fleming's work proves to be a carefully constructed alternative to *Hercinie*. Much of Fleming's love poetry is appealing because it lacks a certain misogynic element latent or patent in the love poetry of many early modern authors, Opitz included. In the wedding pastoral of 1635 it is apparent both that Fleming was aware of this misogynic element, which lies just beneath the surface of *Hercinie*, and that he preferred love poetry that depicted a different relationship between the sexes, one based on equality and on reciprocal fidelity or *Treue*. *Treue* is a central concept in Pyritz's delineation of

Fleming's development, and the analysis of the pastoral of 1635 suggests a corrective to Pyritz's argument that the value of fidelity came into prominence only towards the end of Fleming's career.

Recent studies of Renaissance and baroque poetry emphasize that the Renaissance "Entdeckung des Menschen" (Jacob Burckhardt) could occur only in prose genres, verse genres being too strongly controlled by traditional forms with corresponding traditional content. The humanist verse epistle, which shares many traits with its prose counterpart, represents one of the few exceptions to this rule and provides a forum for the informal consideration of topics, including the examination of personal problems normally confined to prose. The fourth chapter focuses on the four verse epistles written during Fleming's journey to Persia; these show the poet exploiting the potential of the genre to be exploratory, personal, and confessional, and this to a far greater degree than Opitz. At the same time, it is noticeable that even and especially in this genre he never abandons—as has often been claimed—the literary and intellectual conventions of the period. Despite his geographical distance from Europe during the journey to Persia, Fleming was still steeped in European culture and intellectual and poetic traditions. One of the most remarkable characteristics of the poems turns out to be their pervasive neo-Stoicism and their affinity to the neo-Stoic *consolatio*, with its two-part structure of complaint and consolation. This consolatory structure is far more frequent in Fleming's later writings than has heretofore been recognized and offers an historical explanation for much that has been perceived ahistorically as Fleming's departure from the traditions that formed him.

My presenting the works chosen for study in chronological order might suggest that I have my own version of Fleming's development to offer, but this is not the case, or it is the case only insofar as I am attempting to show that many of Fleming's themes and characteristics were present earlier than generally realized. I have used the chronological scheme because any other seemed perversely unfriendly to those who like to use biography as a convenient mnemonic framework, and also because it created appropriate junctures where I could address questions of biography that seemed to me in need of reappraisal. Thus chapter 1 includes remarks on the Schönburg family and Fleming's still somewhat obscure relations to them, while chapter 2 offers some speculations on Saxon patronage of Fleming's work and on Fleming's reasons for leaving Leipzig and embarking on the journey. Chapters 3 and 4 include similar sections related to Fleming's participation in the voyage to Russia and Persia. I have attempted to adopt an attitude of thoroughgoing skepticism as a counteragent to the speculation and surmise that has thrived on meager documentation, and to insist upon sorting out that which can be in some way independently attested from that which cannot. Occasionally I have been able to supply overlooked evidence relating to Fleming's life or references to such in neglected secondary literature.

Some readers will miss extended discussion of Fleming's better-known poems. My not including these poems reflects a deliberate decision. Poems such as *An sich* (So.III.26), *Elsgens treues Herz* (O.V.30), *In allen meinen Taten* (O.I.4), and the *Grabschrift* (So.II.14) have become heavily freighted with interpretation linking them to the view of Fleming developed by Lappenberg and Pyritz. In attempting to interpret these poems anew, the weight of the intervening secondary literature tends to define the terms of one's argument in advance, leaving little space or energy for a fresh viewing; attempting to come to these poems free of the older readings is, even with the best will, extremely difficult. Additionally, many of the better-known poems cannot be accurately dated (attempts to do so notwithstanding), thus rendering any attempt to explore their historical and biographical context particularly risky. For these reasons I concluded that an effort to gain an historically more accurate view of Fleming's verse, one stripped of the myths behind which much of his work has become obscured, would be most successful if it involved unaccustomed avenues of approach via some of his lesser-known and less often interpreted works. It is my hope that the picture of Fleming and his work that emerges from this effort will eventually allow us to return to the better-known poems with new and clearer vision.

A few words on Lappenberg's edition of Fleming's poetry are in order. The edition has not lacked detractors. Albertus Bornemann, writing a scant two decades after Lappenberg's edition of the German poems appeared, argued that Lappenberg erred in using wherever possible the *Prodromus*, the preliminary selection of Fleming's poems first printed in 1641, rather than the *Teütsche Poemata*, the later, undated (1646) complete edition.[13] Pyritz agreed with Bornemann and characterized Lappenberg's edition as "nicht immer zuverlässig" and "textkritisch falsch fundiert" (p. 11). Liselotte Supersaxo devotes an entire chapter of her dissertation to a "schonungslose Kritik an Lappenbergs Ausgabe" (p. 202).

How serious are the accusations of this chorus? The initial answer is that we cannot yet entirely know. Bornemann's arguments—which at times consist more of heat than of light—need dispassionate reexamination and reevaluation, and at least three substantial philological works that treat Fleming's language and spelling and that were unavailable to Bornemann and Lappenberg need to be taken into account.[14] In the meantime it may be remarked that, even should Bornemann's thesis prove tenable, Lappenberg's work would not therefore be shown to be useless, for the *Prodromus* includes but fifty-six poems, while the *Teütsche Poemata* has over five hundred—that is, only about fifty-six poems are affected by Lappenberg's choice of the earlier source. Furthermore, of course, Lappenberg's critical edition supplies variant readings, so that one may choose according to one's taste. To condemn the edition as "textkritisch falsch fundiert" is to be unreasonably exacting.

Some of the vehemence of Pyritz's judgment may have arisen from the at times frustratingly labyrinthine character of Lappenberg's edition. Lappenberg originally wished to combine the German and Latin poems in a single edition, but bowed to the pressure of his publisher and public to separate them. Constant cross-referencing between the two editions is the result, sometimes made particularly difficult by his having changed his mind about the numbering system he would use for references to the German poems after the edition of the Latin poems, with all its cross-references, was completed using the earlier system. He was also obviously receiving and incorporating new material when it was impossible to include it in the body of the edition, so that much information is buried in the notes. Thus Gerhard Dünnhaupt lists in his bibliography of Fleming an imprint containing poems for the poet and rector of the Elisabeth-Gymnasium in Breslau, Elias Major, and remarks "fehlt bei Lappenberg." But in fact Lappenberg was aware of the imprint, though not in time to include it in his bibliography; it is described in the notes to Fleming's German poem (P.W.IV.7) for Major.[15] The errata list must also be consulted faithfully. Two of Supersaxo's most scathing denouncements of Lappenberg relate to his apparently inconsistent dating of an epicedium for Polycarpus Leyser (O.II.11) and a propempticon for Adam Olearius (Sy.II.12): "Wir haben damit ein Beispiel [the dating of Sy.II.12] aufgedeckt, wie Lappenberg auf Grund einer zu starren, voreiligen Interpretation zuverlässige Tatsachen, hier das überlieferte Datum in einem Einzeldruck, mißachtet und unbelegt ausschaltet" (p. 26). Lappenberg quietly corrected both printer's errors in the errata list.

Information in Lappenberg's edition is thus perhaps less easily accessible than one might wish, and even great familiarity with it may not ensure its efficient use. And yet, in this apparent weakness lies its strength: in his complex but meticulous and extensive annotation Lappenberg provided the primary resource and foundation for any historical commentary on Fleming's poems. As such, Lappenberg's edition, supplemented by information and texts that have come to light since its publication, forms the necessary starting point for the following investigations into the generic and historical contexts of Paul Fleming's poetry.[16]

1. Roots and New Beginnings: The *Arae Schönburgicae* and Fleming's Earliest Surviving German Poems (1629–1630)

In the biography he appended to his edition of Paul Fleming's German poems, Johannes Martin Lappenberg writes that "was er [Fleming] vor dem zwanzigsten Jahre [that is, prior to 1630] in deutscher Sprache gedichtet haben mag, scheint gewissenhaft zerstört zu sein."[1] Whether the destruction really was "gewissenhaft," like many questions relating to Fleming's life and work, cannot be answered authoritatively, given the paucity of relevant records. It is true that we have almost nothing in German that can be dated prior to 1630, while Fleming's earliest datable Latin poem, an epicedium (E.V.1) for Johann Hermann Schein's wife, is from 1624. But the absence of earlier German poetry could simply be an accident of textual transmission. Perhaps earlier poetry existed only in manuscript form and Fleming, for whatever reason, never had it printed. In that case, the loss of the earlier poetry would occasion no surprise: few holographs of seventeenth-century poetry have survived. Or perhaps some poems written prior to 1630 were printed, but only in ephemerally small editions. Why, in any case, would anyone take measures to ensure the survival of vernacular poetry by an as yet unknown Leipzig student? The lists Fleming made of "verlorene Gedichte" show that Fleming wrote much that has not come down to us; in addition, a note at a certain point in the manuscript of Fleming's Latin poems directs the printer to insert there various poems not actually transcribed into the manuscript, including "Varia, domi apud parentem."[2] These have not been located.

Of the German poems that did survive, it is impossible to say with certainty which are the earliest, but the most likely candidates are those included in the cycle *Arae Schönburgicae*, one of only two surviving imprints from the year 1630 with poems by Fleming.[3] The date of the occasion for the *Arae Schönburgicae*, the death of Maria Juliane von Schönburg-Waldenburg, is a matter of dispute, but may have occurred as early as 1629, and probably not later than February 1630.[4]

The only other imprint with a poem by Fleming surviving from 1630 is a funeral sermon for Johann Hermann Schein; sermon and appended epicedia would, of course, not have been written until after Schein's death on November 19 of that year. Another German poem from the same year, So.III.1, preserved only in the *Teütsche Poemata*, can be dated to June 1630 or later, as it was occasioned by a sermon that the poet and pastor Martin Rinckart delivered during centennial celebrations on June 25–27 commemorating the Augsburg Confession. Finally, two other poems by Fleming can be assigned to his very early period (there are about two hundred of Fleming's approximately five hundred German poems that cannot be dated with any certainty) and might conceivably have been written earlier than the *Arae Schönburgicae*. For one, O.IV.1, only a *terminus ad quem* can be determined; Fleming mentions Johann Seußius (secretary to the Saxon elector), who died in the spring of 1631, as still alive. The other, O.IV.2, mentions the year 1630 in its title, but cannot be dated more precisely.[5] The German poems of the *Arae Schönburgicae* are in any case certainly among the earliest of Fleming's preserved German poems and may actually be the oldest of his German poems to come down to us. They thus offer a convenient starting point for investigating the beginnings of Fleming's vernacular verse.

The Fleming Family and the House of Schönburg

The Fleming family had been closely associated with the House of Schönburg since at least the time of the grandfather for whom Paul was named. The senior Paul Fleming (d. 1603) held various administrative positions in the town of Lichtenstein, the residence and only town in the Schönburg domain of the same name, one of their most ancient.[6] The connection to the Schönburg family may go back much farther: in the twelfth century, as *Reichsministeriales* under Emperor Friedrich Barbarossa, the Schönburgs were among those charged with clearing forest from the *terra Plisnensis* (as the large east Middle German *Reichsterritorium* centered around present-day Altenburg was called) and bringing in settlers.[7] The occurrence there of such village names as "Flemmingen" suggests that some of the settlers in the newly cleared territory were from the Low Countries and prompts speculation that the poet's family might have such an origin. If so, their connection with the Schönburgs was perhaps one of long standing.[8]

To return to the immediate family: Fleming's father, Abraham (1583–

1649), like the senior Paul, lived and was employed in Schönburg lands. Destined for the ministry, he probably studied theology in Leipzig; an "Abr. Fleming" from Lichtenstein appears in the Leipzig matriculation lists for 1601.[9] Soon after Fleming's birth (1609) he was promoted from *ludi moderator* (schoolmaster) to *Hof- und Stadtdiaconus* in the town of Hartenstein, the official seat of the Schönburgs' *Grafschaft* of the same name.[10] Hartenstein had been the inheritance of Maria Juliane's father, Hugo II von Schönburg (1559–1606), and it was there that Hugo's widow, Gräfin Katharina, still resided.[11] Fleming's mother (d. 1616) served as a *Kammerjungfer* to her; the Gräfin and another member of the Schönburg family, probably her cousin by marriage, Wolf III of Schönburg-Penig, were among Paul's godparents. There is evidence to suggest that in the course of moving from one ecclesiastical post to another—Topseiffersdorf in 1615 and the more important pastorate of Wechselburg in 1628—Abraham Fleming was gradually distancing himself from the dynasty with whom his family had so long been associated, perceiving perhaps that their resources and power were gradually dwindling for a variety of reasons, and that he was instead moving closer to the more powerful ruler of Saxony.

Little is known for certain about Maria Juliane herself, not even her exact birth or death dates; that she is known at all is due mainly to Fleming's commemoration. She was probably born in 1600,[12] one of the younger of the fifteen children from Hugo von Schönburg's two marriages. When she died in 1629 or 1630 she was engaged to her second cousin, Johann Heinrich von Schönburg-Remse, the speaker in many of the poems in the *Arae Schönburgicae*.

Fleming's Strategic Use of Models for the *Arae Schönburgicae* Cycle

There can be no question that Fleming, at the time he was composing the poems in the *Arae Schönburgicae*, was familiar with Opitz's poetic precepts and practice, or that he was familiar with the poems by other poets in Julius Wilhelm Zincgref's 1624 anthology.[13] More important as models for the overall conception of the *Arae Schönburgicae*, however, were cycles of epicedia in neo-Latin by Julius Caesar Scaliger (1484–1558) and Daniel Heinsius (1580–1655). Pyritz's studies of the *Suavia*, Fleming's cycle of love poems from 1631, show Fleming to have been an avid reader and imitator of the neo-Latin love poetry issuing from Paris and Leiden in the second half of the sixteenth and early part of the seventeenth centuries.[14] Tracing the models for the *Arae Schönbur-*

gicae shows, not surprisingly, that Fleming's familiarity with these poets encompassed their work in other genres as well, although, as will be seen, the formulas and language of the amatory verse play a disproportionately large role.

The funerary poetry best known to the student of seventeenth-century German poetry is of that type whose structure and themes Hans-Henrik Krummacher illuminated in his study "Das barocke Epicedium"; that is, the single poem divided rhetorically into three parts, containing, in turn, praise, complaint, and consolation.[15] Against this background Fleming's *Arae Schönburgicae* appear at first decidedly exceptional. They are a collection of twenty-two poems, none of which exhibits the three-part structure, most consisting almost exclusively instead of lamentation, and many seeming more nearly amatory than funerary. Krummacher notes, however, that he chose to study but the most common type of funerary poetry of the seventeenth century with the most clearly marked features. "Die sonstigen Erscheinungsformen der Grabdichtung im 17. Jh.," he observes, require "einer weitausgreifenden, genaueren Untersuchung" (p. 98, n. 19). Perhaps equally fruitful would be an investigation of the other forms of funerary poetry written in neo-Latin in the preceding eras, for the humanist repertoire of themes and genres was notably reduced and standardized by the baroque, the tripartite epicedium that Krummacher studied having survived and proliferated, while other types declined into vestigial remnants. Many factors—cultural, political, intellectual—can be cited as bringing about the reduction and conventionalization of genres. Perhaps a sociological one accounts for the scarcity of funerary poem cycles like Fleming's in the German baroque: the majority of epicedia were written to be appended to funeral sermons, and space restrictions probably helped establish the convention that most persons could be represented by but a single poem, generally a short one.

While a funerary cycle such as the *Arae Schönburgicae* was exceptional in the German baroque, it was less rare in neo-Latin poetry of the late Renaissance. Julius Caesar Scaliger wrote such a cycle on the death of the Italian humanist and poet Hieronymus Fracastorius (Gerolamo Fracastoro, 1478–1553).[16] It is probable that Fleming knew this cycle and was aware of it as he composed the *Arae Schönburgicae*. The title, *Arae Fracastoreae*, may have suggested Fleming's title (*ara* "altar; monument of stone, tombstone"); titles of individual poems within Scaliger's twenty-seven-poem cycle are also echoed in Fleming's:

Scaliger no. 2: *Ad Charitas*; Fleming no. 2: *Ad Charitas*
Scaliger no. 4: *Ad Parcam*; Fleming no. 6: *Ad Mortam* (the names of the Fates are Nona, Decuma, and Morta)

Scaliger no. 5: *Ad Auroram*; Fleming no. 7: *Ad Auroram sponsus*
Scaliger no. 9: *Allocutio*; Fleming no. 16: *Alloquutio*
Scaliger no. 17: *Ad Solem*; Fleming no. 8: *Idem ad Solem*

And there are also clear verbal and thematic echoes of Scaliger's poems in Fleming's; they are not sustained but are striking enough that it seems unlikely that the similarities between the two cycles are accidental or are simply independent echoes of common sources.[17]

Even more important as models for Fleming's *Arae Schönburgicae* were cycles composed by Daniel Heinsius (who himself undoubtedly knew Scaliger's *Arae Fracastoreae*) on the deaths of three of his Leiden colleagues, Janus Dousa (Johann van der Does the Elder, 1545–1604), Justus Lipsius (1547–1606), and Joseph Justus Scaliger (1540–1609), son of Julius Caesar Scaliger. Initially published as single imprints in 1605, 1607, and 1609, respectively, the cycles appeared together in reverse chronological order in the editions of Heinsius's poems from 1610, 1613, and 1617. In the 1621 edition their appearance was essentially the same, but Greek poems in the homage to Scaliger had been removed and placed with Heinsius's other Greek poems.

The *Manes Lipsiani* and the Latin poems of the *Manes Scaligeri* are written, with one exception, in the meters most widely used in neo-Latin poetry, that is, in hexameters, elegiac distichs, hendecasyllables, and iambic lines (senarii and septenarii). *Lusus ad Apiculas*, the seventh poem in the *Manes Lipsiani*, is the exception; it also represents a departure from the generally dignified tone of the surrounding verse. Written in short lines of varying length and no set pattern, this playful poem, in which bees, "mellificae volucres," are exhorted to surround the tomb of the mellifluous Lipsius and to sting repeatedly his detractors, has been variously censured by modern critics as an infelicitous breach of decorum and praised for the sprightliness that distinguishes it from the other poems of the cycle.[18] Fleming was evidently very taken with it, for he also wrote and included as the thirteenth poem in the *Arae Schönburgicae* a *Lusus ad apiculas*, also in free verse, in which the bees, "rorilegae Cereris puellae," are admonished to take their honey to the tomb of Maria Juliane, and to offer their nectar to anyone who there sheds a tear for her; the stinging bees of Heinsius's poem, who "vndique & vndique & vndique & vndique" fly to sting the critic, in Fleming's "iterumque iterumque iterumque iterumque" fly off to gather honey and return.

Whereas *Lusus ad Apiculas* represents, both with respect to tone and form, an anomaly in Heinsius's cycles of 1607 and 1609, metrical variety and a lighter tone, sometimes including the vocabulary of amatory verse, are the rule in the earlier *Manes Dousici*, and it is this cycle that seems to have exerted the greatest influence on Fleming in shaping the *Arae Schönburgicae*. The similarities between the two cycles are striking. Both include the same number of poems: the *Manes Dousici* cycle, with twenty-two poems, is the longest of Heinsius's three cycles (the *Manes Scaligeri* cycle has fifteen and the *Manes Lipsiani* nine poems); it seems unlikely that the identical number in the *Arae Schönburgicae* is coincidental. (Fleming's cycle has, additionally, a prose epitaph, which is lacking in the cycle by Heinsius.) Both cycles are tours de force of formal variety: Heinsius uses lesser asclepiadian lines, ithyphallics, archilochius major lines, distichs composed of iambic trimeters and hendecasyllables, free verse, and other forms, in addition to the usual hexameters, senarii, elegiac distichs, and hendecasyllables: twelve different verse forms all told. Engaging in a traditional type of poetic rivalry, Fleming tops Heinsius by using fifteen forms, including two different types of free verse. Some of the distichs may be forms of his own devising; they do not, in any case, appear in the classical poets.[19] In addition to such formal similarities, there are thematic and verbal reminiscences of some of Heinsius's poems in the Fleming cycle, as well as similarities in the structure and linguistic composition of the cycles.

The verbal and thematic reminiscences initially become apparent about one-third of the way through the cycles, where in each cycle a poem in senarii entitled *Ad Solem* is situated. In both of these poems, a long list of epithets is used to invoke the sun (Heinsius's begins "AVriga lucis"; this phrase opens line 3 of Fleming's poem). In Heinsius's poem the epithets lead up to the epigrammatic closing "Cras e lacertis Tethyos tuae rursus / Redibis: at nox occupat meum solem"; Fleming's poem closes: "cras, cras redibis: at meus sol non item." Heinsius's *Ad Solem* is followed by another invocation of heavenly bodies. The course of the stars is described in *Ad Sidera* and this again leads up to the epigrammatic point based on cyclical return: there is no reason for the stars to return, for "non videbitis Dousam." Fleming's *Ad Solem* is followed also by the invocation in *Ad Lunam* of another heavenly body; it is *Ad Auroram sponsus*, however, which precedes *Ad Solem*, that is most like Heinsius's *Ad Sidera*. In it the coming of dawn is described, leading up to the closing "frustra venis: Thaumantidem numquam meam videbis."

"Thaumantis" was the name Julius Caesar Scaliger used in his love poetry to refer to his beloved; Scaliger himself—like countless neo-Latin poets—had written a poem for his beloved entitled *Ad Sidera*, and Heinsius's poem of that name was probably based on Scaliger's.[20] Scaliger also wrote an *Ad Auroram*, which opens with the same epithet as does Fleming's: "Matuta mater." The purpose of mentioning these connections is not so much to demonstrate the imitations and borrowings inevitably found in Renaissance verse, with its principle of *imitatio*, as to point out, if it is not already evident, that Heinsius and Fleming, in their poems addressed to natural elements, are resorting to the vocabulary and thematics of Renaissance love poetry. Their funerary poems to the sun, moon, and stars, are free *Kontrafakturen* of love poems such as Scaliger—and they themselves, for that matter—had written. Fleming quite explicitly acknowledges his use of this tradition when he borrows the name "Thaumantis" to refer to the deceased Maria Juliane.

There is, however, a notable difference between Heinsius's use of amatory motifs and Fleming's. Whereas Heinsius exploits the themes and language of amatory lyric in only a few of his poems lamenting Dousa, by far the majority of the poems in Fleming's cycle are of this type; indeed, it seems almost to be a cycle of lover's complaints, not an offering of mourning. The reasons for this more visible presence of love poetry in Fleming's cycle are not far to seek and concern poetic strategy and decorum. Dousa, founder of Leiden University and hero of the city, was well known to Heinsius; they were colleagues who shared interests literary, philological, religious, and political. Heinsius thus had vast amounts of material ready to hand for the fashioning of his poems, and the neo-Latin tradition of *Gelehrtendichtung* provided the vocabulary and endorsed the themes. Fleming's acquaintance with Maria Juliane, on the other hand, was of a completely different nature: they were separated by differences of class and gender, and, regardless of the extent of their personal acquaintance, there simply existed no poetic genre that would have allowed Fleming to dwell on whatever they might have had in common. In his own voice he could only praise her in rather staid language as a member of a ruling house and as a woman of virtue and beauty (which, of course, she may or may not have been). The fact that she was betrothed when she died, however, provided the possibility—of which Fleming took excellent advantage—of writing in the persona of the bereaved bridegroom. This strategy then permitted Fleming to write what were essentially love poems, and this had advantages. Love poetry is traditionally the forte of young poets, and in the baroque period it was known as a kind of training ground for *angehende Dichter*. Fleming thus followed a long-established convention, and perhaps also his natural inclination, in exhibiting a predilection for love poetry. The same predilection shows up in the *Suavia* cycle that he published in 1631, which more than the *Arae Schönburgicae* constituted his debut on the stage of the *respublica litteraria*. Amatory verse permitted the poet to show off the inventive wit treasured by neo-Latin poets: Opitz notes that poets "niemals mehr sinnreiche gedancken vnd einfälle haben/ als wann sie von jhrer Buhlschafften Himlischen schöne/ jugend/ freundligkeit/ haß vnnd gunst reden."[21] In addition to the challenge and pleasure afforded by the "gedancken vnd einfälle" that would come with composition of love poetry, the opportunity to display metrical skills doubtless also added to the charms of writing love poetry. Traditional epicedia and epitaphs were generally written in elegiac distichs, but love poetry could be clothed in more varied metrical forms. Such metrical exhibitionism is evident in the influential cycle of neo-Latin love poetry by Janus Secundus, the *Basia*, which was Fleming's model for his *Suavia* cycle.

A brief glance at the later fortunes of Heinsius's and Fleming's cycles offers further evidence that these works were considered to be part of the apprenticeship of the young poet. While the *Manes Dousici* cycle was printed, as noted above, in a section devoted to the three funeral cycles in the editions of Heinsius's poems from 1610, 1613, 1617, and 1621, it was always in last place. In the edition of 1640, edited by Heinsius's son Nicolaas, it was relegated along with much other verse composed before 1610 (but not including the cycles for Lipsius and Scaliger), to the end of the volume in a section entitled *Elegiarum Iuvenilium Reliquiae*; the other poems in the section are largely love elegies. Fleming did not include the *Arae Schönburgicae* in the manuscript of his Latin poetry prepared shortly before his death, nor are they named among the poems he asks to be included if found; they have come down to us only in the original imprint. Though possibly simply an oversight, it is also possible that the omission was intentional, that Fleming came to regard the *Arae* as essentially a youthful exercise, a prolegomenon to more serious and more polished verse—as Nicolaas, and presumably also Daniel Heinsius did the *Manes Dousici*. Heinsius printed youthful indiscretions, as many poets of the period did, under a title that at once excused them and emphasized his precocity; perhaps Fleming would have done the same with his cycle had he lived to prepare further editions of his poems.

In addition to the metrical variety that Heinsius's and Fleming's cycles share, and in addition to the amatory language they have in common, the two cycles resemble each other in their overall structures. (See below a parallel listing of the poems in the two cycles.) Heinsius's cycle opens with dedicatory poems in which he states his theme and purpose, and these introductory poems are then followed by two subcycles.[22] The eight poems of the first subcycle are lamentations addressed to the faculty of Leiden University, to the Muses (Leiden's and Dousa's), to the deceased (the two poems entitled *Threnus*), and to elements of nature; the poems to the sun and the stars mentioned above are included here. The second subcycle, initially set off from the first with a separate numbering, consists of laudatory poems in which the poet recounts Dousa's achievements and in many of which he addresses the deceased. Finally, in an epitaph, the first of three final poems that close both the second subcycle and the cycle as a whole, a passerby is apostrophized; in the next the poet narrates Dousa's apotheosis; in the last he speaks of Bertius's oration for Dousa and the difficulty of repaying Leiden's debt, political and poetic, to the deceased.

Heinsius: *Manes Dousici*

[Dedications]
 1 *Nobilissimis Clarissimis Viris Stephano Francisco Diderico Dousis. paternae virtutis haeredibus*

 2 *Ad Manes*

[First subcycle]
 3 I. *Ad Academiae Lugdunensis membra*
 4 II. *Ad Musas Lugdunenses*
 5 III. *Threnus*
 6 IV. *Ad Solem*
 7 V. *Ad Sidera*
 8 VI. *Threnus*
 9 VII. *Ad Echo Dousicam*
 10 VIII. *Ad Musas suas*

[Second subcycle]
 11 I. *Iano Dousae veritatis assertori*
 12 II. *Iano Dousae libertatis vindici*
 13 **III. Eidem de columbis, quibus in obsidione vsus est [Greek]**
 14 IV. *Eidem de ijsdem*
 15 V. *Iano Dousae Victori*
 16 VI. *Iano Dousae, viro [b]eatissimo votum pro felicitate, ad Manes eiusdem*
 17 VII. *Iano Dousae Venerum & Cupidinum sacerdoti*
 18 VIII. *Eidem*
 19 IX. *Eidem, de puro eius iambo, ex Hippo[na]cteis puris iambis*
 20 X. *Epitaphium*
 21 XI. *In harmoniam, quam paulo ante obitum audire sibi visus est Dousa*
 22 XII. *In Orationem Petri Bertij, Diuis manibus Iani Dousae SS*

Fleming: *Arae Schönburgicae*

[Dedication]
 1 **Sonnet. An das hochedle Haus Schönburg**

[First subcycle, Latin]
 2 I. *Ad Charitas*

 3 II. *Sponsus ad Sponsam*
 4 III. *Idem ad Hyemem*
 5 IV. *Ad Parcas Sponsus*
 6 V. *Ad Mortam*
 7 VI. *Ad Auroram sponsus*
 8 VII. *Idem ad Solem*
 9 VIII. *Ad Lunam*
 10 IX. *Sponsus ad Venerem*

 11 X. *Ad Violas*
 12 XI. *Sponsus ad Aedones*
 13 XII. *Lusus ad apiculas*

 14 XIII. *Ad Zephyros sponsus*
 15 XIV. *Idem ad Charontem*
 16 XV. *Alloquutio*

[Second dedication; 2nd subcycle]
 17 **I. Elegie an das traurige Hartenstein**
 18 **II. Epigramma**
 19 **III. Der klagende Bräutigam. I**

 20 **IV. Der klagende Bräutigam. II**
 21 *Epicedium*

 22 *Ad viatorem*

The *Arae Schönburgicae* have a parallel structure. Fleming's cycle also opens with a dedicatory poem that sets the theme. There then follow two subcycles. The first consists of fifteen Latin poems in which either an impersonal voice, or, as is the case in most of the poems, the poet in the voice of Maria Juliane's grieving bridegroom, addresses mythological figures, the deceased, and elements of nature. The second subcycle, considerably shorter than the first—or than either of Heinsius's, for that matter—differs from the first in that, as in Heinsius's second subcycle, elements of nature no longer function as addressees. Instead, in three of the four poems the deceased herself is apostrophized, as Dousa often is in Heinsius's second subcycle. Fleming offers an *Epicedium* to close the entire cycle and then, as in Heinsius's cycle, a passerby is apostrophized in an epitaph.

There is one further significant point of similarity between Heinsius's and Fleming's commemorations, and that is that in the second subcycle of each work the poet introduces a new language: Heinsius offers one poem in Greek, while Fleming switches from Latin to German for all four poems of the subcycle. Heinsius's inclusion of the Greek poem suggested the use of two languages within a cycle; Fleming then exploited this precedent in order to do something at once similar and more daring. There could be no objection to a poet's mixing some Greek in with his Latin if he was able—Heinsius was noted for his ability to write Greek verse well.[23] To mix German and Latin verse in the manner that Fleming does, on the other hand, was unusual.[24] Moreover, while Fleming was, on the one hand, emulating the Heinsian model and using it to legitimize his own bilingualism, he was at the same time vying with it, for his substitution of German for Greek suggested that the vernacular had or could have the same stature as the ancient language. A poet taking such a position might be expected to buttress it in some way or other, and an examination of the placement of the Latin and German poems within the cycle reveals traces of a strategy aimed at justifying the use of the vernacular.

To trace that strategy, it is necessary to look more closely at the cycle structure of the *Arae Schönburgicae*. The entire cycle opens with a dedicatory sonnet in German to the mourning House of Schönburg. The dedication is followed by the fifteen poems in Latin that constitute the first subcycle. The German poem that follows, *Elegie an das traurige Hartenstein*, closes the frame opened by the dedicatory sonnet; the poet reverts to the vernacular and again addresses a collective audience of mourners. At the same time, *Elegie* opens another frame, this one enclosing the second, shorter subcycle made up of German poems, the principal speaker in which is, again, the bridegroom. Whereas the addressee of *Sonnet* had been the ruling house, the poet speaks in *Elegie* to their subjects, the people of Hartenstein. The social hierarchy that dictates the order of the addressees—first rulers in *Sonnet* and then subjects in *Elegie*—is mirrored by the choice of languages in the two subcycles: the first and longer one in sophisticated Latin, and the second much shorter one, preceded by the address to the subjects, in the vernacular.

The positioning of the short German subcycle within the *Arae Schönburgicae*, the limited number of poems within that subcycle, and, most importantly, the linking of German to the lower rungs of the social hierarchy, thus initially suggest that the German poems occupy a subordinate position vis-à-vis the Latin. The opening and closing of the cycle, however, and above all the very presence and the technical sophistication of the German poems, relativize this appearance. *Sonnet*, which opens the entire cycle, is, significantly, not in Latin but in German: the vernacular is thus given a position of prominence from the very beginning, despite its numerical inferiority in the cycle. At the end of the cycle Fleming returns to Latin, to close the smaller cycle and simultaneously the whole *Arae*. In an epitaph, the twenty-second poem, he addresses a collective audience for a third time; this time it is posterity in the figure of the passerby, the *viator*, who is exhorted to peruse the Latin inscription of the gravestone. As the passerby is potentially of any class, the class distinctions that separated earlier addressees disappear. Simultaneously, the distinguishing mark of language is expunged: the passerby is asked to read the Latin inscription of the gravestone if he is clever in Latin; if he is not, it doesn't matter, for he can seek the "puellum," the "vernam"—this perhaps refers to a boy working in the graveyard—who will convey to him the inscription.[25] Fleming thus calls attention to language in a way that undermines the distinction of Latin as the preeminent one: either language can memorialize Maria Juliane von Schönburg-Waldenburg.

In this cycle Fleming thus called into question the traditional hierarchical preeminence of Latin, first by opening the cycle with a German and not a Latin poem and, second, through strategic interplay between the placement of poems in Latin or German and the social class of addressees. Fleming adapted his Heinsian model in such a way as to help legitimize the use of German in sophisticated circles.

It was no small thing in Leipzig in 1630 to offer German poems on an occasion such as the death of a member of the nobility. Latin was still the standard language for commemoration. Opitzian German, usually traceable to Silesian connections, had just begun to appear in collections of epicedia for important members of the Leipzig bourgeoisie with ties to the academic community, and German was otherwise still confined mainly to student songs and light pastoral love poetry such as Schein wrote.[26] The production of broadsheets using alexandrines, which would become significant in Leipzig in 1631, appears to have been minimal or nonexistent there in 1630.[27] Evidently aware that he was departing from all but the most innovative practice, Fleming carefully prepared the way for his German language debut. He did not attempt to make German stand completely on its own by offering a cycle of exclusively German poems; he also did not simply offer German translations of Latin poems, which might suggest German as a mere vehicle for understanding Latin. Instead, he embedded his German-language poems within a cycle of Latin poems; the juxtaposition enhances the status of the German, as does the fact that they are replacing a poem in Greek in the Heinsian model for the cycle. The Latin poems in the cycle are virtuoso performances; Fleming outdoes Heinsius by offering even greater metrical variety. The German poems are equally virtuoso, displaying both technical excellence and formal variety. Finally, in case there might be any lingering doubt as to the legitimacy of offering poems in German on such an occasion, Fleming carefully adapts Heinsius's cycle structure in a way that revises the linguistic hierarchy and puts German on an equal footing with Latin.

The *Arae Schönburgicae* thus constitute a significant document in the growing self-confidence of a German poet and a milestone in the long development of German as a serious literary language. In offering this bilingual cycle to the Schönburgs on a solemn occasion, Fleming deliberately and successfully sought to establish German as a language capable of commemorating major events and thus a language worthy of patronage.

Formal Characteristics of the German Poems

Although there are only five German poems in the *Arae Schönburgicae*, there is already represented in them essentially the complete, limited range of forms employed by Fleming in his short career: the sonnet, the longer and the shorter alexandrine poem, the epigram, and the ode.[28] Just as in the Latin poems of the cycle Fleming showed off his ability to write in a wide variety of forms and meters, so in the German poems he displays his skill at composing in several different forms in the as yet less highly developed vernacular medium. He was not the very first to offer a formally varied cycle in German, and in writing it he may, in fact, have been inviting comparison with the only cycle of poems in Zincgref's 1624 *Anhang*, five poems written by Caspar Kirchner on the occasion of a marriage.[29] The similarities between the two cycles are far less marked than those noted between Fleming's Latin poems and Heinsius's *Manes Dousici*, but Fleming's unmistakable borrowings from a poem by Kirchner that immediately follows the bridal cycle argues for Fleming's awareness of it. Fleming's improvements on his model, if Kirchner's cycle did indeed serve as such, include his use of the standard fourteen-line sonnet form where Kirchner had used an old-fashioned twelve, and his higher standards of decorum vis-à-vis Kirchner's bawdy humor.[30]

One formal trait in Fleming's cycle might seem uncharacteristic in light of his clear allegiance to Opitzian standards rather than the often old-fashioned standards of the "andere Poeten" in Zincgref's anthology, and that is the choice of elegiac alexandrines (alexandrines rhyming *a b a b*, *c d c d*, etc.) rather than heroic alexandrines (couplets) for *Elegie*, the longest German poem in the cycle. Elegiac alexandrines are used in only six of Fleming's extant poems (there is also a poem in *vers communs* with this rhyme scheme), and they all were written in 1630–31 or in 1636.[31] While the sparse use of the rhyme scheme is in itself not especially remarkable, Fleming's choice of funerary subject matter for his *Elegie* stands out when compared to Opitz's practice. Friedrich Beissner notes that Opitz also wrote comparatively few poems in elegiac alexandrines, and in practice essentially reserved both this rhyme pattern and the genre designation "Elegie" (which did not always coincide) for poems treating amatory topics; he probably took the restriction over in part from the poems entitled *Elegie* in his Dutch models.[32] Fleming's deviation from Opitz's practice suggests his relative neglect of Dutch-language poetry and his correspondingly greater attention to neo-Latin models, which consistently used elegiac distichs not only for love poetry, but also for epicedia and meditative poems such as poetic epistles.[33] It was not clear initially what the German version of the elegiac distich was to be, but Opitz used two separate forms, elegiac and heroic, depending on subject matter, and his example eventually prevailed. Fleming, in contrast, like Johann Rist, seems to have given consideration to using the elegiac alexandrine to represent the full range of neo-Latin elegiac distich genres, as in his use of it here for an epicedium.

Technically, the German poems in the *Arae Schönburgicae* are nearly flawless; Fleming had clearly absorbed Opitz's metrical precepts and profited from the study of his model poems. This is worth noting, for perfect mastery of mature Opitzian metrical principles could not be assumed in Leipzig in 1629 or 1630. In both occasional poetry and broadsheet verse one finds alexandrine lines that exhibit a general understanding of the line, but in which not all difficulties have been overcome. In an epicedium from 1629 by Adam Olearius for Herman Hütten (a Leipzig merchant who had given financial assistance to pupils at the Thomasschule) the opening line is above reproach: "WJe schmertzlich kömpts doch vor/ wenn Freunde wollen scheiden." But in many of the lines regular alternation of stressed and unstressed syllables is achieved only through addition of ungrammatical vowels and the use of syncope, both of which Opitz disallowed ("Von vns in ferne Landt/ odr vns gar müssen meyden"), and in all too many lines, trochees replace iambs at the caesura ("Viel nasser Augen gibts/ alles in Trawren lebt").[34] Problems are also to be found in poems in alexandrines by both Silesians and Saxons among the German epicedia appended to Johannes Höpnerus's funeral sermon for Zacharias Schürer in Leipzig in 1629.[35] Two years later, in 1631, there still appeared poems in which the poets strove without success to achieve Opitzian purity, as evident in this line: "Ein sehr heimliche klage voll bitter angst undt zähren."[36] In her examination of alexandrines in broadsheets Lang notes (p. 78) several instances of alexandrine verse from 1631 or 1632, presumably of Saxon, and perhaps Leipzig, provenance, that betray imperfect mastery of the new form.

The German poems in the *Arae Schönburgicae*, in contrast, include very few lines that could have offended the mature Opitz. The first word ("Schönburg") of *Sonnet. An das hochedle Haus Schönburg* would seem to require being read as a trochee rather than as an iamb, but this is the position in the line most amenable to such variations as reversal of stress; perhaps also the secondary accent in such compounds was stronger in seventeenth-century pronunciation than it is today.[37] There is a similar situation after the caesura in line 35 of *Elegie an das traurige Hartenstein*: "weil dieses Tyrannei endlos gar gerne währet."[38] These, however, are the only lines that might not measure up to the strictest Opitzian standards, and the problems in them are slight and few compared with those in, for example, the poems by Olearius and Ritsch cited above.[39] The beginnings of lines such as line 6 of *Sonnet* ("ich, der ich ohne dich in lauter Trauren bin"; similarly, *Elegie*, ll. 3 and 7) are difficult to read iambically, but technically such lines were correct, monosyllabic words being acceptable in either stressed or unstressed positions.

Fleming also succeeded almost entirely in meeting Opitz's demand for pure rhymes in these poems. The rhyme "Leid" : "Freud" at the end of *Elegie* is at variance with modern standards of High German, but Opitz himself pronounced most words with *eu* as *ei* and used the rhyme frequently in the 1624 *Poemata* and sporadically in the later revised editions.[40] Fleming, in whose Saxon dialect *eu* was—and still is—also pronounced as *ei*, continued to use the rhyme throughout his career. Only twice does he resort to forms that would have been perceived as unequivocally archaic or dialect by most of his Opitzian contemporaries in order to create a rhyme: in lines 13–14 of *Der klagende Bräutigam. I*, he uses "han" for "haben" to rhyme with "an," and in lines 2–3 of the next poem the rhyme "ward" : "verkahrt" appears; Fleming did not use "han" or "verkahrt" again in the extant poems.[41]

Sonnet and *Elegie*

In the dedicatory poem *Sonnet. An das hochedle Haus Schönburg*, which opens the *Arae Schönburgicae* cycle, the poet offers his work, asking rhetorically how he could possibly not mourn, when all the "Meißner Welt" is brought low by the death in the House of Schönburg. He devotes the first seven and a half lines to the general sorrow and his own. The latter he describes in terms that once again point to the young poet's being most at home in the medium of love poetry: "ich, der ich ohne dich in lauter Trauren bin / und gleichsam lebe tot" (l. 6) recalls the Petrarchan lover. The next two half lines bring the monetary metaphor often employed to describe the relationship of poet to patron in this period: "ich, den du mich vorhin / mit Gnade dir erkauft." The turning point of the poem comes, in violation of what has come to be normal sonnet structure, before the end of the octet, in the middle of this eighth line: "Drumb weil mir deine Plagen / und übergroßes Leid durch Herz und Seele geht, / wolan, so nimb von [mir], . . . / . . . die Schrift zu einem Pfande / der reinen Dankbarkeit" (ll. 8–12).[42] The poem closes with a patriotic exhortation: "Was förder dich betrifft, / so scheine, schönes Haus, dem lieben Vaterlande!" The annominatio recalls the wordplay in the opening line: "Schönburg, du schönes Haus," thus tying beginning and end together.

Underlying, and to some extent undermining, the emotional vocabulary of this sonnet is a rational argumentative structure such as often characterizes poems in alexandrines (as opposed to ode form). The hypotactic conjunctions ("indem," "darvon," "Drumb," many relative pronouns) highlight logic rather than sentiment: "All are sad; therefore I must be sad; therefore I offer you this token of my sadness." Repetitions flesh out the arguments: sometimes they amplify (e.g.: "die Schrift, die Trauerschrift," l. 12), sometimes they simply offer an alternative formulation ("ein großes Teil von deiner Schönheit fällt / und wird gerissen hin," ll. 2–3); the resulting syntax is choppy. Both argument and amplification seem to be exhausted before the end of the poem; the ending, with its prosaic "Was förder dich betrifft," introduces a new topic, uneasily tied to the rest of the poem only by the verbal reminiscences of the first line.

On the whole it cannot be said that this sonnet constitutes an auspicious beginning to Fleming's career as a German poet. *Elegie*, which opens the German subcycle, is much more impressive. Fleming structures it on the popular Italian Renaissance genre, the *paragone* or comparison, in which one exercised one's wit and command of rhetoric to argue for one of two alternatives posed, and of which there are late examples in Georg Philipp Harsdörffer's *Frauenzimmer Gesprächspiele*. As in a parlor game turned suddenly grim, Fleming poses the question "which is preferable, death or war?" and then brings to bear all his rhetorical forces on the side of war.[43] The specific case of Hartenstein, the addressee of the poem, prompts the debate and opens the poem: Was it not enough that Hartenstein should be tormented by Mars? Did fate have to send death as well? The death referred to is, of course, that of Maria Juliane. In fact, the war had not severely affected Hartenstein thus far, but the Schönburg lands had suffered from the Saxon military in 1623, and in 1628 Imperials had threatened to use violent means to bring the inhabitants back to the Catholic faith. These were no doubt unpleasant events at the time, but mild compared with sufferings of other areas, or of all of Germany in the later years of the war.[44] After the brief sketch of Hartenstein's individual situation in lines 1–8, Fleming proceeds in lines 8–24 to the more general question regarding whether war or death is to be preferred, and evidence is marshalled to demonstrate death's greater implacability. Three proofs of war's relative tractability vis-à-vis death are offered: "Mars lässet weisen sich," (l. 8); "Mars ändert seinen Rat," (l. 13); "Mars, ob er gleich will sein der stärkste Gott der Erden / . . . oft werden ihrer mehr; / der steckt ihn in den Sack, der jenes [des Todes] Herr kan werden" (ll. 17–19). The anaphoric use of the word "Mars" highlights the argumentative structure; the case for death's superiority is punctuated by nearly identical exclamations: "so bistu nicht, o Tod!" (l. 10); "O Tod, so bistu nicht!" (l. 14). There is a certain potential for monotony in the structure Fleming uses here: three comparisons of *a* to *b*, each using similar phrasing. He averts this, however, through stylistic variation. The first member of the anaphoric series ("Mars lässet weisen sich,") appears in the second half line, while the others appear in the first, and, more importantly, the third and final comparison is extended over eight lines rather than just four. It forms a climax to the argument, rather than being simply one more comparison of equal importance. Particularly effective in lending weight and insistence to this final member of the series of comparisons is the exclamation "o Tod, o starker Tod!" in line 20. The phrase "den Tod, den rauhen Tod" had appeared in the first half of line 8, just preceding the section of comparisons. There it is an accusative object that has been delayed until the end of a relatively long sentence, and when it finally appears it carries a sense of finality—and indeed, it brings to a close the first subsection of the poem. In the second appearance of the phrase there is a distinct verbal reminiscence of the first, but also a verbal variation ("stark" for "rauh") and, more importantly, a variation of tone. It is here an exclamation and an apostrophe introducing a despairing, rhetorical question posed to death: "o Tod, o starker Tod! wes ist, wes ist das Heer, / wer ist, wer ist der Herr, der dich mög' überwinden?" The repetitions and annominatio underscore the urgency of the question.

The evidence demonstrating war to be the lesser of two evils having been presented, the poet turns in the second part of the poem—its forty-eight lines are divided precisely in half—to Hartenstein and asks which of the two, war or death, seems preferable. The poet applauds the unhesitating choice of war, "Er war gar leicht zu wählen" (l. 29). He now concedes that at times one is tempted to prefer death as a release from the tyranny of war (a consolatory argument frequently used in epicedia) but—and he again addresses Hartenstein—such a choice would be out of the question here because of the "Liebe, die du trägst zu deiner Obrigkeit" (l. 38). The argument has returned from the general back to the specific case of Hartenstein, and to the general arguments favoring war over death is now added the love of subjects for their rulers: Mars has never caused Hartenstein as much pain as has irrevocable Death in killing the daughter of the ruling house.

In the final four lines of the poem Fleming comes to speak of his own sadness: he, too, must mourn Hartenstein's double burden of war and death, and this despite the distance—Fleming had for some years been in Leipzig, first at school and now at university. The closing lines, like those of the sonnet, open out on the future, this time in a manner better integrated into the mood and content of the poem: Fleming asks despairingly when Hartenstein's sorrow will ever give way to joy.

In *Elegie* we find Fleming capable of writing a highly structured and tightly argued poem that, if anything, errs on the side of density rather than the prolixity to which baroque poetry in alexandrines was susceptible. The conspicuous logic and hypotactic syntax that seemed distracting and unmotivated in *Sonnet* find their more appropriate use in the rhetorical argument on which *Elegie* is based. It is notable that Fleming in this earliest extant example of his efforts at sustained alexandrines already avoids the rhythmic monotony latent in the line. This he achieves in part by avoiding the parallel structures and wording in adjacent lines that weakened a good deal of Opitz's early verse.[45] He also avoids consistent coincidence of verse units and syntactic units. The end of line 8, for example, forms a natural boundary at the end of a quatrain, but the sentence begun at the caesura continues beyond it; this restless enjambment reflects the intensity of the grim argument. Fleming's frequent use of hypotaxis with subordinate clauses starting at points other than the beginning of the line or the caesura tends to counteract the natural rhythm of the alexandrine (for example, ll. 3 and 7). Fleming uses a relatively high number of monosyllables in the first halves of lines, while producing correspondingly fewer first half lines beginning with a monosyllable and two trochaic disyllabic words, the use of which in much of Opitz's verse tends to set up a strong rhythm too early in the line. These two prosodic characteristics help bring about a generally more flexible line. Combined with the syntactical factors, they allow Fleming to fend off that singsong rhythm to which much of Opitz's verse is prey if not read with considerable good will. Fleming's lines here are not sweet or flowing; they tend instead to abruptness and, as in *Sonnet*, choppiness, but in *Elegie* these characteristics suit the subject matter and rhetoric employed.

The argument of *Elegie an das traurige Hartenstein*, that war is preferable to death, is uncharacteristic of Fleming: one of the most frequent consolatory arguments that he uses in his epicedia is that death is a release from war. Fleming's argument in *Elegie* was probably chosen in part out of deference to the deceased's social class. That the death of a member of the nobility was a far greater loss than the death of a subject or a burgher was a given; Fleming's argument that it was so great a loss that war would have been preferable to it is flattering hyperbole. It is not, however, an argument he uses in late 1631 when commemorating Maria Juliane's second cousins, August Siegfried and Elisabeth (O.II.1 and 2),[46] and it is possible that the first direct experience of war in the autumn of that year rendered it unpalatable.

But while this particular consolatory argument does not become a standard part of Fleming's repertoire, the subject of war itself does, and to this extent *Elegie* is indeed characteristic of Fleming's poetry, epicedia and other genres alike.[47] While he was still in Leipzig, war formed the background to congratulatory poems such as *Auf Herrn Johan Michels sein Doctorat* (P.W.IV.8): "Was ist Gewissers doch bei diesen wilden Zeiten, / da sich die Pest der Welt, der Mars, pflegt auszubreiten / so weit die Luft umarmt was Land und Wasser heißt, / und, wie der böse Krebs, stets um sich frißt und beißt" (ll. 1–4). In a poem for Christoph Buhle about his beloved (O.IV.14), Fleming notes the couple's departure from the city—many fled the threatened siege in the autumn of 1632—and wonders:

> Schöne Stadt, ich trag' Erbarmen
> über deinen schweren Fall,
> daß dich Furcht und Tod umarmen
> hier und da und überall.
> Wenn, ach! wenn wol wirds geschehen,
> daß wir dich in Frieden sehen?
>
> (ll. 25–30)

Despite his geographical distance from the war, it continued to intrude frequently into Fleming's writing after his departure for Persia. It forms the starting point for the first German poem we have from him that is not specifically occasional, the meditative *In Groß-Neugart der Reußen, M.Dc.XXXIV"* (P.W.IV.20):

> Indessen daß der Mars bei zweimal sieben Jahren
> annoch nicht grausam satt berennt und angefahren
> mein wertes Vaterland, vor aller Länder Kron',
> itzt ihr verdammter Haß und angepfiffner Hohn,—
> er geht noch täglich fort, Gradivus, der Verheerer,
> mit seiner bösen Schaar der geizigen Verzehrer,
> . . .
>
> (ll. 1–6)

Even on the shores of the Caspian, over four years distant from Germany, Fleming still agonized over the war in one of his most moving poems:

> Zu dem erschrecken mich die oft besorgten Posten,
> was sich mein Vaterland anitzt noch lasse kosten,
> um nur verderbt zu sein; es freue sich der Pein
> und wolle noch nicht tot in seinem Tode sein.
> So große Lust ich vor mich hatte weg zu machen,
> um des Gradiven Zorn von fernen zu verlachen:
> . . . .

> so groß und größer Grauen
> befällt mich itzund nun, da ich soll näher schauen
> mein durch fünf ganze Jahr' entschlagnes Meißner-Land,
> das von der Kriegesglut zu Pulver wird verbrant.
> (P.W.IV.51, ll. 21-36)

In addition to the pervasive preoccupation with the war, there is another aspect of *Elegie* that foreshadows a characteristic trait of Fleming's poetry. Lowry Nelson noted that "a movement toward the future . . . is the commonest movement to be found in the Baroque lyric"; such movement is certainly evident at the close of both *Sonnet* ("Was förder dich betrifft") and *Elegie* ("wenn wird einmal der Gnaden-Phöbus scheinen / und einst abtauschen dir dein großes Leid mit Freud'?").[48] But also frequent in Fleming's poetry is a change of focus at the end of a poem from the "you" (that is, the addressee or subject of the poem) to either a collective "we" or "I," that is, to Fleming himself. Often the shift of focus involves a comparison or contrast and gives the poem a sense of closure. Although the first person singular is brought into *Elegie* halfway through the poem, in line 25, it is at that point entirely impersonal, simply the vehicle for putting the choice between war and death before the subjects of Hartenstein. In the last four lines, however, the reference to the geographical distance of the speaker from the mourners makes it clear that the "ich" is Fleming himself, and this brings a slightly surprising, but, to modern ears, pleasing sense of the individual, one that is lacking in the protestations of grief put forward by the "ich" of *Sonnet*.

Another early example of this type of closure occurs in the poem Fleming wrote on the death of Katharine Schürerin Götze in September 1631.[49] The first twenty-nine lines of the thirty-four-line poem depict the gorgeous splendor of the deceased's heavenly raiments, followed by the assertion that in the divine chorus she will surely be singing of "was GOtt an vns gethan / In dieser Monats frist," that is, the Protestant victory in the Battle of Breitenfeld. The closing four lines contrast her situation with that of those still living:

> Nun, einmal sind wir durch. Du aber hast stracks künnen
> Auff einmal aller Angst vnd Eitelkeit entrinnen,
> Glückseliger als wir. Wir sehen ferner zu,
> Vnd müssen furchtsam seyn. Du bist in deiner Ruh.

There is a similar closing to the poem for the brother of Katharine, Christoph Schürer (O.II.10) and also in an epithalamium (O.III.4), in which the happily married couple is contrasted in the last strophe with those still single:

> Wir, die wir noch müßig stehn,
> die wir dem gelobten Knaben
> uns noch nicht vermietet haben
> und in wüster Irre gehn,
> wündschen euch Heil und Gewinst,
> uns auch balde solchen Dienst.

The contrast between those who are, or might be fortunate, and those who are not is much grimmer, and related specifically to Fleming alone, in the closing strophe of the epicedium for Michael Thomas from November 1631, not long after the death of Fleming's friend Georg Gloger:[50]

> Vielleichte wird dein grämen
> Ab mit den Tagen nemen/
> Vnd lernen nicht mehr sey[n];
> Nur mein Harm/ mein Betrawren
> Wird ewig müssen tawren/
> Vnd keine Zeit gehn ein.

In a later poem (P.W.IV.23), written in 1634 in Moscow for Georg Wilhelm Pöhmer, who was returning to Germany, Fleming praises Pöhmer and wishes him well for sixty-six lines. He closes by contrasting Pöhmer's plans with his own:

>   Ich werde weiter müssen.
> Mein Sinn ist unvergnügt an Moskau ihren Flüssen,
> will stärker Wasser sehn, ist wie schon auf der Rha,
> in Amphitritens Schoß, der Göttin von Sala,
> und was er itzt nicht weiß. Gott gebe seinen Segen!
> Ich ziehe förder hin, Matuta, dir entgegen.
> Sei Titan mir geneigt! Ich beuge mich vor dir,
> wann du aus Thetis Schoß zu Morgen tritst herfür.

A more poignant example comes from four years later, from the closing of an epicedium for a child (O.II.17):

> Wol dir, kleiner Freund, für dich!
> Ich bin fertig dir zu folgen,
> will es Gott, noch von der Wolgen,
> die mich lange stößt von sich,
> daß die Meinen mich empfangen,
> wo sie vor mir hin sind gangen.

It is, of course, not only in the closings of his poems that Fleming refers to his own situation, be it as a resident of wretched Leipzig, a bachelor, or an eager or weary traveler. But the closings do provide something of an index for comparison: if one looks at the closing of Opitz's poems, one seldom finds similarly specific and individual self-references, and it is thus not surprising that in general, throughout his poems, we find more of a sense of Fleming as an individual than we do of Opitz in his. It is notable that this individual detail is present already in Fleming's earliest poetry—a trace of it in *Elegie*, fully developed in the ode for Michael Thomas.

Epigramma and *Der klagende Bräutigam. I*

The other poems in the German subcycle resemble the Latin poems more closely than does *Elegie*, for in them Fleming returns to the amatory language that characterizes most of the Latin poems. Of the three, the last one, *Der klagende Bräutigam. II*, is the most interesting, but some brief comments on *Epigramma* and *Der klagende Bräutigam. I* are in order first.

Epigramma carries reminiscences of several other poems. Its opening lines ("Die, die da war allhier ein Spiegel aller Tugend, / ist mit der Frülingszeit im Früling ihrer Jugend / von uns gerissen hin"), though more ornate with their vowel harmonies and annominatio, recall a brief passage from a poem by Opitz, first printed in 1622 and included in the 1624 *Poemata* (no. 40), his *Begräbnuß Gedichte. Auff den tödtlichen abgang Jhr Fürstl. Gn. Hertzog Jörg Rudolffs in Schlesien vnd zur Lignitz Ehegemahlin*, in which lines 89–91 read "Auch so, jhr wahres Bild vnd Spiegel aller Tugendt, / Hat das Verhängniß euch, noch eben in der Jugendt, / Von hinnen weggerafft." It is quite possible that the similarity of wording arose unconsciously and bears witness to how closely Fleming studied the 1624 anthology, retaining its phrases and cadences even when he did not set out to imitate them deliberately. The remainder of *Epigramma* suggests a highly condensed version of a poem by Weckherlin, *Vber den frühen Todt &c. Fräwlin Anna Augusta Margräffin zu Baden*, in the *Anhang* of Zincgref's 1624 anthology. Lappenberg noted that Fleming had translated this poem with one of the Latin poems of the *Arae Schönburgicae*, the *Alloquutio*. Both Weckherlin's poem and Fleming's *Alloquutio* consist of long lists of generally beautiful examples of mutability, which are rapidly recapitulated at the ends of the poems and offered as images for the implicitly beautiful, explicitly short-lived deceased. *Epigramma* also resembles the Weckherlin poem in listing examples of mutability, but it is at the same time more subtle. Within five lines Fleming offers four examples of mutability (spring, violets, sunshine, leaves), but he initially avoids parallelism, so that the reader only gradually realizes that this is not just a narrative of the deceased's life, but also an enumeration of emblems of brevity. By also drawing upon a metaphor used in two of the Latin poems, Fleming adds a dimension to his examples of mutability that is not present in either Weckherlin's poem or his own *Alloquutio*. In *Ad Auroram sponsus* and *Idem ad Solem*, the poet contrasts the ever-repeating cycles of nature with the noncyclical termination of human life: the dawn and the sun always return but the beloved does not. In *Epigramma*, spring, violets, sunshine, and leaves change from being signs of mutability to being signs of cyclical nature, from which the beloved is excluded: "Doch Früling, Veiligen, Schein, Blätter finden sich / mit Zeit: o welche Zeit wird wiederbringen dich?" The German poem differs from the Latin ones in that the elements of nature cited, in contrast to the dawn and sun, are not of cosmic dimensions, and the beloved, who is compared to them, seems more tender (spring) and fragile (violets), but also vital (sunshine and green leaves) because of them.

Epigramma appears anomalous in Fleming's German-language *oeuvre* if one looks for its like among the poems explicitly labelled epigrams; Fleming's collection of *Überschriften* is small and unimpressive. The reason for this probably lies in the resemblance between the epigram and the sonnet, which, similarly short, had a well-established tradition of an epigrammatic closing. It was to this form that Fleming most often turned for a German equivalent of the Latin genre, and it is among his sonnets that one finds poems constructed like *Epigramma*, with an exposition occupying a large part of the poem followed in the final lines by a summary and a new light on the problem. Fleming did not employ the rather mannered device of listing and rapid recapitulation very frequently, but he did use it in a sonnet for one of the leaders of the Persian expedition, Philipp Kruse (So.III.22), and twice in sonnets in P.W.III.6, the *Schäferei* for Reiner Brokmann.[51]

The next poem in the German subcycle, *Der klagende Bräutigam. I*, strives to express with rhetorical means the anguish of the bridegroom as he regards his deceased bride. In terms presumably borrowed from *memento mori* descriptions, the groom names parts of her body made nearly unrecognizable to him by the hand of death and, in questions made insistent by anaphora and other repetitions, asks where her former radiance is now. His description of the grief evoked in him by the sight of her entails a similar listing of parts of his own body and their pain which, like the list relating to the bride, strives for a cumulative effect: "Herzquälen, Augenangst, Hauptschmerzen, Seitenstechen" (l. 8); this list is repeated ("drumb hab ich steten Schmerzen / in Augen, in dem Häupt', in Seiten und im Herzen," ll. 11–12), and the insistence of the repetition underscores the intensity of the bridegroom's grief. A further device draws attention to the groom's sorrow: the lists in lines 8 and 12 do not offer perfect sequential correspondences as one might expect, but instead place the heart first and last, embracing the other, lesser *loci* of pain. The climax of the poem resembles the preceding *Epigramma*: the bridegroom here also wishes he could be reunited with his bride. Now, however, in his overwhelming personal grief, he desires not that she had not died, but that he might die and join her beyond the grave.

Der klagende Bräutigam. I demands considerable tolerance of the modern reader. It is hard to accept, other than intellectually, that a deliberately crafted style with many rhetorical devices can express genuine emotion, and this is precisely the premise of this poem. The circumlocutions seem especially distracting, but it is worth recalling that "Schmerzens-Töchter" was a fairly standard way of referring to tears and probably seemed less forced to Fleming's contemporaries than it does to us. Similarly, "Fenster" was a common and not particularly elevated locution for "Augen" and "das Auge bricht" an idiom for "stirbt."[52] As to the groom's "Seitenstechen," it can at least be reported that Fleming, to his credit, never refers to them again.

Der klagende Bräutigam. II

The last German poem in the *Arae Schönburgicae*, the ode entitled *Der klagende Bräutigam. II*, is much more appealing than the preceding. In his notes to the poem, Lappenberg points to Fleming's model for it, Caspar Kirchner's *Epigramma*, number 24 in the *Anhang* to Zincgref's 1624 anthology. (For ease of comparison, Kirchner's and Fleming's poems are reproduced below.) Fleming's poem does not just draw on Kirchner's poem for some of its wording and ideas, it is a contrafactum of it, that is, it uses the same meter and form as Kirchner's oddly-named *Epigramma*, as well as some of the same phrasing, while transforming it from a poem about the lover's burning heart into a poem of mourning. Fleming's retention of so much, especially formal aspects of the original poem, provides us with an unusual opportunity to compare his work with that of a highly sophisticated older contemporary and mentor of Opitz, under, as it were, controlled conditions.[53]

Kirchner	Fleming
Epigramma	*Der klagende Bräutigam. II*

PHoebus pfleget jetzt zu rennen,	Phöbus mit sehr großem Zagen,
Durch deß runden Himmels Saal,	weil die schöne Dafnis ward
Da er pfleget vberall	in den Lorberbaum verkahrt,
Den Erdboden zuverbrennen.	täte Tag und Nacht sich plagen:
Doch brennt Phoebus nicht so sehr,	doch zagt Phöbus nicht so sehr,
Weil mein Hertze brennt viel mehr.	weil ich zage noch viel mehr.
Hat doch Troja nach zehn Jahren,	Orpheus hochgerühmbter Gaben
Nicht durchs gantze Griechenland,	gosse manchen Tränenbach,
Sondern durch Ulyssis brand,	weil er (diß sein Ungemach!)
Seinen vntergang erfahren.	seine Liebste nicht kunt haben:
Doch brennt Troja nicht so sehr,	doch weint Orpheus nicht so sehr,
Weil mein Hertze brennt viel mehr.	weil ich weine noch viel mehr.
Die hochtrabenden Poeten,	Arcas seufzet über Maßen,
Setzen einen Berg genand	als er Juliana nicht
Aetna der durch seinen brand,	kont' bekommen zu Gesicht',
Die Beywohner solte Tödten.	auf die er sich ganz verlassen:
Doch brennt Aetna nicht so sehr,	doch seufzt Arcas nicht so sehr,
Weil mein Hertze brennt viel mehr.	weil ich seufze noch viel mehr.
Bleibet Phoebus gleich im rennen,	Bleibet Phöbus gleich im Zagen,
Troja gehet auff im brand,	Orpheus in dem Weinen lebt,
Aetna brennt durchs gantze Land:	Arcas in dem Seufzen schwebt:
Phoebus, Troja, Aetna, brennen	Phöbus, Orpheus, Arcas klagen
Alle drey doch nicht so sehr,	alle drei doch nicht so sehr,
Weil mein Hertze brennt viel mehr.	weil ich klage noch viel mehr.

The similarities between the two poems are, as indicated, considerable. Both use a six-line strophic form rhymed *a b b a c c* with trochaic lines of four feet, catalectic (masculine) in the *b* and *c* lines. The form, from the melody *Si c'est pour mon pucellage*, was introduced into German from the Dutch. There are five songs in *Den Bloem-Hof van de Nederlantsche Ieught* (1608 and 1610) that use it, and Heinsius used it in one of his best-known songs, his *Pastorael* in the *Nederduytsche Poemata* (1616).[54] After Opitz used it in his *COridon sprach mit Verlangen* (no. 109 in the 1624 *Poemata*), it became a favorite vehicle for pastoral plaints in German. It is quite possible that Kirchner himself brought it to the attention of Opitz and of the other new writers of German verse, for Kirchner had direct contact with Heinsius as early as 1617 when he was studying in Leiden, and Heinsius had at that time persuaded him to take writing verse in the vernacular seriously. Kirchner is in any case the only poet in the 1624 edition other than Opitz to use it.

Fleming borrowed much from Kirchner's poem in addition to its form. He uses most of the wording of the refrain; he retains "Phoebus" as one of the examples and as the opening word of the poem;

and he retains the essential structure of the argument, that is, the intensity of the speaker's emotion (or sensation) is demonstrated by describing three well-known extreme examples of the emotion, all of which the speaker's emotion is said to exceed. In particular, the use of the same opening word creates the impression that Fleming deliberately sought comparison with Kirchner's poem.[55]

One of the more obvious merits of Fleming's poem compared to Kirchner's is its greater thematic and argumentative directness. It is not until the end of the fourth line of Kirchner's poem that we discover the attribute of Phöbus that prompts his being introduced; Fleming connects Phöbus with unhappiness in the first line. Moreover, much of what Kirchner says in the first four lines does little to further his argument. Insofar as he needs examples of intense conflagration to underscore the intensity of his heart's burning, he is wasting time (or filling in metrical feet) by describing how Phöbus now customarily runs through the round dome of heaven. Fleming, in contrast, instead of marking time for any part of the four lines at his disposal, uses each line to evoke the sorrow of Phöbus. With deft compression he introduces Phöbus mourning, in two lines sketches the fate of Dafnis, and then tells of Phöbus's unceasing sorrow. Fleming's rhyme words effectively underline his tale: "Zagen" and "plagen" stand on either side of the central episode, while in the middle two lines the transformation of Dafnis from one line to the next is underscored, one might even say mimicked, by the transformation of "ward" to "verkahrt."

An essentially similar analysis can be made of the second and third strophes in the respective poems. While neither the strophe about Orpheus nor the one about Arcas achieves the same compression and density as the first, both are more focused and to the point than their counterparts in Kirchner, who in each case devotes two lines to extraneous background before mentioning the fire that destroyed Troy and that Aetna spews forth. It seems probable both that Kirchner lacked Fleming's control over his medium and that the display of learning was as important to him as exploiting the full possibilities of a form for expressing a theme.

Not only are the arguments of Fleming's individual strophes more cohesive and direct than Kirchner's, but his overall argument, as supported by his examples and their order, probably appealed more immediately and powerfully to his audience. It is not entirely clear whether anything beyond their common incendiary nature motivated Kirchner's choice of examples or their order. Assuming he wished the listener to think not simply of the sun, but also of the sun god when Phoebus is mentioned (although the actions described are more reminiscent of Phaeton), one could guess that he chose one example divine, one example human (the city of Troy), and one natural (the volcano Aetna). Perhaps the descent from celestial to earthly to subterranean fire is intended to help organize the examples. What is entirely lacking is any way in which such a progression might emphasize the climax of his argument. There is no obvious progression to greater intensity that could then be trumped by the speaker's own burning heart, and the progression divine-human-natural seems irrelevant to the point of the poem.

Fleming's choice of examples suggests that he recognized the sense behind Kirchner's progression, while also seeing that it lacked the inner coherence that would make it an integral part of the argument. In his own poem, he transforms the progression into a much more effective one. He, too, starts with a divine figure, Phoebus, and proceeds in his second example to the (legendary) human, Orpheus. By keeping the element of the male lover constant, the move down the scale from divine to human figure is clearer than it is in Kirchner's poem with its change from a single divinity to the human collective of the city. In the climax of his progression, Fleming brings yet a third plaintive lover, Arcas, the unhappy shepherd suitor of Juliana in the late sixteenth-century pastoral novel, *Les Bergeries de Juliette*, by Nicolas de Montreux.[56] The reference to Arcas provides an effective culmination to Fleming's progression. As the poem progresses from god to legendary human to human, the exemplary lovers become ever more like the reader, who is thus increasingly able to comprehend and sympathize with their grief. Simultaneously, by citing from a contemporary work, Fleming brings his series of examples closer to his audience in another way. The last example is taken not from classical literature and myth, but from a work of modern literature. Moreover, the sources written in Greek and Latin are exchanged for one written in the vernacular. The contemporary readers must have felt a pleasant shock of recognition in the third strophe of the poem, for everyone would have learned in school to identify figures from classical myth and literature, but here a poet asked that the reader recognize a figure from a contemporary work.

The readers who not only recognized the source but had also read it will have realized how very apt a choice Fleming made when seeking a climax to the examples illustrating the immensity of the bridegroom's grief. Arcas, once he has transferred his affections in Montreux's novel from Magdalis to Juliana, proceeds to repine at his unrequited love for Juliana off and on for literally thousands of pages. The coincidence of names made the choice doubly appealing: the speaker in the poem, the bridegroom Johann Heinrich, laments the loss of *his* Juliane even more than Arcas does his—no small claim.[57]

The greater coherence and effectiveness of Fleming's poem compared with his model is evident not only in the way the theme is handled, but also on the levels of sound and syntax, particularly in the way Fleming uses repetition and variation. Fleming repeats little (other than the refrain—and even that in slightly varied form) from one strophe to the next or within one strophe in the first three. It is only in reserving the first word of each strophe for the name of the lover that there is a type of repetition; the placement permits Fleming to present the person in question to the listener or reader immediately and precludes the sort of circuitous route to the name taken by Kirchner. The first four lines of Fleming's first three strophes are marked by a variety of syntax and vocabulary, making the refrain contrast that much more sharply, as it should. Kirchner, on the other hand, uses considerable verbal repetition, none of it for rhetorical effect. His use of "pfleget" twice in the first strophe adds nothing to the meaning of the strophe, and the use of the short phrase "durchs gantze" in lines 8 and 21 suggests poverty of vocabulary and not deliberate echoing. His use of "doch" twice in the second strophe weakens its intensity in the refrain. But most important, he uses "brennen" and "brand" a number of times ("brand" appears three times as a rhyme word) without allowing them to accumulate any intensity or to structure the poem as clearly as they might have. The summation in the last strophe is particularly disappointing. There he is able to connect Troy and Aetna with burning, but not Phöbus, for he has to have Phöbus "rennen" in order to avoid duplicating "brennen" in the fourth line of that strophe.

Fleming avoids the problem of meaningless repetitions—especially repetition of "brennen"—in part by using carefully chosen synonyms or near synonyms: the three mythical lovers all mourn, but Phöbus "zagt," while Orpheus "weint," and Arcas "seufzt." The first three strophes lead up to the climactic summation in the final strophe, where yet a new verb is introduced, "klagen." The progression of verbs lends weight to the last: the effect is one of the accumulation of separate, related emotions, rather than the progressively less meaningful repetition of "brennen" in the Kirchner poem. By leading up to "klagen" with the three related but distinct emotions associated with the three exemplary lovers, Fleming makes the final summarizing verb more complex. It expands to embrace all the individual forms of suffering of Phöbus, Orpheus, and Arcas. The fourth verb must also logically be associated with the fourth lover in the poem, the speaker, so that beyond experiencing all the accumulated suffering of the other three figures, he gains an added dimension, a fourth summarizing, but also superadded pain.

It is not just clarity of argument, controlled variation, and an elegant structure that make Fleming's poem more pleasing than its model. I have already mentioned the weakness of Kirchner's rhymes and pointed to the effective use of rhymes by Fleming in his first strophe. Fleming's poem also has a lightness and smoothness lacking in Kirchner's. Fleming's slightly higher number of monosyllables and disyllables as opposed to words of three and four syllables probably helps him achieve this, as does his avoidance of heavy consonant clusters such as are to be found in line 8 of Kirchner: "Nicht durchs gantze Griechenland." In general, Fleming seems to have ensured that the reader's (or singer's) mouth could move easily from word to word.

One further problem with the poem by Kirchner has to do with scansion. For the most part, Kirchner offers perfectly regular trochaic lines, but he seems to have had problems where Opitz himself also sometimes did in 1624, that is, in using three and four syllable words, especially compounds. Lines 4 ("Den Erdboden"), 13 ("Die hochtrabenden Poeten"), and 16 ("Die Beywohner") are impossible for us to read today as trochees. Although Opitz, in the 1625 edition of his poems, changed many similar places in his own poems, he did not change all of them. We must assume both that a slightly stronger secondary accent in compound words and a certain perplexity in the face of a then little understood linguistic phenomenon allowed Opitz and other poets to continue using in trochaic (or iambic) lines compounds that seem to us to demand dactylic or spondaic treatment.[58]

It is difficult to know just how much credit to give Fleming for having completely avoided this problem in *Der klagende Bräutigam. II*, but it is clear that he did. While he uses compound words, one of four syllables, he has chosen ones that fit easily into a trochaic line: "Lorberbaum" (l. 3), "hochgerühmbter" (l. 7), and "Tränenbach" (l. 8). In his choice of "hochgerühmbter" and his placement of it at the beginning of a strophe, Fleming may have been inviting comparison with Kirchner's "hochtrabenden," where the present participle precludes the easy trochaic scansion allowed by the past participle. Fleming had the advantage over Kirchner in that he could have studied Opitz's revised poems from 1625 where, as mentioned, many of the problematic lines had been revised. But it is important to remember both that Opitz did not revise all such lines, and that the problem was nowhere discussed and described. Thus Fleming's metrical success here could well be the result of his own ear and instinct.

Something that Fleming definitely could not have learned from precept is his handling of larger units of rhythm in this poem. Again, the first strophe—which seems the most successful in Fleming's poem in many ways—illustrates his skill. In the first line, Fleming, rather than setting up the insistent and untempered beat that Kirchner does, softens the trochaic rhythm of the second foot by placing a long-vowelled word that calls for some sentence stress ("sehr") in the unstressed position; as a result, the foot reads as a light spondee, bringing some variation into the line. The significant words of the line—the words that characterize Phöbus as a mourning lover—"großem Zagen," then stand out that much more in contrast when they return to the trochaic rhythm; their long vowels in the stressed syllables permit added emphasis through prolongation. There is a similar rhythm in the second line: the easily pronounced and relatively unimportant first three words quickly lead up to the word that takes the emphasis, "Dafnis." The vocalic echo (the short *a* in "Dafnis" and the long one in "Zagen" and "ward") also points up the name, just as rhyme would, but more subtly. (This *a* assonance, with slight variations, recurs in each line, lending emphasis to the significant words and tying the strophe together.) In Kirchner's second line, in contrast, there seems to be no clear signal as to stress. This is partly due to Kirchner's lack of focus; he hasn't yet in this line of the poem gotten to his topic. Even if he had, it seems doubtful whether he could have guided the reader much: is the important word in the line "runden" or "Himmels"? The unmellifluous "durch des" precludes moving quickly to the emphasized word, and one worries whether, given the *d* in "runden," there is significance to the alliteration. And what of the *r* in "rennen" and "runden"? In fact, these sounds are ornamental at best, accidental otherwise, and don't guide the reader to a particular intended sense or rhythm.

Again, in Fleming's third line there is no question as to the significant word. Here it is not just that one moves quickly past the function words "in den" and that variations on the assonance set up earlier mark the important words ("Lorberbaum," "verkahrt"); there is also a neat parallelism between lines 2 and 3 that puts the laurel where Dafnis was earlier, just before the rhyming verb. The parallelism and the rhyme move the third line quickly forward, as does the (comparative) preponderance of longer words. Fleming then is able to use the rapidity of the third line—which suggests the speed of Dafnis's transformation—as a background for the slow, preponderantly monosyllabic, fourth line, which mirrors the longevity of Phöbus's complaint, where the drawn out "Tag und Nacht" take the place, with added weight, of the "Lorberbaum" of the previous line.

Scansion in poetry of this early period does not bear too close scrutiny. Having barely gained a sense for accentuation in polysyllabic words, the poets had not yet consciously developed any principles of sentence stress or expressive meter. Nonetheless, this earliest of Fleming's odes suggests that, without necessarily being able to express it theoretically, Fleming had a better sense than some contemporaries for the use of meter to support meaning, and that was part of the reason he could surpass Kirchner. The trochaic meter may mask the subtlety of Fleming's metrics from modern readers. The modern ear, accustomed to the use of trochees in joyous contexts, may be repelled by the use of trochees in a poem that is supposed to convey mourning. Such considerations seem to color Gellinek's reaction, for example, to Opitz's trochaic *Trostlied*: "Rhythmus und Ton sind zu leicht, . . . um den Eindruck berechtigter Trauer und die Erhebung daraus zur echten Freude zu ermitteln" (p. 194). But decorum and the evocation of appropriate emotions are the responsibility of rhetoric in this period, with metrical form providing a generally neutral framework—as the popularity of *Kontrafakturen*, such as this one by Fleming, attests.

Der klagende Bräutigam. II is the high point in the German subcycle of the *Arae Schönburgicae*. Already in this very early poem, Fleming shows that "Zu Oden . . . habe ich besser Glücke als zu anderer Art Versen" (P.W.III.6, p. 93). He is able here to transform Kirchner's rather diffuse poem into one that is tightly constructed, in which each word and its position carries significance; his instinct for meter and euphony already surpass what can be explicitly learned from Opitz's rules in the *Buch von der Deutschen Poeterey*.[59] While painting an effective picture of the bridegroom's grief, which surpasses that of distant gods and heroes of the past and of the more intimately known characters of immense emotional capacity from current literature, Fleming at the same time, by insisting that the reader be acquainted with Arcas in order to comprehend the poem, skillfully incorporates an appeal for the vernacular that parallels his overall strategy in the *Arae Schönburgicae* cycle.

The *Arae Schönburgicae*, Epicedia, and the Beginnings of Fleming's Neo-Stoicism

The discussion of the *Arae Schönburgicae* opened with considerations of genre; I noted there that poems in this cycle differ markedly from the tripartite type of the epicedium that Krummacher investigated in "Das barocke Epicedium." A brief glance at some of the epicedia

Fleming wrote after the *Arae Schönburgicae* indicates that this was not an isolated occurrence. Krummacher noted that in a number of his German epicedia (P.W.II.3, 4, and 11; O.II.5–8, 12, 13, 15–17) Fleming departed from the praise-lamentation-consolation structure of the traditional epicedium by radically shortening or dispensing altogether with the *laudatio* and moving rapidly to the lamentation. In two poems (P.W.II.3 and 4) he neglects even the lamentation, so that the poems consist entirely of consolatory passages: "Bei Fleming gibt es, in Alexandrinern wie in Liedform, einerseits Stücke, die strenger . . . die Gesetze des Epicediums befolgen, andererseits aber auch solche, die reine Consolationes mit einem einleitenden Klageteil ohne jede laudatio sind" (p. 129). The two-part poems Krummacher suggests to be closely related to the neo-Stoic genre of the *consolatio*. The presence in Fleming's work of both epicedium and *consolatio*, as well as "mancherlei stoisch gefärbte Argumente" in the *consolatio*-like epicedia, he argues, "bestätigt wiederum, daß Flemings Stoizismus mehr ist als eine nur beiläufige Frucht einer allenthalben wirksamen geistigen Strömung der Zeit" (p. 130).

What is particularly interesting about the poems in the *Arae Schönburgicae*, both German and Latin, is that they depart from the usual structure of an epicedium not in the direction of the *consolatio* and Stoicism traced by Krummacher, but in the direction of pure lamentation. While a *laudatio* is often implicit in the description of the departed bride in many of the poems, consolation is entirely absent. The pervasiveness of lamentation probably arose in part from Fleming's using the persona of the bereaved bridegroom as pining lover. The influence of Fleming's models and perhaps the rank of the deceased (an abbreviated *consolatio* was sometimes considered appropriate for public figures) may also have contributed to the absence of consolatory arguments.[60] But Fleming also wrote a number of other epicedia for people closer to his own rank in which consolation is less explicably attenuated or absent. *Auf eben selbiges [Glogers Ableben] unter eines Andern Namen* (P.W.II.8), for example, is lamentation from the beginning to its last lines: "Was fangen wir nun an, was sollen wir beginnen, / wir, Deine noch wie vor, wir ewig Deine wir? / Wer aber stellt sich uns, wie du getan hast, für?" Another poem, *Auff Absterben der Edlen vnd vieltugentsamen Frawen Marthen-Elisabethen/ geborne Heroldin* offers a relentless, rhetorically powerful description of the wretchedness of earthly existence, which then contrasts with the blessedness of the deceased in heaven.[61] The juxtaposition is not explicitly presented as a consolation, and such consolation as it could have offered is overset by the closing of the poem, which consists of the widower's lamentation (based on an anagram of the deceased's name): "Am Rathe warstu reich: Am Rathe mangelts mir/ | Nun du so eilest weg. Ach Rath/ Ach bliebstu hier! | Ach Liebste/ bester Rath/ wer wird nun Rathen künnen?" In a poem (P.W.II.12) Fleming wrote for a young boy he had tutored, Hans von Löser, the adversative "aber" in the final sentence initiates an abbreviated and indirect consolation: "Dir aber, jüngrer Sohn, du einziger der Deinen, / in dem sie schauen an, nicht aber ohne Weinen, / des selgen Brudern Geist, erlängre Gott dein Ziel / und setz' an deine Zeit, was der zu frühe fiel!" This is overshadowed by the rest of the poem, which concentrates on lamentation (ll. 1–24, 40–54), with an excursus (ll. 25–40) praising the *puer senex*; the effect is that of one protracted lamentation. Fleming's poem on the death of the church official Polycarpus Leyser (O.II.11) offers anything but consolation: the poet calls to mind first the fate of the Israelites after the death of Moses, and then the fate of Leipzig after the death of the churchman Vincentius Schmuck in 1628, from which time Fleming dates the misfortunes of pestilence and war that befell the city. His cheerless conclusion from this typological prefiguration is that the death of another important church leader bodes further ill:

> Vater, euer frühes Ende
> macht, daß wir uns fürchten mehr.
> Wir verkehren Haupt und Hände
> und tun kläglich mehr als sehr,
> sehr, daß ihr uns seid entnommen
> mehr umb das, was drauf mag kommen.
>
> (ll. 79–84)

The most striking example of an epicedium that offers minimal consolation while simultaneously demonstrating Fleming's awareness of the requirements of the genre, is the previously mentioned ode that Fleming wrote for the death of Michael Thomas on November 14, 1631; it is reproduced below in its entirety:

1
SO wil denn noch kein schwitzen/
Für vnsre Fieber nützen?
Kein Bezoar seyn gut?
Kein Salben/ kein Artzneyen
5   Wil vnsrer Stadt gedeyen/
Vnd wehren dieser Glut.

2
Des faulen Herbstes Lüffte
Beäthmen sich mit Giffte/
Vnd hauchen vns jhn ein.
10   Bey wem der Zunder fänget/
Wird plötzlich so versänget/
Daß er auch todt muß seyn.

3
So manchen manchen Jungen
Hat vnlängst eingeschlungen
15   Der nimmersatte Fraß!
So manchen/ manchen Frischen
Kan nochmals Er erwischen/
Vnd strecken in das Graß.

4
Man hört die heisern Glocken
20   Zu Grabe täglich locken;
Man trägt jhr stündlich aus.
Jn Flor' vnd schwartzem Trawren/
Fast gantzen Leipzigs Mawren
Es wehklagt jedes Hauß.

5
25   Der Feind hat vns vmbschlossen/
Die Bäwe wol durchschossen/
Doch bang' vns nur gemacht.
Jetzt steht frey alles offen/
So werden wir betroffen/
30   Vnd hämisch vmbgebracht.

6
Erzürnter Gott/ halt' jnne/
Brich doch dem strengen Sinne
Mit linder Gnaden ab.
Sol den durch wildes Sterben
35   Das gantze Volck verderben/
Vnd abziehn in ein Grab.

7
Heut' ist es an dem Deinen/
Nechst traff die Reye Meinen/

>   Ach! meinen Andern Mich.
> 40   Wer weis was jnner heute
>   Vnd morgen gehn für Leute/
>   Wo Du must hin/ vnd Ich.
>
>   8
>   Dir solt' ich zwar verbieten/
>   Das vbermachte wüten
> 45   Vnd thun vmb diesen Mann.
>   Doch könt' ich andre lehren/
>   Was ich mir selbst nicht wehren
>   Vnd angebieten kan.
>
>   9
>   Vielleichte wird dein grämen
> 50   Ab mit den Tagen nemen/
>   Vnd lernen nicht mehr sey[n];
>   Nur mein Harm/ mein Betrawren
>   Wird ewig müssen tawren/
>   Vnd keine Zeit gehn ein.

Here Fleming dispenses entirely with the *laudatio* and doesn't even refer to the deceased—a jurist acquainted with the cultural and intellectual elite of Saxony survived by a wife and seven children—until the seventh strophe, where Thomas simply fills in one half of the tag "hodie tibi, cras mihi" (modified slightly to reflect Gloger's prior death, but retaining the essential message of universal vulnerability).[62] In place of praise, Fleming describes and bewails in harrowing images the fate of Leipzig, which in the autumn of 1631 had been taken by the Imperial general Count Johann Tserklaes von Tilly before being freed by the Swedish king, Gustav Adolf, and which was periodically swept by the plague; he implores God to be more merciful. In the second to last strophe, after this grim jeremiad, Fleming acknowledges his duty to insist on moderate lamentation, but also that he can hardly ask of others that which he cannot demand of himself. The poem closes with a halfhearted suggestion that the grief of those addressed might lessen with time; his own will not.

That Fleming wrote not only epicedia that conformed to the conventional tripartite type, but also ones which, as Krummacher shows, are closer to *consolationes*, and, as just outlined, ones in which *lamentatio* predominates, points firstly to his ability to offer variations within a genre that was difficult not only because it was highly conventionalized, but also because poets were called on so often for it. In reading Fleming's epicedia one encounters remarkably little repetition. There may also be a second factor, other than Fleming's gift for invention, that accounts for the mix of *consolatio*-like epicedia and ones that more closely resemble *lamentationes*. The *Arae Schönburgicae* and the five epicedia just mentioned were all written early in Fleming's short career: the *Arae Schönburgicae* are from 1629 or 1630, and the latest of the other five, O.II.11 for Polycarpus Leyser, is from January 1633.[63] This would suggest that the profound neo-Stoicism for which Fleming is known, and which Krummacher deduces from such poems as Fleming's epicedium for Barbara Kruse (P.W.II.14, written in 1634) took firm root only around the time of his departure on the journey to Persia, that is late 1633.[64] It is notable that in the face of what was apparently the most deeply felt loss of his life, the death of Gloger on October 16, 1631, Fleming decidedly did not respond with neo-Stoic fortitude. The last three strophes of his epicedium for Michael Thomas, in which Fleming describes his own disproportionate grief, which he cannot restrain or control, are witness to this. Fleming's extraordinary reference to his own loss in that epicedium, whose very presence constitutes a breach of decorum, is repeated in a number of other poems from the period. The sonnet for the octogenarian Gedeon Hanemann (d. October 25, 1631) was written even closer to the date of Gloger's death than the one for Michael Thomas. In it Fleming's grief at his own loss serves as a foil for the traditional argument that it is good to die at the end of a productive life, but simultaneously overshadows the occasion of the poem, the death of an old man:

> DJch/ Vater/ klaget man/ daß/ da dich nun vmbhangen
> Der greisen zeiten Schnee; da dich geehrt gemacht
> Dein dickbejahrtes Häupt/ vnd in die Weisen bracht/
> Du außgetreten bist/ vnd hin zu vielen gangen;
>   Jch wein' vmb einen Freund/ den auff hat können fangen
> Der vnbedachte Todt in rother Jugend tracht/
> Da seiner Ehren Schmuck in voller Rose lacht/
> Eh' er die reiffe Blüt in gantzem kunt' erlangen.
>   Nun/ ob dein sanffter Fall die deinen schmertzt/ vnd mich;
> Doch wein' ich billicher vmb meinen/ als vmb dich
> Die deinen thun/ vnd ich. Du hast den Lauff vollendet/
>   Vnd warest Lebens satt. Was du hier guts gethan/
> Vergisset keine Zeit. Er/ meiner/ fieng' erst an/
> Vnd ward vmb nützlich seyn am Leben stracks gepfändet.[65]

This obsessive and inconsolable reference to Gloger's death is not confined to epicedia—or to the *Libri Manium Glogerianorum*, Fleming's explicit tribute to his dead friend. In a propempticon (M.V.21) from

November 1631 for Salomon Steyer, who was making a brief visit to his native Silesia and leaving his fiancée in Leipzig, Fleming admonishes the woman to moderate her sorrow at Steyer's departure. In language reminiscent of poems in the *Arae Schönburgicae*, Fleming assures her that Steyer will return—in contrast to Gloger, who will not: "Ibit et, et tua vita pia cum sorte redibit; / ivit, at aeternum non mea vita redit." When Gustav Adolf's wife Marie Eleonore visited Leipzig in December 1631, Fleming wrote for her both a German ode (O.IV.3) and a Latin epigram (Sy.IX.11). In the latter he describes the entire city turning out to see her, while he alone broods at home, for how can he see her, when his eyes are blinded with tears for Gloger: "Solus ego torpesco domi. Quid, diva, videret, / lacryma quem longis exoculavit aquis?" The *Klagegedichte über das unschuldigste Leiden und Tod unsers Erlösers Jesu Christi* (P.W.I.9), a major work by the young poet that was printed as an *Einzeldruck* in early 1632, opens with Fleming invoking Melpomene, the muse of tragedy, to whom he confides that only she remains to him because, as she knows, he is alone. This and the following lines make it almost certain that this is again a reference to Gloger's death, and it is hard to read the body of the poem, a *vita Christi* culminating in his passion, without suspecting that in mourning Christ, Fleming was simultaneously mourning his friend. This poem closes—after a particularly repugnant passage on the role of the Jews in the crucifixion—with an ecstatic realization of the miracle worked by Christ's death, that death is the beginning of eternal life. Again one senses that this Christian consolation was sought as comfort as much for Gloger's death as for Christ's.[66]

The example of a number of early epicedia that lack neo-Stoic consolatory arguments, as well as that of the many instances in which Fleming appears unable to restrain his grief at Gloger's death indicate, as suggested above, that in the very early thirties Fleming had no profound commitment to neo-Stoicism, and that unlike Opitz, some of whose earliest poems, those in the *Aristarchus*, exhibit neo-Stoic thinking, he was not strongly attracted to this philosophy while very young. Beginning in 1632 one can cite epicedia that contain clearly neo-Stoic consolatory arguments. O.II.8 for Beata Maria Möstel, O.II.6 to the widow of Peter Kuchen, and O.II.5 for the three von Wirth daughters, all from 1632, not only use some neo-Stoic argumentation, but also exhibit the two-part structure of the *consolatio*. For two of these, however, there are external reasons that would account for the reduced structure: they are for children or infants. Traditional rhetoric, which had highly developed schema for praising adult men, offered less assistance when the object of a *laudatio* was very young, and it was understood in any case that *aptum* required one to concentrate more on consolation when the deceased was a child than when he or she was an adult.[67] Thus it seems likely that the two-part structure exhibited here is more the result of suiting the poem to the object than a demonstration of Fleming's natural inclination at this point to the Stoic form of the *consolatio*. The arguments themselves in these two poems have a hollow ring. They form a seemingly endless catalog of reasons why one should not mourn overly much, and the one for the three von Wirth daughters is particularly superficial, though, to be fair, it is hard to conceive what could be said in any age to comfort for such a loss. The same technique, one *Trostgrund* per strophe never ending, is carried over to the poem to the widow of Peter Kuchen. After three strophes of introduction, Fleming devotes the bulk of this ode to enumerating reasons for not sorrowing, including: "Ihr kommt zu früh' in Witwenstand? / Was mehr? Gott hat ein großes Land, / er kan euch ferner noch beschenken" (ll. 103–5).

The majority of Fleming's other German epicedia from the terrible year 1632, however, do not exhibit neo-Stoic philosophy, but rather, when they offer consolation at all, use arguments Christian or humanist in origin. It can, of course, at times be difficult to separate these two traditions from Christian- or neo-Stoicism, but there are a number of instances where the dominance of Christian or humanist rather than neo-Stoic argumentation is fairly evident.

Among the poems in which Christian consolation dominates is the ode (O.II.7) that Fleming wrote on the death of Frau Kuchen (whom in O.II.6 he rather clumsily comforted for her husband's death). Fleming consoles the parents with the fact that their daughter is where she desired to be:

> Laßt uns ihren Glanz besinnen
> und das Himmlische beginnen,
> Anfangs nun, nun Endes bloß!
> Wer will ihre Lust beschreiben,
> die sie wird ohn' Ende treiben
> in des Allerliebsten Schoß'?
>
> (ll. 25–30)

The somber closing of this epicedium, in which the poet paints the lot of those Helene Kuchen has left behind her in the world, contrasts sharply with Stoic teachings of *apathia*:

> Sind wir hier im Leben lange,
> so ist uns auch lange bange,
> leben desto minder doch.
> Und wem solte fast gelüsten,

mehr zu irren in der Wüsten,
mehr zu ziehen dieses Joch?

Phöbus kürzt nun ab die Tage,
doch darmit nicht unsre Plage,
die rings um uns schläget ein.
Nun der Sommer ist entwichen,
kömt der faule Herbst geschlichen,
sagt, es werde Winter sein.[68]

Essentially the same Christian message—that the deceased now lives in an infinitely better world—forms the argument of consolation in an alexandrine poem, *Auf eines von Grünental Leichbestattung* (P.W.II.2). The name of the deceased provides the basic metaphor of the poem, which is the contrast between the beautiful but transient valley of life and the beautiful eternal one in which Grünthal now dwells.[69]

　　　　　Diß haben wir zu hoffen,
daß noch ein grüner Tal uns allen stehet offen,
da zwar auch Blumen sein, nicht aber die vergehn;
. . . .
　　　　　In diesen ist versetzet
auch unser Grünental; er ists, der sich ergetzet,
der fromme Gottes-Freund, in einer solchen Lust,
die er zwar oft genant, doch aber nie gewust.

(ll. 51–58)

Probably the most striking example of this type of explicitly Christian consolation, however, is in the poem *Auf Jungfrau Magdalena Weinmans Ableben* (O.II.4), in which *Jesusminne*, briefly glimpsed in lines 28–30 of the poem for Helene Kuchen (O.II.7), constitutes the main source of images for most of the poem. In lines 46–54 the poet shows us the soul of the young woman being received by her bridegroom, Christ:

Komm, Seele, keusche Braut!
Dich hab ich mir vertraut
durch mein Erbarmen.

Dein Malschatz bin selbst ich,
du meiner. Meine mich,
wie ich dich herzlich meine!
So solstu ewig sein
was ich bin. Du bist mein',
ich allzeit deine.

The poem closes with the poet's entreaty to Magdalena that she intercede with her bridegroom on behalf of those she has left behind in a world filled with war and plague.

In several epicedia Fleming offers consolation that is humanistic rather than Christian neo-Stoic. The greater portion of the poem written in his own name on the death of his friend Georg Gloger (P.W.II.7), from 1631, consisted of intense lamentation. Such a resolution as the poem has comes from the poet's vow to perpetuate Gloger's name in his poetry, and this humanistic topos, one presumes, constitutes a sort of *Trost*. The classical and humanist background is even more evident in a poem from 1632, in the promise to preserve the name of Maria Schürer (O.II.3):

> Im Übrigen will ich,
> wie ich denn soll, durch meiner Verse Preis
> geschäftig sein umb dich,
> will wenden an nicht ungelehrten Fleiß,
> daß die, so dieses lesen,
> auch melden meinen Sin,
> daß ich dir hold gewesen,
> du keusche Schürerin.
>
> Ihr Andern, zündet an
> die teure Myrrh' und fremdes Benzoe,
> daß von dem Oliban
> und Aloë ein süßer Dampf entsteh'!
> Inmittelst will ich tönen
> die weise Melodei,
> daß auch das Grab der Schönen
> nicht ohne Freude sei.
>
> (ll. 57–72)

Consolation in the form of a promise of everlasting fame is offered Georg Seidel (P.W.II.10), who died defending Leipzig, and August Siegfried von Schönburg (O.II.1), who died of wounds sustained at Breitenfeld:

> Dein Gedächtnüß, werter Held,
> soll dort neben Phöbus stehen,
> auf und nieder mit ihm gehen
> und der Welt sein vorgestellt.
> Du wirst nicht vergessen sein,
> weil wir haben seinen Schein.
>
> (ll. 79–84)

It is not until around 1634 that we can find in the extant German poems substantial and sustained passages of neo-Stoic philosophy, and from this time on, they and the characteristic two-part structure of lament and consolation can be found not just in epicedia such as that for Barbara Kruse, but also in meditative poems such as *In Groß-Neugart der Reußen* P.W.IV.20), or in poetic epistles, and even in love poetry (for example, O.V.31), where it is surely neo-Stoic attitudes that underlie what Pyritz called the "latenter Optimismus der Flemingschen Natur."[70] All this suggests that, though acquired rather late—later than some descriptions of Fleming and his poetry imply—neo-Stoic habits of mind became, as Krummacher argues, a profound and pervasive aspect of Fleming's thinking. It is not clear whether there was a particular event or influence that prompted this.

The Fleming Family and the House of Schönburg Again

Fleming wrote several other works for the Schönburgs, the most notable being the similarly bilingual *Taedae Schönburgicae*, which includes a long alexandrine epithalamium, *Früelings-Hochzeitgedichte* with a beautiful description of nature in May.[71] In the same year (1631), he dedicated his metrical renderings of the penitential psalms to Countess Katharina von Schönburg, mother of Maria Juliane and his own godmother. In late autumn he wrote the German epicedia for August Siegfried (O.II.1) and Elisabeth (O.II.2) von Schönburg. These are the last poems we know of that Fleming wrote for the Schönburgs. While it is possible that this is an accident of textual transmission, it seems likely that Fleming realized that his best chances for patronage lay elsewhere.

The Schönburgs had been at the height of their prosperity in the fifteenth and first half of the sixteenth centuries, when they were able to draw upon profitable agriculture and the rich mines of the Erzgebirge. A general and never reversed decline began around the mid-sixteenth century. Its sources seem to have lain, first, in the Schönburgs' never establishing a principle of primogeniture and, second, in their failure to make consistently clear who was the feudal overlord—Saxony or the emperor—of their many individual, variously acquired and variously enfeoffed, lands. Schönburg lands were last united under a single head under Ernst II. When he died in 1534 his lands devolved upon his four sons, who had numerous offspring, who in turn did likewise; Ernst had at least nine grandsons and fifteen great-grandsons. The marriages between cousins, such as Maria Juliane's with her cousin Johann Heinrich, may have been belated attempts to recentralize the rule. The mere cost of maintaining so many courts became a significant drain on the treasury.

A not surprising result of this multiplication of rulers was a lack of coherent policy for the various lands and a tendency to seek outside support, not always to the good of the whole. In the course of the late Middle Ages the Schönburgs, with respect to some of their lands, had been able to enter into favorable feudal relationships with the Bohemian crown—soon Imperial—which provided protection against the ambitious Saxon Wettins. In the course of the sixteenth century, however, Saxony was able to press sometimes real, sometimes spurious claims on Schönburg lands with increasing success, in part precisely because the Schönburgs failed to insist upon the Imperial overlordship where it existed. In disputes among family members, for example, adjudication was sometimes sought in Saxon courts even when, the overlord of a particular land being Imperial, the appeal should have been to the Imperial court. Saxony was naturally happy to oblige, as this strengthened its case for jurisdiction in lands historically fiefs to the emperor. The most sensational instances involving the shortsighted appeal to the "wrong" overlord occurred in 1617 and 1628. In 1617 Wolf Ernst von Schönburg's younger brothers (among whom was Maria Juliane's fiancé, Johann Heinrich) appealed to the Saxon court to bring Wolf Ernst to justice for murdering his brother, Otto Wilhelm; in 1628 yet another brother, the already mentioned August Siegfried, murdered his cousin Friedrich, and Saxon courts were appealed to once again. Both incidents naturally strengthened Saxony's claim to jurisdiction in Schönburg lands. (Fleming, in his epicedium [O.II.1], tactfully neglects to mention the murder.)

Fleming and his family must have been aware that the Schönburg dynasty was on the wane. The history of the Schönburg lands and the sequence of posts held by Abraham Fleming would suggest that the ties between the Flemings and the Schönburgs, including ecclesiastical ones, weakened in the course of the early seventeenth century, and that the Flemings' ties with Saxony, conversely, were strengthened. While Lichtenstein, Abraham's birthplace, was clearly a sovereign Schönburg land, Hartenstein was a land in which control over the church was a matter of dispute between the Schönburgs and Saxony. The church in Topseiffersdorf, where Abraham held a position from 1615 to 1628, was subject to some control from the (Saxon) Consistorium in Leipzig.[72] The church in Wechselburg, a fief which the Schönburgs held from Saxony, and where Abraham was called in 1628, was probably more directly answerable to the Saxon church.

Whether the gradual move to lands more and more closely linked to Saxony was deliberate or not is not clear; what is clear, however, is that the Schönburgs were, for the reasons outlined above, becoming less and less prosperous, and that for Abraham Fleming and his son to begin cultivating contacts with more powerful and wealthier Saxony would not have been foolish. It is notable that after 1631 we find no reference to the Schönburgs in Fleming's preserved works and no further poems dedicated to them or commemorating occasions affecting the house.[73]

2. Politics and Poetry in Saxony: The Policies of Elector Johann Georg of Saxony and the *Schreiben vertriebener Frau Germanien* (1631)

In the spring of 1631 Fleming, now a student in his third year at the University of Leipzig, published a poem of 208 lines in elegiac distichs under the title *Germaniae exsulis ad suos filios sive proceres regni epistola*. The Latin poem was followed by a German version in 300 lines with the title *Schreiben Vertriebener Fr. Germanien an jhre Söhne/ Oder die Churf. Fürsten vnd Stände im TeutschLande*.[1] As the titles indicate, the poems purport to be letters written by Germany personified as a woman.

Germania first addresses to the "Churfürsten, Fürsten und Stände" of Germany the fervent plea to accept her letter if they still regard her as their mother. She describes the misery that brings her to write. Driven to the outermost edge of Germany, she huddles now on the stormy North Sea coast, trembling with cold and fear. Possessing neither pen nor ink, she writes with a reed dipped in a clod of earth moistened with her tears. For a desk she uses her knee. Since she has been impoverished, she must live in a simple hut constantly threatening to collapse in the slightest wind. She has only a much-patched skirt to clothe herself. She has no maidservants. Her sorrows have aged her prematurely: wrinkles, gray hair, sunken cheeks, and loose teeth have replaced her earlier beauty: "Ach! ach! ich Schöneste der allerschönsten Frauen, / wie bin ich so verjagt, so ungestalt, so bloß!" (ll. 39–40). The depth of her fall can be measured against her proud past. Once she was mighty enough to ban emperors from her realm, and her Arminius beat back the Romans. But the wheel of Fortune has turned. Her once-free people must suffer the interventions of foreign rulers; her war-devastated earth has absorbed so much blood that it can hold no more, and the rivers must help bear the blood away. Heaven has decreed this fate; although completely innocent of any crime, she cannot escape the fateful sign under which she was born: she is the plaything of Fortune. Above all she is pained by the "dreigespaltne Riß in der Religion" (l. 124): she is ready to fight bravely against any enemies, but that her sons are made enemies by internal strife is beyond her endurance. Again she considers history, not German this time but that of the great empires, Assyria,[2] Persia, and Greece—all fallen. Must she not also one day fall? An exile, her glory past, she resembles Nebuchadnezzar, reduced like him to a bestial existence. She too seeks her sustenance in field and forest; her only companions are a dolphin (in the Latin version "Delphini") and birds. Her sisters, the other kingdoms of Europe, avoid her; it was her own sister, Bohemia, who began this disorder in her lands. Germania regrets that the great princes of yore—she names several from Saxon and Brandenburgian history—are no longer alive.

After this wide-ranging *lamentatio*, which constitutes the major portion of the epistle (ll. 1–224), Germania addresses a request to her sons. This *petitio* is the purpose of the letter. She begs them by all that they must hold sacred—God, the empire, natural law, custom, and ancient German faith—to come to her aid. She names a number of her sons—Saxony, Brandenburg, the Palatinate, Hesse, Lüneburg, Anhalt, Mecklenburg, Baden, and Württemberg—whose current reputations and past histories should spur them to assist her. She notes that the Netherlands were able, by dint of united struggle, to free themselves from Spanish tyranny; her sons should seek to emulate such unity. They are her only hope; they should pray to God and send a petition to their brother the emperor. Perhaps they might yet, by such means, rescue their mother. With a reiteration of her request for their unified assistance and a cautious expression of hope, the poem closes.

As a motto for the Latin version of the poem, Fleming chose a sentence from a work by the Tübingen jurist Thomas Lansius: "Pax Romana, ipsorummet Romanorum judicio, nullo vinculo fortius connectebatur, quam Germanorum inter se odio; ut Tacitus solenne votum in haec verba conceperit (in de morib. Germanor.): Maneat, quaeso, duretque gentibus si non amor nostri, at certe odium sui, quando urgentibus imperii fatis nihil jam praestare Fortuna majus potest, quam hostium discordiam" ("The pax Romana, in the judgment of these same Romans, was held together by nothing more strongly than by the mutual hatred of the Germans among themselves, as Tacitus also said in *De Germania*, when he expressed his wish in these words: 'May there remain, I pray, and continue [among the Germans] if not love for us, then at least mutual hatred; for with the oppressive circumstances of the Empire, fate can offer us nothing greater than the discord of our enemies.' ")[3] The first edition of Fleming's poem (1631) carries the signature "Allervnterthänigst vnd demütigst vbergeben von Paull Flemmingen."

The *Schreiben vertriebener Frau Germanien* has evoked different, mutually contradictory, reactions in the secondary literature. A relatively recent critic has faulted it for lacking any political *engagement* whatsoever, while others have seen in the poem a lively partisanship on behalf of the Protestants. Occasionally expressed in passing is the view that the poem advocates a nonpartisan or suprapartisan stance. An examination of the sources of these understandings and, more importantly, a glance at the political situation in Leipzig in the early 1630s indicates that the third view, though in need of elaboration, is most nearly accurate.

The view that the poem lacks an adequately developed political dimension was put forward by Heinrich Dörrie in his study of the heroic epistle.[4] Dörrie, as Beissner (*Geschichte der deutschen Elegie*, p. 50) had done more briefly before him, calls attention to the poetic tradition in which the poem stands: that of the Ovidian heroic epistle, as transformed by humanists into a vehicle for contemporary political comment. The transformation dates back to Petrarch, who replaced Ovid's fiction of a correspondence between pairs of famous lovers with a fictive correspondence between the personified church or the city of Rome and the pope. Many other poets of the Renaissance and Reformation expressed their political and religious convictions in this form: Ulrich von Hutten, Helius Eobanus Hessus, Georg Sabinus, Michael Helding, and Johannes Stigel, to name but a few German neo-Latinists before Fleming.

Fleming's poem is the first and one of very few poems in this tradition to appear in German. (That Fleming's was the first in the German history of the genre is noteworthy, for he by and large confined himself to the genres that Opitz had already introduced into German. Perhaps in this instance he wished to emulate Opitz's efforts to enrich the variety of types of poems in German.) Dörrie considers the *Schreiben vertriebener Frau Germanien* epigonal: Fleming " 'flüchtet' sich in die Aufgabe, eine bedauernswerte Frau zu schildern, was wortreich und in gesuchten Bildern geschieht. Einen Beitrag zu den drängenden Fragen jener Zeit findet man nicht" (p. 470). "Einzig das Reformationszeitalter scheint die Möglichkeit geboten zu haben, daß man sich in dieser Form zu den großen Fragen der Zeit äußerte, ja auf die Entscheidung dieser Fragen einwirkte" (p. 463). The poem, Dörrie believes, is merely "eine Suasorie ohne Programm" (p. 470).

In this opinion Dörrie stands alone; somewhat more often one encounters the interpretation of the poem put forth by Hermann Stölten in his "Gustav Adolf und seine Zeit in Paul Fleming's Gedichten." Stölten considered it in the context of the Swedish king Gustav Adolf's landing in Germany during July 1630 and of his attempts, in the next fourteen months, to persuade the Protestant princes of Germany, including the Saxon elector Johann Georg I, to ally with him against the Catholic Imperial forces. Stölten points out that Fleming was the son of a Protestant pastor, and, as an intimate of Georg Gloger, the friend of a man who had been driven from his Silesian home by Imperial troops. Stölten believes that Fleming expresses in this poem the desire of German Protestants for an alliance with Gustav Adolf, the savior of German Protestantism and archenemy of the Catholic empire. The friendly dolphin who comforts Germania in her distress Stölten presumably takes as a play on the name of the Swedish king, for he suggests it may be a sign for the Swedish army waiting near the coast of Germany for the invitation to land.

This understanding of the poem has not been explicitly disputed. In his article from 1941 Hans Rodenberg presented a similar interpretation; he alludes to Gustav Adolf's landing in Germany and comments "Auf ihn konzentrierten sich die Hoffnungen Flemings (wie wohl die der meisten Protestanten in Deutschland)." In the *Schreiben vertriebener Frau Germanien* he sees one of the poems of the period in which Fleming "zum bewaffneten Widerstand aufrief, [und] die Tatenlosigkeit Sachsens bitter kritisierte," that is, condemned Elector Johann Georg's hesitation to enter into an alliance with the Swedes.[5]

The third view of Fleming's poem has been proffered with minimal elaboration by Varnhagen von Ense and Schlesinger in their biographies of the poet. Varnhagen, although he does not date the poem but simply discusses it along with Fleming's poems for Gustav Adolf in the general context of the Thirty Years' War, noted that it and several others of Fleming's poems were distinctly nonpartisan: "Doch wendet sich die Theilnahme des Dichters, über die streitenden Partheien hinaus, entschiedener auf das gemeinsame Schicksal des Vaterlandes"; he notes Germania's respectful attitude to the emperor and characterizes the sentiment of the poem as "dem Partheiwesen entrückte Vaterlandsliebe."[6] Schlesinger goes slightly beyond Varnhagen when he notes—in addition to characterizing Fleming as "kein protestantischer Eiferer"—that Fleming's seeking to avoid partisanship in the poem was consonant with the politics of Saxony.[7]

Neither of the first two views of Fleming's poem—Dörrie's that it lacks a political stance and Stölten and Rodenberg's that it takes a decidedly Protestant one—seems untenable at first glance. Scholars have often stressed the contrast between the humanists' lively political partisanship and the lack of political *engagement* in seventeenth-century poetry—which is the central point of Dörrie's interpretation.[8] On the other hand, Fleming's enthusiasm for Gustav Adolf has often been recalled, and several eulogies of Gustav Adolf from the years 1632 and 1633 seem to confirm the judgment of Marian Szyrocki that Fleming was an "eifriger Parteigänger des Protestantismus," who placed "seine Hoffnungen zuerst auf Gustav Adolph."[9]

But this plausibility is deceptive. Both these interpretations mistake the political situation in Saxony at the time the poem was written, and thereby misconstrue it. Dörrie used an early edition of Fleming's collected works, and did not know the individual printing of 1631. He thus saw only the sad state of Germany in the 1630s as the general background, and it is no wonder he perceived no reflection of concrete events or political opinions in the poem. Stölten and Rodenberg knew the date of the poem's first appearance (1631) and Stölten, for reasons I mention below, was able to date the poem even more precisely, to early spring 1631. But neither Stölten nor Rodenberg takes account of the important shifts in the Saxon political climate during the course of that year: they project the great enthusiasm for Sweden triggered by Gustav Adolf's victory over Tilly at Breitenfeld in September backward into the first months of the year. But before the victory the Swedish king was not met with uniform approval.

To see that, contrary to Dörrie's contention, Fleming was indeed adopting a specific political stance in his poem and to recognize that, as Varnhagen and Schlesinger indicate, this stance was not that of Protestant partisanship, it is necessary to date the poem precisely and look at the political events in Saxony that surrounded its composition. I noted that the *Schreiben vertriebener Frau Germanien* can be dated to spring 1631. The main evidence for this is an argument *ex silentio*: in May 1631 Tilly took Magdeburg and burned the city to the ground, an act that deeply shocked Protestant Germany. In September he took Leipzig and shortly thereafter was defeated by the Swedes and Saxons at Breitenfeld. Fleming mentions neither event, which suggests that neither had yet occurred when the poem was composed, for their effect on contemporaries was so profound that it is scarcely credible that Fleming would have passed over them in silence if they had happened. A second suggestive bit of evidence lies in the title: Germania writes to "ihre Söhne oder die Churfürsten, Fürsten und Stände in Deutschlande." From February 6 to April 5, 1631, the so-called Leipziger Konvent of Protestant electors, territorial princes, and estates was in session in Leipzig, where it had been called by the Saxon elector Johann Georg. These are without doubt the addressees intended by the poem's title, and Leipzig the city from which Germania feels herself so distant (l. 7).

The historical background for Fleming's heroic epistle is to be found, indeed, precisely in the Leipzig Conference. Older historians, especially Protestants, have often portrayed the conference as a failed attempt by the elector of Saxony to placate Emperor Ferdinand II; Johann Georg also did not lack critics in his own time among Catholic and militant Protestant propagandists alike.[10] Considering the events that immediately followed the conference—the fall of Magdeburg and the Battle of Breitenfeld—historians have generally agreed that Saxony would have done better to ally with Gustav Adolf immediately in early 1631 or even 1630. Stölten, who, as noted, correctly perceived the connection between the poem and the Leipzig Conference, shared this view. He portrays the conference as a missed opportunity for the Protestant princes to ally themselves with Sweden—an opportunity lamented, he thinks, by good Protestant patriots like Fleming.[11] Such retrospective judgments on historical events have their value, of course, but they are more hindrance than help in attempting to grasp the historical and political dimension of a poem like Fleming's, for Fleming can have had no such retrospective insight into events. It will be more useful to describe how the situation must have appeared at the time to a Saxon like Fleming. Such a description, including a review of the course of Saxon policy before and during the conference, will illuminate the political posture in Fleming's heroic epistle more precisely and historically more accurately, than has heretofore been done.[12]

Johann Georg, who had been elector of Saxony since 1611, followed from the beginning the policy of his predecessors in combining Lutheran belief with loyalty to the emperor. Wedgwood says of him that "he wanted above all peace, commercial prosperity, and the integrity of Germany" (p. 60). He regarded with suspicion anything that might endanger the unity of the empire, since peace was inevitably also endangered thereby; in this light it is comprehensible that he neither greeted nor supported the uprising in Bohemia. After the outbreak of the Thirty Years' War, Johann Georg avoided all alliances with other Protestant princes, especially any entente with the Calvinists, which would have branded him an enemy of the emperor. The success of this essentially neutral policy may be recognized from the fact that until 1631 Saxony had suffered very little from the war. In the late 1620s, however, the signs of strain between Saxony and the empire grew. The campaigns and victories of the Imperial armies in Protestant areas gave one pause, but the major motivation for Saxony to modify its posture arose from the Imperial Edict of Restitution of 1629. In that edict, the emperor decreed that all bishoprics, abbeys, and other church lands secularized since the Treaty of Passau in 1552 were to be returned—a severe blow to the treasuries of Protestant princes and to converted subjects in the affected areas. Still there was no final break: in Saxon centenary celebrations of the Confession of Augsburg in 1630—whether as wishful thinking or gestures of reconciliation is unclear—Emperor Ferdinand II was invoked as protector of the Lutheran Church.[13] Johann Georg was nonetheless aware that some response was needed, and in the spring of 1631 he convoked the Leipzig Conference so that the Protestant princes could discuss the latest events and formulate an answer to the Edict of Restitution. Johann Georg had decided to insist on a conciliatory answer. In his invitation he describes the purpose of the council: "[die] wiederbringung des zwischen den Catholischen vnnd Evangelischen Ständen hoch nötigen vnd fast zerfallenen/ rechtschaffenen/ alten/ deutschen/ sicherem Vertrawens/ so wol [die] beförderung des so lang desiderirten/ verlornen/ edlen/ werthen/ allgemeinen Friedens."[14] Some Protestant princes already wanted to ally themselves with the Swedes, but Johann Georg regarded any such alliance with a foreign power as disobedience to the emperor, a disobedience that would put Saxony irrevocably on the side of the emperor's enemies and draw her into a war from whose depredations the land had thus far remained free. In addition, Johann Georg and most North German princes regarded Gustav Adolf with some mistrust, since behind his efforts to rescue Protestantism they suspected an attempt to enlarge Sweden's territory at the expense of Germany's. (Fleming, in Sy.III.4, written in the autumn of 1631 after the Battle of Breitenfeld, devotes nine lines to protestations that Gustav Adolf was not interested in gaining Germany's wealth and territory; the strained effort to revise a common perception of the Swedish ruler's motivations arouses in the modern reader more suspicions than it allays.) In the conference's petition to the emperor, Elector Johann Sigismund of Brandenburg complains that "auch zweyen gantze Creyß/ als die Newe: und Vcker Marck in des Königs in Schweden Hände gerahten [seien]."[15] It is significant that not only the Lutheran but also the Calvinist princes and the representatives of the Calvinist cities were invited to the conference, given that Johann Georg had hitherto avoided all alliances with the Calvinists. One may see in this avoidance the influence of his Imperial-minded, anti-Calvinist court chaplain Hoe von Hoenegg. But the events of the late 1620s had persuaded even Hoenegg that the Lutherans and Calvinists could no longer afford the luxury of a divided front, and thus Calvinists were invited to the conference as well as Lutherans. At the same time, Lutheran and Calvinist theologians (Hoenegg among them) met informally in an attempt to settle the doctrinal differences that divided them. In this fashion the Leipzig Conference gained an explicitly irenicist character, that is, agreement and peace were sought by means of overlooking nonfundamental differences in confession and stressing everything held in common.[16]

Thus, in the spring of 1631, when Fleming was writing the *Schreiben vertriebener Frau Germanien*, Elector Johann Georg was working on the one hand for reconciliation with the Calvinists, while on the other still striving to avoid a breach with the emperor. In the acts of the conference one reads repeatedly of the participants' wish to create peace and unity in the empire, of their readiness to negotiate with the Catholic princes, and above all of their efforts to remain true to the emperor. The main results of the conference were the aforementioned petition to the emperor, which requested him to rescind the Edict of Restitution and end the mishandling of Protestants by Imperial troops, and the decision to raise an army in case their pleas went unheard.

With this background, it is possible to discern that Fleming's poem reflects a number of aspects of Johann Georg's policy before and during the Leipzig Conference. In the *Schreiben vertriebener Frau Germanien* one finds, for example, the mistrust of any intervention by foreign powers in the affairs of the Holy Roman Empire, particularly the mistrust of Sweden's intervention that Johann Georg shared with North German rulers. One also sees reflected in Fleming's poem Johann Georg's faithfulness to the emperor and the empire and his wish to save the unity of the empire. Furthermore, Fleming, like Johann Georg, displays a readiness to overlook partisan confessional differences for the sake of the unity of the empire. Finally, it is possible to detect similarities in the specific measures Germania, on the one hand, and Johann Georg, on the other, prescribe. Each of Fleming's reflections of Johann Georg's policies merits fuller delineation.

Fleming expresses his aversion to foreign interference in Germany in two passages of his epistle. In lines 74–76, Germania asks "Wie kunt' ich fürderhin das Elend schauen an, / wie mir mein freies Volk die fremden Herrscher treiben, / wie vor mir täglich weint mein armer Untertan?" And in lines 119–20 she complains: "Ich muß zu meinem Leid' auch Einen mir versühnen, / der mich nicht Mutter heißt, der mich ohn' Ende plagt." In themselves these lines could apply to several European powers that had intervened in German affairs between 1623 and 1631—primarily Denmark, France, and Sweden. But Denmark had been forced to withdraw from the struggle after its defeats of 1626, and France had only intervened indirectly: the French supported the Swedes financially but raised no army of their own. One may thus confidently connect these two passages in the poem directly with the Swedes, who were the only foreign power actively threatening any part of Germany at this time.[17] In any case—whether Fleming's words are directed specifically against a Swedish intervention or merely against foreign intervention in general—in the context of Johann Georg's anti-Swedish position at the time, they argue strongly against Stölten's interpretation of the friendly dolphin on the North Sea coast as a symbol for Swedish troops, as well as against the opinion encountered frequently in secondary literature that Fleming welcomed Gustav Adolf's entry into Germany from the very beginning.[18]

The striving for unity, the second characteristic of Johann Georg's policy, appears repeatedly in Fleming's poem, often expressed eloquently *per contraria*, when Germania depicts the effects of strife on her people and land. The theme appears no later than the motto of the Latin poem: the quotation from Tacitus provides historical confirmation that Germany's enemies have welcomed her disunity because their own position was strengthened by it: "May there remain, I pray, and continue [among the Germans] if not love for us, then at least mutual hatred; for with the oppressive circumstances of the Empire, fate can offer us nothing greater than the discord of our enemies."

Germania similarly recognizes that her situation is bad enough when her enemies threaten her, but becomes insupportable when her own children attack her:

> Und wolte, wolte Gott, es wäre nur der Feind,
> den ich noch nie gescheut! So muß allein' ich klagen,
> daß ich an diese soll, die meine Kinder seind.
> Ich muß mich arme Frau noch selbst zum Stabe bringen
> und mein Schergante sein, das nie kein Feind getan.
> Ich selbst und durch mich selbst muß mich an Eisen zwingen
> und mir an meinen Hals die Koppeln legen an.
>
> (ll. 142–48)

Germania is ashamed of the internal enmity of her realm and foretells dire consequences: did not even great Rome fall through disunity?

> Nicht einig wollen sein, das tut mich so beschämen,
> Und wer nicht glauben will, daß diß die Zwietracht kan,
> und daß noch selbst die Welt so werd' ihr Ende nehmen,
> der komm' und sehe dich, du armes Rom, nur an!
>
> (ll. 149–52)

The desire for the unity necessary to preserve the German nation is also expressed positively in the poem, through the leitmotiv of family metaphor: Germania appears as a mother in the poem, the princes as her children. Although, as noted above, the circumstances of the poem's composition point to the Protestant princes taking part in the Leipzig Conference (several of them named explicitly in ll. 239–46) as the poem's immediate addressees, there is nonetheless no sectarian restriction of the circle of addressees or of the family image in the title: Germania considers all princes of Germany, of whatever religious persuasion, as her children. At one point she refers to the emperor as her son (l. 272), and at another, when summoning her various sons, she calls for and praises "die schöne Pfalz von wegen ihrer Treu'" (l. 242; there is no reason to believe the words are intended ironically). The mother-son metaphor suggests that the fidelity of the emperor, electors, princes, and estates should be directed first of all to Germany and should be stronger than any other ties, including those of confession.

This leads to the third characteristic of Johann Georg's policy also reflected in Fleming's poem: the readiness to seek agreement across confessional boundaries. That Fleming's poem—in an age of the bitterest religious polemics—should be without any confessional partisanship has its significance, and can only be understood against the historical background of the Leipzig Conference and the policy of Johann Georg. Frau Germania mentions at no point any preference for those of her sons who profess a particular creed. The sole mention of the different sects is to be found in the lines lamenting the existence and consequences of the religious divisions: "Mich schmerzt auf allen Seiten / der dreigespaltne Riß in der Religion" (ll. 123–24). Germania does not see the root of her distress in any of the three confessional groups; the reason for her misfortune, rather, is the whim of fate:

> Das Glück ist mir so feind, daß mirs auch könte gönnen,
> daß ich bis ans Gewölk' und an die Sterne kam,
> auf daß es mich mit Fug' hat tief gnung stürzen können,
> und zusehn, wie ich da mein elend Ende nahm.
> Ich bin der Götter Spiel und Kurzweil, . . .
>
> (ll. 153–57)

This is but one of several passages in which Germania attributes her fall to a supernatural agency, and twice she insists she is innocent and undeserving of her fate (ll. 117, 270). Taken together, the passages suggest that she wishes at all costs to avoid locating the guilt in any one of her sons, since this would weaken the appeal to family ties and her call to unity. Only once does she name a specific territory as partially responsible for her situation: her sister Bohemia, she says, threw the sparks of conflict upon her (ll. 209–10), a poetic paraphrase of Johann Georg's outrage over Bohemia's betrayal of the emperor. (Fleming reiterates this attitude towards Bohemia in a poem for Johann Georg, Sy.III.3, from the autumn of 1631.) By making Bohemia a daughter of Europa and thus a sister of Germania, not a son, Fleming moves the source of the conflict out of the circle of addressees and thus avoids blaming any German prince. One might suspect that the accusation against Bohemia reflects an anti-Calvinist resentment, but this is unlikely given Germania's reference to the (Calvinist) Netherlands as a model of peace and unity and her remark in line 243 that "an Hessen hab ich Trost" (the ruler of Hesse, Landgraf Wilhelm V, was a staunch Calvinist), as well as the above-mentioned reference to the Palatinate. Indeed, the text suggests that Fleming knew of and was supporting Johann Georg's new policy of reconciliation with the Calvinists.

Further similarities between Fleming's poem and Johann Georg's politics are recognizable in the measures for the reinstatement of peace that each suggests; these may be coincidental or, more likely, reflective of logical conclusions independently drawn from the same set of circumstances. Germania (ll. 262–66) urges her princes, first, to pray to God for help, and, second, to petition the emperor for her:

> so müßt ihr Alle stehn
> mit Räuch- und Opferwerk' und aufgehabnen Händen
> und eurer Seufzer Brunst von Herzen lassen gehn
> zu Gott und himmelan. Klagt auch von meinetwegen
> mein großes Herzeleid dem hohen Ferdinand',
> . . .

In the *Abschied/ Deß zu Leipzig/ von den Evangelischen Protestirenten Chur-Fürsten/ Ständten vnd Herrn Abgesandten/ gehaltenen/ vnd den 2. Aprilis dieses 1631. Jahrs/ geschlossenen Convent-Tags* the assembled princes similarly advise prayer; the institution of "Bett vnd Buß Täg" is recommended, in the hope that God will thereby be propitiated (fols. A2r–A2v). The second measure agreed upon by the Leipzig participants was practical: they, as Germania urges, turned to the emperor, asking for, among other things, the revocation of the Edict of Restitution. The third measure recommended by the participants has no correspondence in Fleming's poem: the Protestant princes determined to join together and raise an army for the purpose of defending Protestant lands in the event of an attack by Imperial troops.

These parallels between Fleming's poem and Saxony's attempt in this period to pursue a policy of neutrality indicate that the *Schreiben vertriebener Frau Germanien* does indeed advance a particular political agenda. However, far from offering evidence for Fleming's being an "eifriger Parteigänger des Protestantismus" who from the beginning welcomed Gustav Adolf as the savior of Protestantism, the poem instead shows him urging a cessation of interconfessional hostilities and favoring reconciliation based on the underlying unity of Germans and the irrelevance, for these purposes, of confessional differences. Germania's appeal to her sons when she begs the princes and estates to join together and end the bloodshed is essentially an irenicist one, and the religious and political ideas that Fleming expresses in the poem are clearly more irenicist than partisan.[19]

The Iconography of Fleming's Frau Germania and Connections to Other Irenicist Works

The *Schreiben vertriebener Frau Germanien* was far from being the only poem written on the occasion of the Leipzig Conference. There was a veritable flood of occasional poems, mostly panegyrics for the participants and *laudationes* predicting the success of the conference.[20] Fleming himself wrote two further poems in connection with the conference: *Auf Herrn Johann Casimir, Herzoge zu Sachsen, Namenstag* (P.W.IV.2) and *An den Durchlauchtigsten, Hochgebohrnen Fürsten vnd Herren Herren Johann Georgen, Hertzogen zu Sachsen. . . .*[21] In the poem to Johann Casimir, Fleming strikes a defiantly Protestant note as he describes the proud past of Saxony as the cradle of the Reformation, but this gives way to the same expressions of longing for peace that characterize the poem for Johann Georg.

One broadsheet in the deluge that accompanied the conference merits particular attention, for it suggests that Fleming was not isolated in his irenicist inclinations. It bears the title *Europa qverula et vulnerata, Das ist/ Klage der Europen/ so an jhren Gliedern vnd gantzem Leibe verletzet/ vnd verwundet ist/ vnd nunmehr Trost vnd Hülffe begehret* and comprises, like the majority of broadsheets, an illustration and a poem.[22] The engraver was a Leipzig artist, Andreas Bretschneider.[23] The poet, one Elias Rudel or Rudelius, is almost unknown, but the many occasional poems Rudel dedicated to Johann Georg suggest that he was somehow connected with the Saxon court. One source identifies him as David Schirmer's predecessor in the position of court poet to Johann Georg.[24]

Bretschneider's engraving depicts Europe personified as a woman. She is standing on a small pedestal of earth. On her left she is attacked by soldiers; above the soldiers are storm clouds. On her right the sun is rising over a city on a river in a peaceful landscape; somewhat farther to her right are some people apparently deep in conversation. Europa herself stands in a desperately pleading posture with tousled hair and dirty, ragged clothing. Rudel's poem of sixty alexandrine lines opens with the poet asking Europa how she came to this state. In her response she first laments her lost beauty and then describes how all her food has been taken from her, how all her fields lie fallow. She asks herself where all her strength has gone: her enemies now mock her descent and her birth. But the greater part of her response is made up of her fervent plea for unity and peace:

> Wo ist die Einigkeit? denn wo dieselbe wohnet/
> Mit Vnglück/ bösem Raht vnd That man wird verschonet:
> . . . .
> Wo die Vereinigung geschehen der gemühter/
> Erfolget auch gar bald vertheidigung der Güter;
> Es wird das gantze Landt vnd Reich in sicherheit
> Vnd Einigkeit gesetzt/ davon die Frewdigkeit.
> Das Mittel ist allein das man so sey verbunden/
> Als wie der alten Bund/ zu meiden alle Wunden/
> Zu bleiben in der Still/ zu suchen Friedes gunst/
> Zu meiden Neid vnd Grull/ das ist die gröste Kunst.
> Es folget den auch bald/ wie der gerechte Friede
> Weit vor zu zihen sey mit einem schönen Liede;
> Wie der Poeten Kunst vnd Freyheit hat bedacht:
> Den Friede wollen wir/ der Krieg kein Heyl hat bracht.
>
> (ll. 37–52)

As in Fleming's poem, all polemics against specific parties are lacking here, and no one is singled out as responsible for Europe's destruction. Instead, the necessity for unity and peace is stressed.

The similarity of content—above all the common use of an allegorical female figure advocating irenicism—prompts the question whether Fleming's poem is in some way connected to the broadsheet of Bretschneider and Rudel, especially since the illustration of Europa in the broadside resembles the portrayal of Germania in Fleming's poem in several important points. The postures of the two figures are different: standing elevated and exposed to her enemies' arrows, Europa recalls Saint Sebastian, while Germania, bent over her knee as she writes, recalls, appropriately, traditional depictions of acedia and melancholy best known from Dürer's *Melencolia I*.[25] The more general attributes of the two figures, however, are quite similar: in both the female figure is isolated, having fled to the water's edge, an unnamed river in Europa's case, the North Sea in Germania's; in both she wears poor and tattered clothing and is close to starvation; and in both she is the desperate prey of her enemies. Purely literary models for Fleming's Germania may be found, since the portrayal of Germany as a suffering woman was a humanist commonplace. But if one considers the strong pictorial element and the wealth of realistic, often visually oriented details in Fleming's poem, one may with justice suspect a pictorial rather than a literary source for the poem. Bretschneider's engraving is a logical suspect: it is the only portrayal of a land or continent as a suffering woman that I have been able to find from the period before 1631.[26]

An iconographic tradition of portraying Germany as a woman does indeed exist, but all the examples I have found from before 1631 depict what one might call Germania *triumphans*: Germania clothed richly, with orb and scepter. She is portrayed thus at the Stuttgart court festivals of 1616, in a broadsheet of 1620, and on the title page of an edition of Sebastian Münster's *Cosmographia* from 1628.[27] The earliest graphic representation of Germania *in extremis* known to me appeared in 1647 on the title page of Johann Rist's *Das Friedewünschende Teütschland*, where she is portrayed as a beggar woman surrounded by threatening soldiers. The scarcity of graphic representations of Germania *in extremis* contrasts with her frequent depiction in verse. In 1638 Rist offered a brief glimpse of her as "deß Türken Magd" in the peroration to his admonitory poem *An die Christliche* [sic] *Fürsten vnnd Herren in Teutschland*, and two years later Justus Georg Schottel portrayed "Die höchstbetrübte Germania" in a long-winded imitation of Fleming's poem.[28] She again puts in a pathetic appearance in Harsdörffer and Klaj's *Pegnesisches Schaefergedicht* of 1644 (pp. 14–17), in which the mad shepherdess Pamela believes herself to be war-torn Germany. There appears to be a lack of art-historical research on the iconography of the Germania figure. It would perhaps be worthwhile to investigate the development of the tradition of Germania images and discover whether Bretschneider's portrayal of a threatened Europe contributed to the transformation of Germania *triumphans*, who continued to be portrayed as long as the idea of a German empire seemed viable, into a Germania *in extremis*, at the time when the concept had become questionable.

Whether Fleming in fact knew the broadsheet of Rudel and Bretschneider and was inspired by it—or the reverse—must remain in the realm of speculation. Fleming's epitaph for Bretschneider (M.VII.19) is proof that he either knew or knew of the artist, although, since it is undated and Bretschneider's death date is unknown, it gives no indication of the dates of Fleming's acquaintance with Bretschneider's work. Neither the broadsheet nor Fleming's poem can be dated so exactly as to allow us to say with certainty which appeared first. In the broader context of investigating the political content of Fleming's poem, the impossibility of proving dependence conclusively one way or the other is in any case less significant than the fact that both the broadsheet and the poem demonstrate the existence of nonpartisan or suprapartisan irenic sentiment in Leipzig in early 1631.

Means of Persuasion Employed by Frau Germania

Thus far the focus has been on some particularities of Fleming's poem that throw some light on its political attitude, to the end of establishing that the poem is not, as Dörrie described it, "eine Suasorie ohne Programm" but that, on the contrary, Fleming takes a political position very similar to that of Elector Johann Georg. But Dörrie is quite right in pointing out the elements of the *suasoria* in the poem: it is not merely a description of Saxon policy. On the contrary, the poem is a passionate appeal to its addressees: Fleming attempts to arouse compassion and to persuade princes and estates of the worrisome condition of Germany. Two of the many persuasive techniques with which Fleming makes his case are of particular interest: the vivid personification of Germany and the use of a well-known biblical myth of world-historical development.

The use of a symbolic figure representing a country or a society as the speaker has the advantage, for a poem like Fleming's, that the figure can, as representative of a group, put forward her opinions with more weight than can the poet speaking in his own voice. Fleming exploits this characteristic of the heroic epistle significantly more than his predecessors in the genre. In earlier poems of this type the speaker is named in the poem's title, but is endowed with little in the way of individual or human features; the personified speaker thus remains rather abstract.[29] Fleming, on the other hand, seeks to strengthen Germania's words by allowing her to describe herself and her situation in detail: we know where she is, how she lives, and what she looks like. In lines 1 through 40 Germania introduces herself, mother of the German princes, and describes her location and her extreme poverty with a wealth of pitiful realistic detail, such as her means of making ink from dirt and tears. This initial description culminates, in lines 33–40, in the physical self-portrait of an aging, withering woman at once realistic in its specificity—she is wrinkled, consumptive, hollow-eyed, etc.—but at the same time possessed of powerful symbolic overtones pointing to the themes of vanity and *memento mori*.[30] Then, for a time, Germania turns to speak of past glories, but from line 185 to 204 and then again beginning with line 273 in the *peroratio* Fleming has her return to speak of her own miserable situation and to add new details—how she weeps in her lonely wilderness and is mocked by magpies and even trees, how her tears blotch her writing. Fleming thus repeatedly brings before the reader his central, pathos-laden image of a threatened, anxious, once-proud woman begging her sons for help. When Germania turns from self-portrait of herself as a woman to a description of what she stands for allegorically, that is, to a description of the lands she represents (e.g., ll. 81–100), the narration never becomes an objective or impersonal description of events, for we see everything through Germania's agonized eyes. She stands perpetually before us and points repeatedly and fixedly at herself and at the consequences of the war for herself, that is, for Germany.

The vivid personification of Germania gains an added rhetorical power when Fleming exploits the grammar of the first person narration: Germania draws repeated attention to her own personal fate through the reiteration, often anaphoric, of the first-person singular pronoun:

> Ich, königliches Kind, wie bin ich so gefallen!
> Die ich die zärtste war in meiner Schwestern Schar,
> da ich die zwölfte bin, ich, die ich vor für allen
> der Mutter höchste Lust, die allerliebste war,
> die ich so mächtig war, . . .
>
> (ll. 41–45)

In a passage that resembles Fleming's description of his own internal discord in a poetic epistle to an unnamed friend (P.W.IV.50), the tragedy of Germany's internal disunity is represented by the painful, schizophrenic doubling of the first person singular pronoun described as being at war with itself; the individuality of the persona serves to point up the irrationality of division within that which is supposed to be unified, that is, the German empire:

> Ich muß mich arme Frau noch selbst zum Stabe bringen
> und mein Schergante sein, das nie kein Feind getan.
> Ich selbst und durch mich selbst muß mich an Eisen zwingen
> und mir an meinen Hals die Koppeln legen an.
>
> (ll. 145–48)

Fleming further enhances the rhetorical appeal of Germania's pleas by having her excuse the symptoms of her own sincerity in a pathetic humility formula: her distress has prevented her taking the usual care with *elocutio* and *dispositio*:

> Die Zährenbach, die ich hierüber ausgegossen,
> die ließe mir nicht zu der Sätze Zierlichkeit.
> So ist die Schrift auch selbst zusammen ganz geflossen,
> daß man kein' Ordnung sieht. Wie mir mein Angst und Leid
> es haben vorgesagt, so hab' ich nachgeschrieben,
> ohn' aller Worte Wahl, die billig sein sonst soll.
>
> (ll. 281–86)

This is a bit disingenuous on Fleming's part, but in fact the poem is less highly structured than, for example, his *Elegie an das traurige Hartenstein* in the *Arae Schönburgicae*, which it resembles in the use of the elegiac alexandrine for a (nonamorous) lamentation. Whereas the *Elegie* was neatly divided into two halves, with the first half in particular highly structured by repetitions of phrases that underscored the argument, the *Schreiben vertriebener Frau Germanien*, in keeping with its epistolary nature (see chapter 4) as well as the need to reflect the distress of the speaker, is more associative in its thought. Germania focuses now on her current situation in the wilderness, now on her past glories, now on the arbitrariness of fate, and now on the devastation in her lands. There are a few fairly clear divisions: there is the long *lamentatio* and short *petitio*, and a distinct pause for a regrouping of forces at line 100, but Fleming has not striven for verbal or motivic echoes like the repeated references to Mars and death that organize the *Elegie*. One of the very few echoes that does occur comes, curiously, from the very medium responsible for the disorder of the poem. The tears mentioned at the outset (l. 11) as enabling Germania to write her lament reappear at the end of the poem (ll. 281–84), making the ink run together and destroying the structure of the letter—but thematically tying beginning and end together. How seriously we are to take the notion of the tears' preventing Germania from arriving at "der Sätze Zierlichkeit" is unclear. "Zierlich" or not, Fleming's sentence structure and length are here generally effective. As in the thematically related *Elegie*, he varies both length and structure and thereby wards off the potential monotony of a comparatively long piece. At times this variety serves as an effective means of emphasis, as when a fairly long, complicated period is followed by a sentence of a mere half line, which stands out by contrast (see, e.g., ll. 5–9).

The effectiveness of Fleming's Frau Germania rests not only on his use of personification per se, but upon his success in maintaining the fiction of Germania as author throughout the whole poem, both stylistically and thematically. The use of Germania as speaker ultimately appeals not only to patriotism but also to the compassion of the addressees.

A second significant means of persuasion that Fleming employs is a particular version of a biblical myth of historical development. Fleming's Germania refers her listeners repeatedly to world history, by singling out great men of the past as models for her princes. At one point, however, the historical allusion serves a different purpose. When she speaks of the fall of Syria (sc. Assyria), Persia, and Greece, she speculates: "Vielleicht wird nun die Reih' und das Verhängnüß kommen / auf unser krankes Reich" (ll. 169–70). At first sight it seems hardly amazing that Germania should interpret history typologically and regard the fall of earlier empires as predicting her own fall, the fall of the Holy Roman Empire of the German Nation. But it was not usual, in early seventeenth-century Protestant Germany, to interpret the relationship of Assyria, Persia, and Greece to Germany in this way. That Germania nonetheless does so is all the more foreboding for reasons that become clear against the background of the so-called myth of the empires.[31]

The myth is based on the story of Nebuchadnezzar's and Daniel's dreams in the Book of Daniel (chapters 2 and 7); for Fleming's poem Nebuchadnezzar's dream in chapter 2 is of particular significance. In it the king sees a gigantic statue of a man whose head is of gold, whose breast and arms are of silver, whose stomach and loins are of brass, and whose feet are of iron mixed with clay. A stone destroys the statue's feet, then breaks it into pieces, and finally grows into a mountain that fills the world.

Daniel interprets the parts of the statue as four empires, Nebuchadnezzar's and three yet to come. The stone that destroys the statue, he continues, is the kingdom of God, which will put an end to all earthly kingdoms and last forever. Christian theologians and historians have in the course of time identified the four empires in different ways, gradually settling on Assyria, Persia, Greece, and Rome. Rome, as the last kingdom, represented the bulwark of history against the coming of the Antichrist and the end of the world; the decline and collapse of the Roman empire created tremendous anxiety and prompted new interpretive efforts to prove its continuance, and thus the delay of the end of time. The crowning of Charlemagne as emperor was interpreted as a renewal of the old empire; the Holy Roman Empire came to be understood as the continuation of the fourth kingdom represented by the statue's iron and clay feet, the final earthly realm (a version of this interpretation is found in Luther's preface to the Book of Daniel). Since no other earthly kingdom follows the fourth before the stone (that is, the Kingdom of God) grinds the statue to dust, the dream of Nebuchadnezzar came to be understood as prophesying that the Holy Roman Empire of the German Nation would last until the end of time. This is the understanding of world history and of Germany's role in it that Daniel Caspar von Lohenstein, for example, uses at the end of his *Sophonisbe* in order to pay a compliment to his Habsburg patrons: the personification of Fate appears and considers which of the four empires deserves the "guldner Siegs-Krantz." In the end the crown is awarded to Austria, which is honored as Rome's heir by the other empires—Assyria, Persia, and Greece—since only Austria is immortal: "Nimm/ Oesterreich/ den Siegs-Krantz hin. | Dein Stamm wird ewig uns stehn für."[32] The prerequisite for this scene in honor of the House of Habsburg is a view of history that sees in the decline of the preceding empires not a prediction of Germany's decline but transitional phases preparing the way for an empire that will last until the end of the world.

Whether or not Fleming personally placed credence in this interpretation of the Book of Daniel and the four kingdoms is moot. Certainly as an enormously widely read young man he was aware of other possibilities. In his moving epicedium (O.II.14) for the daughter of the Reval gymnasium teacher, Timotheus Polus, he invokes Assyria, Persia, Greece, and the city of Rome simply as examples of earthly ephemerality (ll. 37–42). But his rhetorical purpose in the current situation called for a more powerful argument. Rist, seven years later, would evoke the humiliating image of Frau Germania serving as maid to the Turks; Fleming's tactic is perhaps even more effective. He initially invokes a myth specifically developed as reassurance of the continuity and continuance of the fourth kingdom. Then, in a rapid reversal, he has Germania say "Vielleicht wird nun die Reih' und das Verhängnüß kommen / auf unser krankes Reich," thus conjuring up two frightening possibilities. Either the prophecy and its interpretation were mistaken, and the empire, merely one more emblem of vanity, simply has no special position in the universe, or, far worse, at a moment when humanity, preoccupied by war and gain, is least prepared, the Apocalypse is at hand. Either way, Germania vividly conveys how desperate her situation is and how badly she, the empire, needs the united assistance of her princes.

Fleming's Politics, His Search for Patronage, and His Decision to Leave Germany

At least two factors might be adduced to cast doubt on the assumption that the *Schreiben vertriebener Frau Germanien* directly and simply reflects Fleming's own independent political sentiments, and that the coincidence of Germania's irenicism and concern for the empire with Johann Georg's political strategy is purely fortuitous. There is, first, the likelihood that Fleming hoped for patronage from Johann Georg (to this topic I return below) and second, the strict censorship of the age, which would have made it difficult to publish sentiments other than the accepted over a genuine signature (which, of course, does not prove that Germania's sentiments are not Fleming's, but points to the unlikelihood of our hearing opposing sentiments if Fleming had them). Nonetheless, some evidence outside the *Schreiben vertriebener Frau Germanien* suggests that while censorship and the desire for patronage undoubtedly played a role, some of the sentiments of the poem were nonetheless not just the product of momentary expediency.

Stölten (p. 401) makes Fleming's friendship with Georg Gloger, whose Lutheran family had been persecuted by Catholic Silesian authorities, part of his argument that Fleming's sympathies must have been heartily pro-Lutheran and pro-Swedish. It is indeed true that in a poem (Sy.II.1) for Gloger written in August 1631, just two and a half months before Gloger's death, Fleming describes how Gloger reacted manfully to the slings and arrows of fortune: to the death of his parents, the confiscation of all the family property, and expulsion from Silesia on religious grounds.[33] The historical background to these tribulations would have been clear to contemporary readers: Karl Hannibal Burggraf von Dohna oversaw the forced reconversion of Protestant Silesia in the late 1620s. On the basis of this history one might expect—and Stölten clearly does—that Fleming, and Gloger especially, would harbor considerable rancor for the agents of excessively repressive Imperial Catholic policies, that is, for Dohna, and for those associated with him. And yet the young poets' admiration for Opitz, who from 1626 to 1632 or 1633 was the Burggraf von Dohna's private secretary and who was thus implicated, at least to all appearances, in Dohna's policies, knew no bounds, and they were most eager to meet with him when, in 1630, he was briefly in Leipzig on his way to Paris on a mission for Dohna. Some years later Fleming, in a poetic epistle to Adam Olearius (P.W.IV.44, l. 141), names Dohna as a source of inspiration and assistance to Opitz and ranks him with

Virgil's and Horace's patrons; never does he speak slightingly of the Burggraf. Opitz's politics, or lack thereof, have been regarded as requiring criticism or apology since the middle of the last century. But many of his own contemporaries, including Gloger and Fleming, in a time of violent religious partisanship, seem to have admired him without reservations based on his politics. Fleming's friendship with Gloger, then, although certainly informed by an awareness of harsh measures taken by the Imperials, simultaneously provides evidence for Fleming's at times being less troubled by confessional-political boundaries than might be expected. It suggests further that the nonpartisan, irenicist stance in the *Schreiben vertriebener Frau Germanien* was genuine, and not assumed just for the occasion.

It may also be noted that Fleming did not, as one might expect, relinquish his sense of loyalty to the emperor once the actual break between Saxony and the empire came in the autumn of 1631. He speaks positively of Ferdinand II in a poem for Heinrich Nienborg from 1634 (P.W.IV.21, l. 27ff.), and in 1637 in an epitaph (E.V.50) he calls him "patriae pater." There is also an undated panegyrical epigram for Ferdinand III (E.IV.26). One ought not to place too much weight on these items, since the list of Fleming's addressees resembles a "Who's Who" of the early modern period. Nonetheless, the recurrence in Fleming's works of positive references to the emperor certainly argues that the idea of the empire—necessarily entailing Catholics as well as Protestants—and not just a strictly Protestant Germany, attracted his loyalty.

The topic of patronage, postponed earlier, can now be addressed. The available information suggests that while, as just argued, the *Schreiben vertriebener Frau Germanien* does to a significant extent represent Fleming's own views, the coincidence of the views expressed in the poem with the thinking of Saxony's ruler suggests that the poem may also have represented a bid for patronage, probably not an isolated one. Since Elias Rudel, poet of the irenicist broadsheet cited above for its similarities to Fleming's poem, was apparently attached to the Saxon court, it is probable that the sentiments of his broadsheet were expressly approved by Johann Georg and his deputies and that the broadsheet may even have been part of a campaign to persuade the populace of Leipzig and the assembled princes to adopt Johann Georg's policy and to counteract the Swedish propaganda, which had increased in Germany since Gustav Adolf's landing. Although Fleming had no official ties to the Saxon court, it is not unreasonable to suppose that he hoped his support of the Saxon position in the *Schreiben vertriebener Frau Germanien* might come to the attention of the court. He simultaneously addressed directly to the elector a poem (see note 21) in his own voice in which a similar policy is outlined and in which, of course, Johann Georg is extravagantly praised. It was noted above that the 1631 printing of the *Schreiben vertriebener Frau Germanien* bore the signature "Allervnterthänigst vnd demütigst vbergeben von Paull Flemmingen." There is no dedication, but the obsequious formulation suggests the addressee of the poem was of high rank—perhaps the elector himself. Fleming probably hoped that this poem and others dedicated to Johann Georg might lead to financial help with his studies, or perhaps even a position at court. There are other indications that he sought Saxon patronage; a charming ode from 1631 or earlier (O.IV.1) to Magnus Schuwart, a Saxon court official, opens with a breathless inquiry about the Saxon elector's sentiments regarding him and his verses:

> Freund der dreimal dreien Schwestern!
> Kan es wol geschehen sein,
> wie du mich berichtetst gestern,
> als ich gienge zu dir ein,
> daß der Sachse günstig sei
> mir und meiner Feldschalmei?
>
> Ist denn nun mein Dorfgeheule
> auch bis in die Stadt erschallt,
> der ich mich doch, wie ein' Eule,
> stets im Wald' und Finsterm halt'?
> Hat denn auch der Fürst erhört
> das, was Pan die Bauren lehrt?
>
> (ll. 1–12)

Although he says he would feel like "eine Gans bei Schwänen" (l. 26), he longs to be among the intellects of the Saxon capital: "doch verlangt mich sehr dahin" (l. 28). In 1632 he addressed himself to the Dresden Kapellmeister, Heinrich Schütz, and again touched upon the topics of Johann Georg's favor and of his desire to live amidst the sophistication of the court city:

> Hilft mir Gott und will mein Glücke,
> daß mirs auch noch wol soll gehn,
> daß ich nicht so stets zurücke
> und in schlechter Acht muß stehn,
> so ist deines Fürsten Gunst
> mir nicht, hoffe, gar umsonst.

> So will ich einmal auch kommen,
> wo ihr schönen Leute seid.
> Was ich mir schon vorgenommen,
> das eröffnet jene Zeit.
> Diß ists, das ich sagen will;
> dort ist meiner Hoffnung Ziel.
>
> (O.IV.15, ll. 37–48)

The lines "so ist deines Fürsten Gunst / mir nicht, hoffe, gar umsonst" suggest that Fleming was already actually enjoying some kind of patronage from the elector. Information for a year later is somewhat more certain: in his biography of Fleming, Walter Schlesinger—who offers no source, but who presumably had access to Leipzig archives and whose work is usually reliable—indicates that in 1633 Fleming received "ein kurfürstliches *stipendium medicum*, . . . das auf drei Jahre berechnet war" (p. 141). Fleming's apparent success at gaining at least some patronage makes one wonder why he nonetheless, in the autumn of 1633, joined the Holstein expedition to Persia, which he must have realized would not be without perils, even if he could not realize he would never see his native land again.

Fleming's reasons for leaving Germany have been a topic of speculation in the secondary literature for over a century. Lappenberg commented that "über den Wendepunkt in Flemings Leben, welcher ihn veranlaßte, seine Studien in Leipzig aufzugeben und sich der Gottorper Gesandtschaft nach Rußland und Persien anzuschließen, herrscht einiges Dunkel" (Fleming, *Deutsche Gedichte*, p. 865), and well before this, Varnhagen von Ense, in his early biography of Fleming, thought that the undated poem *Nach seinem Traume an seinen vertrautesten Freund* (P.W.IV.50) reflected Fleming's inward struggle over the decision (pp. 20–22). At the turn of the century Albert Bornemann and more recently G. L. Jones devoted studies specifically to the question why Fleming left Germany; the topic is also almost inevitably touched upon in more general studies of Fleming.[34] There is at times a defensive tone to these discussions, a concern that Fleming might be seen as having left Leipzig and abandoned his compatriots from cowardly motives. Schröder, for example, insists that Fleming's departure was not "feige Flucht von dem gemeinsamen Schicksal, sondern . . . eine Sendung im Dienste des Vaterlandes" (p. 627). Bornemann methodically lists Fleming's reasons: interest in travel, gathering material for his poetry, and gaining the favor of princes, and then states that "Die kriegerischen Unruhen des Jahres 1633 konnten für Fleming nicht Veranlassung zur Reise bilden . . . Erst in den späteren Gedichten macht Fleming, der seine Beteiligung an der Reise immer mehr bereut, jene Kriegsunruhen als Veranlassung zur Reise geltend" (p. 12).

Fleming's motivations will never be known unequivocally. It seems far from unreasonable, though, to surmise that the deteriorating conditions in Leipzig, mainly the result of the war, played a major role in his decision to break off his medical studies and leave. That Leipzig "was far from being a pleasant town to live in," as G. L. Jones (p. 126) puts it with considerable understatement, was touched upon in the preceding chapter in connection with Fleming's descriptions of war and his epicedia. Fleming's agonized question, when will Leipzig again be at peace, was quoted from his poem for Christoph Buhle (O.IV.14). In three successive autumns the city was besieged, and war made pestilence, seldom a stranger to cities of this period, an even more frequent visitor to Leipzig. The first siege especially, following as it did on the heels of Gloger's death, must have seemed to Fleming like the continuation of a nightmare. During this period, in the early 1630s, university functions were interrupted by the war even when the city was not directly under attack; Fleming was to have received his Magister in January 1633, but this was delayed until May. Worst of all must have been the most direct consequence of war and pestilence: the soaring mortality rate. Ernst Kroker examined the death and marriage rates for Leipzig in the 1630s and discovered the curious statistic that in each of the years 1633, 1634, and 1638, more weddings were celebrated than in any single year between 1595 and 1680. The grim fact that accounts for this situation is that in each preceding year the mortality rate reached unprecedented highs, leaving enormous numbers of widows and widowers desirous of new spouses (the *vitae* appended to funeral sermons from this period bear witness to how promptly spouses tended to remarry each of the often several times they were bereaved).[35] It was probably no exaggeration when Fleming wrote in his epicedium for Michael Thomas "Man hört die heisern Glocken / Zu Grabe täglich locken" (ll. 19–20). The year 1632 was especially deadly, and in that year Fleming wrote more epicedia than in any other. That he was not similarly productive in 1633 (1634 saw a record number of marriages) is in all likelihood due only to his having left the city before autumn.

A Leipzig epithalamium from 1634 provides unexpected corroboration of the thesis that Fleming departed Leipzig in large part to escape the effects of the war. It was written by "Amandus Jägern," probably a pseudonym for Fleming's close friend Martin Christenius, a native of Jägerndorf.[36] The opening of the epithalamium, a long pastoral narrative (eleven octavo pages), describes the devastation in Leipzig and the effect on the citizenry:

> Jetzt wann man sie betracht
> Jst sie an Reichtumb arm/ an Lobesstat veracht/
> An schönen Baw verstört/ an Volcke fast verstorben/
> Jn Summa gantz vnd gar durch Feindes Grimm verdorben
> Vnd gar nicht Leipzig mehr. Daher durch die Gefahr/
> Die sich erstreckte fast in etlich gantzer Jahr
> Der Musen grösser Theil/ auch andre viel bewogen
> Zu meiden diese Noth/ wo anders hingezogen
> Vnd Sicherung gesucht. Worunter dann zugleich
> Der Nympffen waren viel an Hab' vnd Gütern reich
> Vnd Schönheit ferr berühmt; auch viel von AdelStammen
> Vnd sonst belobte mehr/ die hier gesampt beysammen
> Besonders Sylvius/ der beydes an Gemüth'
> Vnd Gaben hochgepreist/ durch sondre HimmelsGüt/
> Jngleichens mit vnd bey der schönen Zunfft gewesen:
> . . .
>
> (ll. 11–25)

Sylvius was a pastoral name that Fleming used for himself in a number of his own poems (O.IV.6, 18, 19). It becomes clear that it designates him in this work as well when at the end of the poem we are told of a messenger arriving with a "Hochzeitlied" from Sylvius: it is Fleming's *Hortulan und Lilie* (O.III.10).

Fleming's eventual success in gaining patronage from Johann Georg in 1633 may have simply come too late, after Fleming had seen too much chaos, death, and destruction to believe that his art could flourish in Saxony. Before Saxony entered the war, seeking patronage was a reasonable course (although even in the late 1620s the electoral treasury had begun showing signs of strain), but in the 1630s, in the midst of the war effort, the elector distinctly did not represent a reliable source of income. It was mentioned that Fleming approached Johann Georg's Kapellmeister, Heinrich Schütz, in 1632 (O.IV.15); perhaps Schütz or some other well-wisher pointed out to him that Schütz's salary had for some time been irregular in the extreme.[37]

3. Baltic Pastoral: Fleming's *Schäferei* for Reiner Brokmann (1635)

The pastoral tradition that reached from Theocritus and Virgil down through the Renaissance and into the seventeenth century metamorphosed (one is tempted to say metastasized) into numerous overlapping literary genres: pastoral novels and novellas, pastoral operas, neo-Latin eclogues more or less resembling Virgil's, pastoral dramas, and shepherd songs in abundance and variety. Several of these highly sophisticated forms were first introduced into German by Opitz: he wrote the libretto for an opera, *Dafne*, whose music by Schütz unfortunately did not survive; he edited a translation of Sidney's *Arcadia*; he wrote a number of songs based on Dutch pastoral songs based in their turn on French sources. And with his *Schäfferey von der Nimfen Hercinie* he introduced yet a further variation on pastoral's possibilities: the *Schäferei*, a novella-length prose genre in which the poet and several friends, thinly disguised as shepherds, peregrinate, discourse on topics of interest, and periodically burst into song, often to celebrate some occasion central to the work.[1]

Opitz's efforts at introducing various forms of pastoral into German aroused considerable interest and activity in Leipzig circles. Adam Olearius met a number of times with Opitz when the latter stopped in Leipzig on his way to Paris in 1630, and, among other topics, they discussed translating Virgil into German; Opitz especially urged Olearius to translate the eclogues. This Olearius did not do himself, but he did encourage the young Oswald Beling (1625–46) in the endeavor and, three years after Beling's death, Olearius saw to the editing and publication of the edition, which was augmented by his own "Hirten Gespräch."[2] Olearius may have written other pastoral poems. One "Andinum d'Orliens"—clearly a pseudonym, perhaps for Olearius—published a "Corydon-Lied," a song in the pastoral tradition for the 1633 wedding of Andreas Bachmann and Catharina-Isabella Bergerin (the bride's last name evidently provided the initial inspiration).[3] Other Leipzig writers also exploited pastoral motifs when writing epithalamia, among them one who signed himself sometimes "Amandus Jägern," sometimes "Mauritius Schinstern," and was probably Fleming's friend Martin Christenius from Jägerndorf in Silesia. His *Con-*

tinuation der jüngst beschehenen . . . *Hirten-Lust* for Martin Schörkel and Margarethe Putscher of 1633 and his *Ernewerte Hirten-Lust* for Friederich Kühlewein and Rosine Vetzerin (the latter was quoted in the preceding chapter in reference to Fleming's reasons for departing Leipzig) are narratives describing the activities of the wedding guests and the bridal couple on the wedding day; poems are inserted at strategic points.[4] Christenius departs from Opitz's practice in his *Schäferei* by using more or less opaque pastoral names, rather than real ones, and by employing alexandrines throughout for the narrative instead of prose. A lack of obvious scholarly pretensions further sets these early Leipzig pastorals off from Opitz's. There were also attempts to follow Opitz's example more closely: Gottfried Finckelthaus, another close friend of Fleming's, used the *Schäferei* genre to commemorate Thomas Leonhart Schwendendörffer, who died in 1635. Anthony Harper has argued persuasively that Finckelthaus is also the author of a further *Schäferei, Floridans Lob- vnd LiebesGedichte*, written at about the same time, of which more below.[5] And a final witness to Leipzig interest in the pastoral: the first German pastoral novel, the *Jüngst-erbawete Schäfferey/ Oder Keusche Liebes-Beschreibung/ Von der Verliebten Nimfen Amoena, Vnd dem Lobwürdigen Schäffer Amandus*, was published pseudonymously under the name Schindschersitzky in Leipzig in 1632 and enjoyed considerable popularity.[6]

Fleming's own contributions to pastoral fall mainly under two headings: the individual pastoral ode and the *Schäferei*. Characteristically, he excelled in two pastoral genres in which some autobiographical content was sanctioned. Opitz, in his Corydon-Lieder, particularly in *Galathee*, wrote of himself and his affairs of the heart under the thin disguise of pastoral names; in the *Schäfferey von der Nimfen Hercinie* he dispensed entirely with pseudonyms to write directly of himself and his friends. In many of his pastoral odes in the Dutch-French tradition favored by Opitz (as opposed to the Italianate tradition of Fleming's translations from the *Pastor fido*), Fleming also offered considerable autobiographical detail, but in contrast to Opitz and many others, he used the form largely to commemorate occasions affecting his circle of (male) friends, rather than to treat of love affairs. Two of his pastoral odes, for example, are recognizably based on *Galathee*, but one celebrates a friend's wedding (O.III.17) while the other mourns a friend's departure from Leipzig (O.IV.19). Passages of lamentation for dead or departed (male) friends (often identifiable despite the pastoral names) frequently temper the occasional or celebratory character of Fleming's early pastoral poems (see O.IV.4–7, 10, 19), and when read chronologically, they provide an index of Fleming's increasing unhappiness in the troubled city.

Just as Fleming characteristically chose potentially autobiographical genres, so too it is not surprising that when he came in Reval to essay a more substantial pastoral work he should disregard the variety of pastoral genres with which he must have been acquainted in Leipzig and go directly back to Opitz, for whom all his life he harbored deep admiration, in order to write a work modeled on *Hercinie*. Now a traveler himself, Fleming may have been attracted to his source by its pervasive theme of travel. Since the above-mentioned works by Finckelthaus were not written until the autumn of 1635 and winter of 1635–36, and since Christenius's epithalamia are not directly related to Opitz's *Schäferei*, Fleming's work constitutes the first known imitation of *Hercinie*.

Fleming's Journey to Reval, His Contacts There, and His Friendship with Reiner Brokmann

The story of Fleming's journey has been told many times, so that I can confine myself here to a sketch of the steps that brought him as far as Reval.[7] In the latter part of 1633 Fleming, along with his friend and mentor Olearius, entered the service of Friedrich III, Duke of Holstein, as members of the proposed embassy to Russia and Persia, headed by ambassadors Otto Brüggemann and Philipp Kruse, and charged with negotiating with the Czar and the Shah agreements permitting Holstein to establish an overland trade route from Persia through Russia. The expedition departed from Hamburg on November 6, 1633, arrived in Riga on November 14, and proceeded by sled via Dorpat to Narva (January 3, 1634), where they awaited the arrival of a similar Swedish embassy. Negotiations with Sweden were a *sine qua non* of the expedition, as the Germans needed to travel through Sweden's Baltic territories. Additionally, the Swedes themselves had unstable plans for diverting the silk trade overland, and they vacillated between partnership and rivalry with the Germans in negotiating with the Czar. Relations were, however, by no means acrimonious between members of the respective embassies, as can be seen in poems (O.II.13 and E.VI.18) Fleming wrote somewhat later, in 1635, for Peter Crusbiorn, who had traveled with the Swedish embassy to take up his post as Swedish resident ambassador in Moscow, and in Fleming's friendship with Krußbiorn's secretary, the Nuremberg patrician Georg Wilhelm Pöhmer. The wait in Narva for the Swedish ambassadors proved to be so long that a substantial part of the expedition was sent ahead to Novgorod, under Fleming's leadership, before the spring thaw made the roads impassable, and the ambassadors themselves and twelve others had go to Reval for six weeks when provisions ran low. Finally, after many meetings with the tardy Swedes and extended negotiations with Moscow, the ambassadors joined Fleming's contingent at Novgorod, and at the end of July the Holstein expedition was able to proceed to Moscow, arriving on August 14. During their four-month sojourn in the Russian capital Fleming and his companions sought out and socialized with the German-speaking residents of the city, including the Lutheran pastor, Martin Münsterberger. The ambassadors meanwhile reached a moderately satisfactory agreement with Czar Michael Romanov, but were required by him to supply further documents from Duke Friedrich himself before proceeding through Russia to Persia. The embassy therefore left Moscow on December 24, 1634 and traveled back to the Baltic; on January 10, 1635 they arrived in Reval (present-day Tallinn), where most of the members of the initial expedition, including Fleming, installed themselves. The ambassadors and a few others, including Olearius, set out on January 30 for the rest of the journey back to Gottorp. Fleming remained in Reval throughout 1635; in December the ambassadors finally returned with documents and reinforcements—for they had realized that the size of the initial group was much too small for so long and arduous a journey—and everyone set off once again in early March 1636 for Moscow and Persia.

Fleming's long stay in Reval from January 1635 to March 1636 was less of a sojourn in a foreign land than it might at first appear.[8] While the city and surrounding Estonia were under Swedish dominion—Russian attempts to take the town in the sixteenth century having failed—most of the important and well-to-do families were German. Olearius notes that the indigenous populations, the Estonians and Latvians, were referred to collectively as "die Undeutschen" (*Reisebeschreibung*, p. 107). Some of the Germans traced their roots back to the German orders of knights that had controlled Livonia into the sixteenth century, and many others were descended from German merchants. The *raison d'être* of the town, as far as this dominant nonindigenous population was concerned, was trade, for Reval's situation on the Baltic with an excellent harbor made it a logical mediator between Russia and Western Europe, and many merchants from Northern Germany, especially from cities of the Hanseatic League (to which Reval belonged), had emigrated to Estonia to facilitate and profit from the mediation. By the seventeenth century and the time of Fleming's stay there, Reval was no longer as prosperous as before. The emerging centralized Russian state was a more difficult neighbor and trading partner than the Reval merchants of the fifteenth century and earlier had known, and deadly famine and plague in 1602–3 had seriously affected the population. The hostilities between Sweden and Poland also disrupted trade and contributed to the decline of the economy. Even in its decline, however, the city was sufficiently prosperous to offer a pleasant stopping place for the travelers. The fact that ambassador Otto Brüggemann was related to one of the important families of the area, that of Johann Moller (Möller, Müller), seems to have ensured that those staying in Reval would have entrée into the society of at least one leading family. And since Olearius notes (*Reisebeschreibung*, p. 103) that particularly cordial relations existed among the various leading men of Reval—the members of the city council, the teachers at the gymnasium, and the religious leaders of this Lutheran city as well as the landed gentry—contact with the Mollers doubtless led in due course to the Western European Germans' introduction to *le tout* Reval.

This period was probably the most productive in Fleming's career. There are many undated love poems—sonnets and odes—that were most likely written in Reval, as well as numerous occasional poems for citizens of the town and members of the expedition, some written in Fleming's own name, some in the name of well-wishers. The eight Moller children seem to have been particularly successful in drafting Fleming to write for them. The two major works from this period, the *Schäferei* for Reiner Brokmann's marriage and the *Gymnasium Revaliense*, were written, or at least begun in April 1635, indicating how quickly Fleming had been integrated into Reval's intellectual and social circles. They also show how little distance the journey had put between Fleming and European culture, classical or modern: the *Gymnasium Revaliense* was modeled on a cycle of poems written by the fourth-century Latin poet, Ausonius, while the epithalamium was, of course, based on Opitz's work.

Fleming's title for his epithalamium—I shall use the more convenient, albeit inelegant, designation P.W.III.6—is *Auf des ehrnvesten und wolgelahrten Herrn Reineri Brockmans, der griechischen Sprache Professorn am Gymnasio zu Reval, und der erbarn viel ehren- und tugendreichen Jungfrauen Dorotheen Temme Hochzeit*; the title marks this pastoral as an occasional work more explicitly than Opitz's title does his. Of Dorothea Temme nothing is known;[9] Brokmann is better documented. The same age as Fleming, he studied at Hamburg and Rostock before becoming a professor of Greek at the recently founded Reval Gymnasium in 1634. In 1639 he assumed a country pastorate not far from Reval, and he moved farther up the ecclesiastical hierarchy before his death in 1647.[10] Brokmann took an intense interest in the new Opitzian poetry, even attempting alexandrines in the Estonian language,[11] and his initial inscription in Fleming's *Stammbuch* (B.II.30) attests to his admiration for this follower of the new school of poetry. Fleming, in P.W.III.6, warmly recalls that Brokmann was the first of the town's intellectuals to inquire for him. The exact date of Brokmann's marriage is not known, but the opening of Fleming's work indicates that it was shortly after the middle of April.

Structural Correspondences between P.W.III.6 and Opitz's *Hercinie*

Fleming's P.W.III.6 has received almost no attention from Fleming scholars, and little from students of the German pastoral. Among the earlier generation of the latter, Heinrich Meyer, Ursula Schaumann, and Ernst Günter Carnap contented themselves with short, not always accurate, plot summaries, while more recent surveys of *Schäfereien* mention it briefly or not at all.[12] The main reason for this neglect is probably that Fleming's work appears initially too much like a pale copy of Opitz. P.W.III.6, while borrowing the interwoven prose and verse, the general plot, the character configuration, and some phrasing, lacks both the marvelous dazzle of Hercinie and her cave, and the uncanny drama of the encounter with the witch. Fleming's—and all later *Schäferei* poets'—failure to follow Opitz's example of imparting humanistic learning, which makes him seem less weighty than his model,[13] seems not to be offset by the innovations or elaborations in landscape, plot, and types of poetry that are associated especially with the *Schäfereien* coming out of the Nuremberg school.

This unflattering assessment of Fleming's work as a wan imitation arises in part, paradoxically enough, from an unawareness of how carefully Fleming studied the *Schäfferey von der Nimfen Hercinie*. Comparison of the two works reveals that Fleming did not borrow themes and motifs in a superficial fashion, but rather adapted and transformed to his own ends fundamental aspects of *Hercinie*. An examination of Fleming's adaptation has the interest of disclosing one important contemporary's understanding of *Hercinie* and highlights differences between Fleming and Opitz. Moreover, it indicates a fundamentally different direction the *Schäferei*, and perhaps the novel, might have taken had Fleming's model been more influential. To anticipate briefly: comparing and contrasting the two works and the ways in which certain corresponding aspects are transformed by Fleming reveals that Fleming's work is a more coherent and unified one, that it focuses on bourgeois values, that it is more realistic, and that the understanding of love between the sexes represented in it is more egalitarian and reciprocal than that depicted by Opitz. None of these characterizations need represent a value judgment—although the fact that for the modern reader they often do is consonant with the fact that modern readers often find Fleming more appealing than Opitz.

I said above that Fleming studied Opitz's work carefully, and I believe his care can initially best be demonstrated by showing how the poems in his work create a structure that in most places corresponds very closely to one in Opitz's work. An awareness of this structural similarity—partly masked by the prose narrative in which the poems are embedded—will then become helpful in comparing and contrasting the two works, for it makes manifest correspondences that otherwise might be overlooked and that occasionally prove more important than such obvious correspondences as that between Opitz's Hercinie and Fleming's Muses.

Anyone who has read both *Hercinie* and P.W.III.6 recognizes immediately that the opening quatrain of Fleming's work ("Den Nächten gieng das Liecht") and the immediately following prose ("Mit Kurzem, es war zu Mitten des Aprils") imitate the quatrain and subsequent prose that set the season at the beginning of Opitz's work ("Der Monde machte gleich," "Mitt einem worte: Es war zue ende des Weinmonats").[14] Fleming thus at the outset quite openly alludes to his model. Formal similarities in the closings of the works are less immediately obvious, but nonetheless recognizable: each work ends with three sonnets contributed by the poet's three friends, followed by an ode by the poet himself. Such parallels based on form or speaker, or both, exist throughout the two works. Fleming's work, although much shorter than Opitz's, has very nearly the same number of poems (the identical number, thirty-four, if one consistently counts offset single lines, couplets, and quatrains in each work as well as Fleming's dedicatory sonnet); there is often a one to one correspondence between individual poems in the respective works, and much of the time at least a general correspondence between groups of poems (see parallel listing below).

Hercinie	P.W.III.6
	1 Dedicatory sonnet, l. 1ff.[15]
1 Quatrain: *Der Monde machte gleich*, p. 9	2 Quatrain: *Den Nächten gieng*, l. 15ff.
	3 Genethliacon for Kruse, l. 19ff.
	4 Genethliacon for Brüggemann, l. 29ff.
	5 Genethliacon for Brüggemann, l. 81ff.
	6 Single line on Tantalus, l. 117

Baltic Pastoral 85

2 Sonnet: *Weil mein Verhengniß wil*, p. 10
3 Sonnet: *Es ist gewagt*, p. 11f.
4 Love ode: *Ist mein hertze*, p. 14f.

5 Venator's misogynic epigram, p. 17
6 Another, p. 17

7 Hercinie's welcome, p. 26
8 Portal inscription, p. 31

9 Portrait epigram, p. 34
10 Portrait epigram, p. 34
11 Portrait epigram, p. 35
12 Portrait epigram, p. 36
13 Portrait epigram, p. 36
14 Portrait epigram, p. 37
15 Portrait epigram, p. 37

16 Panegyric on Schaffgotsch, p. 38ff.

17 Invocation of Berggott, p. 46
18 Witch: *Ist dann kein mittel*, p. 49f.
19 Witch's spell, p. 50
20 Witch's spell, p. 51
21 Witch's spell, p. 51
22 Witch's spell, p. 51
23 Witch's spell, p. 51

24 *Das liecht wardt schwartze nacht*, p. 51f.
25 *Ist jenes dann das feldt*, p. 52ff.
26 Ode: *Meine Frewde die mich bindet*,
  p. 55f.
27 *Sechstine*, p. 57f.
28 *Sonnet über die augen der Astree*, p. 58
29 Nüßler's epigram, p. 59
30 *Du Hochberedter mann*, p. 60f.

31 Nüßler's sonnet, p. 63
32 Buchner's sonnet, p. 63f.
33 Venator's sonnet, p. 64
34 Opitz's ode, p. 64f.

7 Love ode: *Laß es sein*, l. 118ff.

8 Polus's misogynic epigram, l. 166ff.

9 Ode for Polus, l. 178ff.
10 Ode for Münsterberger's nameday,
  l. 286ff.

11 Epigram on the desert, l. 340ff.
12 Olearius on barbarian lands, l. 344f.

13 Clio's wedding epigram, l. 346f.
14 Melpomene's epigram, l. 348f.
15 Thalia's epigram, l. 350ff.
16 Euterpe's epigram, l. 354f.
17 Terpsichore's epigram, l. 356f.
18 Erato's epigram, l. 358ff.
19 Calliope's epigram, l. 362f.
20 Urania's epigram, l. 364f.
21 Polyhymnia's epigram, l. 366f.

22 Fleming in Brokmann's *Stammbuch*,
  l. 368ff.

23 *R. Brockman an seine Dorothea*, l. 376ff.
24 Brokmann's epigram, l. 392ff.
25 Brokmann's epigram, l. 396ff.
26 Brokmann's epigram, l. 400ff.
27 Brokmann's epigram, l. 404ff.
28 Brokmann's epigram, l. 408ff.
29 Brokmann's epigram, l. 412ff.
30 *Daß er unbillich getan*, l. 416ff.
  [*Wie er wolle geküsset sein*]

31 Olearius's sonnet, l. 426ff.
32 Pöhmer's sonnet, l. 440ff.
33 Polus's sonnet, l. 454ff.
34 Fleming's ode, l. 468ff.

Opitz's first poem, the quatrain in which he sets the season, is followed by a set of love poems—two sonnets and an ode. Fleming's work deviates slightly here from Opitz, (this deviation is discussed below) for immediately succeeding the quatrain in P.W.III.6 he includes three poems in praise of the ambassadors and only then brings a love poem, an ode in the same form as Opitz's. In each work there follows a misogynic poem or poems by one of the poets' friends based loosely on Catullus or the *Anthologia Latina*. Shortly afterward, each work has a number of very short poems or epigrams whose origin is supernatural, written by mythical female beings. In Opitz's work, these are the inscriptions on the portraits of the Schaffgotsch family; in Fleming's, they are the work of the Muses. In *Hercinie* the portrait inscriptions lead to the center of the work, to the long panegyric for Hans Ulrich Schaffgotsch, to whom the work is dedicated. In P.W.III.6 the Muses' verses similarly lead to a panegyric for the person for whom the work is written, that is, to Fleming's brief entry in Brokmann's *Stammbuch* (the discrepancy in length between the two panegyrics is discussed below). Parallels continue immediately after this central point: in each work there now follows a group of mainly epigram-length poems emanating from someone who is not of the central group of four friends. In *Hercinie* the first of these is by a supplicant of the "Berggott," the remainder are by the witch; in P.W.III.6 they are all by Brokmann. After the mention, but not the reciting of *Wie er wolle geküsset sein*, Fleming's work moves rapidly towards its closing with the sonnets and ode by the four friends; in *Hercinie* there are several more intervening poems in various forms by the friends before the closing sonnets and ode.

To summarize, while there is not always a one to one correspondence between the poems of one work and those of the other—although frequently this is the case—there is a general correspondence in form and speaker of groups of poems. Each work contains an initial set of poems (at least the last of which is a love poem) by the poet, followed by misogynic verses by one of his friends. There follows shortly a set of epigrammatic poems by benign mythical female beings that leads to a panegyrical poem to the person to whom the work is dedicated. This is followed by another set of mainly epigrammatic poems, these again by persons outside the group of four peripatetic shepherds. The works close with three sonnets and an ode. These similarities in structure can hardly be accidental, particularly given that Fleming's work is considerably shorter than Opitz's, and proportionality would argue against the inclusion of enough poems to create a parallel structure unless it were done deliberately. Fleming had studied *Hercinie*, particularly its poems, much as he did Heinsius's *Manes Dousici*, and the example of the *Arae Schönburgicae* suggests that we can look for more than simple copying when Fleming sets out to write his own version of *Hercinie*.

The Panegyrical Poems in Fleming's and Opitz's *Schäfereien* and Fleming's Focus on Friendship

In investigating how Fleming borrowed and transformed the structure of Opitz's work for his own purposes, two places where Fleming actually departs noticeably from this structure provide a convenient starting point. First, there is the initial discrepancy towards the beginning of P.W.III.6 where Fleming has put nonamorous verses before his love poem, while Opitz has love poems only, and second, the discrepancy in length and character of the panegyrics (the long poem to Schaffgotsch and the *Stammbucheintragung* for Brokmann) at the centers of the works. The two differences prove to be related. For if we look for a poem or poems in P.W.III.6 whose general characteristics seem to correspond more closely to Opitz's panegyric on his patron than does the *Stammbucheintragung*, we come precisely to the three seemingly anomalous poems towards the beginning in which Fleming praises *his* patrons (*Kom, schöner Tag* for Kruse, and *Herr, wer er auch wird sein* and *Ist er itzo schon von hinnen* for Brüggemann). Fleming has simply moved the panegyrics for his patrons from the middle to the front of the work. Calling attention, probably deliberately, to the correspondence between his three poems and Opitz's panegyric is a verbal reminiscence of Opitz in Fleming: Opitz's alexandrine panegyric opens "Brich an/ du schöner tag/ vndt komm/ du edles kindt/" (p. 38) while the first of Fleming's poems for his patrons opens "Kom, schöner Tag, und du, o süßer Schein."

Fleming's gain from this adjustment is twofold. He now has the opportunity to put a very different type of poem in the central position in his work (more on this below), and he is able to compliment his patrons without interfering with the focus of his epithalamium. If one regards the dedicatory sonnet and the quatrain setting the season as preliminaries, then the three panegyrical poems occupy the place of honor at the beginning of the work. At the same time, by making them part of the scene-setting material that precedes the celebration of the true occasion of the work—Brokmann's imminent wedding—Fleming permits himself, once the topic of Brokmann's wedding is raised by the Muses' poems, to concentrate exclusively on that event and the themes suggested by it. This contributes to a unity and coherence in Fleming's work not found—and probably not striven for—in Opitz's. While the center of Opitz's work is Hercinie's cave and the praise of Schaffgotsch that occurs therein, it is surrounded on either side by themes—love and travel—and displays of encyclopedic learning that hardly relate to it, and often not to one another. Fleming, in contrast, brings all the topics not arising directly from the occasion—praise of patrons, travel, praise of friends other than Brokmann—towards the beginning of the work as his friends gather about him and then, once all are there, leads into the closely interwoven themes that occupy the rest of the work.[16]

Even while deviating from Opitz's structure by bringing his panegyrics up towards the front of his work, Fleming pays Opitz the compliment of imitating him: the first of the two poems for Brüggemann, *Herr, wer er auch wird sein, der etwas auf wird schreiben*, is modeled after Opitz's 1623 *An eine Hochfürstliche Person/ vber den von deroselbten gestiffteten Orden . . . der Vertrewligkeit*, which begins "HErr/ wer der auch wird seyn/ so künfftig ewer Leben."[17] Like Opitz, Fleming uses a device similar to *praeteritio* to lead into his praise of his patron, saying "whoever it will be who will write [of you] for posterity will say"; the poet himself then takes over the role of that future scribe by recounting the virtues of his patron. Gellinek has pointed to the stylistic deficiencies of Opitz's panegyric, which shares with many of his early poems the tendency to pile up a long series of similarly structured clauses (see esp. ll. 28–36).[18] Opitz also has a difficult time coming to the point in a way that suggests he wasn't in complete control of his medium:

> HErr/ wer der auch wird seyn/ so künfftig ewer Leben
> Der Zeit die nach vns kömpt/ wird zu erkennen geben/
>   Daß ewres Namens Lob berühmbt sey weit vnd breit/
>   Als wie jhr dann verdient/ O Hoffnung vnsrer Zeit;
>
> . . .
>
> (ll. 1–4)

Only after these four lines does Opitz arrive at the main verb: "Wird sagen."

While borrowing from Opitz the basic concept for his poem, Fleming avoids these stylistic difficulties. His sentences are more numerous and thus shorter (twenty-two in fifty-two lines vs. seven in the same number of lines in Opitz) and more varied; he avoids the monotony of an extended series of similar clauses (the longest series is in ll. 49–53); his use of fewer relative clauses contributes to a sense of forward motion in his poem as opposed to the sense of standing in one place that one has in Opitz's; and he is altogether more direct:

> Herr, wer er auch wird sein, der etwas auf wird schreiben,
> das bis zum Ende hin der grauen Zeit kan bleiben,
> das seinen Tod verlacht, der wird auch zeigen an,
> . . .
>
> (ll. 29–31)

Opitz's poem is a very early one, and Gellinek has shown how he later moved away from some of his early stylistic characteristics, gradually providing more attractive models for his followers. It is thus not unreasonable that Fleming's poem, composed twelve years after Opitz's, should have benefitted from the intervening years and be better written. But it is worth noting that Fleming was sufficiently confident of his own, better style that he was not drawn into imitating that of the early Opitz, even while imitating the overall idea of his poem.

Despite its stylistic superiority, Fleming's poem is curiously awkward in its construction, for the poet has not been able to integrate the purely panegyrical passages (ll. 29–39 and 49–65) with the passages celebrating Brüggemann's nameday (ll. 39–48 and 65–72). The transitions from one mode to another in the middle of line 39 and the middle of line 65 are so abrupt that they arouse the suspicion that two independent poems have been merged, as does the fact that the panegyrical passages speak of both Brüggemann and Kruse equally, while the nameday passages clearly refer only to Brüggemann. The last lines, 73–80, in which the old year is urged to make way for the new, seem hardly related to any of the preceding except insofar as the half line "November werde Mai" names the months of Brüggemann's nameday and Kruse's birthday. Lappenberg (Fleming, *Deutsche Gedichte*, p. 875) notes that this poem from Fleming's *Schäferei* was never reprinted and suggests this was due to the ill repute Brüggemann had achieved by the end of the expedition; perhaps the simpler explanation is that Fleming was aware of the defects of the poem.

Fleming's short poem in *vers communs* for Kruse's birthday that precedes the alexandrine poem for Brüggemann was also not reprinted, perhaps overlooked due to its brevity. The second poem for Brüggemann, this one for his birthday, was, however, reprinted in the *Teütsche Poemata*. It represents the only part of this entire *Schäferei* with even a remote connection to shepherds; in the *Teütsche Poemata* it becomes part of a *Chor der Hirten* (P.W.IV.25). Written in Fleming's favorite ode form, which he used equally for epithalamia and epicedia, it is far more attractive than the alexandrine poem and shows us the expedition members celebrating Brüggemann's birthday even in his absence. Barbara Becker-Cantarino has discovered an autograph letter from Fleming to Brüggemann dated March 14, 1635 which includes this poem;[19] it lacks the fifth strophe, which in P.W.IV.25 and P.W.III.6 makes reference to the season ("Der beschneite Hornung"). Perhaps the original version of the alexandrine nameday poem to Brüggemann also lacked the closing lines that set the season, and they and the strophe in the ode were added in the work for Brokmann in order to underline the fact that these poems were being recalled from earlier times. That and Fleming's reference to Moscow, where the long alexandrine poem was written ("das Gedichte, so . . . in Moskau . . . gemacht wurde," prose preceding l. 29), have the effect of making the work live in a larger and more definite—if exotic—landscape: it is not the description of a random single day but is firmly anchored at several points in the time and space of the journey.

While the three poems for the ambassadors correspond to Opitz's long panegyric by virtue of being written to honor patrons and, in the case of the second one, by virtue of similarities in form and tone, there remains Fleming's inscription in Brokmann's *Stammbuch*, which corresponds to Opitz's poem by virtue of its position at the center of the work and because it is also a poem praising the man to whom the work is dedicated. In most other respects, however, the poems are obviously vastly different, and the differences help pinpoint where Fleming's aims diverge from Opitz's.

Opitz wrote his poem for a member of the nobility on whose estate he had stayed and whose further patronage the poem encouraged; its considerable length accords with the principles of epideictic rhetoric governing the composition of panegyrics for important men. The fiction that the poem, composed by the Fates, was picked out in diamonds upon a black crystal wall is intended to suggest that the poem is eternal. It also argues for the verity of the poem: it was written by those who control events and thus know their truth, and it was written in materials so noble that they cannot be associated with falsehood.

Fleming's poem, whose brevity is dictated by the diminutive page of an *album amicorum*, is from one member of the learned bourgeoisie to another: equal to equal. Originally written in Latin in Brokmann's *Stammbuch*, the form of inscription does not so much ensure its imperishability, in the manner of Opitz's diamonds, as it ensures that the poem be comprehensible to and shared by all members of that international fraternity, the *respublica litteraria*, without regard to national and linguistic boundaries. In his brief, pithy praise of Brokmann, Fleming does not concern himself with ancestry and deeds of valor, but instead commends three traits: Brokmann's learning, his love of poetry, and—surpassing these two—his friendship.

This delineation of differences between the poems may seem to belabor the obvious: the poems must inevitably show such differences, given that they honor persons of such different status. But this objection begs the question. Fleming had ample opportunity to write a work such as P.W.III.6 for a highly placed person or member of the nobility, for Brüggemann or Kruse, for example, or for Duke Friedrich. He was also perfectly able to write an epithalamium for Brokmann without modeling it on Opitz's *Schäferei*. But when he came to imitate Opitz's *Hercinie* he chose to do so when celebrating the wedding of someone of his own station with whom he shared interests and friendship. The difference in station between the persons honored in the two works and the resulting differences in the central panegyrics are thus in and of themselves significant. By placing the *Stammbucheintragung* in the central position of the work, making it correspond in placement to the most important poem in Opitz's work, Fleming draws attention to the differences between the works and the different values that characterize the world of learned friendship, on the one hand, and those governing the relationship of poet to patron on the other.[20]

The spirit of friendship among equals in which P.W.III.6 was written colors not just the sections specifically concerning Brokmann, but also all the passages depicting interaction among the four central characters. The conversations among Opitz, Venator, Buchner, and Nüßler in *Hercinie* are barely disguised philosophizing, and the topics are either related to Opitz's difficulties or are of general scholarly and antiquarian interest. The impersonal and elevated discourse necessarily used in connection with the patron seems to pervade the work. In contrast, the conversations in P.W.III.6, while not lacking in learned references, seldom become highly abstract and philosophical, and there is in them more of the back and forth of conversation as opposed to the sustained sequential monologues that for long stretches pass for dialogue in *Hercinie*. Additionally, in the conversations in P.W.III.6 the narrator is only occasionally the center of interest: Fleming's putative love life is touched on in his conversation with Timotheus Polus, but they pass quickly to the difficulties Polus is having at the gymnasium. Fleming and Pöhmer then talk about Fleming's apparently not having written, and not long thereafter Polus defends Livonia from Olearius's suggestion that it is just a little backwards, who in turn defends the journey into barbarian lands; they then speak of Brokmann. The overall effect is of friends discussing in a fairly haphazard and natural manner topics of interest to any and all of them—as opposed to learned men holding forth on philosophical topics touching none or, at most, a single one of them, personally. In both *Hercinie* and P.W.III.6 the cast of characters is a group of learned friends; in Opitz's work the emphasis is on "learned"; in Fleming's it is on "friends." Similarly, in Opitz's work the four men are clearly equals, but the attention focuses on Opitz, his love life, and approaching journey, and we gain little sense of the other three except insofar as they respond to Opitz's problems in characteristic ways or display expertise in particular areas. In Fleming's work, not only are the friends equals, but there is also a sense of reciprocity among them: they take turns being the focus of interest and focuser of interest. The ultimate effect is to make them more identifiably individuals: we know that Polus is worried about politics at the gymnasium and that he is defensive about Livonia's apparent backwardness; that Pöhmer and Fleming had been together in Moscow and that Pöhmer has missed hearing from Fleming, whose poetry he is fond of; that Olearius is inclined to look down his nose somewhat at Livonia, but that he is fascinated by the strangeness of foreign lands and values the comradeship of the journey.

There was, of course, one very good reason why Opitz did not need to flesh out the characters in his work, and that is that they were sufficiently well known to his audience—both to his noble patron and to the scholar-poets keenly interested in Opitz's vernacular poetry. There was no need to identify them or to make them individual: the names were sufficient, and their presence fulfilled a representational function—leading learned men of Germany were gathered to praise the house of Schaffgotsch. Fleming, choosing to write for the wedding of a schoolteacher, had an audience both more bourgeois and more local, one that had personal contact with at least Polus and Olearius, if not Pöhmer, and that probably took pleasure in seeing them appear not merely as names but as people whose known interests and concerns were depicted. Insofar as Fleming was also writing for the broader audience of his friends in Leipzig and friends of the new poetry in Germany—and the work was sent back to Leipzig for printing—interest in the work was probably ensured by its exoticism, by the very notion of a German poet writing in the Opitzian manner at the border with the barbarians.

Fleming's Realism

It is not only Fleming's explicit departures from Opitz's work that point to basic differences between P.W.III.6 and *Hercinie*. Examination of places where he has at some level retained the structure of *Hercinie* can also lead to fundamental distinctions between the works. One point of apparent similarity is Fleming's retention, as indicated earlier, of two sets of mainly short poems or epigrams on either side of the central panegyric and his use of similar speakers for these. In *Hercinie*, Opitz and his three friends read the inscriptions on the portraits of Schaffgotsch ancestors put there, presumably, by the nymphs. In the corresponding place in P.W.III.6, Fleming and his three friends read the poems inscribed by the Muses on a tablet. The sets of short poems in *Hercinie* and P.W.III.6 that follow the central panegyric share a similarity in authorship with each other and with those that precede the panegyrics. Unlike most of the other poems in the two *Schäfereien*, none of these short poems is the work of any of the four friends. In *Hercinie* the second set consists of an invocation of the mountain spirit and the witch's incantations. These correspond in P.W.III.6 to poems written by Brokmann for his betrothed. The implications of the latter correspondence—two sets of poems concerning love—are particularly interesting for what they tell of the concept of love in the respective works. For the moment, however, it will be useful to start with a more obvious aspect of contrast highlighted by these passages in the respective works, that is Fleming's greater realism vis-à-vis Opitz.[21]

In *Hercinie*, the sets of short poems emanate from one certainly and one possibly supernatural source, nymphs and a witch, who, moreover, put in appearances in the narrative. In Fleming's work the supernatural element is toned down. In one case the poet is clearly human (Brokmann), and in the other, where the Muses are the source of the poems, the supernatural poets remain offstage; Fleming allows a description of their distantly heard sweet music to suffice. The immediate effect of Fleming's transformation of these passages is to give his narrative as a whole greater verisimilitude: there is little one can point to, as one can in *Hercinie*, that openly attests that the *Schäferei* might not have actually occurred. This is in keeping with Fleming's greater realism in other areas: the shepherd costumes of Opitz's work are vestigial; in Fleming's they are suppressed entirely—no sound of pastoral pipes heralds the arrival of his friends, and they carve no poems on trees. Small concrete details add to the verisimilitude of the narrative, as when Fleming makes a joke of the disparity in size between himself and Olearius, and when Pöhmer, who had never been in Reval, willingly undertakes to sing a sonnet for Brokmann, but nevertheless observes that he is "der verlobten Personen Bekanter nicht" (p. 92).

Fleming's more realistic narrative and setting are, however, not simply an artless attempt to describe a real event. An element of piquancy is added to his demonstrable capacity for realistic and credible narrative when one realizes that despite all the verisimilitude, what he depicts could not actually have taken place; Fleming twice slyly calls attention to the impossibility. It will be recalled that just before the appearance of Hercinie in Opitz's work, Nüßler remarks "Aber . . . was halten wir vnsere gäste mitt anderen reden auff" (p. 25), a reminder that Buchner and Venator, who are not Silesians, are enjoying the hospitality of Opitz and Nüßler, who are.[22] Fleming copied this configuration of hosts and guests precisely—again an indication of how closely he studied *Hercinie*. He and Polus are the short- and long-term residents of Reval welcoming Pöhmer and Olearius, both of whom were not only nonresidents, but could in fact not possibly have been in Reval at the time assigned to the narrative.[23] Olearius had left for Gottorp two and a half months before, and Pöhmer had left Moscow for Germany the previous autumn. Hence the astonishment with which Fleming and Polus greet the arrival of the other two is only apparently exaggerated. Many in Fleming's first audience must have realized that the appearance of Olearius and Pöhmer was fantastic, and must have enjoyed the way Fleming forestalls Olearius's explanation of his presence. Polus asks (for the second time) how Olearius and Pöhmer come to be in Reval: "Olearius wolte gleich seine Frage beantworten, als wir vor uns in dem Püschlein ein liebliches Getöne . . . erhöreten" (p. 86). Fleming, whose narrative skill turns out to be considerable, has arranged for an interruption by the Muses just in time. Similarly, Fleming tantalizes the reader further at the end of the piece when the four men go to supper at Polus's, "Darbei denn Olearius und Pöhmer ihrer Ankunft und anderer Sachen halben uns Bericht gaben" (p. 94)—a report not imparted to us.

Fleming's work has, in a sense, not just one but two "unerwartete Begebenheiten" (as the apparition of "das geflügelte Gerüchte" is characterized in the *Pegnesisches Schaefergedicht*): one patent—hearing the Muses and finding their tablets, and one hidden—the miraculous appearance of Olearius and Pöhmer.[24] The two apparitions are fundamentally similar. Upon hearing the sweet, fading music from an as yet unknown source, Olearius jokingly suggests "daß die Musen ihren Parnaß verlassen und in diese Gegend sich verfügt hätten" (p. 86); this is the topos of the migration of the Muses, who conventionally were said to travel to distant sites when poetry flourished there. Similarly, Olearius and Pöhmer have migrated from their homes in Germany to distant Reval, and what has brought them is the spirit of friendship. On the level of structure, it can be argued that the visits of the Muses and of Olearius and Pöhmer are interchangeable in that both correspond to the *unerwartete Begebenheit* of Hercinie's appearance. The Muses do so by virtue of their being benign deities, and Olearius and

Pöhmer by virtue of their miraculous arrival upon the scene at very nearly the same point in the narrative line as Hercinie, that is, after the exchange about love has come to an end and other topics have been discussed for a time. But at the same time that the two events in Fleming's work correspond to the appearance of Hercinie, they also both correspond equally to the arrival of Buchner, Venator, and Nüßler in *Hercinie*. The arrival of Opitz's friends is heralded by sweet music, "welche . . . entweder der Musen söhne/ oder auch die Musen selbst zue sein schienen" (p. 12). Fleming has distributed the components of this single scene—friends, music, the Muses, and the Muses' sons—between two scenes in a way that retains a certain unity while also eliminating elements of the fantastic. The arrival of Olearius and Pöhmer is indeed the arrival of the Muses' sons, for like Opitz's friends, they were very much interested in German poetry.[25] In contrast to Opitz's friends, however, they are not accompanied by unlikely music, which is left instead, appropriately, to the Muses themselves.

The interconnectedness of the arrival of Fleming's friends and the visit of the Muses points to a further aspect of Fleming's work that distinguishes it from Opitz's and reinforces some of the differences mentioned earlier. In *Hercinie*, Opitz has selected from classical and Renaissance sources the nymph and the episode of the cave because they are appropriate to his patron, who has warm springs on his estate; they have no particular symbolic or thematic connection with other parts of the work and form no particular link to Buchner, Venator, and Nüßler. In Fleming's work, the Muses similarly are appropriate and complimentary to Brokmann because of Brokmann's interest in poetry. For Fleming to indicate in P.W.III.6 that the Muses have actually migrated to Reval is to suggest that Reval has poets, Brokmann, for example, with talent enough to lure them there and to be their representatives. Olearius makes this connection explicit when he, hearing the fading music, jests about the Muses' migration to the environs of Reval. At the same time poetry, love of the Muses, is an essential part of the friendship of Fleming, Polus, Olearius, and Pöhmer, so that the explicit central event of P.W.III.6, the visit of the Muses, constitutes not just homage to the addressee of the work, as does the visit to Hercinie in Opitz's work, but also symbolizes the tie binding the entire group of men in friendship.[26] This linking of the four friends, the Muses' visit, and the person to whom the work is dedicated, is another way in which Fleming has endowed his work with a coherence and unity that is not to be found in Opitz's *Schäferei*. While the themes of love and travel do form a recurrent motif in *Hercinie*, they do little to join the parts of the work concerning Schaffgotsch to the parts concerning only the four friends. Poetry and friendship in Fleming's work, on the other hand, become part of the structure and fabric of the work in such a way as to weave the entire work into a unified whole. The skill apparent in the very early *Der klagende Bräutigam. II*, where verbal and motivic correspondences served to transform a rather ragged model into a polished and highly compact, unified new poem, is here at work on a larger scale, using carefully chosen themes and significant plot elements to produce a similarly meaningfully organized work.

To return briefly to the question of the realism of P.W.III.6: Fleming's inclusion of an impossible event in the form of Olearius's and Pöhmer's visit does not conflict with its realism in the way the appearance of a supernatural being does in *Hercinie*. Opitz's realism in the depiction of landscape has attracted considerable attention, and his carefully localized description of the setting of *Hercinie* at the opening of the work became a standard part of *Schäfereien*. Garber has noted how this sometimes led to contrasts that strike the modern reader as odd, for, in addition to the local landscape, the later poets generally also took over the splendid chambers of Hercinie's grotto: "Aber die Nachfolger verlegen diese Prunkräume häufig aus den unterirdischen Zonen in die Schäferlandschaft. Und in ihr treten sie deshalb besonders kraß hervor, weil die Landschaft gelegentlich sehr genau beschrieben wird und durchaus nicht immer eine Phantasielandschaft darstellt"; one might add that they also took over the introduction of nymphs and divine and allegorical figures into the narrative. Garber goes on to say, "Aber das Zeitalter war es gewohnt, die Natur allegorisch auszustatten und auszulegen. Es nahm keinen Anstoß an dieser Mischung aus realer Landschaft, allegorischen Gestalten und kunstvollen Räumen, weil ihm die Natur durchweg Geistiges verkörperte, so daß man sie mit bedeutungsvollen Gestalten bevölkern konnte."[27] Later *Schäfereien* thus incorporated both Opitz's landscape realism and the fantastic aspects of *Hercinie*. Fleming's work shows that this was not in any way imperative; had his example attracted more attention, the seventeenth century might have produced much more prose depicting idealized but nonetheless recognizably realistic interaction among members of the bourgeoisie in realistic surroundings.

Fleming's Epithalamium as a Critique of Opitz's Depiction of Love

Opitz, or the character called Opitz, is in *Hercinie* very much preoccupied with his love life; how he is to come to terms with leaving his beloved in order to travel forms a leitmotiv of the work. Although not as extensively or obviously thematized in P.W.III.6, the question of the proper relationship between lover and beloved is also important in Fleming's work. In fact, in an unobtrusive way, Fleming's epithalamium offers a response to questions about love raised in *Hercinie*. Carefully maintained correspondences between the two works once again suggest points of entry for investigating the concept of love espoused by Fleming as a contrast to that of Opitz.

The first poem about love in Fleming's work, *Laß es sein, mein Sinn, und schweige*—given the title *Philyrena* in the *Teütsche Poemata*—appears considerably later than the first love poem in *Hercinie* (sixth poem versus second), but it is related by more than just a common theme to the three love poems (two sonnets and an ode) at the beginning of *Hercinie*. *Philyrena* alone of a number of odes in P.W.III.6 is in the same form as the ode, the fourth poem in *Hercinie* that begins "Ist mein hertze gleich verliebet," while verbal echoes in Fleming's prose following *Philyrena* ("Ich hatte die letzten Worte noch nicht recht ausgesungen") link it to Opitz's third poem, a sonnet (*Es ist gewagt; ich bin doch gantz entschloßen*), which is followed by the phrase "Ich schnitzte noch über dem letzten worte" (p. 12). Moreover, it will be recalled that Fleming's three poems for his patrons represent an intrusion into the structure found in *Hercinie*, which places panegyrics at the center of the work, not the beginning. If one disregards the three panegyrical poems, *Philyrena* becomes the first poem following the season-setting quatrain, and thus corresponds to Opitz's sonnet *Weil mein Verhengniß wil*," the first poem in *Hercinie* after the time and place are set. While these correspondences may individually appear coincidental, their accumulation argues otherwise. They suggest that what we find in P.W.III.6 is not simply a love song, *Philyrena*, randomly placed and vaguely imitative of sentiments in *Hercinie*, but rather a love song that by its position, by its situation in the narrative, and by its form, deliberately invites comparison with the three love poems by Opitz.

Opitz's sonnets each depict with different imagery the lover who resolutely acquiesces to the need to leave his beloved and then rapidly falls apart. In the first poem fate is invoked as the cause of parting, and "So giebet zwar mein sinn sich mitt gedult darein." But by the final tercet, the Petrarchan lover, robbed of his sun, can no longer see and is bereft of everything but misery and himself, who lives in misery. In the intervening prose before the next sonnet Opitz convinces himself not to blame fate for his predicament, as he is leaving by his own choice. But as to how to deal with the pain of parting from his beloved, he can only think that in order to regain his treasured freedom he must change himself and become, like Odysseus's men, impervious to the siren song of woman. The second sonnet makes it clear that such stoic indifference is not quickly achieved. In it the poet himself now claims responsibility for the decision to part from his beloved: "Es ist gewagt; ich bin doch gantz entschloßen," but once again the loss leaves him in chaos: "ich bin selbselbst verlohren | Verlier ich sie: verbleib' ich dann allhier | So ist doch nichts als wanckelmuth an mir" (pp. 11–12).

Something like a resolution to all this emotional conflict is achieved in the next poem in *Hercinie*, the ode *Ist mein hertze gleich verliebet*. Venator, Nüßler, and Buchner have arrived upon the scene. Venator, whose long lecture on how to select a worthy object of love is yet to come, has espied the second sonnet carved in a tree and ventures to guess that Opitz has sacrificed his freedom to the seemingly pleasant service of love. Opitz does not answer directly, but remarks that Venator has hit upon the meaning of his next song, which he proceeds to sing, after asking indulgence for its simplicity, which is suited to its object.

The most striking aspect of the song is its insistent justification of the lover's choice of a beloved from simple circumstances.[28] The first strophe asks "Ist mein hertze gleich verliebet | In ein schlechtes [sc. schlichtes] mägdelein/ | . . . | Soll ich darumb vnrecht sein?" And again in the fourth strophe: "Niemandt wirdt mir vnrecht geben; | Hohe brunst bringt furcht vndt neidt" (pp. 14–15). Her lack of means becomes a source of Petrarchan oxymoron: she is the poet's "reiches armutt" (strophe 4). What justifies the choice of a simple maiden is that the poet has discovered in her "Trew" (strophe 3) and "sicherheit" (strophe 4). There is little sense that she has similarly found reassurance in him; the depiction of the relationship is one-sided, showing its effects on the lover, but not the reverse. In its closing, the ode refers explicitly to the theme of freedom and servitude already touched on in the image of Ulysses's men and in Venator's reaction to the second sonnet. Opitz assures his beloved that "Meine freyheit soll allein | Deiner liebe dienstbar sein," a paradoxical promise that carries one last reminder of the difference in station, for part of the paradox is that the man of higher station will be serving the lower-class woman.

Gellinek discusses this ode against the background of a group of Opitz's love sonnets. In these "konnte Opitz . . . aus einer immer kleiner werdenden Pendelbewegung zwischen Ablehnung und Bejahung der Liebe heraus eine Art Gleichgewicht herstellen," while the ode *Ist mein hertze gleich verliebet* represents the pendulum finally coming to rest in "eine harmonische . . . Liebesauffassung," allowing Opitz "in dem Idyll die Standarte der wahren Liebe, das ist der treuen, beständigen, beinahe ehelichen Liebe zu tragen" (p. 167). This view of the ode makes sense against the background of Opitz's earlier love poetry, but it requires qualification when compared to Fleming's poem.

Fleming's eight-strophe poem, *Philyrena*, falls into two equal parts: the first four strophes correspond thematically to those initial parts of Opitz's sonnets that display neo-Stoic resolve to accept a painful situation, while the last four strophes recall especially Opitz's ode. It is this last correspondence that is most interesting. Both the four final strophes of Fleming's poem and Opitz's entire ode seem to portray the lover buoyed up by similar relationships of "treue, beständige, beinahe eheliche Liebe." And yet Fleming's portrayal entails an equality, reciprocity, and maturity that are absent from Opitz's. In *Philyrena* there is no mention of the beloved's simple circumstances. On the contrary, the ending, with its wish for the beloved's perpetual presence, implies that lover and beloved are close enough in station to marry. Where Opitz worries about others' reaction to his relationship with a woman beneath his station, Fleming asserts his confidence in the beloved: "Mißtreu ists, so wir verzagen, / sie ist allzeit ähnlich ihr. / Wahrer Liebe treue Pflicht / mindert sich durch Absein nicht" (ll. 144–47). In Fleming's poem, the lover is able, unlike Opitz of the sonnets, to gain lasting strength from the neo-Stoic arguments presented in the first four strophes, and he does not seek solace or safety in the beloved in a one-sided manner, but rather recognizes the pain of their separation as a sign of their love that must be born by them both: "Dieses, was du nennest Schmerzen, / ist der rechten Liebe Lohn, / die sie fühlet gleich wie du / und noch duppelt mehr darzu" (ll. 150–53).[29] What ultimately makes the separation bearable is a fundamental awareness of the reciprocity of their love: "Philyrena, die du liebest, / liebet dich noch wie vorhin" (ll. 154–55). Fleming's poem does not close with an Opitzian promise of paradoxical servitude, but with a wish for the arrival of the day when lover and beloved can be united in perpetuity, not as servant and mistress, but as husband and wife.

That the Petrarchan disintegration of the lover depicted in Opitz's sonnets has no counterpart in Fleming's poem is not coincidental but rather inherent in the conception of reciprocal and equal love that Fleming offers in place of what is represented in Opitz's three love poems. Petrarchan love entails by definition an unequal relationship. It is so devastating in part because the beloved is more powerful than the lover and robs him of his freedom of action and thought. It is a natural tendency to express such a power relationship metaphorically in terms of social station, thus making the beloved highborn and the lover her servant. What passes for Opitz's resolution of the enslavement to the Petrarchan beloved in his first two sonnets involves the lover's reversing the power relationship in that initially merely metaphorical sphere, that of social station. The reversal of the relationship from servant and lady to upper- or middle-class lover and common girl strips the beloved of at least some of her power and makes the relationship more bearable, thus making the surrender of freedom to the beloved's servitude a harmless paradox by comparison.

The love relationship depicted in Fleming's poem resembles neither Opitz's Petrarchism nor the mirror image counterpart of Petrarchism that Opitz offers and that seems on the surface deceptively like "treue, beständige, beinahe eheliche Liebe." Instead, Fleming offers a brief but consistent portrait of love that can survive distances because it is based implicitly on equality and explicitly on deeply felt reciprocal love. The correspondences of placement and form between his poem and Opitz's suggest that this ideal is presented deliberately as an alternative to the understanding of love in *Hercinie*.

The argument that Fleming was responding consciously to Opitz is strengthened by the example of a contemporary author who was moved in his own *Schäferei* to respond to Opitz's depiction of his simple maid. Instead, however, of simply offering an alternative as Fleming did, he broadly parodied the unequal love relationship in Opitz's *Hercinie*. Gottfried Finckelthaus, in his *Floridans Lob- vnd Liebes-Gedichte* from 1635, includes a portrait of the narrator's lovesick friend Dorilus, who is clearly based on the character Opitz in *Hercinie*, but whose difficulties arise from his loving a woman above—not below—him in station.[30] While such a difference in rank would lend itself to exploitation as a metaphor for the devastating remoteness of the Petrarchan woman, Finckelthaus prefers to mine its potential for parody, in the modern sense, of the Opitzian situation.[31] Dorilus's contrafactum of Opitz's *Ist mein hertze gleich verliebet* outlines the reversed positions (vis-à-vis Opitz's poem) of lover and beloved, as can be seen in the first and last strophes:

> ACh/ Mein Hertz ist hoch verliebet
> Jn ein hohes Mägdelein!
> Die mich nur allein betrübet/
> Vnd vmb diß muß vnrecht seyn.
> Liebste deiner Hoheit Liecht
> Gleicht sich meiner Einfalt nicht!
> . . . .
> Wer dich wird besitzen können/

> Hat den Trost vnd höchste Ruh:
> Sey in solchen trewen Sinnen/
>   Liebste/ wie ich jetzund thu.
>   Meine Einfalt sol allein
>   Deiner Hoheit Diener seyn.
>
> (fols. B7v–B8r)

This prepares the way for Dorilus to parody Opitz's similar song, *WOl dem der weit von hohen dingen*, which had appeared in the 1624 *Poemata*.[32] The refrain of Opitz's poem is "Ein jeder folge seinem Sinne, / Jch halts mit meiner Schäfferinne." The first, sixth, and seventh strophes of Dorilus's song run as follows:

> WOhl dem/ der tracht nach hohen Dingen/
>   Vnd nicht tritt auff der Einfalt Bahn!
> Wer sein Gemüth nicht hoch wil schwingen/
>   Der kömmt auch nimmer oben an.
> Ein jeder folge seinem Sinne:
> Ich halt's mit keiner Schäferinne.
> . . . .
> Zu der/ so ist vom hohen Stande/
>   Nur einig sich mein Sinn hinstellt.
> Hat sie auch keinen Sitz im Lande/
>   So ist nichts da/ das mich jhr helt.
> Ein jeder folge seinem Sinne:
> Ich halt's mit keiner Schäferinne.
>
> Wenn sie nicht glentzt von thewren Sachen/
>   Glentzt auch nicht jhrer Augenlicht.
> Die Hoffart muß sie schöne machen/
>   Ein schlechter Glantz behelt mich nicht.
> Ein jeder folge seinem Sinne:
> Ich halt's mit keiner Schäferinne.
>
> (fols. C1v–C2r)

Finckelthaus offers no specific alternative to the unequal Opitzian love relationship, and he to a large extent seems to share Opitz's distrust of women, as will be discussed below. His main purpose seems to have been simply to make fun of the person who has gotten himself in the position of mooning over someone of a different rank. It was up to the more respectful Fleming, for whom broad parody of Opitz would have been out of character, to propose the alternative to the unequal love relationship.

The themes of love and the proper relation of man and woman recur periodically in *Hercinie* and P.W.III.6, and these other passages merit some attention in light of the above discussion. The most striking and explicit treatment of love in *Hercinie* is the one offered by Venator early in the work. Venator's view, in essence, and stripped of the Platonic and neo-Platonic vocabulary that has lent authority to similar disquisitions for centuries, describes love and women as very often deceptive and frighteningly powerful because of their appeal to what are regarded as baser instincts. It is incumbent upon the lover to struggle mightily to see through deception and to dominate through reason rather than succumb to the senses; he must always seek an object worthy of him. It is difficult to determine the extent to which the passage expresses Opitz's own authorial or personal sentiments. His joking references to "eine stattliche rede" and to the obvious philosophical sources of the speech suggest that it is not to be taken too seriously. There is probably, however, some dissimulation here, and Gellinek is probably correct when she suggests that Opitz is able in *Hercinie* to achieve the appearance of some equanimity vis-à-vis his love life only "durch die Aufspaltung seiner eigenen widerstrebenden Haltungen der Liebe gegenüber" and through writing "die moralischen Einwände und scholastischen Argumente gegen die 'Liebestorheit'"— that he to some extent endorsed—into Venator's part (p. 167).[33]

The scene with the witch in *Hercinie* provides a further, more certain, index to aspects of Opitz's attitude towards love and women, one that tends to confirm that the sentiments expressed in Venator's speech originate in Opitz's own view on the topics. In this scene an old woman mutters spells and performs mysterious actions whose purpose is to make an unwilling man fall in love with the woman who is in love with him. The old woman is unattractive and her doings mysterious and repulsive—and the four observing shepherds are terrified. They flee from her, Opitz first, when she conjures up a thunderstorm, the culmination of the spells she has recited in order to arouse the passion of the reluctant lover. While the immediate cause of the shepherds' flight is the storm itself, the ultimate source of their terror is the witch, for the storm appears as a natural correlative to the power she tries to exercise over men through her witchcraft. It is hard to escape the conclusion that the witch functions as a projection of Opitz's own fear of succumbing to certain kinds of love and women: she represents all that is apparently irrational, powerful, and thus threatening in them.[34] Once at a safe distance from the scene of the conjuring, Opitz remarks in the narrator's voice that the devil is not everywhere master, thus making a clear connection between the witch's activities and the realm of evil. By allying the witch with the devil, Opitz, in the long-standing Christian tradition, is able to separate what he feels is worthy love from that which he finds too disturbing, and to remove from himself any burden of guilt for the latter. Its source is the Evil One, not himself, and succumbing to it can be ascribed to the overwhelming power of its source.

Against this interpretation of the encounter with the witch it might be argued that Opitz was there as elsewhere simply following his sources. But Opitz was far from being a slave to his sources: he used them as a storehouse of motifs and phrases that he felt free to mold, diverse as they were, to his own purposes. In fact, by following one of his main sources for the scene with the witch more, and not less, closely than he did, he would have created a more sympathetic picture of the woman who has commissioned the witch to help her.[35] Theocritus's second idyll, told by the neglected woman, deflowered and unmarried, who attempts to concoct her own magic love potion, is poignant in its depiction of her despair. Of all this Opitz retains only traces, two references to the woman's faithfulness: the witch says "Zue rhaten deiner trew/ o jungfraw/ derer schmertzen/ | . . . mir dringen selbst zue hertzen" and "So mußen gleichfalls auch deßelbten sinnen brennen/ | Der von sich selbst nicht wil den trewen sinn erkennen" (p. 50). Opitz, unlike Theocritus and his other major sources, Virgil in his eighth *Eclogue* and Sannazaro in his *Arcadia*, does not actually permit us to see the person in love. Instead, he separates this person from the caster of spells, thus permitting the latter to stand for the naked and frightening power of love stripped of the humanity and pitifulness that might attach to the slighted or unsuccessful lover. It might also be objected that it is risky to ascribe too much importance to the episode of the witch. Certainly the encounter of the three shepherds with the witch is routinely passed over in silence or with the briefest of mentions in studies of *Hercinie*.[36] But when one considers that the shepherds on their walk encounter only two major figures, and that one of them is the witch, this argues for her importance. In fact, if one steps back from the work and looks at its architecture as represented by its characters, one sees the four shepherds moving through a structure anchored by two figures, Hercinie and the witch. The two are equivalent insofar as they are both female and extraordinary; they also balance one another insofar as Hercinie is represented positively as appealing to order (especially in the guise of the social hierarchy) and rationality (with repeated caveats in the form of fables of hubris—Arachne, Midas, etc.—not to overstep human limitations), while the witch is presented negatively as trying to summon up the disordering effects of the irrational senses. Purely from the point of view of themes, the witch episode must also be considered important. Garber, one of the few interpreters to regard it as integrated into the work by more than just a generic requirement for the occult, draws the connection between it and the earlier extensive discussion of love: "Die . . . Zauberin-Episode muß . . . in ihrer kontrapunktischen Funktion zur humanistischen Liebeskonzeption, wie sie auch in der *Hercinie* sich abzeichnet, begriffen werden".[37] In fact, the scene of the witch shows the shepherds precisely that kind of irrational, deceptive, and overpowering love that Venator had warned Opitz against at great length in his early monologue.

In Fleming's work we find something quite different from the witch and all she represents. At the point following the discovery of the Muses' tablet and the brief panegyric to Brokmann, that is, at the point which corresponds to Opitz's scene with the witch, we find not a depiction of the frightening and irrational power of love, but instead a celebration of love in the form of poems by the bridegroom himself. This is, of course, in keeping with the occasion of the work, but as I argued above, Fleming was in no way constrained to make his imitation of *Hercinie* an epithalamium, and thus to offer a depiction of a very different kind of love from that depicted by Opitz. That he did choose to make the occasion of P.W.III.6 a wedding and that he chose to offer the groom's poems at a point in the work that strategically corresponds to the scene with the witch argue for his deliberate focus on an alternative notion of love and the relationship between man and woman.

What we find in Brokmann's nine poems (an ode, six epigrams, a short alexandrine poem, and *Wie er wolle geküsset sein*—only the title of the latter is cited) and the surrounding dialogue is a version of the love relationship similar to that offered in *Philyrena*. Its basis is equality and mutual affection, and it is expanded to include some of the intensity of the Petrarchan relationship, which is, however, not debilitating precisely because not predicated upon the unattainability of the woman. In fact, the very pleasures of the senses that are forever off limits to the Petrarchan lover are broadly hinted at.

Just before Polus reads the first song written by Brokmann, he remarks upon the equality and reciprocity of the love match: "Er ist ihrer, sprach Polus, und sie seiner wol wert. Ist auch kein Zweifel, daß aus Vermählung so ähnlicher Gemüter eine gewündschte Ehe ersprießen wird. Sie meinen einander von Herzen" (prose following l. 375). The remark ensures that two of Brokmann's epigrams in particular, *Auf der Liebsten Demant* and *Als sie im Schnee sich erlustirete*, with their Petrarchan images of the bride's hardness and coldness, will be read as playful conceits rather than a description of the true state of the couple's affections. Brokmann's own two songs, *R. Brockman an seine Dorothea (Ja, Leben, ich bin angezündet)* and *Wie er wolle geküsset sein*, which frame the six Petrarchan epigrams and a short love poem, fulfill a similar function. They each contain reminders of the physical passion that the bridal couple may enjoy and that is always denied to the Petrarchan lover. The potential agonies of the Petrarchan relationship depicted in the framed poems are thus relativized; they are at most temporary, more likely purely fictional. *Wie er wolle geküsset sein* is, of course, a splendidly explicit and lengthy set of instructions for an act Petrarchans enjoy fleetingly, if ever, because it presupposes the woman's cooperation, and the borderline salaciousness of the poem allies it with the neo-Latin epithalamic description of the bridal night—and may account for its being only mentioned but not printed in P.W.III.6. In *R. Brockman an seine Dorothea* the groom delights in having discovered in his bride that beauty of soul or mind that Venator says is rare but essential. Unlike the mistrustful and ascetic Venator, Brokmann delights equally in "Leib und Geist," and at the close of the poem eagerly summons the bride that he may enjoy (or possess) her.[38]

R. Brockman an seine Dorothea carries reminiscences of an ode in *Hercinie* in which Opitz reiterates his allegiance to his "schlechtes mägdelein" after the encounter with the witch. The feminine rhymes of the first two strophes of *Meine Frewde die mich bindet* appear in *R. Brockman an seine Dorothea*: "bindet" : "angezündet," "beisammen" : "flammen." The feminine rhymes of the third strophes are similar, though not identical: "begehren" : "Gebärden" and "beschweren" : "werden." The endings of the first strophes of the respective poems express similar ideas: Opitz writes "Daß mein sinn sich jhr ergiebt/ | Kömpt daher weil sie mich liebt" (p. 56), while Fleming writes "Was meine freien Sinnen bindet, / das sind die Ketten deiner Gunst" (ll. 378–79).

Opitz's *Meine Frewde die mich bindet* represents the last we learn from him about the problem—the incompatibility of travel and love—that threads its way through *Hercinie* (there are two further love poems, *Sechstine* and *Sonnet über die augen der Astree*, but they are not clearly connected to the dilemma of the character Opitz). Rusterholz, in the afterword to his edition of *Hercinie*, remarks of *Meine Frewde*: "Durch die Hexenepisode wird dem Dichter klar, daß die Liebe, die ihn bindet, nicht dämonisch, sondern 'der list vndt kräuter frey' sei und deshalb auch in der Ferne Treue bewahren könne" (p. 79). This is too sanguine an interpretation of the poem: there is no mention in *Meine Frewde* of the problem of parting and its being resolved. There is also no reason to think that Opitz has discovered the nature of his girl's love through the encounter with the witch, rather, his assertions in the poem that she is free of witchcraft protest too much: it seems more likely that the insistence arises from the wish, not the knowledge, that they are true. The closing strophe is equivocal in its logic: Opitz asserts that anyone impervious to the charms of his girl would also be impervious to magic—the unspoken corollary being that whoever is susceptible to her charms might also succumb to magic. Garber notes that in this song Opitz returns to an earlier theme—which Garber calls, incorrectly I believe, "schlichte Gegenliebe"—embodied in *Ist mein hertze gleich verliebet*.[39] This thematic similarity, as well as the reuse of the same strophic form, suggest that *Meine Frewde* represents an insistent reassertion rather than a newly gained position.

Fleming's poem in Brokmann's voice, while sharing rhyme words and the same initial idea that the lover is bound by his beloved's affection, presents a much more confident lover who delights in and is happily inflamed by all his beloved's various perfections. For him there is not even the awareness of the possibility that her ability to attract him might be false or that she might enslave him to his own detriment. Here as elsewhere in P.W.III.6, with the exception of the brief reference to those who tempt their lovers but withhold their embrace (p. 77), the understanding of love and the relation between man and woman is a remarkably positive one.

The view of women presented by Opitz in *Hercinie* may not be explicitly misogynic, but it certainly involves considerable fear and distrust of women. This potential for misogyny that Opitz left latent in the genre of the *Schäferei* did not go unnoticed or unexploited by Finckelthaus in his *Floridans Lob- vnd LiebesGedichte*. The narrator, Floridan, with varying degrees of earnestness, laments the falseness of his beloved and describes women, as they are and as they should be, in terms clearly borrowed from Venator's speech.[40] He recites to his friends Alcandre and Dorilus a long alexandrine poem indicting the women of Leipzig for lying and capriciousness, and this poem reminds Dorilus of a history he has just read.[41] In it a young man, Clerio, happens upon a woman, Vinzia, who is bound hand and foot to a tree and is being tortured by three men, one with a bodkin for gouging out her eyes, one with a knife for cutting off her hand, and one who is fanning coals preparatory to reheating an iron for purposes easily imagined but not specified. The reason for her punishment, it turns out, is that she has by her beauty attracted many lovers whom she has played off against one another; her final sin, says one of her torturers, was marrying a worthless fellow who possessed all the faults she had objected to in other lovers. Clerio, after listening to the catalog of her sins, eventually, though with no great show of eagerness, sees to her release, pledging that she will mend her ways. Dorilus regards the story as an excellent cautionary tale for women who might be tempted to misbehave; Alcandre remarks that the woman's punishment was well deserved and inquires whether she did indeed reform. Dorilus reports disgustedly that the continuation of the tale indicates that she did not, and that this so provoked him and inflamed him with the same desire for revenge that had possessed the three young men that he couldn't bring himself to finish the tale and learn of her pitiful demise.

It is not clear that the tale, whose narration constitutes a major episode in Finckelthaus's *Schäferei*, is intended to be understood as the author's earnest statement on the nature of women. The earlier parodies of Opitz's poems show that *Floridans Lob- vnd LiebesGedichte* is partly humorous, Dorilus's narration of Vinzia's grisly punishment is followed by poems in praise of a woman in Leipzig who writes poetry in the Opitzian manner. Given, however, that the narration of Vinzia's story takes place within the context of a speech clearly based on Venator's, it seems justifiable to conclude that Finckelthaus was showing us a scenario that would follow logically from Venator's, and implicitly Opitz's, assumption that women exert almost irresistible attraction while being generally false, that is, showing us with gruesome explicitness the desire for revenge on the woman who can be neither resisted nor trusted.

It seems similarly probable that Fleming also sensed the potential for misogyny inherent in Opitz's portrayal of women and the relationship between men and women. Where Finckelthaus chose to present Opitz's attitude in its most extreme (and possibly caricatured) form, Fleming proffered an alternative which, based on different assumptions, excluded the potentially devastating emotions latent in Opitz's work. Fleming proposed instead the notion of a relationship between man and woman based on equality and upon reciprocal *Treue*.

That Opitz was Fleming's starting point but also his point of departure when the topic of love arose is underscored in the closing poems of P.W.III.6. In the earlier discussion of structural resemblances between *Hercinie* and Fleming's work, I noted the similarities of their endings. Each is rounded out by three sonnets putatively contributed by the poet's friends, followed by an ode from the poet himself. There is an additional link to Opitz here: Fleming's sonnets all recall love poems published by Opitz in 1624. The first, *Was tun doch wir, daß wir die süßen Jahre*, is ascribed to Olearius. The phrase "lassen Fuß für Fuß" in the second line echoes "Der schönen Schönheit gaben Fliehn fuß für fuß" from Opitz's famous *ACh Liebste laß vns eilen* (no. 141 in the 1624 *Poemata*), while Olearius's theme, "what is appropriate behavior when one is confronted with the rapid and irreversible passage of time?" also recalls Opitz's poem. In responding to this question, however, Olearius—and thus Fleming—departs from Opitz in characteristic directions. Unlike Opitz, he does not entertain the possibility of physical pleasure unsanctioned by marriage, but instead takes as a given that there are those who are unmarried and chaste and those who are married and thus parties to licit pleasure. In the closing tercet, Olearius argues that contemplating the happiness of a married couple is one of the few privileges of the unmarried and implies that married happiness is the proper end for all. The unmarried assume the role of burning but chaste Petrarchans—but Olearius/Fleming, in contrast to Opitz's practice most of the time, paints their suffering humorously: they are "Fels und stählerner als Stahl, / bestürzt, verwirrt." The oxymoronic psychology of the Petrarchan, who is both steadfast and mercurial, is cast in an image at odds with itself. The reader visualizes the strength of rock and steel but must then laugh when the descriptive adjectives of the next line so patently—and so abruptly—contradict this image.

Pöhmer offers the next sonnet, *Die warme Frühlingsluft macht ihren Himmel klar*, which recalls *Ihr/ Himmel/ lufft vnnd wind/ jhr hügel voll von schatten*, the translation of a poem by Ronsard that Opitz used to illustrate the sonnet in chapter 7 of the *Buch von der Deutschen Poeterey*. Both poems use recapitulation schemes in which aspects of nature named in the first eight lines are rapidly renamed in the final tercet; they differ in the use to which the natural elements are put. Opitz invokes them hoping that they may bid adieu to his beloved Flavia for him, as his own courage and senses desert him when he must depart from her. Fleming's poem, though so clearly modeled after Opitz, is no plaintive request and does not depict parting; rather, he confidently asserts that the natural elements, the exuberant and fecund macrocosm, celebrate the union of the bridal couple.

The third and final sonnet, *Wie? Ist die Liebe Nichts? Was liebt man denn im Lieben?*, ascribed to Polus, takes up the topic that Opitz treated in *JSt Liebe lauter nichts, wie daß sie mich entzündet?* (no. 20 in the 1624 *Poemata*). Opitz's poem, a skillful rendering of Petrarch's *S'amor non è* (*Canzoniere* 132), in which good use is made of the antithetical possibilities of the alexandrine line, is a *locus classicus* of Petrarchism. The final lines reflect the schizophrenia of the tormented lover: "Ich weiß nicht was ich will, ich will nicht was ich weiß, / Im Sommer ist mir kalt, im Winter ist mir heiß." Fleming's sonnet initially appears to be heading in the same direction as Opitz's, that is, to an expression of perplexity and helplessness, an inability, occasioned by the effects of love, to answer the question "what is love?" The question remains unanswered in Fleming's poem also, but not because the persona is bewildered by being in love, but precisely because he has not had the experience of love. In the end, after recapitulating all the "wrong" answers in a manner that recalls Pöhmer's poem and its Opitzian model, Polus/Fleming turns to the bridal couple as the ones most likely to be able to give him an answer.[42] Once again, Fleming shifts the focus from the deleterious effects of love to reciprocal love sanctified by marriage. Both Opitz's and Fleming's poems, although ostensibly leaving the question "what is love?" unanswered, offer definitions *ex negatione*, and even in these they differ. Opitz, with the misogynist's mistrust of the libido, wonders how love could be good, since it brings "böse Lust"; Fleming, who is able to incorporate an affirmation of the physical into his concept of love, denies that love is "Böse," for, he thinks, "nichts Solches macht Begier."

Sources and Development of Fleming's Concept of *Treue*

Fleming's portrayal of a non-Petrarchan love relationship, particularly in the odes for Elsabe and Anna Niehus, has attracted attention at least since 1925, when Günther Müller, in his study of the German *Lied*, contrasted Fleming's love songs with the Petrarchan tradition: "[Fleming] schafft neue Form und neuen Gehalt im Liebeslied. Persönliche Zärtlichkeit und Innigkeit ist das, was er hereinbringt. Gerade das Entscheidende des bisherigen Liebesliedes, die Unverbindlichkeit der Huldigung, das Verhältnis der geistigsinnlichen Polarität, die Koketterie und das Schmachten, den Selbstwert der Spannung zwischen dem Du und dem Ich hat Fleming auf der Höhe seiner Lieddichtung, in den Liedern an Elsabe Niehus, im wesentlichen beseitigt."[43] Fleming's turning away from the Petrarchan conventions to verse celebrating *Treue* became the ultimate focus of interest in Hans Pyritz's studies of Fleming's love poetry. In his chapter "Überwindung der Tradition" he argues that under the influence of his attachment, first to Elsabe, then to Anna Niehus, Fleming abandoned the Petrarchan images of the lover pining from unrequited love for a cold and distant woman and wrote poems that corresponded more closely to his own personal sentiments and situation. One senses in Pyritz's own emotional language his extraordinary admiration for these poems. In the crowning section of his work, "Der eigene Ton," he writes:

> Es bleibt die letzte Aufgabe unserer Motivanalyse, das Herzstück von Flemings Liebeslyrik sichtbar zu machen, den geheimen Mittelpunkt ihres eigentlichen Lebens, in dem am stärksten und unmittelbarsten das Seelentum ihres Dichters sich bezeugt, in dem die Metamorphose vom Nachahmer zum produktiven Gestalter vollzogen und besiegelt ist, die gattungsgeschichtliche Bedeutsamkeit des Flemingschen Werkes begründet liegt und seine noch heute mögliche Wirkung ruht. Was Paul Fleming über allen Petrarkismus hinaus zu geben hatte, was er schließlich geben mußte, um sein menschliches und künstlerisches Wesen zu erfüllen, das Beste, was er überhaupt gegeben hat, es kreist um das Motiv der Treue, vollendet sich im Werbungs- und im Sehnsuchtslied.[44]

Almost immediately after the original publication of Pyritz's work in the early 1930s, Richard Alewyn, ever sensitive to ahistorical thinking in literary criticism, to applying the criteria of *Erlebnisdichtung* to the poetry of earlier eras, reviewed Pyritz's book with admiration, but also with reservations about the very concept of "overcoming tradition" in the seventeenth century. He pointed out that Pyritz himself had noted that Fleming, in his late odes, was in fact still writing in a tradition, albeit no longer the Petrarchan. Pyritz, a little with the air of one pulling a rabbit from a hat, says at the end of the chapter on "Überwindung der Tradition" that Fleming may in the late odes have been returning to his beginnings and the type of poetry cultivated by his teacher at the Thomasschule, Johann Hermann Schein, that is, to the *Gesellschaftslied*, for "Werbungs- und vor allem Treue-Thematik stehen im Mittelpunkt der erotischen Lieddichtung von Regnart bis Schein."[45]

This notion, proposed more or less as an afterthought by Pyritz and emphatically affirmed by Alewyn, that Fleming's best love poetry, the non-Petrarchan love poetry celebrating *Treue*, may have roots in the *Gesellschaftslied*, particularly as practiced by Schein, is repeated or quoted from time to time in the rather sparse annals of Fleming scholarship since Pyritz, most recently by Jörg-Ulrich Fechner. Fechner notes the importance of *Treue* in Fleming's love poetry and cites Alewyn to the effect that this concept cannot be considered a personal achievement of the poet, but that it partakes of an existing tradition. Echoing Pyritz, Fechner goes on to assert that "Die Treue steht, angelehnt an das Vorbild der italienischen Lieddichtung, als bestimmender

Wert im Mittelpunkt des sächsischen Liebeslieds von Regnart bis Schein."[46] Beyond such brief references, the relationship of Fleming to Schein and to the tradition of the *Gesellschaftslied* has not been explored, in part, it must be said, because Pyritz's understanding of Fleming's development as an overcoming of tradition has had, despite Alewyn's critique, wide, if often tacit, acceptance.[47] It seems appropriate here, in light of the preceding discussion of love as depicted in P.W.III.6, to look more closely at Fleming's relationship to the sources posited, Schein and the *Gesellschaftslied*, to determine whether other traditions might have influenced Fleming's notion of *Treue*, and, finally, to consider whether the concept really appears so suddenly in the odes to Elsabe and Anna Niehus or if—as P.W.III.6 might lead one to expect—the ground has been prepared in some of Fleming's earlier verse.

Circumstantial evidence certainly points to Schein's having influenced Fleming and his poetry. From about 1622 until he was regularly matriculated at the University in 1628, Fleming was a pupil at the Thomasschule in Leipzig, where Schein was cantor from 1616–30. Fleming wrote a number of poems, all epicedia, for Schein and for members of his family (Sy.III.1, M.VII.5, P.W.II.6, E.V.1 and 3, and one printed on p. 857 of the *Deutsche Gedichte*). Lappenberg remarks that "Zu [Schein] . . . mochte Fl. sich sehr angezogen fühlen, wie die poetischen Beweise der Theilnahme an dessen traurigen Familienereignissen darlegen" (Fleming, *Deutsche Gedichte*, p. 857). In one of the more reliable biographies of Fleming from this century, Lappenberg's "mochte" becomes "muß": Walter Schlesinger states that "Fleming muß Schein besonders nahegestanden haben; ein lateinisches Gedicht . . . auf den Tod von Scheins erster Gattin . . . ist sein frühestes erhaltenes dichterisches Erzeugnis. Auf Schein selbst verfaßte Fleming mehrere Gedichte."[48] But the argument from the existence of epicedia is less convincing than it seems, for if a moderately good poet of the seventeenth century were to have "stood close" to all those for whom he wrote epicedia, life would have been excessively crowded. In fact, it would have been far more remarkable had Fleming gone so far as to forget his duty and to fail to write poems when an important public figure, or his wife or children, died.[49] Rather than looking to epicedia for indications of Fleming's personal relationship to Schein, a more accurate index is obtained by noting whether Fleming voluntarily makes reference to Schein—as he does so often to Opitz—on occasions when it is not simply social custom that requires it. And here the results are disappointing; only in his *Liefländische Schneegräfin* (P.W.III.7) does Fleming mention the composer: "Wir tönen nach dem

Besten / ein Waldlied aus dem Schein, und sein Studentenschmaus / muß ganz von vornen an gesungen werden aus" (ll. 126–28). The references are to mature compositions of Schein's, the *Musica boscareccia* and a collection of drinking songs. Significantly, Fleming is not speaking here of his literary indebtedness to Schein or admiration for his verse, but rather is describing the entertainment of guests at a wedding. When the opportunity arises to refer to great poets or composers, Fleming passes over Schein in silence. In P.W.IV.15 (*An Herrn Johan Klipstein*), for example, whose theme is the power of music and poetry, Fleming praises Opitz, Schütz, and Nauwach—but not Schein. Very possibly Fleming's enthusiasm for Schein's work was restrained because Schein, who was both poet and composer, wrote verse not entirely in conformity with the Opitzian reform, while Schütz and Nauwach provided settings for poems from the master himself.

Fleming's personal relationship to Schein as pupil to teacher at the Thomasschule must remain a matter of speculation. Lest, however, one be tempted to paint Fleming's situation as a *Thomaner* under Schein in rosy hues, it should be noted that being at the Thomasschule, an *Armenschule*, was no picnic, and that health, discipline, and standards were particularly bad during the Thirty Years' War under Schein and his successor Tobias Michael.[50] The main duty of the pupils in the 1620s, as it had been since the founding of the Thomasschule as a church school in the thirteenth century, was to sing at church services, funerals, and weddings. The boys' health suffered severely. They were required to stay through the entire service when they sang in cold churches and churchyards in winter. At funerals, they had to wait outside in the rain or snow until the long funeral procession had entered the church, and then find places to sit and kneel on the cold stones. They were vulnerable to the epidemics that visited Leipzig in the 1620s and 1630s. All the boarders lived together in cramped quarters, and there was no separate sick room. The situation was no better with regard to academics than it was to health—indeed, that Fleming was so well-read must have been more the result of native talent than the Thomasschule education. Well into the thirties, singing at funerals took precedence over classes, so that Schein's successor, Michael, complains "er habe propter funera fast noch keine Syntaxstunde in seiner Tertia gehabt."[51] Before and during Schein's tenure pupils far too frequently skipped class and choir practice, sometimes crossing the palm of the preceptor to ensure impunity; discipline in general was poor. Schein seems to have allowed pupils to be accepted who were not good singers, with obvious consequences for the choirs. Schein himself was severely overburdened, being required, as were all of those who held the office of cantor at the Thomasschule before Tobias Michael, to teach a regular schedule of humanistic and theological courses in addition to directing the musical program and conducting the first choir. His requests to be released from this went unfulfilled.

Knowing no other, a high-spirited and intelligent boy in Fleming's time may have coped with conditions such as these without ill effect. But it is also possible that the Thomasschule occupied no very firm place in Fleming's affections and that there is a reason for his not referring to Schein more often in his preserved poetry or to the rectors of the school during his time there (Sebastian Crell and Johann Merck) ever.

Fleming's official musical activity while a Thomaner consisted largely of singing Protestant hymns and church music in general, so that, even if he was in Schein's own choir (the other was directed by the rector of the school), this does not necessarily argue for firsthand work with Schein on the composer's secular songs. Nonetheless, it is clear from the *Liefländische Schneegräfin* that Fleming knew the *Musica boscareccia* and the *Studenten-Schmauss*, which he must have learned of during his student years at the latest. The scant biographical information on the connections between Fleming and Schein exhausted, we can now turn to the relationship between the compositions of the two men.

In the statements of scholars who have gone beyond simply asserting, on the basis of the pupil-teacher relationship and Fleming's epicedia, that Schein *must* have been important to Fleming, one finds some inconsistency. Pyritz, as stated, suspected that in his late odes for the Niehus sisters (especially O.V.28–32), with their emphasis on *Treue* and their avoidance of Petrarchan motifs, Fleming was returning to his beginnings, to Schein and the *Gesellschaftslied*. Supersaxo points to an undated poem that she believes to be quite early, So.IV.1, and that she characterizes as "in fröhlich unbeschwertem Tone gehalten, der in uns die Scheinschen Verse wachruft" (p. 121). Günther Müller does not mention Schein when, anticipating Pyritz, he sketches out Fleming's poetic development in the later love odes, but rather refers to the composer in connection with Fleming's O.V.15: "Und der Scheinschen Leichtigkeit kommen Lieder nah wie das berühmte 'Wie er wolle geküsset seyn'."[52] Walter Brauer looks specifically at the question of where Schein's influence on Fleming might be detected and, before ultimately responding that it is nowhere significantly evident, remarks "Es läßt sich wohl etwa eine Liste von Flemingschen Gedichten aufstellen, die den Gedanken an Scheinsche Lyrica wachrufen: Oden III, 21; IV, 13, 18, 19, 28, 32, 36, 37; V, 7, 12, 35."[53] More recently, Gerald Gillespie has suggested that one of the "two poles of the lovesong tradition in Fleming's work" as represented by O.V.20, *An die Stolze*, is like Schein's songs, "half-plea, half-accusation . . . with motifs of desperately sweet pain and outcries against the cruelty of love" (p. 77).

Altogether this is a motley collection. O.V.28–32 are poems to Elsabe Niehus in which Fleming continually reasserts their mutual fidelity despite the distance that separates them. So.IV.1 (*An Ambrosien*) is notable for its short verse line and playful imagery and language. O.V.15 (*Wie er wolle geküsset sein*), magisterial and sensual, entails an intimate understanding between lover and beloved. Brauer's selections include birthday poems, epithalamia, and love songs; they have in common the use of pastoral names. O.V.20 (*An die Stolze*) is the desperate complaint of a pastoral Petrarchan lover whose beloved spurns him. That Schein is cited as a possible model for such diverse poems testifies to the difficulty of perceiving his influence with any high degree of resolution, and, indeed, whereas one can point to individual Opitzian models and their forms or phrasings for specific Fleming poems, one simply cannot do this with Schein.[54] Whether the "musicality" or "Leichtigkeit" of Fleming's verse actually comes from Schein is a question that cannot be dealt with here, other than to remark that the means by which Fleming achieves his musicality must be precisely described before its relationship to Schein's can be determined. The analysis of *Der klagende Bräutigam. II* in chapter 1 may suggest some starting points, as may Konrad Unger's examination of "Flemings Dichtungen ihrer Form nach."[55] But the question of whether Schein exercised influence on Fleming's themes and their treatment, specifically, whether he provided a model for Fleming's depiction of a relationship based on *Treue*, is explored below.

One reason for the diversity of opinion regarding Schein's influence on Fleming must lie in part in the diversity of Schein's own work. He published three major collections of secular love songs, the *Venus Kräntzlein* of 1609—to which we will return below,—and the two quite different and very popular collections of the 1620s, the *Musica boscareccia*, published in three parts in 1621, 1626, and 1628, and the *Diletti pastorali* of 1624.[56] The last two, which, as modern works, would have been of most interest to a young poet like Fleming, are strongly Italianate and, as the titles imply, thoroughly pastoral. Brauer remarks: "Mit einemmal, über Nacht, hat der Leipziger Musikdirektor Arcadia nach Sachsen verpflanzt" (p. 388). The cast of the fifty songs of the *Musica boscareccia* are Filli and her Corydon, Silvio, Eremio, and Rosildo, Mirtillo and Delia, Cupid working his mischief on various of the shepherds and shepherdesses, and nymphs and satyrs, with Bacchus and Mopsus as extras. Many of the songs are lovers' complaints, some present joyful festivities, some describe the tricks played by Cupid on the unsuspecting, and several celebrate the weddings of fortunate shepherds whose shepherdesses have had a change of heart (some of these latter songs were originally written for Leipzig weddings). There are occasional thematic parallels between some of Fleming's poems and some of these songs: it was probably shepherds' complaints such as *Filli deine lieb Euglein klar* (*Musica boscareccia* I, 3) that Gillespie had in mind when he suggested that some of Fleming's songs, such as *An die Stolze* (O.V.20), resembled certain of Schein's. This similarity, as well as, of course, the use of pastoral names and typical pastoral situations in both Fleming (e.g., O.V.1–3, 5, 7) and Schein, is as likely to be the result of independent use of common pastoral sources as of Fleming's reliance on Schein. In the case of O.V.20, there is at least one poem by Opitz (*ALhier in dieser wüsten Heydt*) that Fleming's *An die Stolze* resembles as much as it does Schein's *Filli deine lieb Euglein klar*, and it seems likely from the occasional verbal reminiscences that Opitz's poem was indeed Fleming's main source.[57] The differences in vocabulary and phrasing between Schein's pastoral songs and Fleming's—Schein tends both towards preciosity, particularly but not only in the use of foreign words and diminutives, and occasional inelegance—make him an unlikely direct source for Fleming. Most importantly, though, nowhere in these poems of Schein's is there any depiction of fidelity between lovers, parted or otherwise, that resembles the depiction in Fleming: this is simply not part of the Italianate pastoral convention that governs the *Musica boscareccia*. There is reciprocal love represented in the wedding songs that punctuate the two works, but readers can judge for themselves whether such can have been close ancestors of *Elsgens treues Herz*:

> Sieh da, mein lieber Coridon,
> wie sehr dich Venus liebet,
> dieweil sie dir ein solchen Lohn
> für deine Treu jetzt gibet.
> Ihr Söhnelein
> Cupido klein,
> so dich hat tun verwunden,
> hat heute dich

mit leidentlich
nun wieder selbst verbunden.

O Coridon, o Coridon,
Das ist ein Tag der Freuden,
Heut scheinet dir die liebe Sonn',
Vergiß nun alles Leiden!
Weil deine Braut
Dir wird vertraut,
Die Braut-Meß Phoebus singet,
Die Musen all
Tönen mit Schall,
Daß es im Wald erklinget.

Darum, o lieber Coridon,
Nun wirst du selbst wohl wissen,
Wie du dein liebste Filli schon
Sollst in die Arme schließen.
Sie wird sich auch
Nach Liebsgebrauch
Wohl wissen zu bequemen
Und dich dergleich
Ganz tugendreich
In ihre Ärmlein nehmen.

(*Musica boscareccia*, pt. 1, no. 4)

It is not just the mythological and pastoral cast of characters that make such poems as this differ so much from Fleming's poems to Elsabe and Anna Niehus, it is also the one-dimensional nature of the characters and emotions. Not only in poems such as this, in which the lovers have found one another, but in all of them, the characters and their feelings are painted in a few bright primary colors: unclouded joy when Filli smiles, despair when she is cruelly indifferent. They are actors and actresses who, behind their tragic or comic masks, betray no individual psychological history. (Günther Müller, p. 24, makes a similar observation about the way motifs are treated in these poems: "Mit den überkommenen Motiven wird wie mit Schachfiguren gespielt, und nicht die Figuren, sondern das Spiel mit ihnen ist das eigentlich Tragende.") Schein does not attempt to depict something as complicated as the lover resolute in the face of adversity deriving his strength from the memory of and confidence in his beloved's faithfulness. It may also be noted that many of Schein's poems depicting happy lovers are written in the third person: Schein allows us to overhear the sufferings of unrequited love, but reciprocal love seems less inclined to be personally articulate.

In addition to songs celebrating the end of the lover's sufferings, there is one song in Schein's *Musica boscareccia* that depicts a lover parting from his beloved, and here one might hope to find some anticipation of Fleming. This is not, however, the case, for the parting is that of a rather endearing pastoral-Petrarchan shepherd from his hard-hearted shepherdess, and it bears no resemblance to separations depicted by Fleming:

O Scheiden, o bitter Scheiden,
wie machst du mir so großes Leiden!
O schöne Äugelein,
ach soll eur Blickelein
ich denn so gar fort meiden!
O süßer Mund,
dein Lippen rund
tun mir mein Herz zerschneiden.

O Filli, ich muß doch sterben,
Wo ich dein Gunst nicht kann erwerben,
O harter Demantstein!
Ach laß den Diener dein
Doch nicht elend verderben,
Ein Liebesblick,
So mich erquick,
Laß mich von dir ererben!

Ach, wird dir doch nichts entnommen,
Wenn mir zu lieb und Liebesfrommen
Viel tausend Schmätzelein
Von deinen Lippelein,
Ein süßes Labsal, kommen.
Ach, edles Hertz,
Bedenk mein Schmerz,
Den du oft hast vernommen.

(*Musica boscareccia*, pt. 1, no. 15)

The songs of Schein's *Diletti pastorali* are madrigals; forms as well as themes go back to the verse of Tasso and Guarini. Unconstrained by the repetitiveness of strophic form, Schein excels at brilliant, rapid narrative, perhaps best represented by *Aurora schön mit ihrem Haar*. The cast of characters, the tone, and the situations, however, are very similar to those of the *Musica boscareccia*, and the poems of both works can only be said to bear a general family resemblance at best to some of Fleming's Italianate pastoral poetry.

Schein's earliest collection of secular songs is, as mentioned, quite different from his work of the 1620s. The *Venus Kräntzlein* was published in 1609 while he was still a student. Although Cupid and Venus, along with other classical gods, put in appearances, these poems show little influence from the Italian pastoral but rather recall much more strongly the indigenous German song tradition—as is particularly evident in such motifs as wearing flowers with names like "Vergißmeinnicht" and warning the beloved of Neidthardt's machinations. It is in these poems that songs with themes anticipating Fleming's are to be found: songs about requited love and faithfulness during separation. Schein's use of acrostics like Fleming's underscores the thematic resemblances. Most of the acrostics are unique, but Schein uses the name Sidonia in three of the poems, and, since his first wife's name was Sidonia Hösel, it is tempting to conclude that these poems form a little narrative about Schein's courtship of her. Arthur Prüfer describes them: "In Nr. 2 lacht das junge Liebesglück des Dichters über die frohe Aussicht auf den baldigen Besitz der Geliebten, in Nr. 11 ergeht er sich in Klagen über die Trennung von ihr, in Nr. 14 hält er gar ihre Untreue vor" (Schein, *Sämtliche Werke*, vol. 1, p. xi). In another poem, which uses the acrostic "Anna," we also learn of the sufferings and hopes of a lover parted from his beloved:

1
Ach, edles Bild,
Von Tugend mild,
Wie thust Du mich so kränken?
Dass Du nicht hier,
Bist stets bei mir,
Mein Herz will sich versenken.
Ach, wenn ich doch,
Dich sehe noch,
O süßer Schatz, mein Leben,
Wollt' ich gar weit,
Mein' Traurigkeit,
Dem Meer thun übergeben.

2
Nun liebst Du mich,
Gleichwie ich dich,
So laß es doch auch merken,
Und gegen mir,
Ach, schönste Zier,
Beweis es mit den Werken,

Von Herzen tief,
Schreib' mir ein Brief,
Weil mir weit sein gescheiden,
Und thu damit,
Nach meiner Bitt',
Lindern mein großes Leiden.

3
Nach dir mein Sinn
Thut seufzen hin,
Kann aber nicht geschehen,
Dass ich sobald,
Mein Aufenthalt,
In Freuden dich mög sehen,
Dieweil das Glück,
Mit seiner Tück,
(O weh, o weh, o Klagen,)
Mich schwitzend heiß,
Von meiner Reis',
Thut wieder zurück jagen.

4
Ach liebstes Herz,
Bedenk den Schmerz,
Den dieses Lied dir klaget,
Und dir mein Treu,
Ohn Heuchelei,
Ganz trauriglich ansaget,
Bald mich gewähr',
Was ich begehr',
Schaff', daß ich Labsal finde,
Ob ich schon leid',
Wünsch ich dir Freud',
Dem lieben Himmelskinde.

(*Venus Kräntzlein*, no. 9)

Schein here paints no Petrarchan reproaching his lady for her hardheartedness, no lovelorn shepherd; it is circumstance and fortune that bring separation and unhappiness. Although the opening lines of the second strophe are a conditional, there is nothing in the poem to suggest that they could not also be a simple statement of the couple's mutual affection: "Nun liebst Du mich, / Gleichwie ich dich." The song itself is a witness of the lover's faithfulness: "Bedenk den

Schmerz, / Den dieses Lied dir klaget, / Und dir mein Treu, / Ohn Heuchelei, / Ganz trauriglich ansaget." Little is said of the beloved's beauty; it is her virtue and the hope that she will alleviate the pain of separation with a letter that the lover focuses on. This is surely the type of *Gesellschaftslied* "von Regnart bis Schein" that Pyritz and Alewyn had in mind when positing that rather amorphous *Lied*-genre as the tradition in which Fleming was working when he wrote many of the poems to Elsabe and Anna Niehus. It is precisely not that modish, Italianate pastoral strand of it that Fechner mentions and for which Schein and Regnart are known, but rather the type that was much closer to indigenous German traditions and the *Volkslied*, and that Schein cultivated in obscurity at the beginning of his career and Regnart at the end of his.

This being the case, there is no reason to assume that Schein's 1609 collection in particular was important for this phase of Fleming's poetry. Schein simply used the same motifs as were used in scores of poems of love and parting from the sixteenth century, and his rough metrics and forms, and the occasionally clumsy vocabulary and syntax, entirely pre-Opitzian as they are, did not significantly distinguish his early songs from those of other poets of *Gesellschaftslieder* and cannot have recommended these songs in particular as models for Fleming.[58] Here I believe the case for Schein's direct, tangible influence on Fleming at any phase of his career breaks down.[59] But if Pyritz and Alewyn are nonetheless correct that the themes of some of Fleming's love songs do hark back to the themes of the (non-Petrarchan, non-Italianate) *Gesellschaftslied*, the question arises of how Fleming was able suddenly, in the latter half of his career, to reach back to the thoughts and vocabulary and phrasings of such a rough form and recast them in the Opitzian elegance and the eloquence and suppleness that we find in the poems to Elsabe and Anna Niehus?[60]

Some of the aspects of P.W.III.6 sketched out in previous sections suggest starting points for answering this complicated question. First, the poem *Philyrena* in P.W.III.6, with its theme of faithfulness during separation, points to the fact that this and related themes did not in fact appear suddenly in the odes to Elsabe and Anna Niehus, but were already part of Fleming's poetic range somewhat earlier—in fact, much earlier, as discussed below. Pyritz himself pointed to *Philyrena* as a predecessor of the central odes of his interpretation (pp. 267, 285), although he was so intent upon discovering the new in Fleming that he did not lay stress on the continuity this poem implies. More importantly, P.W.III.6 as a whole suggests that it is not just in love poetry that one might find the depiction of a non-Petrarchan relationship based on reciprocity, equality, and *Treue*, that is, it points to genres other than love poetry (which was dominated by Petrarchism) in which Fleming could work with the themes and vocabulary of *Treue*. In P.W.III.6 Fleming shows us relationships of mutual affection existing among the four men and between Brokmann and his bride; this suggests that we might expect to find depictions of relationships based on *Treue* in poems of friendship and in epithalamia.

Dürrenfeld noted that Fleming's ode *Als etliche seiner Freunde von ihm zogen*, is "ein bezeichnendes Beispiel für die Herübernahme petrarkistischer Motive und Gestaltungsweisen aus der Liebes- in die Freundschaftsdichtung," and Unger remarks that Fleming sings of Gloger "wie man eine Geliebte besingt."[61] Fleming is far from being the first to use the vocabulary of Petrarchism in friendship poetry. One can point to instances in the neo-Latin tradition, for example, Simon Grunaeus's *Ad Meliorum Laubanum abiturientem Dantiscum*, in which only the name of the addressee reminds readers they are not reading a love poem.[62] It is, however, not just from the reservoir of Petrarchan protestations and eroticism that the young Fleming "borrowed" for his friendship poems. In a poem from 1632, *Auf eines guten Freundes Geburtstag* (O.IV.4), for example, we find passages celebrating the *Treue* that exists between like-minded and like-hearted friends and that resembles sentiments to be found in Fleming's late, non-Petrarchan love poetry for Elsabe and Anna Niehus:

> Bruder, meine mich mit Treuen,
> so du treu es meinen kanst!
> Zoilus sein falscher Wanst
> berste, wie er will, von neuen!
> Ehrlich, treulich, standhaft Lieben
> ist für Neide stets doch blieben.
>
> Deiner Tugend weise Gaben
> locken, Lieber, mich zu dir.
> Nun so komm! Du solst an mir,
> was die Liebe wündschet, haben.
> Wenn ein Herz ein Herze krieget,
> das ihm gleicht, so ists vergnüget.
>
> . . . .
> Ach wie selten kan erreichen
> ein treu Herze seinesgleichen!
>
> (ll. 31–42, 47–48)

If one changes "Bruder" to "Schwester," a term of affection which Fleming used when addressing Elsabe Niehus (O.V.27 and 28), and removes a few phrases linked to humanistic learning, the result is a fragment of a love poem celebrating already in 1632 the values we associate with Fleming's attachments to the Niehus sisters. There is, in fact, a long classical and Renaissance tradition of writing about male friendship that stresses values similar to those found in Fleming's odes for Elsabe and Anna Niehus. Cicero, in his *De amicitia*, the main source of Renaissance theory about friendship, points to the importance of *fides*, loyalty, which is fostered by similarity between friends, and which in turn ensures constancy: "Firmamentum autem stabilitatis constantiaeque est eius quam in amicitia quaerimus fides est; nihil est enim stabile, quod infidum est. Simplicem praeterea et communem et consentientem, id est, qui rebus isdem moveatur, elegi par est; quae omnia pertinent ad fidelitatem" ("Now the support and stay of that unswerving constancy, which we look for in friendship, is loyalty; for nothing is constant that is disloyal. Moreover, the right course is to choose for a friend one who is frank, sociable, and sympathetic—that is, one who is likely to be influenced by the same motives as yourself—since all these qualities conduce to loyalty").[63] Heinz Wilms, in his dissertation on friendship in neo-Latin and German baroque poetry, brings a number of examples from neo-Latin friendship poetry, especially propemptica, in which *fides* and assurances of loyalty play a major role.[64] As early as 1617 we find Opitz seeking ways to express this classical and Renaissance philosophy of friendship in the vernacular:

> Was in der welt die Sonn'/ in der Sonn' ist das licht/
> In dem licht' ist der glantz/ in dem glantz' ist die hitze:
>   Das ist vns Menschen auch die wahre libes pflicht/
>   Vnd ein getrewes hertz': es ist nichts nicht so nütze.
> O wie glückselig ist auch in dem höchsten schmertzen/
> Der dem ein trewer Freund mit liebes brunst von hertzen
>   Ohn falsch ist zugethan. ein solchen in der noth
>   Vnd wiederwertigkeit halt' ich für einen Gott.[65]

Lines 4 and 5 call to mind one of Fleming's best-known love poems, *Elsgens treues Herz* (O.V.30), with its refrain "Mir ist wol bei höchstem Schmerze, / denn ich weiß ein treues Herze"; it is sung today not as a love poem, but as a poem of friendship. Pyritz's reactions to Opitz's epigram and Fleming's poem, whose similarity of phrasing he noted, is interesting. He found it odd that Fleming's poem is now sung as a friendship poem (it was also, according to Lappenberg's notes, used as a wedding song as early as 1649): "[O.V.30] ist das einzige außergeistliche Lied Flemings, das heute noch gesungen wird, merkwürdigerweise zwar nicht mehr als Liebeslied, sondern als Freundschaftslied" (p. 281), and notes of Opitz's epigram that "charakteristisch genug handelt es sich da um F r e u n d e s treue!" (Pyritz's emphasis, p. 282). When Pyritz goes on to point out ways in which Fleming's poem is more melodic and less abstract than Opitz's epigram, he is certainly correct. But in differentiating Fleming's poetry from Opitz's and Fleming's own late poetry from that which preceded it, he turned a blind eye to the path of continuity signaled by the near interchangeability of some friendship poems and some love poems, to the fact that Fleming was able to acquire and explore the concept, the vocabulary, and the themes of *Treue* in his poems of "Freundestreue" before turning to love poetry.

The relationship of such friendship poetry to *Gesellschaftslieder* is not clear. It is possible that Opitz, in seeking vernacular vocabulary in which to express the sentiments of neo-Latin friendship poetry, may have, despite his general disdain for the indigenous tradition, wittingly or otherwise absorbed some of the vocabulary of the *Gesellschaftslied*. Hoffmann von Fallersleben prints in his collection of *Gesellschaftslieder* several poems in which the phrase "ein treues Herz" is used, most notably one (no. 102) from a collection originally published in Breslau that opens "Ein treues Herz ist ehrenwerth." It seems possible then, that Fleming, when writing of "Freundestreue," was at times writing within two by now inextricably entwined traditions, that of the *Gesellschaftslied*, which supplied some of the vernacular vocabulary, and Renaissance friendship poetry, which supplied the main philosophical impetus.

The epithalamium also plays a role in Fleming's developing the idea and language of love based on equality, reciprocity, and *Treue*. Unger pointed out (p. 14) early in this century that Fleming's *Elsgens treues Herz* (O.V.30) bears a resemblance to an epithalamium by Petrus Denaisius, number 7 in the *Anhang* to Zincgref's 1624 anthology. This poem for the wedding of Georg Michael Lingelsheim and Agnes Loefenius (or Jörg Michael Lingelsheimer and Agnes Löfenijn, as the title identifies them) in 1597 opens:

GLückseelig muß man preisen,
Die gleiche lieb vnd trew
Einander thun erweisen,
Stetigs vnd ohne rew,
Jn Noth vnd schweren zeiten
Tröst eins deß andern leidt,
Jn lieb vnd frölichkeiten
Mehrt eins deß andern frewdt.

Although Pyritz also noted (pp. 282–83) the similarities between this poem and Fleming's *Elsgens treues Herz*, he again was more concerned to show the superiority of Fleming's relatively late poem to Denaisius's and did not consider that some of Fleming's own epithalamia might form intermediaries. While many epithalamia by Fleming and his contemporaries take their cues from the names of the betrothed couple or focus on the bridal night, some, like Denaisius's in its opening strophe, focus on the mutual consent or reciprocity that is assumed to underlie any engagement, and that is so unlike the imbalance of the Petrarchan relationship. Perhaps pragmatic realities—bride and groom are usually from the same class; marriage can be ended only by death—account in part for the stress on equality and faithfulness of the couple in some epithalamia. These qualities are also reminiscent of the theory of male friendship, and bride and groom are at times depicted as friends, as in Denaisius's poem, as well as lovers. In any case epithalamia, by the nature of the occasion celebrated, offer an obvious forum for references to reciprocal love, equality, and steadfast faithfulness.

In an early epithalamium, O.III.1 for Daniel Döring and Rosine Schwendendörffer (1632), Fleming points to a natural law of "Brüderschaft," with which the bride and groom are in accord by virtue of their similarity or equality, and which will ensure the longevity of their union:

> Kein stärker Bündnüß ist auf Erden,
> als wenn sich Gleich und Gleich gesellt.
> Diß Ganze, was wir nennen Welt,
> muß gleichsfals so beweget werden.
> Was außer solcher Brüderschaft,
> hat langen Taurens keine Kraft.
>
> Du hast dir ein Gemahl erkoren,
> so dir gemäß in Allem ist,
> in der du dir recht ähnlich bist,
> in der du selbsten dich verloren.
> Ietzt wirst du, Werter, doppelt reich:
> du findest dich und was dir gleich.
>
> (ll. 43–54)

The importance of such sympathetic equality between bride and groom is highlighted in an epithalamium Fleming wrote in the following year for the widowed, middle-aged Martin Schörkel and his young bride, Margarethe Putscher (O.III.2).[66] The disparity in age prompts an insistence that they are nonetheless equal: "Gleiches Paar, doch nicht an Jahren! / Ihr laßt uns an euch erfahren, / daß auch Ungleich gleiche sei" (ll. 37–39). A much later poem of Fleming's, one of the love poems to Anna Niehus, O.V.37, echoes the early epithalamia when expressing this same principle of equality: "Wahre Liebe steht vergnüget, / wenn sie ihres gleichen krieget" (ll. 5–6).

In an undated epithalamium (O.III.9) from Fleming's Leipzig years, the fact that the groom has recently lost family members prompts Fleming to write, in terms that recall Denaisius and anticipate *Elsgens treues Herz*, of the mutual comfort husband and wife give by their loyalty:

> Doch so ist diß auch nichts Neues,
> daß die Sonn' im Regen scheint.
> Also lacht man, wenn man weint,
> wer nur auch hat etwas Treues,
> das mit ihm die Wage hält,
> wo die leichte Schal' hinfällt.
>
> Ein vertrauter Freund im Leben,
> der halbirt uns unser Leid,
> duppelt gleichfals alle Freud'
> und versichert uns beineben,
> daß die Not, so uns betrübt,
> ihm auch gleiche Stöße giebt.
> . . . .
> Helfe Gott, daß diese Treu'
> alles Traurens Ende sei!
>
> (ll. 31–42, 83–84)

Fleming also writes of equal and reciprocal relationships between man and woman in poems for engaged couples who were parted, a frequent theme in *Gesellschaftslieder*. In 1632 the sadness of a lover whose fiancée has left Leipzig (for safety?) prompts him to portray the deserted *locus quondam amoenus* in terms that recall the Petrarchan pastoral tradition: "Weiln auch deine Charitille / nicht bei uns zugegen ist, / so ist Alles öd' und stille, / Alles hat sein Leid erkiest" (O.IV.14, ll. 37–40). But the underlying assumption is that this is but a temporary sadness that the faithful lover can and will bear:

> Zweierlei hat man vom Lieben,
> so man standhaft ausverharrt:
> in dem Absein das Betrüben,
> Freuen in der Gegenwart.
> Lust und Leid ist der ergeben,
> wer in treuer Brunst will leben.
>
> (ll. 61–66)

Four years later, Fleming expresses with epigrammatic conciseness the difficulty and the reward of faithful but separated love when he apostrophizes Elsabe Niehus at the closing of *An Basilenen, nachdem er von ihr gereiset war* (O.V.27): "Sei gegrüßt, bald Trost, itzt Qual." In a later poem to Anna Niehus (O.V.40) there is a further variation upon the theme of separation and reunion, when Fleming urges her to embrace their current circumstances as a pledge of future happiness: "Ists wahr, daß alle Frölichkeit / wird süßer nach dem Leiden, / so schicke, Schatz, dich in die Zeit. / Wir sehen uns mit Freuden!" (ll. 29–32).

Perhaps the most striking instance of Fleming's early exploration of the non-Petrarchan theme of fidelity is to be found in a poem that incorporates the theme of separation into an epithalamium. This is in an ode for Salomon Steyer and Anna Junghansinn written for their wedding on July 3, 1632. The groom, like many of his fellow Silesians, had come to Leipzig to study; there he met Anna Junghansinn and became engaged. In the late autumn of 1631, he returned to Breslau—Fleming's propempticon for him (M.V.21), with its despairing reference to Gloger's more permanent departure, was mentioned in chapter 1—probably to assume duties as a pastor, and returned only in the following year, to be married.[67] Fleming's poem for the couple, unknown until recently, is reproduced below in its entirety.[68]

1

   LJebster Freund/ nachdem du liessest
   Deine prächtig' Oder stehn/
   Vnd entgegen stracks zu gehn
   Vnsrer Pleisse dich befliessest/
5 Weil du dir gebildet ein/
   Samb sie solte schöner seyn/

2

   Hat dir alsobald gefallen
   Sampt dem Ort' ein feines Bild/
   Daß dein reiffer Sinn denn hielt
10 Als die schöneste für allen.
   Was sich in sich schicken sol/
   Thut dem ersten Blicke wol.

3

   Vnser Phebus war dir günstig/
   Vnd gab dir den thewren Krantz;
15 Dich zu führen an den Tantz
   War nicht minder Hymen brünstig.

Beyder Götter werthen Lohn
Trägstu völlig jetzt darvon.

4

20 Du hast deine Gunst gesetzet
Jn des fernen Meissens Schoß.
Leipzig war dir einig groß.
Breßlaw wurde schlecht geschätzet.
Breßlaw die belobte Stadt/
Die so schöne Jungfern hat.

5

25 Liebe lest sich nicht verbinden
An gewissen Ort vnd Stand;
Auch nicht an das Vaterland.
Sie ist vberall zu finden.
Jhre Heymath ist die statt/
30 Wo sie Gegenliebe hat.

6

Einmal hat des Winters Kummer
Der gesunde Lentz gelegt/
Vnd das schwangre Feld gehegt/
Einmal wird es gleich nun Sommer/
35 Seit daß du dich hinverwandt
Jn dein grosses Vaterland.

7

Vnverhoffter dieser Zeiten/
Doch vmb so viel lieber mehr/
Sey willkommen/ vnd rück her
40 An der Liebsten hertze Seiten.
Dein Pfand/ Du/ bist noch bey Jhr/
Wie auch Jhres/ Sie/ bey Dir.

8

Weil du aussen bist gewesen/
Bist du auch zugleich' aus dir.
45 Dein Hertz' hauste stets in Jhr.
Ohn sie kuntst du nicht genesen.
Du ohn Sie/ vnd Sie ohn Dich/
Kunte keines frewen sich.

9

Sie hast du aus Jhr genommen/
50 Gleich als wie sie dich aus dir.

Sie war in dir/ du in Jhr.
Keines mochte zu sich kommen.
Diß war nur der sichre Stand/
Eines war des andern Pfand.

10

55 Wahre Liebe wil nicht trügen/
Sie helt vber jhrer Pflicht.
Was sie einmal schon verspricht/
Kan/ vnd sol/ vnd muß sich fügen.
Muß es gleich geschieden seyn/
60 Sie setzt sich zum Bürgen ein.

11

Du hast vns ein sattes gnügen/
Trewer Schlesier/ ertheilt/
Vnd nach mügligkeit geeilt
An die zarte Brust zu liegen/
65 Die sich dir/ wie du dich Jhr/
Hat so hoch versprochen hier.

12

Mars der war dir sehr zu wider/
Sperrete fast allen Paß;
Amor legte dieses Haß
70 Doch zu deinen Füssen nieder.
Könt' er seyn von dem vmbringt/
Den er allzeit doch bezwingt?

13

Wen die starcke Liebe wirbet
Vnd zu jhren Fahnen stellt/
75 Der wird ein behertzter Held/
Dem sein Anschlag nie verdirbet;
Der frisch in die Feinde setzt/
Vnd sie trennet vnverletzt.

14

Schöne Braut/ was hats geschadet/
80 Daß er ist von euch gereist/
Nun sein wiederkomner Geist
Euch mit dopler Lust begnadet.
Für des Abseyns kurtzes Leid
Habt jhr ewge Frewdenzeit.

15
85 Rechte Liebe wird nicht funden
    Allzeit im zu gegen seyn.
    Gleichsfalls ist sie nicht allein
    An den lieben Leib gebunden.
    Offt erkieset sie die Flucht/
90 Daß sie gebe süssre Frucht.

16
    Sie ist eine Krafft der Selen/
    Die sich schwinget weit vnd breit/
    Die sich in den Träumen frewt/
    Vnd zu weilen auch muß quelen;
95 Doch nichts minder ist sie früh'
    Aus dem Leibe kommen nie.

17
    Wenn die dicken Nebel brechen
    Titans seiner Strahlen Krafft/
    Vnd sie nehmen in verhafft/
100 Kan man auch in Warheit sprechen/
    Daß mehr sey kein Cynthius?
    So/ wann Lieb von Liebe muß.

18
    Euch wird förderhin nichts scheiden/
    Zwey an Leibern/ Eins an Brunst;
105 Wir gehn jrre dieser Gunst/
    Wallen zwischen Lust vnd Leiden
    Jn Gedancken/ leicht als Wind.
    Sind ab/ wo wir leiblich sind.

Fleming offers here an account of the couple's history, punctuated in every fifth strophe by short disquisitions on the nature of "Liebe," "Wahre Liebe," and "Rechte Liebe." In the first of these, prompted by the Silesian (Steyer) having fallen in love with a Leipzigerin, Fleming insists that reciprocity is the constitutive characteristic of love, geography being no object: where one finds one's love returned, that is one's home. In the following four strophes the history of Steyer and Junghansinn's courtship moves Fleming to speak of another way in which they have rendered null the barrier of geography: during Steyer's return to Silesia, he and his fiancée carried one another within themselves as pledges.[69] Beneath the wittiness of expression and the paradox and antithesis fitted precisely to meter and line, these strophes, with their theme of separation, recall the ingenuously expressed theme of parting lovers in the *Gesellschaftslied*, while simultaneously preparing for the odes in which it is Fleming himself who is the one separated from his beloved. In the poem entitled *Als Einer von seiner Liebsten verreisete* (O.IV.35), which Lappenberg surmises was actually about himself, Fleming describes the exchange of hearts, and in a phrase frequently used in *Gesellschaftslieder*, promises that happiness will follow, as sunshine upon rain:

> desto freier zieh' ich hin,
> weil ich stets doch bei euch bin.
>
> Dieses Pfand, mein treues Herze
> nehmet hin, wie eures ich!
> Was uns itzund zwingt zu Schmerze,
> soll ergetzen euch und mich!
> Freude folgt auf Angst und Pein,
> wie auf Regen Sonnenschein.
>
> (ll. 29–36)

In *An Basilenen, nachdem er von ihr gereiset war* (O.V.27), Fleming confidently asserts that he and his beloved will remain with one another despite separation:

> Ist mein Glücke gleich gesonnen
> mich zu führen weit von dir,
> o du Sonne meiner Wonnen,
> so verbleibst du doch in mir.
> Du in mir und ich in dir
> sind beisammen für und für.
>
> (ll. 1–6)

In strophe ten of his epithalamium for Steyer and Junghansinn, Fleming again, as in the fifth strophe, offers some general observations on the nature of love. Here he states that it is never deceptive and that it offers itself as security in times of separation; the descriptions of the hardships that Steyer underwent to keep his promise and return to his bride illustrate this maxim. This theme of honest faithfulness in separation is implicit in much of Fleming's later love poetry, and explicit in *Treue Pflicht* (O.V.32) for Elsabe Niehus; in *An Anemonen, die Liebste* (O.V.41), the theme is summed up in the last line of the second strophe: "Wahre Liebe hält ihr Wort."

In the fifteenth strophe of his ode for Steyer and Junghansinn, Fleming offers further propositions about the nature of love, arguing that it can still thrive when lovers are apart precisely because it is not solely associated with the body, but is, rather, a power of the mind; dreams can mediate between those who are parted. His assertions in this poem from 1632 are couched in more cheerful terms than are found in most of the odes that treat of his own separation from his beloved, but the underlying philosophical notion is the same. In *An Basilenen, nachdem er von ihr gereiset war*, he apostrophizes dreams to act as mediators between them: "Ihr, ihr Träume, sollt indessen / unter uns das Beste tun" (ll. 19–20).

The example of some of the friendship poetry and epithalamia from Fleming's Leipzig years demonstrates that the notion of reciprocal love and *Treue* between equals was not just a product of Fleming's poetry for the Niehus sisters, but that it was a concept that appealed to Fleming and that he found ways of expressing from very early on. When he came to write the pastoral epithalamium for Brokmann halfway through his career, he was able to go so far as to offer the concept of reciprocal, faithful love as an explicit alternative to the unequal relationship that was Opitz's best effort at surviving within the Petrarchan system of love. How Fleming's alternative concept was rooted in his own personal experiences and personality we can hardly know, except to note that his own poetry and the testimony of his friends suggests that he had a gift for friendship. The literary roots of the concept and the language used to express it are clearer: they are, first, the *Gesellschaftslied*, as Pyritz and Alewyn suggest, but more precisely, the native German strain, and second, the classical and Renaissance theory and poetry of friendship. How influential epithalamia were is unclear, but the example of Denaisius indicates that equality and fidelity appeared in them as themes, and Fleming certainly extended this convention.

In a sense Fleming's love poetry for Elsabe and Anna Niehus forms a logical extension of his earlier poetry. While he could always resort to the conventions of Petrarchan poetry to depict a love relationship, the mutual consent supposed to obtain between real men and women who were engaged called for the depiction of the different, non-Petrarchan relationship of *Treue*, such as that which we find in some of his early epithalamia and in the work honoring Brokmann's marriage. When Fleming himself then became engaged, first to one sister, then the other, this epithalamic convention of *Treue* logically suggested itself. It was made even more compelling by thematic parallels between his own situation and the theme of separated but faithful lovers in the *Gesellschaftslied*. Fleming's poems for Elsabe and Anna Niehus are thus in a sense just as conventional as Fleming's Petrarchan poetry, although the predominance of the Petrarchan value system in the

German baroque as a whole makes Fleming's poetry of *Treue* seem fresh by comparison.

The substantial autobiographical element in Fleming's late love odes further contributes to the appearance that these poems depart from conventional love poetry.[70] The inclination to autobiography, however, like the theme of *Treue*, is not something that puts in a sudden appearance in Fleming's late poetry. In connection with Fleming's *Elegie*, I noted that the closing of that extremely early poem, in which the poet explicitly contrasted his own situation with that of the addressee, was like the endings of many of his later poems; such autobiographical references are remarkably common in Fleming. A particularly vivid example is the epicedium for Michael Thomas, in which the poet concentrates upon his own grief to the point of failing in his duty to comfort others who are bereaved. Some of Fleming's early pastoral odes also have a strong autobiographical element (see esp. O.IV.4, 5, 6, 7, 10, and 19). The epithalamium for Steyer and Junghansinn shows the poet offering considerable biographical detail, rather than simply painting a conventionalized portrait of an ideal bride and groom. Fleming thus from his early poetry onward exhibits a tendency to offer more particularized biographical and autobiographical detail than do many poets of the age. Like the theme of *Treue*, then, this tendency actually has deep roots in his own writing, but when the theme of *Treue* and autobiography appear together, the initial impression they make is that the poet has done something extraordinarily new. There is, finally, a strong admixture of neo-Stoicism in Fleming's poetry of *Treue* for the Niehus sisters, and this, which we do not encounter in, for example, the Steyer-Junghansinn epithalamium, adds an additional dimension that again makes these late poems seem new against a background of Petrarchistic poetry, though not against the background of Fleming's poetry as a whole.

4. Epistolae ex Persia: The Poetic Epistles Written during the Persian Journey (1636–1638)

In early March 1636, after a fourteen-month stay in Reval, Fleming and the now somewhat enlarged embassy left the Baltic city for Moscow. From there they departed in June, finally underway to their real destination, Persia; this journey and the return would take nearly three years. There is a commonly held assumption, whose roots are already perceptible in Gervinus and Goedeke, and which was important in Pyritz's work, that during the long journey Fleming was cut off from European letters and society and that, thrown back upon his own inner resources, he perforce produced personal, unmediated poetry.[1] Pyritz wrote: "Indem der Dichter den bisherigen Wirkungsbereichen entrückt war, in denen sein Schaffen wurzelte, fand er vor gänzlich verwandelte innere Bedingungen sich gestellt. Abgeschnitten von literarischen Quellen, herausgerissen aus dem Stromkreis der Gesellschaft, des Gemeinschaftsantriebs und der vollen Resonanz beraubt, war er im wesentlichen mit sich allein" (p. 311). This dramatic image dissolves under scrutiny.[2]

Tropsch, in *Flemings Verhältnis zur römischen Dichtung*, documented Fleming's frequent borrowings from classical writers in poems written in the period from 1636 to 1639 and thereby demonstrated that Fleming was not cut off from European literary sources during the journey. Manfred Beller has similarly pointed to Fleming's "Pflege hoher Stillagen und das auffällige Hervortreten mythologischer Ausdrucksformen gerade in den Jahren 1636 bis 1638."[3] Whether Fleming could incorporate classical learning because of a well-trained memory, a commonplace book, or a small library—or all three—is immaterial: what is clear is that he and the other well-educated members of the expedition carried with them physically or mentally much of the baggage of European culture. That Fleming was "mit sich allein" during the journey—literally or figuratively—is nonsense. The final roster included nearly one hundred men (not counting the soldiers), including Olearius, one of the foremost intellects in Germany; Hartmann Grahmann, a sophisticated court physician skilled in the by now modish Paracelsian chemical medicine; Nuremberg patricians Hieronymus

Imhof and Georg Pius Pöhmer, brother of Georg Wilhelm; and others just as deeply rooted in European culture.

The expedition, in fact, was intended as a representation of European civilization. Its form of organization was that of a European court, as is clear from the *Hofordnungen* promulgated by Duke Friedrich and the ambassadors and printed by Olearius in the *Reisebeschreibung* (pp. 85–100).[4] Members of the expedition were given traditional court titles and positions, for example, *Marschall, Stallmeister, Kammerherr, Hofjunker, Kammerpage,* and *Lakai,*[5] and fulfilled the corresponding practical and ceremonial duties. Fleming, for example, as a *Hofjunker* or *Truchseß* (or both; the designation is unclear), was expected to accompany the ambassadors to table and to take turns with the other *Junker* in the duty of carving. The ceremonial duties were not the only ones (although in Fleming's case, it is not clear whether he had other regular tasks, or if he was simply expected to hold himself ready for orders from the ambassadors as needed), but they were important ones, as they would be in any court, and particularly so during this expedition when the impression made upon the foreign hosts could determine the success of the mission.[6] There is a telling passage from Duke Friedrich's *Hofordnung*: "[it is ordered that] Jnsonderheit aber *in praesents* frembder Leute/ der Marschall nebenst den hohen Officirern und Hoff Junckern jederzeit auffwärtig seyn/ Sie die Herren Gesandten in geziemender Ordnung aus und ins *logier* begleiten/ jhnen allen/ ob wäre Jhre Fürstl. Durchl. selbst zu gegen/ gebührenden *respect* erweisen/ und sich also bezeigen/ darmit bey jedermann/ bevorab aber den Frembden Jhre Fürstl. Durchl. hoher Name und *respect* desto mehr *aestimiret* und geschätzet werde/ weil auff die *Legationes* alle Völcker genawe achtung geben/ und daraus der abwesenden hohen Potentaten Stand/ *Grandezza*, Qualiteten und hohe tapffer Gemühter zu *colligiren* pflegen" (*Reisebeschreibung*, pp. 95–96). Far from being cut off from the culture of Europe, Fleming was in continuous contact with it during the journey, both in the form of highly intelligent and sophisticated men, and in the form of the social hierarchy that structured their behavior and interactions.

This reminder is particularly timely when interpreting Fleming's four German poetic epistles, at least three of which were written in the course of the journey. The four are: P.W.IV.50, *Nach seinem Traume an seinen vertrautesten Freund* (undated); P.W.IV.44, *An Herrn Olearien vor Astrachan der Reußen in Nagaien* (September 1636); P.W.IV.49, *An einen seiner vertrautesten Freunde auf dessen seiner Buhlschaft ihren Namenstag* (November 25, 1636); and P.W.IV.51, *An Herrn Hansen Arpenbeken, vertrauten Bruders, auf dessen seiner Liebsten ihren Namenstag in Gilan begangen* (February 1, 1638).[7] Heinz Wilms, discussing these poems under the general rubric "Freundschaftsdichtung," remarks: "In diesen Dichtungen ist Fleming wie vor ihm [Petrus] Lotichius [Secundus] Wegbereiter einer individuellen Lyrik, die das echt persönliche Erlebnis zum Anlaß und Gegenstand hat. Hier dient die Dichtung nicht mehr einem bestimmten offiziellen Anlaß, der Thema und Gegenstand festlegt, sondern sie entsteht aus einer besonderen Gelegenheit und deren innerer Nachwirkung."[8] Wilms is correct that P.W.IV.44, 49, 50, and 51 are not official occasional poetry, but what the thematic rather than generic designation "Freundschaftsdichtung" obscures is that these four poems, like many of Lotichius's elegies, are poetic epistles, a humanist genre with its own tradition and conventions and one in which it is expressly permitted for the poet to concentrate on subject matter of his own choosing, including his own experiences, rather than on some standard or official external event. Thus it only appears that in such poems the poet, Lotichius or Fleming, "überschritt die Grenzen der zeitgenössischen Dichtung" by concentrating on himself as Wilms claims (p. 156). A glance at the history and theory of the poetic epistle provides a context for these poems and establishes that while later poets may have written verse reminiscent of Fleming's poetic epistles by reason of also focusing upon the individual and his experience, Fleming was not prescient and did not anticipate them by writing outside of all established canons. In these poems, despite his physical distance from Europe, Fleming continued to write within the normal confines of European poetic theory and practice contemporary with him.

History and Theory of the Poetic Epistle

The tradition of writing poetic epistles reaches back to classical times, to Catullus, Horace, and Ovid. Of these, Ovid, with his *Tristia* and *Epistolae ex Ponto*, exerted the greatest influence on later writers of poetic epistles down to the eighteenth century, Horace's influence being confined mainly to his odes. In the Middle Ages the genre flourished especially in the Carolingian period, when Alcuin and his circle cultivated learned friendships in verse letters. It once more became important in the Renaissance and served as a means of communicating humanist ideals; Petrarch's sixty-four *Epistolae metricae* provided the impetus for many later humanists. In Germany many of the reformers in Erfurt and Wittenberg, including Helius Eobanus Hessus, Georg Sabinus, and Jacob Micyllus, wrote verse letters, modeling them largely after Ovid's. Other sixteenth-century poets who wrote poetic epistles include Janus Secundus, who composed two *libri epistolarum* as well as his better-known *Basia*; Lotichius, whose elegies, as noted, generally take the form of verse letters; and Caspar Ursinus Velius, whose *Poematum libri quinque* include a book of *epistolae*, some in hexameters, some in elegiac distichs. When in the seventeenth century German poets with pretensions to Renaissance elegance such as Opitz and Fleming began writing in their native language, they had a long tradition of poetic epistles to draw upon; the neo-Latin poetic epistle of the sixteenth and early seventeenth centuries formed the immediate background to their own. They themselves, of course, continued to write neo-Latin poems as well, including poetic epistles; the transition to writing them in German was a natural one.

In addition to the neo-Latin tradition, there had also been a tradition of vernacular poetic epistles in the preceding centuries. The genre flourished especially in the first half of the fifteenth century in France among Clément Marot and his followers. At mid-century, however, Marot was eclipsed by the poets of the Pléiade, and these, in their reaction to him, turned away from the poetic epistle, which they criticized for not being sufficiently elevated, for treating "choses domestiques et familières."[9] (When in Holland, an equally important source of models for the Opitzians, the vernacular came to be regarded as a worthy vehicle for poetry in the early seventeenth century, poets seem to have followed the Pléiade in their neglect of the vernacular poetic epistle.) The poems of Marot and his school were not in themselves particularly important for the German poetic epistle, but are of interest because the vogue of the French poetic epistle and the attendant difficulties of creating an appropriate vernacular equivalent for a classical form coincided with early efforts to articulate theoretical norms governing the writing of poetry in French. Thomas Sebillet's *L'Art poétique françoys*, which appeared in 1548, was the first treatise on poetry to deal extensively with the poetic epistle. The theoretical background of the genre is thus worked out more fully in the French than in either the neo-Latin or the German traditions.

From an examination of this sixteenth-century French discussion of the genre and also of Renaissance (prose) epistolographic theory and practice, supplemented by consideration of other sources—references to the poetic epistle in the treatises of Julius Caesar Scaliger (*Poetices libri septem*, 1561), Jacobus Pontanus (*Poeticarum institutionum libri tres*, 1594), and Opitz (*Buch von der Deutschen Poeterey*, 1624)—the theoretical outlines of the poetic epistle emerge.[10] The poetic epistle was regarded by neo-Latin, French, and German theorists alike as closely related to the elegy. The Latin poetic epistle was, in fact, generally written in elegiac distichs, although hexameters were also used. Poets of the vernacular used a vernacular equivalent of the long lines of the elegy: in German the alexandrine or, occasionally, *vers communs*. The close kinship of the poetic epistle to elegy had important consequences not only for its form, but also for its content. Renaissance theorists considered the elegiac meter suitable for almost any topic, so long as the topic was not too elevated, and the poetic epistle enjoyed this same privilege. At times the poetic epistle actually usurped the prerogative of the elegy to treat a wide range of subjects, for the prescriptive definition of the elegy itself was sometimes narrowed to include only the love elegy, even though the meter was in practice all-purpose.[11]

Developments in Renaissance epistolographic theory similarly point to the freedom of the epistle (both prose and verse, as discussed below) to treat a wide range of subjects. The theory of the prose epistle underwent a radical change in the fifteenth and sixteenth centuries in reaction to the highly restrictive and prescriptive *artes dictaminis* of the Middle Ages. Whereas medieval treatises on letter writing gave explicit precepts (derived from rhetorical theory) regarding the choice of subject matter of letters, the fleshing out of this subject matter (*inventio*), and its arrangement (*dispositio*), Renaissance theorists such as Heinrich Bebel (*Commentaria epistolarum conficiendarum*, 1503), Desiderius Erasmus (*De conscribendis epistolis*, 1522), Joannes Ludovicus Vives (*De conscribendis epistolis*, 1536), and Justus Lipsius (*Epistolica Institutio*, 1591) refused to offer rules for invention and disposition, insisting instead in their treatises that the individuals writing the letter must themselves decide upon the subject matter, its elaboration, and arrangement. Erasmus and Vives cautioned only that decorum required that the words of the epistle be suited to the social standing of the writer and his correspondent. In familiar letters, exchanged among friends of the same social class, the variety of topics that could be treated and the degree of intimacy that could be expressed were considerable.

Although the poetic epistle is not discussed explicitly by any of the major humanist theorists of epistolography, it is safe to assume that their teachings are relevant for verse as well as prose, for composition in both verse and prose was based upon the same rhetorical principles. The poetic epistle differed from its prose counterpart only in that the writer had to observe the rules of versification. French theorists considered the poetic epistle simply "une lettre missive mise en vers,"[12] and Renaissance epistolographic treatises from time to time include among their examples poetic epistles from Horace and Ovid.

The epistolographic treatises of Bebel, Erasmus, Vives, Lipsius, and others represent the attempt of theory to catch up with practice, for the humanist tradition of writing informal letters on a wide range of topics, like that of writing metrical epistles, goes back to Petrarch. With Cicero's *Epistulae ad Atticum* and *Epistulae ad Familiares* as their primary models, Renaissance letters became an important and nearly unique vehicle for self-revelation and autobiography, for there were few conventional restrictions on the subject matter of letters. Petrarch remarks of his own letters: "At times they will deal with public and private affairs, at times they will touch upon our griefs which supply plenty of subject matter, or still other matters that happened to come along. In fact I did almost nothing more than to speak about my state of mind or any other matter of interest which I thought my friends would like to know."[13] Petrarch is being slightly disingenuous, for his published letters were far from being simply spontaneous scribblings. He and the humanists who followed him expected their correspondence to be read by their contemporaries and posterity and took care that the image of themselves that emerged from the style and content of their letters would do them honor. Nonetheless, these letters have far more in them of the writers themselves as individuals and of their personal concerns and circumstances than do works in almost any other Renaissance genre.

Karl Otto Conrady has insisted upon the greater self-revelatory quality of the Renaissance letter compared with Renaissance lyric: "Die neulateinische Lyrik hat mit unvermittelter Ichaussprache wenig zu tun. Die 'Entdeckung des Menschen' [in the Renaissance] äußert sich in andern literarischen Gattungen. . . . Die Lyrik ist so stark an die Tradition, an vorgegebene Aussageweise, überlieferte Thematik und Motivik gebunden, daß das Ich, wenn es ganz von sich sprechen will, all dies erst überwinden oder es sich doch sehr kräftig anverwandeln müßte. Brief und Biographie dagegen . . . werden zu Gefäßen bisher unbekannter Selbstaussprache."[14] The poetic epistle, where letter and lyric come together, offers a rare exception to Conrady's generalization, for it is a verse genre that shares the freedom of the prose letter to express the individual experience of the poet. This does not mean that it is a form or forerunner of *Erlebnisdichtung,* but only that as a genre less restricted with regard to content and disposition by tradition and rhetorical precept than many other genres, it can touch on subjects not usually treated in verse. This is particularly apparent when poetic epistles are compared to occasional poems. Where the occasional poem has its subject dictated by the occasion—a wedding, birthday, death, or journey, for example—the poetic epistle can treat any topic of the poet's choice. The subjects of Petrarch's metrical epistles range from a description of the uneasy state of Europe on the eve of the Hundred Years' War to the familiar theme of his efforts to free himself from Laura's enchantment. The author of an occasional poem resorts to the classical *loci* and the classical models for his *inventiones*, and the same *inventiones* appear again and again in the poems of the same genre (the argument, for example, that it is good to die young, which appears in nearly all of Fleming's epicedia for children and infants). The writer of a poetic epistle, in contrast, can include details and information drawn from his own experience as he sees fit. The disposition of occasional poems tends to standardization and conforms to the rather narrowly defined expectations of its recipients and readers, whereas the poetic epistle can be ordered in the fashion the writer wishes, or simply as his thoughts occur to him. In practice, the persona presented in an occasional poem tends to be little individualized: the focus upon the occasion and the addressee naturally precludes that. In many poetic epistles, on the other hand, the writer, who often takes events and topics of immediate concern to himself as his themes, emerges as a distinct individual with a specific history, often recognizably real surroundings, and sometimes a definite personality.

The Poetic Epistles of Martin Opitz

I have elsewhere discussed in some detail the problems of defining which of Opitz's poems, none of which is explicitly called an epistle, would have been regarded as such by Opitz and his contemporaries.[15] Briefly, the reasoning is as follows: the theory and practice of the poetic epistle in Latin leads one to expect German poetic epistles will be longer poems, written in alexandrines or possibly *vers communs*, the German equivalents of the elegiac distich. Their titles will designate an addressee, someone of approximately the same social class as the poet (poems to rulers entail panegyric and are usually written on an occasion or for a purpose and thus lack the freedom of choice with respect to topic characteristic of the familiar epistle). Neo-Latin practice leads one to expect poetic epistles to be published either under a separate rubric ("Liber epistolarum" or the equivalent) or, if their number is small, in a book of *Sylvae* or *Wälder*, in the most miscellaneous book, if there is more than one. In the 1644 posthumous edition of Opitz's poems, which, as it was prepared by Opitz before his death, may be regarded as an "Ausgabe letzter Hand," the first book of *Poetische Wälder* is such a book. Of the thirty-eight poems in this first book, the last seven are translations; another nine are either sonnets or in *Lied*-form and can be disregarded. Of the remaining poems in alexandrines (or in one case, in *vers communs*), six panegyrical poems to nobles, three dedicatory poems, a propempticon and a *Promotionscarmen* can be similarly eliminated as prompted by an occasion, not by a topic emanating from the poet's own needs and interests. Nine further poems, for various reasons, cannot be considered poetic epistles. *Als er auß Siebenbürgen sich zurück anheim begab* does possess the discursive and reflexive qualities characteristic of epistles, but it lacks a specifically designated addressee. *Antwort auff Herrn Balthasar Venators teutsches Carmen/ an jhn geschrieben* would appear, from its title, to be a more likely candidate, but it is pure anecdote, with no acknowledgment of the addressee. The other seven are very much occasional poems. Although there are no established names for the subgenres of occasional poetry that they represent, the purpose of each of these is clearly that of celebrating an important occasion. In one case the event is the cessation of the plague, in another the fact that a book has remained unscathed by a fire in Leipzig; the remainder celebrate literary, musical, or artistic—or in one case commercial—accomplishments. The two poems that remain, *An Herrn Johann Seußius/ Churf. Sächsischen Secretar* and *An Herrn Zincgrefen* (which fit the formal criteria outlined above) differ from the poems surrounding them because of their informality and the fact that their topics are determined by the mutual interests of author and addressee, not an occasion fixed by the calendar or grounded in an external event; as such they would have been regarded by Opitz and his contemporaries as poetic epistles, letters in verse form.[16]

In *An Herrn Johann Seußius/ Churf. Sächsischen Secretar*, Opitz writes, as Lotichius did in several of his elegies, from an army encampment, and his situation prompts him to meditate upon proper occupation in time of war. Three activities associated with camp life—womanizing, gaming, and drinking—he rejects before endorsing a fourth possibility, writing satirical and commemorative poetry and cultivating learning in general. In these, and more particularly, in the cultivation of Stoic equanimity—to which there is a paean—Seußius serves him as a model; the closing of the poem is panegyrical. In *An Herrn Zincgrefen*, written in Paris, Opitz is even more explicitly concerned with literary questions. He praises Zincgref for his efforts on behalf of the German language and then, in order to incite him to redouble his efforts, describes how bad poets are flooding Paris. The implication is that guardians of the German language must be unflagging in promoting literary activity and keeping it out of the hands of poetasters.

Both of these poems exhibit the salient features of the Renaissance poetic epistle: in neither does an occasion dictate the topic, which is chosen rather because it is appropriate and of interest to both writer and addressee. There is no traditional arrangement of material in either poem; in both poems there are passages in which the arrangement of ideas appears to be purely associative. Such a discursive, spontaneous quality was one of the chief characteristics of Renaissance letters. In both poems, as in familiar letters, we get some sense of Opitz as an individual and of his situation.

Despite these marked epistolary traits, however, Opitz's two German poetic epistles show signs of moving away from the best possibilities of this Renaissance genre. By comparison with the elegiac epistles of sixteenth-century poets such as Helius Eobanus Hessus and Lotichius, the individuality of the persona pales. There is simply less biographical and circumstantial detail offered (this may be partly a function of language; Opitz's Latin poetic epistles, of which there are several in the second book of his *Sylvarum libri tres*, are more intimate). Opitz's choice of topics and way of presenting them also suggests some estrangement from the verse letter of the previous age. In these poems he is really less concerned with communicating his current situation to his addressee than he is with expounding upon two rather lofty topics: poetry and the (neo-Stoic) life of learning. While each is certainly appropriate to the addressee, it is noticeable that Opitz does not choose, as he legitimately could in a poetic epistle, more quotidian or personal topics.[17]

Fleming's Poetic Epistles

Given his general familiarity with Opitz's works, Fleming probably knew at least the poem for Seußius (*An Herrn Zincgrefen* was not published in Opitz's collected poems during Fleming's lifetime), but there is no need to assume that they in particular served him as models for poetic epistles, for he could more easily look to the abundant examples of classical and Renaissance poets writing in Latin. Fleming himself wrote a number of Latin poetic epistles, many of which are to be found in the second book of *Sylvae*. One of the most delightful of these is an early one (Sy.II.3), in which Fleming invites Georg Gloger to accompany him home to Wechselburg. It includes passages on the history of their friendship and Gloger's influence on both his poetic endeavors and his medical studies. In a poem written two years later to Timotheus Swirsen (Sy.II.10), Fleming indicates he is deeply troubled by his parents' misgivings about the potentially dangerous journey he is to embark on. But after presenting this background, Fleming begins to quote Swirsen urging him not to shirk duty and danger and describing the various advantages of travel; the encouraging words wipe away the poet's scruples and he indicates his eagerness to set off. The poem presents features that characterize other of Fleming's poetic epistles. It comprises two parts, in the first of which the poet outlines a troubling personal situation. A turning point leads to the second part, in which the poet finds comfort and courage in the interchange with his friend. Some of Fleming's Latin verse letters to his friends, however, seem to be truncated before the resolutely cheerful part and end less hopefully. In a poem to Olearius (Sy.II.14) written on March 10, 1634 from Novgorod, where Fleming was separated from the main part of the embassy, he complains of his poetic inspiration having deserted him and of the inhospitable nature of the town; he closes averring that Olearius's absence is a deprivation to him. From Moscow two years later he sends a similarly melancholy missive (Sy.II.22) to Timotheus Polus, which is dominated by his worries about the journey, from which he had evidently recently attempted to withdraw.

This poem to Polus appears to be the last substantial poetic epistle Fleming wrote in Latin. There are three short hendecasyllabic nonoccasional poems to Brokmann, Polus, and Salomon Petrus from later in 1636 and 1637, but their verse line and their brevity set these apart from the more discursive type of poetic epistle just discussed. The later poetic epistles are in German. Whether this change of language happened by design or chance, or if it is an accident of transmission, is unclear.

Fleming's four German poetic epistles fall into two subgroups.[18] *Nach seinem Traume an seinen vertrautesten Freund* (P.W.IV.50) and *An Herrn Olearien vor Astrachan der Reußen in Nagaien* (P.W.IV.44) are rather prolix and puzzling. In each the poet expresses concern about some difficulty that seems to be more genuinely and personally troubling than the problems that prompted Opitz to write to Seußius or Zincgref, but in neither of the poems is the topic clear. The remaining two, on the other hand, *An einen seiner vertrautesten Freunde auf dessen seiner Buhlschaft ihren Namenstag* (P.W.IV.49) and *An Herrn Hansen Arpenbeken, vertrauten Bruders, auf dessen seiner Liebsten ihren Namenstag in Gilan begangen* (P.W.IV.51), are lucid and concise, and their subject matter not at all obscure. All four possess a structure more or less similar to that of the poem for Timotheus Swirsen mentioned above, and to the importance of that structure, as well as to other aspects of the four poems, I return after discussing each individually.

Nach seinem Traume an seinen vertrautesten Freund (P.W.IV.50)

Unlike Fleming's three other German poetic epistles, *Nach seinem Traume an seinen vertrautesten Freund* cannot be dated with any certainty; the identity of the addressee is also uncertain, and even the subject matter is obscure. Varnhagen von Ense, as mentioned in chapter 2, speculated that it was prompted by Fleming's difficult decision in 1633 to leave Leipzig and that the addressee was Hartmann Grahmann. Lappenberg assumed a later date, November-December 1636, and thought the poem might either reflect Fleming's private worries about his apparently crumbling relationship with Elsabe Niehus, or else the ill-humor that affected many members of the expedition and that seems to have had its roots in Ambassador Otto Brüggemann's behavior.[19] Lappenberg did not attempt to identify the addressee, but modern scholars have favored Olearius; Wilms and Lohmeier implicitly accept Lappenberg's dating, but Supersaxo suggests that the poem was written later, after Fleming received news in March 1637 of Elsabe Niehus's engagement to Salomon Matthiä.[20]

A further date, April-May 1636, and set of circumstances that have not hitherto been investigated might form the background to the poem. During 1635 Fleming had formed the attachment to Elsabe Niehus while in Reval. In an undated epigram, *Literae Basilenae S.* (E.III.45), Fleming responds to her reproaches that he has broken an oath, perhaps that he would withdraw from the expedition and thus not put them both through the ordeal of an extended separation. The broken oath is mentioned again in *An einen seiner vertrautesten Freunde* (P.W.IV.49), when he laments that he cannot kiss "Balthien, die mich mehr nicht läßt grüßen, / weil ich ihr nicht bei meinen Worten blieb" (ll. 3-4). In the poetic epistle of May 30, 1636 to Timotheus Polus (Sy.II.22), already mentioned, Fleming explicitly says that on his arrival in Moscow (March 30, 1636) he was determined not to continue with the journey, but to turn back. For one reason or another—and it is unclear whether it was his own decision or due to outside pressure—he changed his mind: "Nescio, quae nostro nimis adversaria voto / in placitum rapuit nos Abeona suum" (ll. 17-18). *Nach seinem Traume* may reflect his anguish over this decision. The notion that it is no longer within his own power to alter his choice is expressed in the letter to Polus: "Quicquid erit, quod fata mihi non cognita miscent, / non stat in arbitrio velle redire meo" (ll. 31–32); line 15 ("Es ist kein ander Rat. Ich muß mich geben drein") and lines 19–20 ("Umsonst ists, was ich tu', und tu' ich noch so sehr, / denn mein Verhängnüß wil's") of the German poem may reflect earlier stages in his coming to accept the decision. In favor of this date (April-May 1636) are lines 74–75: "Hast du dir schon allhie sonst können nichts erwerben, / dein Eignes und dich selbst fast drüber eingebüßt." Lappenberg interprets this reference to the addressee's near loss of life as pointing to the shipwreck that occurred on the Caspian Sea in mid-November 1636. However, Fleming himself was endangered by that shipwreck, while *Nach seinem Traume* seems to refer only to the addressee's near loss of life, not to Fleming's. But there had also been an earlier shipwreck in November 1635, involving the ambassadors and their company returning from Gottorp to Reval with the papers required by the Czar; Fleming, awaiting them in Reval, was not involved in it. It is perhaps to Olearius's involvement in this disaster that lines 74–75 refer. One further fact makes it particularly tempting to date the poem April-May 1636. This is Fleming's reference to bad dreams in the above-mentioned Latin poetic epistle to Polus: it is such a dream that is the immediate occasion of *Nach seinem Traume*. There is no reason to suppose that this period was the only time when Fleming was plagued by nightmares, but the coincidence is nonetheless striking.

While this possible dating and background for *Nach seinem Traume* is moderately persuasive, it is not compelling, and certainty in determining the date and subject matter of the poem remains elusive.[21] That such a wide range of dates could be suggested (1633, 1636, 1637) testifies to the relative consistency of Fleming's style throughout his career; it also reflects Fleming's concealing the nature of the problem dealt with in the poem from all but the addressee. Given the uncertainty, it seems best to study the poem more or less abstracted from a specific set of circumstances. Disadvantageous though this might appear to be, it is still possible to examine structures, motif complexes, and their interactions with sufficient precision to see that the poem resembles the other poetic epistles in interesting ways.

The poem falls into two quite different parts. The first forty-four lines are a brilliant, extended description of the poet's unhappy state of mind, the case history of the man who is too troubled by this world to be able to achieve Stoic equanimity. This is followed in lines 45 through the end by a resolute turning away from or overcoming of the difficulty, and the celebration instead of friendship with the addressee. Rescue comes through insight into the illusory and mutable nature of the world and through the discovery of the contrasting eternal values of friendship and poetry. It is the same two-part structure already noted in Fleming's poem to Timotheus Swirsen, in which the poet laments an unhappy situation and then, through a newly gained perspective, is able to put the worry behind him.

In the first eight lines of *Nach seinem Traume* Fleming describes his waking state, and then in conclusion contrasts this with his sleeping. He spends his waking hours tormented by a range of emotions: "Angst," "Kummer," etc., and he is reduced to a state of "wachender Begier." The variety and vagueness of the affects named make it impossible to deduce the nature of his trouble, but the general state is one understood by neo-Stoic thought. Fleming's sufferings, whatever their immediate cause, are those of a person who is too much troubled by the world to achieve apathia, a freedom from emotions and desire. Fleming then describes the contrast which his sleeping hours provide, when his suffering is turned into ridiculous jest and play. This restless sleep, he says, is not only an occasional occurrence, but specifically something that he has just experienced: "als wie mirs heute ging." He goes on to remind the addressee that his troubles are known to him "Du weißt, um was ich traure" (l. 9); the line suggests private knowledge that Fleming does not intend to impart to the general reader of his poems.

While the first eight lines of the poem provide only a brief description of Fleming's troubled state, lines 13–32 redescribe it at greater length. Again, a portion devoted to waking, lines 13–27, precedes a portion in which Fleming tells what occurs when he sleeps. The terms and rhetorical devices used in this passage recall the language of neo-Stoicism. The concept expressed in line 13, "Ich zwinge mich in mir und kan mich doch nicht beugen," recalls similar lines in other neo-Stoic passages of Fleming's poetry: "Ich will mich unter mich mit allem Willen bücken" (P.W.IV.44, l. 183) and "Wer sein selbst Meister ist und sich beherschen kan / dem ist die weite Welt und Alles untertan" (So.III.26, ll. 13–14). Though sometimes difficult to grasp because of the deliberate proliferation of personal pronouns for rhetorical effect, these passages all employ the notion of the self as composed of two parts, one of which is supposed to dominate or tame the other. The great expounder of neo-Stoic thought, Justus Lipsius, describes the relationship between the two, between "Leib" and "Seele," in *De Constantia*: "Die zwey hengen an einander/ aber mit einer vneinigen einigkeit/ vnd können sich nicht leichtlich vertragen/ fürnemlich/ wenns die Oberhand vnnd Dienstbarkeit angehet. Dann sie beyde wollen herrschen/ vnnd fürnemlich das theil/ welches dienen vnd gehorsam sein sol."[22] Ideally the soul, guided by reason (*Vernunft*), should govern the body, which is the source of the emotions and desires and which is guided by delusion (*Wahn*).

Fleming twice attempts to use reason to establish this proper hierarchy; he invokes one of the major insights that, according to Stoic thought, could be gained by the exercise of reason, that is, insight into the inexorability of fate: "Es ist kein ander Rat. Ich muß mich geben drein. / Man fragt nicht, ob ich wil. Es muß vertragen sein" (ll. 15–16), and—with a phrase reminiscent of Opitz's first sonnet in *Hercinie*, which describes a poet in very much the same state of emotional turmoil—"Umsonst ists, was ich tu', und tu' ich noch so sehr, / denn mein Verhängnüß wil's" (ll. 19–20). The insistence on inevitability, however, is not sufficient to put an end to his complaints: "Diß weiß ich mehr als wol, und gleichwol führ' ich Klagen" (l. 17). The result is conflict between a divided self in which neither half gains the upper hand, a situation that Lipsius describes: "Dañenher entstehen in dem Menschen zwiespalt/ vnruhe/ vnd gehet nicht anders daher/ als wann jmmer zwey theil gegen einander zu Felde legen/ vnd alle stunde mit einander scharmützelten" (fol. 12r). Fleming presents precisely this situation, right down to the military vocabulary, in lines 21–27:

> So lieg' ich stets mit mir und wider mich zu Felde,
> verkaufe mich mir selbst mit meinem eignen Gelde,
> bestreite mich durch mich. Der zweifelhafte Krieg
> spricht meinem Feinde bald, bald mir zu seinen Sieg.
> Ich bin mir Freund und Feind. So streitet Streit mit Friede,
> so schlagen sie sich selbst stets an einander müde,
> bis sich mein matter Leib nicht länger regen kan.

In this dazzling description Fleming uses antithesis, annominatio, alliteration, and anadiplosis to evoke the labyrinthine confusion of a self divided against itself.[23] By twice renaming the combatants, the poet develops the controlling metaphor of the soul at war with itself to depict an intensifying struggle. They are initially two parts of the poet, then friend and enemy, and finally peace and war themselves. The struggle thus takes on an increasing urgency and universality. In lines 28–32 Fleming once again, as in lines 5–8, describes what happens when, exhausted by his inner strife, he is overcome by sleep: in his dreams his mind reflects his inner torment in a topsy-turvy mirror, doing everything contrariwise and turning his unhappy confusion into frenzied activity and inappropriate, even mad, laughter.

The first half of line 33, "Und so auch ging mirs itzt," parallels the first half of line 9, "als wie mirs heute ging," and closes off the second description of Fleming's waking and sleeping. (Fleming's insistent references to the freshness of the event make it that much more frustrating that the situation cannot be identified: there is an odd mix of specificity and vagueness.) In the lines that follow, Fleming begins to reflect on and judge the confusion thus far only described. He notes that he has already forgotten the reason why he laughed in his sleep, suggesting that the laughter was senseless. He then says: "Das ganz verkehrte Tun, das mich verzaubert hält, / macht, daß mein eigen Werk mir wachend oft entfällt" (ll. 35–36). The context offers no assistance in determining what the abstract "Tun" refers to, although it is presumably clear to Fleming and his "vertrautester Freund." Conceivably it could refer to a love entanglement, especially given its use in conjunction with the word "verzaubert," and given that the description of his torment and confusion recalls similar descriptions in Petrarchan love poems. This is what led Lappenberg and Supersaxo to assume the poem reflected his unhappy relationship with Elsabe Niehus. The passage is, however, so entirely lacking in explicit references to love and the beloved, that it is possible that it refers to some other, nonamorous, dilemma.

Fleming's description of sleeping and the perverse activities of his dreaming mind gradually leads him to discoveries, presented in the associative fashion of the informal epistle, about his waking life. His dreams had involved false laughter, and he realizes an inverse truth, namely that his waking happiness is a dream: "Mein Frohsein ist ein Traum" (l. 37). This insight then leads him further, to the great truth of the Renaissance world, that life itself is a dream (ll. 37–38). What is so disturbing about the dream-life for Fleming is that it is chaotic and confused, like his dream or nightmare: good and evil are not distinct and, just as the metaphor of his own dream was his crazily laughing mind, so life as a dream resembles a drunken follower of Bacchus. The confusion and disorder Fleming thus describes recall the neo-Stoic concept of the surface appearance or illusion of life as disorder and chance, *adiaphora*. To regain peace of mind, it is necessary to be disillusioned, to penetrate beyond this illusion to a stable and eternal order controlled not by chance, but by fate (or Providence, as fate was interpreted by Christian-Stoics). Fleming initially expresses the notion of piercing through the veil of illusion by means of the metaphor of the theater, saying that one need not sit through an entire performance if one suspects a bad ending; thus can he and his addressee, he says, leave this troubling situation before the end. He then suggests that the illusion can also be banished if one opens one's eyes and learns to see. In both cases Fleming uses imagery that underscores the notion that the unhappy situation that has been tormenting him is mere illusion: it is either theater or blindness and as such can be banished.

The sudden active involvement of the addressee in these lines is puzzling: "Wir wollen, liebster Freund, des Endes nicht erwarten. / Tu' einst die Augen auf und lerne sehn mit mir, / was man so lange Zeit beginnt mit mir und dir!" (ll. 50–52). Everything up to this point has suggested that the trouble, whatever it is, affects Fleming only. Now it would appear to be a mutual difficulty. This passage has prompted the interpretation that the poem is about the growing unhappiness of members of the expedition with Brüggemann's behavior, which even prompted Olearius to consider returning to Europe on his own. Alternatively, it might reflect Fleming's and Olearius's shared worries about the women they left in Reval. In any case, the involvement of the addressee, whatever the historical background, turns out to be crucial for Fleming and the rest of the poem, for it is in friendship that he finds the reality and constancy otherwise lacking in his life.

In lines 54–56 Fleming points to the transience that characterizes the world: "Indeß dreht Klotho hart an unsrem schwachen Faden, / an dem diß Leben hängt. Die Jugend, die wird alt, / die Schönheit schwindet hin, wir werden ungestalt." Again Fleming insists that the realm governed by mutability and illusion can be left behind: "Freund, auf und laß uns gehn! / Auf! es ist hohe Zeit dem Übel zu entstehn. / Versichre dich an mir!" (ll. 59–61). From someone seemingly himself in need of reassurance, the poet has turned into a friend able to offer support, so perfect is the reciprocity of friendship. In the poem to Timotheus Swirsen, the addressee is quoted offering reassurance in the second part of the poem; here it is Fleming himself speaking in a voice transformed by his having recognized a locus of values unaffected by the troubling nightmare world. Fleming now, for most of the remainder of the poem, celebrates friendship, for it in its constancy offers the needed alternative to the labile activity of a mind tormented by chaotic, illogical emotions—emotions aroused by a world whose illusory nature forms a barrier that is overcome only when it is finally seen through.

In his description of his friendship with the addressee, Fleming touches upon major elements of the classical theory of friendship, including the notion mentioned in the preceding chapter in connection with epithalamia, that true friends must be similar: "Du bist mir ähnlich ganz" (l. 83). (Cicero says in *De amicitia*: "[amicus] est enim is qui est tamquam alter idem.")[24] But the main focus of Fleming's celebration of friendship in the second part of P.W.IV.50 is on the enduring quality of his friendship with the addressee. He assures his friend that he will follow him regardless of how far he should travel (ll. 61–68). In lines 98ff. he contrasts the constancy of his affection ("Ich muß beständig lieben") with the fickleness of those who forsake their friends in times of danger; in classical and Renaissance theory, times of trouble were regarded as the true tests of friendships. Similarly, Fleming notes that true friends share laughter and sorrow (ll. 85–86). There is a thematic and partial verbal parallel here to the earlier passages that described the alternating sorrow and irrational laughter of the divided self; the constant presence of someone who lends his support whether his friend is downcast or cheerful offers an antidote to the inconstancy of the emotions.

Cicero closes his conversation with Laelius on friendship by recalling his friendship with an older man, Scipio. Although Scipio is now dead, "vivit tamen semperque vivet," for his virtue still lives, as does his illustrious memory. The notion of friendship lasting beyond the grave was equally present in the Renaissance, and we find it in the ending of *Nach seinem Traume*. Fleming says that the addressee is a "Zeuge meines Tuns, voraus der edlen Kunst," and that this first attracted the addressee's favor (ll. 111–12); the subsequent lines suggest that he means by "Kunst" writing poetry in German. In it he finds an enduring art appropriate to the celebration of his enduring friendship and promises that with his verses he will create a monument to his friend that will ensure his memory living beyond the grave. Such a promise was no empty one: in his epicedium for Gloger (P.W.II.7) Fleming had similarly vowed that Gloger's name would not die, and the *Libri Manium Glogerianorum* are the fulfillment of that vow. A passage in the *Reisebeschreibung* testifies that being commemorated was a genuine concern of the humanistically educated: Olearius describes how he and his companion Albrecht von Mandelsloh made a pact "daß/ wer unter vns am ersten stürbe/ vom andern zum Gedächtniß mit einer Lob-Schrifft geehret werden solte" (p. 380). When Mandelsloh died, Olearius wrote a "Klageschrift" for him and conscientiously edited and published Mandelsloh's travel journal.[25]

Fleming thus finds in the permanence and constancy of friendship and poetry appropriate remedies for his former unbearable condition of mutability and inconstancy. He finds these alternatives through a process of gaining insight into the insubstantiality of certain aspects of experience in order to penetrate to a different, permanent realm of values. While the process of gaining insight is delineated fairly clearly, the actual problem that prompts the search is not. Fleming exploits the prerogative of the epistle to deal with personal matters and focuses on a problem so delicate that it cannot be explained. In contrast to Opitz's two poetic epistles, in which the poet's difficulty is made clear, Fleming offers the reading public only a general and abstract understanding of the central subject matter of his poem.

An Herrn Olearien vor Astrachan der Reußen in Nagaien (P.W.IV.44)

The title of P.W.IV.44 indicates that it was written off Astrakhan, the city on the the delta of the Volga where members of the embassy first set foot in Asia (*Reisebeschreibung*, p. 371). The embassy twice passed several weeks in or near that city: in September and October 1636 on their way to Persia they lay at anchor there, and during the summer of 1638 they passed through the city on their return. The poem belongs to the earlier sojourn, for Fleming remarks in it that three summers have elapsed since the beginning of the journey (November 1633) and that the year was once again turning towards winter (ll. 95–98).

By the time of their arrival in Astrakhan, the embassy had already undergone severe hardships. The shipwreck that befell the ambassadors, Olearius, and some of the other expedition members sailing from Travemünde to Riga in 1635 was mentioned in the preceding section. The journey down the Volga had proven more difficult than anticipated. Navigational problems arose frequently, and marauding bands of Cossacks threatened the ship from the banks of the river. Additionally, ambassador Brüggemann's temper and conduct seem to have caused dissatisfaction and resentment among the other members of the embassy. During the stay in Astrakhan itself, he reportedly embarrassed his companions and perhaps endangered his mission by his lack of tact. He seems to have made himself particularly unpopular with Olearius, the chronicler of the expedition, with consequences as might be expected for his posthumous reputation.[26]

An Herrn Olearien vor Astrachan der Reußen in Nagaien is an enigmatic poem. It is ostensibly a monument, a *Denkmal*, written by Fleming to Olearius to ensure his friend's lasting fame, and yet it contains hints at unhappy circumstances that, as in *Nach seinem Traume*, are never clarified. There are passages in the poem that ally it to celebratory occasional poetry, but also some that thematically link it more closely to religious verse. Dürrenfeld noted in connection with this poem Fleming's tendency to incorporate in a single poem "Elemente verschiedener traditioneller Sphären."[27] The thread that runs through the poem and lends it a certain coherence is that ubiquitous poetic theme, poets and their poetry.

The poem has a well-defined exordium (ll. 1–14) and conclusion (ll. 187–94). These are set off typographically by indentation in both the *Prodromus* and the *Teütsche Poemata*. Lappenberg has carried this over to his edition and has himself introduced the further indentation of line 127. The body of the poem falls into two major divisions, the first beginning at line 15 and running to the middle of line 103; the second half of line 103 through the first half of 109 form a transition to the second half, which runs through line 186. The first half is a panegyric to Olearius, while the second, which includes the hints at unhappiness, is a more personal description of Fleming's own life and character. Each of these major sections in turn falls into two subsections.

In his programmatic exordium (ll. 1–14), Fleming announces what he is writing and explains why he is writing it. His purpose, described in terms reminiscent of Horace's *Exegi monumentum* as well as of the closing of *Nach seinem Traume* (P.W.IV.50), is to create a poetic monument that will ensure the lasting fame of Olearius and himself, a composition "wo nur die Feder zu mit dem Gemüte trifft" (l. 6), presumably an assurance of sincerity. The reason for writing to and about Olearius in particular is that he is the only one present who understands and approves Fleming's industry: "Ob hier gleich Niemand fast auf dieses Wesen hält, / so bist doch du noch da, der dem mein Fleiß gefällt!" (ll. 1–2). "Fleiß" presumably refers to industry in cultivating the new vernacular Opitzian poetry.

In line 9 Fleming invokes his favorite Muse. Thalia, associated with various types of poetry at different times by different poets, is chiefly the Muse of comedy, but also of light verse and of history writing. None of these domains seems especially apt in the context of this poem, but Plutarch, in a passage cited in Renaissance works on mythology, describes Thalia as the goddess of banquets, possessed of the ability to make men companionable, and Fleming may have associated this Muse with conviviality or friendship.[28] He remarks in *Nach seinem Traume* that "Thalia, meine Lust, die hat mich das gelehret, / mit dem ein treuer Freund kan werden recht verehret" (ll. 121–22; see also O.III.22 and So.III.3 and 12).

Fleming commences the first major section of the poem, the panegyric to Olearius, with a repetition of the notion (using similar syntax) that opened the exordium. Olearius is one of the few who have made a name for themselves in Opitzian poetry: "Wie wenig ihrer itzt noch namhaft sind zu machen, / die etwas Düchtigs tun in dieser neuen Sachen" (ll. 15–16). This is at one and the same time part of the panegyric and the start of a brief excursus on the all-important topic, vernacular poetry. Fleming mentions Olearius's love of the Muses and then marvels that they have now learned to speak German: they have migrated from south to north so that "Das edle Latien wird hochdeutsch itzt gelesen" (l. 28).

Fleming combines his description of the migration of the Muses with themes taken from another Renaissance topos, the debate over whether arms or letters are superior. Fleming draws from the arsenal of arguments on the side of letters the assertion that, without poetry to commemorate them, the heroes of arms would be forgotten. He notes that Germany's own past heroes have sunken into oblivion because, until now, they have lacked poets to perpetuate their memory. (Hercinie had made a similar point about the Schaffgotsch family, whose early deeds were inadequately memorialized.) The argument about the mnemonic function of poetry forms a bridge from Fleming's excursus on poetry back to his main topic, Olearius's virtues, for Olearius has broken the night of poetic silence surrounding Germany's military heroes by writing a paean to the "Helden der Alanen." Lappenberg identifies this as a reference to Olearius's *Sieges- vnd Triumffs-Fahne Gustavi Adolphi Magni* of 1633.

Following a protestation that he is so overwhelmed by his subject as to be disoriented (ll. 45–47), Fleming resumes the panegyric proper to Olearius. Sometimes, as Quintilian notes, it is rhetorically more effective to deal separately with the person's various virtues without regard to chronology, but at times the most effective approach for a panegyrist is to treat the subject's life and accomplishments in chronological order, from childhood to maturity.[29] Fleming has chosen the latter approach and traces Olearius's life from the cradle to the present. The description does not, however, simply flow smoothly from one stage in Olearius's development to the next, but falls into two distinct parts. In the first, Fleming treats Olearius's infancy, childhood, and youth, devoting particular attention to his early talents. These are represented in highly allegorical fashion as gifts of the (pagan) gods. Apollo infused him with his arts; Suada, the goddess of eloquence, with the ability to speak well, etc. The *puer senex* topos puts in its expected appearance more than once. All this is the stuff of standard neo-Latin and baroque *Gelehrtenlob*. The section, with its elaborate allegory and learned circumlocutions ("dreibeströmte Stadt" for Leipzig, for example, recalling similar periphrasis in Horace and Ovid)[30] breaks off abruptly with the reference in line 79 to Germany. The mention of war-torn Germany seems to jolt the poet out of the benevolent mythical world with which he has surrounded Olearius's early years, and into the harsher, real surroundings of the Thirty Years' War. Fleming's description of Olearius's maturity in the second half of the panegyric proceeds in a more sober, factual, though still flattering, fashion. Fleming describes how Olearius found the devastation in Germany unbearable and determined to leave by embarking upon the embassy to the East. Fleming intertwines the description of Olearius's travels and duties with expressions of gratitude for Olearius's kindness to himself, both in securing him a position with the embassy and in furthering his poetic talents. This passage seems especially epistle-like, in contrast to the first half of the panegyric to Olearius, which concentrates solely on the addressee and is composed largely of hyperbole and allegory. This latter half of the panegyric includes the interests of both the writer and his addressee, and provides some information about their actual activities and welfare.

In the second major part of the poem (ll. 109–86) Fleming focuses on himself. The change in focus from Olearius to himself is effected in a transitional passage (103–9) in which Fleming reports how the energetic Olearius, constantly busy, nonetheless takes the time to think of him, Fleming. He tells how Olearius turns to him and exhorts him: "'Auf', sprichst du, 'rege dich! / Ich liebe deinen Fleiß'" (ll. 106–07); this concisely expresses Olearius's role as one who fosters and encourages Fleming's talent. Fleming, in response, now turns to report on his own situation and unexpectedly protests his incapacity: "Ich zwinge meinen Sin. / Ich weiß nicht, wie ich itzt so laß zum Dichten bin, / zu Ruhme nicht gedacht." (ll. 109–11). This demur contrasts with the exclamation that preceded the description of Olearius's youth: "Ich weiß nicht, wo ich bin: / es kömpt mir gar zu viel auf einmal in den Sin / von dir, du Sohn der Luft!" (ll. 45–47). It also contrasts with the self-assured tone of the opening of the poem, in which Fleming announced his intention of creating a poetic monument to his friend. Insofar as these statements involve a contradiction—on the one hand, Fleming wants to and does create a poetic monument, while on the other, he says he is too exhausted to write and is unconcerned with fame—they can perhaps be reconciled by assuming that when Fleming protests inability in lines 109–11, he is referring to poetic productivity in general, as opposed to the writing of a piece for Olearius, whose talents and friendship it is no trouble for him to praise. And indeed, this interpretation is borne out by later passages in the poem, which suggest that Fleming is endeavoring to write under unpleasant constraints that may not apply to his writing for Olearius.

The parallel between lines 109–11 and 45–47, both describing the poet's mental state preparatory to writing, is matched by a further parallel between lines 111–26 and the first half of the panegyric to Olearius (ll. 47–79). Each is a biographical, allegorized description of the two men's early years. Fleming emphasizes the similarities between his own early talents and proclivities and Olearius's with the repeated phrase "auch ich" (ll. 111, 115, 117) or its variant "ich auch" (l. 119). As in the first part of the panegyric to Olearius, the allegorical description of Fleming's youth breaks off at a certain point, in this case after a description of success at Leipzig immediately preceding the journey, where, it is implied, Fleming had half finished his medical studies when the war interrupted them: "Das war zu jener Zeit, da für mein würdigs Haar / der dritte Lorbeerkranz schon halb geflochten war" (ll. 125–26).

There follows a passage (ll. 127–47) in which Fleming describes the conditions necessary for poetic creativity; this comes somewhat unexpectedly, but is tied to the preceding autobiographical passage when Fleming concludes the digression by saying "Nun kanst du leicht ermessen, / was ich seit jener Zeit von aller Lust vergessen" (ll. 147–48). "Jener Zeit" recalls the same phrase in line 125 ("Das war zu jener Zeit, da für mein würdigs Haar") and here too presumably refers to Fleming's Leipzig years. The conditions Fleming describes as necessary for a poet are the ones that obtain when a poet has a benevolent patron. Fleming cites the classical examples of Virgil and Horace, who served and were encouraged by Augustus and Maecenas, and the contemporary example of Opitz with his patron, the recently deceased Burggraf von Dohna. When Fleming says, immediately following his catalog of patrons and poets, "Hier muß kein Zwang nicht sein" (l. 143), he seems to be asserting that a noncompulsory relationship must obtain between poet and patron if the poet is to be productive.

This digression on the conditions of poetic creativity, with its discouraged-sounding closing, "Nun kanst du leicht ermessen, / was ich seit jener Zeit von aller Lust vergessen," suggests that Fleming has lacked a favorable relationship to a patron and that he has been forced to write under circumstances unfavorable to literary productivity. Perhaps his obligations as poet for the expedition were becoming too burdensome. There is a passage that expresses somewhat similar sentiments towards the end of Fleming's hodoeporicon to Grahmann (P.W.IV.53, ll. 427–44), and an anonymous poem by a member of the expedition, *Auf der Fürstlichen Holsteinischen Gesandschaft . . . glückliche Zurückkunft* (B.III.18) implies that conditions during part of the journey had become inimical to the Muses, perhaps because of leadership problems. But the precise background of Fleming's complaint in P.W.IV.44 and of the problems sketched in these other two poems is uncertain. The passage, like passages in *Nach seinem Traume an seinen vertrautesten Freund* (P.W.IV.50), seems to have been written more for the addressee, to whom little needed to be explained, than for a wider public.

If the parallel between the two parts of this poem—the part devoted to Olearius and the one concerned with Fleming himself—were complete, Fleming's allegorical description of his early years in lines 111–26 would be followed by a more factual account of his more recent past. We encounter, however, something slightly different: first the laconic reference to his unhappy circumstances just discussed, and then a lengthy self-characterization (ll. 149–86).

Fleming has provided us with a number of self-characterizations, the best known of which is his epitaph (So.II.14), completed shortly before his death. We also tend to think of the hortatory imperatives directed at himself in So.III.26 (*An Sich*) as representative of Fleming's character. Both of these poems have a quality of self-assurance, indeed, of defiance; the latter in particular is couched in the terms of the confident Christian-Stoic: "Wer sein selbst Meister ist und sich beherschen kan, / dem ist die weite Welt und Alles untertan." The self-characterization in P.W.IV.44 is also in the Christian-Stoic tradition, but its tones are muted, and it emphasizes more the humility of the Christian than the defiance of the Stoic. With its seven sections beginning "Ich," it reads like a litany and a credo. The first parts of it, in their sentiment if not their form, are particularly reminiscent of Fleming's religious poetry. "Ich traue meinem Gott und lasse mich begnügen, / der wird es alles wol nach seinem Willen fügen" (ll. 155–56) recalls O.I.4: "In allen meinen Taten / laß ich den Höchsten raten," or even O.I.9, lines 4–6: "Wie Gott es fügt, / so sei vergnügt, / mein Wille!" Fleming's submissiveness to the divine plan is mirrored in the secular realm by his acceptance of his lord's authority: "Ich fürchte meinen Gott und ehre meinen Herren, / der mir nächst ihm gebeut" (ll. 163–64). This recalls the statement that opens the self-portrait in this last section of the poem: "Mein Wundsch ist größer nicht, als ich bin und mein Stand" (l. 149). Fleming's disclaimer of hubris applies equally in the spiritual realm and in the temporal realm with its strict social hierarchy. Coming immediately after the passage implying unhappiness with the conditions of patronage, these lines suggest Fleming's attempt to reconcile himself to conditions imposed by an authority over which he has no control.

There is an elegiac, almost bitter tone alongside the submissiveness as Fleming notes that his youth is rapidly being spent: "nun meine Jugend mir in ihrer Blüte stirbt / und mit der Ernte selbst die Hoffnung mir verdirbt" (ll. 153–54). This sense of spent youth and a pessimistic outlook for the future already appeared in the poem for Timotheus Polus (Sy.II.22) from the spring of 1636, in which Fleming declares he will travel, "sed aetatis non sine caede meae" (l. 20). The sentiment recurs in other poems written during the journey, including the nameday poem for Hieronymus Imhof (P.W.IV.45) and especially the poetic epistle for Hans Arpenbek (P.W.IV.51). This recurrent pessimism seems to stand behind Fleming's reference in lines 157–62 to a possible resumption of his medical studies, which, he says, he almost regrets having begun.

Fleming moves from describing his acceptance of his subordination to authority in lines 149–66 to describing his interaction with others in general. He mentions first his gentleness and honesty in his dealings with others and then touches on Stoic themes of constancy and being true to oneself. The Stoic belief in the self as a refuge from the world and a constant touchstone of virtue is behind Fleming's desire "mich auf allen Fall mir ähnlich stets [zu] erzeigen" (l. 172). The certainty of a clear conscience and virtuous conduct permits indifference to false friends and their slander: "Ich kehre mich nicht dran, was jener von mir zeugt, / der mündlich mich hat lieb und herzlich doch betreugt" (ll. 173–74). Fleming says that, despite the contumely of false friends, his "redliches Verhalten" will vindicate him, and he reiterates the lack of duplicity in his interactions with others. Lines 179–80 suggest that this vindication may not occur immediately, and that he must momentarily tolerate false accusations without being able to clear himself before the world: "Immittelst will ich mich nur selbst zufrieden sprechen. / Der Höchste, der es sieht, wird alle Unschuld rächen." These lines seem to refer to a specific, immediate situation, which, however, once more remains unexplained; like lines 147–48, they suggest that there is some rather serious problem in the background, familiar to Olearius but not to us. A temporary unhappiness is also suggested by the closing lines of the self-portrait, when Fleming indicates he will exercise self-control until a kinder fate shines on him: "Ich will mich unter mich mit allem Willen bücken, / bis mein Verhängnüß mich hinwieder wird erquicken" (ll. 183–84), and when he offers the consolatory topos that happiness can be measured only by contrast with sorrow: "Wer weiß, was Honig ist, der Wermut nicht versucht? / Ie bittrer ist der Stamm, ie süßer ist die Frucht" (ll. 185–86). The entire self-characterization seems to function for Fleming as a reassurance to himself of his own strength and integrity despite surrounding adversity.

In his peroration (ll. 187–94) Fleming reverts to his purpose in writing the poem: it is intended as a testimony of the *Treue* he owes his friend, of that virtue that figures so large in Fleming's poetry of friendship and love. Fleming refers explicitly to the fidelity he owes Olearius, but also, implicitly, to Olearius's reciprocal *Treue* to him: "Laß diß ein Zeugnüß sein der ungefärbten Treue, / die ich dir schuldig bin, o Freund, des ich mich freue / in dieser Traurigkeit!" Fleming's indebtedness to Olearius, of which the poem is testimony, is the consequence of the latter's fidelity to him. Olearius's friendship, "des ich mich freue," his example and his support, are what prevent Fleming from losing courage entirely in the face of "diese Traurigkeit." He excuses himself for being unable to repay Olearius at present with anything other than words but hopes for a better day when he will be able to show his full gratitude.

Despite the structuring parallels I have shown, *An Herrn Olearien vor Astrachan der Reußen in Nagaien* is not a tightly or obviously organized poem. The panegyrical passages to Olearius, for example, seem only tenuously connected to the passages describing patronage. Dürrenfeld's remark that it seems to be composed of elements from different traditional spheres has already been quoted; Wilms (p. 162) has characterized it as a poem in which humanist learning alternates with personal sentiment. A good deal of the apparently patchwork construction of the poem is attributable not to any lack of skill on Fleming's part but rather to his exploiting the prerogatives of the epistle to treat a variety of topics and to do so unmindful of any preordained order. Vives noted of Cicero's letters, "Cicero quum narranda habet multa, non est valde sollicitus, quod primum faciat, quod secundum; promiscue spargit et refert ut veniunt in mentem prius," and Cicero himself remarks in a letter to his brother Quintus "Epistolae nostrae debent interdum hallucinari."[31] In his poem to Olearius at Astrakhan, Fleming wrote of many things that were important to him: Olearius's talents and interest in him, his own youth, from which the journey seems to separate him, worries about conditions for writing, and his sense of himself. Each topic is treated in an appropriate style. The praise of Olearius is in a particularly elevated style, with strings of amplifying relative clauses, circumlocutions, and references to classical myth. The self-characterization is written in a plainer style that proclaims the poet's straightforward nature. The various different sections are linked by an associative train of thought (as when the recollection of his half-completed medical studies makes Fleming think of the importance of proper patronage, which he now lacks). And while the poem "wanders," its various parts nonetheless cohere because of the pervasive themes of poetry and friendship.

An einen seiner vertrautesten Freunde auf dessen seiner Buhlschaft ihren Namenstag (P.W.IV.49)

Although Fleming does not name the addressee of *An einen seiner vertrautesten Freunde auf dessen seiner Buhlschaft ihren Namenstag*, the poem is dated November 25, 1636; from this date Lappenberg deduced that Fleming wrote the poem to Olearius. In his notes to the poem, Lappenberg explains that November 25 is "Katharinentag," and that Olearius's "auserwehltes Lieb," eventually his wife, was Katharine Moller of the Reval Moller family. Fleming, as he frequently did, created evocative names to refer both to Olearius's beloved and his own. "Wirie" is probably taken from the district of Wierland, where the Moller family estate, Kunda, was located, while "Balthie" is presumably derived partly from "Elsabe," partly from "baltisch" or "Balticum." *An einen seiner vertrautesten Freunde* was written at Niasabat (Nisowai) on the shores of the Caspian where the expedition was encamped; they had been recently shipwrecked, and efforts to recoup their losses kept them at Niasabat until December 22.

P.W.IV.49 is the only one of Fleming's poetic epistles in which he uses neither the alexandrine line nor rhyming couplets. It is written instead in the other major long line available to German baroque poets, *vers communs*, and Fleming rhymes these lines alternately *a b a b, c d c d*, etc., forming quatrains. Fleming, like his contemporaries, seldom used the five-foot French line. Opitz had in his own practice demonstrated a preference for the longer alexandrine line and justified this theoretically in the *Buch von der Deutschen Poeterey*. In chapter 7 he notes that Ronsard, sensing that the alexandrine tends to prolixity, preferred *vers communs* as an equivalent for the Greek and Latin long lines, but Opitz finds it rather too short, for the German language, he says, does not permit the compactness of expression possible in French. One might wish that Ronsard had had the final word, for the alexandrine does seem to cater to the German baroque weakness for diffuseness, while the admirable conciseness and density of a poem like P.W.IV.49 suggest that the course of seventeenth-century poetry in German could have been different had the five-foot line formed its base.

The compactness of expression of P.W.IV.49 also results from its rhyme scheme, which provides natural units of four lines, long enough to express a complete thought with a little elaboration, but not so long as to permit amplification ad infinitum. Fleming here—unlike his practice in the alexandrine cross-rhymed *Elegie* in the *Arae Schönburgicae*—makes thought units coincide consistently with the four-line unit of the quatrain; only once, in the opening of the poem, does he permit a sentence to extend beyond the end of a quatrain. With the asymmetrical line of *vers communs* he does not run the danger that lurks in the alexandrine—and which he counteracted in the *Elegie* with enjambment and clauses starting within the half-lines—of having half lines with a monotonously repeating rhythm. The quatrain has the additional feature of being susceptible of division into two equal parts. In the opening, Fleming uses the second half of the second quatrain to provide a succinct summary of the preceding six lines; in other places he uses the two-part structure to express antitheses.

The stylistic compactness of *An einen seiner vertrautesten Freunde* is especially apparent when compared with *An Herrn Olearien vor Astrachan* (P.W.IV.44) or *Nach seinem Traume* (P.W.IV.50). *An Herrn Olearien vor Astrachan*, particularly in the first part, uses numerous relative clauses, fourteen in the first forty lines, most of them starting at the caesura or the beginning of the line, thus doing little to relieve rhythmic monotony. They serve the purpose of descriptive amplification and *insistierende Nennung*, seldom bringing new information, but rather describing in greater detail or simply in different words, often with formulaic phrases, something that has already been said. They retard the forward movement of the poem and create an impression of diffuseness. Alewyn's critical comment, occasioned by one of Opitz's less happy habits as a translator, is also suited to Fleming here: "Ein Wort bezeichnet, mehrere umschreiben."[32] In *An einen seiner vertrautesten Freunde*, by contrast, Fleming has in the entire poem of seventy-two lines used only nine relative clauses, and the result is certainly far more attractive. Similarly, although *Nach seinem Traume* is less plentifully strewn with relative clauses than *An Herrn Olearien vor Astrachan*, Fleming tends in that poem, too, to say the same thing several times in different words. The desired effect is emphasis and an elevated style, but the repetition sometimes seems an unnecessary dwelling on points that actually lose their impact through repetition.

In its structure and themes *An einen seiner vertrautesten Freunde* is remarkably similar to *Nach seinem Traume*. Like that poem, it falls into two distinct parts, in the first of which a problem is described, and in the second of which the problem is resolved. Since it is unclear what *Nach seinem Traume* is about, it seems almost like an abstract presentation of the structure (presentation of a worrisome problem followed by a resolution or reconciliation) of which *An einen seiner vertrautesten Freunde* offers a concrete example. Like *Nach seinem Traume*, *An einen seiner vertrautesten Freunde* opens with a brief exposition of a dilemma that is then described in detail in the remainder of the first part of the poem. We are left this time in no doubt as to the precise nature of the poet's distress. In lines 1–8, the first two quatrains, Fleming describes his own and his addressee's forlorn situation, separated as they are from their beloved "Wirie" and "Balthie." The situation is poignant for both of them. It is the nameday of Wirie, and she is thus particularly on Olearius's mind, who, were he not separated from her by more than a thousand miles, would probably spend much of the day with her and perhaps be allowed the liberty of a kiss in honor of the occasion. Because of the nameday of the beloved of one of his closest friends, the poet himself also has occasion to think of the relationship between lovers and to contrast the strain in his relationship to Balthie with the apparent harmony existing between his friend and Wirie. These matters are suggested in the first few lines of the poem with far greater economy than is possible in the retelling. In the first two lines of the second quatrain, the poet describes the emotional effect upon himself and his friend of this unhappy situation of separation and exile: "so stehn wir hier mit seufzenden Verlangen / und füllen uns mit leerer Einsamkeit." Fleming's use of the oxymoronic pair "füllen" and "leer" is particularly effective, for the apparent paradox draws attention to the vastness of their desolation; by their very sighs of longing, the two lovers breathe in loneliness and increase their own emptiness. The second two lines of the second quatrain indicate that they are so stricken as to be incapable of activity; in their melancholic acedia, they can do nothing but regret their suffering.

The next lines describe the familiar struggle between the two parts of the poet, one resisting, the other recognizing fate. In *Nach seinem Traume* Fleming says: "Es muß vertragen sein. / Diß weiß ich mehr als wol, und gleichwol führ' ich Klagen" (ll. 16–17); here he declares: "Vergeblich ists um alles unser' Denken, / wie sehr wir auch um unser Freude tun" (ll. 9–10). The third through sixth quatrains of the poem offer a series of meditations on the theme that one cannot change what is past; all the while though, despite the apodictic declarations to that effect, a tone of regret and complaint is apparent. The tension between complaint against fate and acceptance of fate remains unresolved. Fleming points to the uselessness of regretful remembrance, which only pains the "Erinnrer." In the fourth quatrain he remarks on the futility of long journeys which, embarked upon by the suffering rememberers in order to forget, themselves become sources of suffering—a painful lesson to which Fleming reverts two years later in his poem to Arpenbek (P.W.IV.51). There is thus little consolation for the rememberers even when they valiantly strive to disengage themselves from their past. The next quatrain tersely recapitulates the baroque metaphor of time flowing as inexorably onwards as rushing water—a metaphor that Fleming had also used in his unhappy epistle to Polus (Sy.II.22). Fleming here not only points to the irreversible forward march of time, but also, by stressing one's bondage to time itself, suggests that the past and memory are themselves inescapably bound to us. In lines 21–24 he draws the consequences of this in lamenting tones: it would be better to have a past that involved no engagement of the affections whatsoever, than to have a past that has involved loss, and hence occasions present grief.

In the next five quatrains, lines 25–44, Fleming offers, instead of the rather abstract wisdom of the preceding lines, a passage of concrete imagery that furnishes a natural correlative to the mental struggle portrayed in the preceding lines. Fleming recounts his experience of the recent shipwreck, which he describes with graphic immediacy (the accuracy of his account is confirmed by comparison with the *Reisebeschreibung*, pp. 399–405), but which, by virtue of its components, necessarily resonates with overtones from the highly developed allegorical tradition of representing life as a voyage. An additional dimension is created when Fleming uses Petrarchan language in the description. The resultant image is unusually complex and powerful.

Fleming first relates how he and Olearius are wont to go down to the edge of the Caspian (Hyrcanum Mare) to contemplate the tempestuous sea; he then apostrophizes the sea, describing its fury and the events that culminated in the shipwreck of the expedition. Finally, Fleming exclaims that he wishes all his unhappiness had been destroyed and sunk to the bottom of the sea in the storm. The image of the sea reflects back on the mental state described in the first six quatrains in several intricate ways. Like the dream image in *Nach seinem Traume*, the turbulence of the sea, its "Rasen," recalls the disturbance of the poet's mind. The dream or nightmare described in P.W.IV.50 had a certain peculiar autonomy, a capricious life of its own separate from the poet; so here does the sea, which is not simply a bit of lifeless nature, but an animated, or better, a personified being, which Fleming can apostrophize but in no way control. On another, more subtle level, the sea takes on the attributes of the Petrarchan woman, and the recounting in lines 29–36 of the perilous journey of the expedition's ship suggests the torment of the Petrarchan lover. The sea is described as "falsch" ("Dein falscher Grund der Seichten und der Tiefen," l. 29); it fills the sailors with "Angst" and makes them "bleich" and "naß." (While literally referring to the sea water, "naß" also translates into Petrarchan tears or perspiration; in O.V.1, l. 12, the Petrarchan lover even sweats tears.) The Petrarchan polarity of laughter and tears, which reflects the mercurial turns of the lover's mood in the face of his beloved's fickleness, is also present, here divided between the weeping, despairing voyagers and the mocking, pitiless sea ("Was wir geweint, das hast du ausgelacht," l. 32). The typical Petrarchan paradoxes and oxymora appear in the form of burning water created by the sea's anger and the cold sweat of those subjected to its heat. Dürrenfeld notes Fleming's use of Petrarchan imagery in this passage; she finds "reizvoll die Tatsache, daß die reale Natur in diesem Abschnitt Gegenstand der Beschreibung ist. Die Dichtersprache unternimmt also den Versuch, vom bloß metaphorischen Bereich, in dem sie sich geübt hat, zur direkten Benennung der Dinge und Situationen zurückzukehren" (p. 145). But Fleming's use of Petrarchan imagery here has a more subtle purpose than Dürrenfeld suggests. If one compares this description of the shipwreck with Fleming's other descriptions of either this or the earlier shipwreck in P.W.IV.46, P.W.IV.53, So.I.19, and So.III.51, one finds some elements that are common to some or all of them: the images of waves as mountains and of being flung up to the stars and down to the abyss (traceable to Ovid's *Tristia* I.ii.19–20, according to Tropsch, p. 128), the sequence of events involving loss of mainmast and mizzen,[33] and the futility of casting out the anchor. Only in *An einen seiner vertrautesten Freunde* does the Petrarchan imagery appear, and surely Fleming employs it here deliberately in order to connect the seascape to the problem of pining lovers that constitutes the main theme of the poem. The sea imagery, precisely because of the metaphorical language used to describe it, itself becomes a "metaphorischer Bereich" that refers back to Fleming's and Olearius's love lives.

It is not surprising that Fleming should have used sea imagery with Petrarchan overtones as a metaphor for the emotional upheaval of unhappiness in love, for one can find this already in Opitz. Lines 11–12, for example, of his well-known sonnet describing the Petrarchan plight, *JSt Liebe lauter nichts, wie daß sie mich entzündet?* (no. 20 in the 1624 *Poemata*), read: "Jch walle wie ein Schiff, daß in dem wilden Meer / Von Wellen vmbgejagt nicht kan zu rande finden." When contrasting bachelors, with their Petrarchan love lives, with the about-to-be-married Johann Mayer and Margarethe Gierlach, Opitz addresses the bachelors and exclaims: "Ihr aber schifft im Meer | Das keinen Hafen hat/ da Vnmuth vnd Beschwer | An statt der Segel seyn/ da Klippen/ Wind vnd Wellen | Der rasenden Begiehr sich euch zugegen stellen."[34] What is remarkable about the passage of sea imagery in

Fleming's poem is that he, in contrast to Opitz, nowhere explicitly identifies the Petrarchan sea imagery as describing his own love life, but allows the reader to make this connection.

Lines 41–44, the last quatrain in the passage of sea imagery, add a further dimension to the way in which this imagery reflects back on what was said in the first six quatrains of the poem. Fleming contemplates the wreckage of the ship and wishes that his unhappiness had drowned in the tempest: "Das tote Schiff liegt nun vor uns ertrunken. / . . . Ach! daß mit ihm nur wäre gleich versunken / all Unglück auch, das nun schon wieder blüht!" (ll. 41, 43–44). This is the problem of the "Erinnrer," trying to do the impossible, to escape the memory of happiness. Like the "dead ship" the memory remains; the happiness, once sweet, is now sour because lost, and it dwells in memory just as the carcass of the once seaworthy vessel lies cast up, inanimate and immobile, on the beach. Past unhappiness carries over into the poet's existence even after the devastating storm. Fleming thus restates here, in a metaphor to which he draws no attention, just as he drew no attention to the earlier Petrarchan overtones, the certainty that memory is an inescapable part of the process of time and that as part of time past it can be neither altered nor erased. The situation seems quite hopeless, and Fleming proceeds in lines 45–48 to reproach the goddess Nemesis, whose main attribute, he says (recalling her original attribute), is supposed to be inconstancy, for failing to change their circumstances once more, this time from ill to good.

In lines 49–50 Fleming refers, as he has done in both of the other poetic epistles discussed, to his friend's familiarity with his plight. In this poem, for the first time, he has given enough information so that it is not just the addressee who comprehends the difficulty. The next two lines then suddenly initiate a reversal of fortune and the overcoming of the stated problem, as the poet resolutely declares: "Ich will forthin mich nur um nichts mehr quälen, / will mich forthin bekümmern nur um mich." This seems at first glance an extraordinary instance of pulling oneself up by one's own bootstraps, as well as a desertion of Olearius. The latter impression, it soon becomes apparent, is false. Fleming means that he will be concerned only about himself as opposed to the problems caused by his romantic entanglement and the vexing assaults of fortune, not as opposed to his friend's well-being; in fact, his friend clearly shares, as he did in *Nach seinem Traume*, in the resolution of the problem. It is more difficult to dispel the other impression—that Fleming's sudden self-assurance and sense that his problems need no longer concern him are too sudden and unmotivated. In *Nach seinem Traume* there was a fairly clearly delineated process of insight and disillusionment leading to a new, maturer wisdom that led to the overcoming of the poet's emotional turmoil. Here this process is not explicitly portrayed, and the only hint at a source for Fleming's sudden strength is his statement in line 52 "[Ich] will mich forthin bekümmern nur um mich." This is perhaps an expression of the characteristic neo-Stoic withdrawal into the self as a source of virtue, constancy, and security, although it is not stated in characteristically neo-Stoic language, in which the idea is generally expressed as "sei deine" or "geh' in dich selbst zurück."

What we do find, however, in *An einen seiner vertrautesten Freunde* that more clearly explains or shows the poet's sudden change in attitude and the resolution of his problem, is the theater metaphor of *Nach seinem Traume* (lines 45–50) translated into natural imagery. In those lines Fleming suggested that his entanglement in his own mental turmoil could be likened to the enthrallment of a person at a play. Because the action is but a play, this person, as audience, is free to leave if not desirous of witnessing the tragic ending. In *An einen seiner vertrautesten Freunde*, the seascape that Fleming tells us he and his friend are observing is treated precisely as though it were a theatrical representation. Fleming exhorts himself and Olearius simply to turn their backs upon it: "Komm, laß uns itzt durch jene flachen Felder, / so viel sichs schickt, nach Lust spaziren gehn!" (ll. 53–54). In the simple gesture of turning away from the sea to walk back through the fields is the implicit assumption that the problem represented by the seascape has a lesser ontological status, that is, it is an illusion, just as the play from which Fleming in *Nach seinem Traume* can turn away is an illusion. In one symbolic gesture the poet withdraws from his entanglement in time and memory to emerge onto a higher plane of reality.

The landscape description that Fleming now offers in lines 55–64 is as extraordinary and complex as was the description of the sea. It suggests a *locus amoenus*, while also portraying with remarkable detail a real locale; most importantly, the landscape provides a symbolic counterpart to the seascape and all that it represents.

The place that Fleming sketches is clearly a "pleasant place." It has meadows and trees; it is fertile, beautiful, and a place of happy companionship. The absence of the brook, one of what Curtius calls the "minimum ingredients" of a *locus amoenus*, is a bit surprising, but there is at least the refreshing snow on the mountaintops even in the hottest months.[35] But it is perhaps almost accidental that this landscape coincides with the topos of the *locus amoenus*, for its characteristics are drawn from a real place. In his *Reisebeschreibung* Olearius describes the natural vegetation of the area around Niasabat and the walks that certain members of the expedition took through this charming landscape: "Als derwegen vnser etliche . . . ins Feld spatzierten/ wurden wir nicht alleine von den schönen gleich als Sommer Wetter/ sondern auch lieblichen grünen Gepusche/ so mit Weinstöcken vnd Granatbäumen zierlich vermischet/ genötiget vns auff einen lustigen Holm/ welchen ein mit einem anmutigen Gereusche krum-fliessender Bach gleich zu einer Pen-[I]nsul machete/ zu setzen/ vnd durch das andencken vnser in Deutschland hinterlassenen guten Freunde vns z[u] ergetzen" (pp. 415–16). This is recognizably the place of Fleming's poem. His "Apfelwälder" are Olearius's "Granatbäume" (or "Granatapfelbäume"), and his somewhat startling reference to "Weinwälder" is a remarkably compact description of a phenomenon noted by Olearius (p. 412): the wild grapevines in this region often grew to enormous heights by clinging to the trunks of trees, whence, having become entwined in the lofty branches, they dangled back earthward, giving the unwonted illusion of a forest of grapevines; one can observe them in illustrations to the *Reisebeschreibung* on pages 413 and 416.

The specificity of this landscape description recalls the similar specificity of the landscape in which Opitz locates his *Hercinie* and contrasts with Fleming's general practice when portraying his natural surroundings during the journey. In his travel sonnets (e.g., So.III.32, 36, and 38) and in the hodoeporicon to Grahmann (P.W.IV.53), natural scenery is adorned with classical references and animated by gods and innumerable nymphs. The landscape features, particularly the rivers, are personified and apostrophized; they tend to lose their individuality in direct proportion to their donning of the trappings of classical allusion. The scenery in *An einen seiner vertrautesten Freunde*, by contrast, is visited by but one god, when the sun almost unavoidably is represented by Phoebus; the classical topos of the *locus amoenus* almost disappears as a real geographical locale emerges.

The difference between the landscape in *An einen seiner vertrautesten Freunde* and those of other poems arises from different functions. The landscapes of travel sonnets and the hodoeporicon are mentioned in order that they may be praised, and this demands all the ornaments of epideictic rhetoric, including hyperbole, classical allusion, and mythology. The function of the landscape in *An einen seiner vertrautesten Freunde*, however, is not to be an object of demonstrative rhetoric, but to provide a symbolic alternative to the image of the sea. It fulfills this function in part by being a *locus amoenus*, but also by being a place whose features contrast precisely with those of the sea. Thus the movement and instability of the seascape find their opposite in the constancy of the landscape, in bushes and forests which will "um und neben uns stets stehn" (l. 56), and in the snow which does not come and go with the seasons, but always covers the mountaintops. These mountains, interestingly enough, are absent from Olearius's description of the place where the expedition members strolled and picnicked; despite Olearius's continual striving for scientific accuracy, his portrayal of that landscape, with its pleasant brook, has a great deal more of the literary *locus amoenus* topos about it than does Fleming's own poetic description.[36] Fleming's inclusion of the mountains reflects his accuracy of observation, for there were such mountains a short way inland from the Caspian. Equally important, the mountains provide a symbolic counterpart to the sea's inconstancy and to its menacing depths: the shining heights of the "hohen Gordieen" are the opposite of the "falscher Grund der Seichten und der Tiefen" that threatened the mariners (l. 29). In archetypal terms, Fleming's landscape permits him to move from the demonic underworld to Apollonian heights; one might term it a sacramental movement that lifts him from despair through purgation to salvation.

In the second to last quatrain of the poem the poet's gaze shifts; rather than taking the measure of the lofty mountains, he surveys his more immediate surroundings and the present moment. He urges his friend to do honor to the day by composing a song for his beloved and himself resolves to do what he can; the melancholic inactivity of the opening lines has been replaced by a resolution to exert oneself as far as possible. Fleming's tone is sober, but no longer despairing. That he is able to offer counsel and to face his situation with a promise of effort, if not with abundant optimism, is the modest result of the transformation from despair to hope symbolically represented by his turning from the seascape to the landscape in the course of the poem.

An Herrn Hansen Arpenbeken, vertrauten Bruders, auf dessen seiner Liebsten ihren Namenstag in Gilan begangen (P.W.IV.51)

Fleming wrote *An Herrn Hansen Arpenbeken, vertrauten Bruders, auf dessen seiner Liebsten ihren Namenstag in Gilan begangen,* during the embassy's return journey from Persia to Moscow and Reval. In his notes to the poem Lappenberg dates it quite precisely: the nameday of Arpenbek's betrothed, Brigitta van Acken, falls on February 1; the reference in line 5 to the three long years of the Persian journey indicate the poem was written when the expedition passed through the fertile land of Gilan on the western shores of the Caspian for the second time, on the way back to Germany in 1638.

Not a great deal is known about the addressee. Olearius indicates in his roster of the expedition's members in the *Reisebeschreibung* that Arpenbek, who had the same rank in the expedition as Fleming, came from Dorpat, through which the expedition passed on the way from Riga to Narva and Reval in 1633 (p. 57). In the seventeenth century Dorpat, like Reval, still bore the marks of centuries of German colonization and settlement, although it was also under Swedish rule at the time of the expedition. Arpenbek served as Russian translator for the embassy's transactions with the Czar when they sought permission to travel through Russia on the way to Persia. Other than this, we know only of his engagement and eventual marriage in 1639 to Brigitta van Acken, whom he presumably met, as Fleming did Elsabe Niehus, during the year-long stay of part of the embassy in Reval in 1635 and early 1636. It is Arpenbek's attachment to Brigitta van Acken that forms the background to all of Fleming's poems to him: this one, the accompanying epithalamium (O.III.21), and a nameday poem (P.W.IV.42); he also wrote a Latin epigram (E.III.48) to Arpenbek's fiancée herself. Since Fleming addresses Arpenbek in *An Herrn Hansen Arpenbeken* as "Bruder," it appears that they were rather close, although this is a bit surprising given that the number of poems for him was small.

From its title, one might surmise that *An Herrn Hansen Arpenbeken* would be very similar to *An einen seiner vertrautesten Freunde*; both were written for the addressee on the occasion of his beloved's nameday. The two poems turn out, however, to be thematically rather different, in part because *An Herrn Hansen Arpenbeken* serves a function not apparent from its title. It is a cover letter for the epithalamium (*Brautlied*, O.III.21) that Fleming wrote for Arpenbek and his betrothed, and it explains why Fleming has written the poem now, rather than closer to the date of the wedding. It thus differs from *An einen seiner vertrautesten Freunde* and from Fleming's other two poetic epistles (as well as from Opitz's) in that it actually conveys information apparently unknown to the addressee. Nowhere in *An Herrn Hansen Arpenbeken* does Fleming say "Du weißt es besser als ich" or the like. The two poems on namedays of friends' beloveds illustrate the difference between occasional poems and poetic epistles, for while both poems were written in connection with a typical, recurrent occasion, a nameday, the occasion serves as an excuse rather than a raison d'être. The poems are thematically determined far less by the occasion than by the circumstances of the poet himself when each poem was written: in one case, Fleming is preoccupied with Elsabe Niehus, in the other, with whether he will live to see Germany again.

Although *An Herrn Hansen Arpenbeken* differs from *An einen seiner vertrautesten Freunde* in theme, on another level it resembles that poem and *An Herrn Olearien vor Astrachan* and *Nach seinem Traume* as well. For a major portion of *An Herrn Hansen Arpenbeken* is also devoted to outlining a troubling situation oppressing the poet, and the final part of the poem presents a resolution of the problem. The poem falls into three distinct parts: an opening section of twelve lines, a middle section of forty lines (ll. 13–52), and a closing section of twelve lines (ll. 53–64). The division between the first two sections was marked typographically in the *Teütsche Poemata* through indentation of line 13; Lappenberg did not retain this.

A major theme is a contrast between the unhappy present and the future. In the opening section Fleming addresses Arpenbek, saying that if Arpenbek survives the year, he will be far happier on his beloved's next nameday, as he will be able to enjoy the day in her company. This opening recalls a nameday poem for Hieronymus Imhof (P.W.IV.45) written nearly two years earlier; there also the conditional clause that opens the poem ("Gönnt Gott inkünftig uns das liebliche Gelücke, / da unser Deutschland uns sieht kommen wol zurücke") gives an indication of the tremendous hardships the embassy had already undergone, severe enough to raise serious question as to their survival. In lines 5–11 of *An Herrn Hansen Arpenbeken*, Fleming expands the contrast between the present and the hoped-for future, saying that with his marriage Arpenbek will be rid of all the suffering undergone during the journey, and that the memories will simply be an occasion for entertaining story telling. Fleming summarizes the contrast in line 12 with an antithesis of the type found in many of his love poems in which he evokes the happiness that follows upon the pain of separation: "es wird dir Zucker sein, was vormals Galle war."

In the second and central section of the poem Fleming comes to speak of himself, introducing a counterpoint theme—his poor prospects in contrast to Arpenbek's probable future happiness. In the nameday poem to Imhof, Fleming speaks of the possibility of surviving the journey in the first person plural, thus suggesting that there is hope both he and his companions will enjoy the future happiness mentioned. In the opening of *An Herrn Hansen Arpenbeken*, however, Fleming speaks only of Arpenbek, using only the second person. When he then comes to speak of himself, it is apparent that he is no longer at all sanguine about his own survival; in fact, he doubts that he will be alive to attend Arpenbek's nuptials. In a very sober assessment of his own situation, expressed in stark, unadorned verse that reads almost like prose, he says:

Ich zweifle sehr daran, daß ich dann werde leben
und dir auch meinen Wundsch mit andern Freunden geben,
weil dieser schwere Zug mich täglich mürber macht
und meinen stärksten Teil schon längst hat umgebracht.

(ll. 13–16)

The contrast between Arpenbek's fairly good chances for enjoying the pleasures of marriage on his return, and his own probable exclusion from such joy due to a premature death, is underscored by the rhyme word in line 13, which echoes the rhyme of the opening line. In each case the rhyme word is "leben," but in the first case it is linked to survival, in the second to probable death.

Fleming indicates two reasons why he is doubtful of being able to return to Germany. The first already adumbrated in lines 15 and 16, is the physical strain of the journey. He expands this thought in lines 17–20 urging, in tones of some exasperation, that those who doubt him undertake such a journey and see for themselves the toll it takes. The second reason, of which he speaks at greater length, is his concern over what will meet him if he returns to Germany, a concern which, it is implied, erodes his strength as much as does the actual physical strain of the journey. News from Fleming's homeland is grim. In his epithalamium for Reiner Brokmann in April 1635, Fleming expressed some satisfaction in the rumors that "Gott mein Meißen mit Friedensaugen gnädiglich wieder angesehen" (P.W.III.6, p. 73); the rumors were probably about the truce agreed upon in February 1635 by Saxon elector Johann Georg and the emperor. But the Peace of Prague, to which the truce led, brought little advantage to the Saxons, whose former allies, the Swedes, turned on them: Saxony hardly fared better in the second half of the 1630s than it had in the first. In lines sadly reminiscent of his *Schreiben vertriebener Frau Germanien* from seven years earlier, Fleming, in the poem to Arpenbek, uses oxymoronic phrasing and polyptoton to convey the masochism he perceives in Germany's perverse persistence in its wars: "es freue sich der Pein / und wolle noch nicht tot in seinem Tode sein" (ll. 23–24). He then embarks upon an extended comparison of the magnitude of his former desire to escape Germany and her wars with the magnitude of his present fear of returning home to the same situation (ll. 25–36). His fear of the latter is as great and greater, for the situation at home has in no wise improved. Again there is a faint verbal echo of the opening passage about Arpenbek, again with signs reversed: Arpenbek will be "in größrer Freude" (l. 2), while Fleming faces "größer Grauen" (l. 33) upon his return home. Accompanying the comparison of his initial eagerness to depart and his present reluctance to return is an implicit commentary on the value of his journey and of his motivations for embarking upon it; in lines 27–33 he recounts his motivations in terms that cast the worst possible light upon them. All of the usual allegiances and responsibilities of a young man he repudiated for the sake of "diese Handvoll Blut," to save his own skin. He forsook his fatherland and family in order to see the world, hoping it would enhance his reputation to be a great world traveler (which was indeed a frequently repeated incentive to travel: "was gilt bei uns ein Man, der nicht gereiset hat?" [P.W.IV.53, l. 62]). The sad result, however, has not been the preservation of his own physical well-being; his travels themselves have ruined his health, and his homeland, on which he turned his back, hoping it might return to normal during his absence, is now as chaotic and bloody as before, or even more so. Neo-Stoic thought is in this passage conspicuous by its absence—not because Fleming here repudiates it, but because he is implicitly saying that he failed to attend to neo-Stoic principles when he set out on his journey. It is left to the reader to measure his actions against neo-Stoic teachings and draw the moral. Lipsius's *De constantia* presented definite neo-Stoic notions about travel and its escape value: the initial motivation of the dialogue is to show that physical journeying to flee a war-torn homeland is an improper course of action. A Stoic's refuge is not a distant land, but his mind, and his mind, conversely, is his world. Fleming was thoroughly familiar with these beliefs; he illustrated them in 1634 in the poem *In Groß-Neugart der Reußen* (P.W.IV.20):

> Es ist ein seltsams Tun, daß wir uns so bemühen
> um Ehre, Geld und Kunst, durch ferne Länder ziehen,
> Frost, Hitze, Hunger, Durst, Angst, Mühe stehen aus:
> . . . .
>   Ich will dirs besser weisen,
> wohin du sichrer solst und mit mehr Nutzen reisen.
> Geh, sieh dich selbsten durch! Du selbst bist dir die Welt!
>   (ll. 113–119)

Fleming, as he portrays himself in lines 25–33 of *An Herrn Hansen Arpenbeken*, has to his sorrow failed to heed precisely this teaching. There is another tenet of neo-Stoicism that Fleming has violated according to this description of himself, or more precisely, that he has perverted. He tells of his thinking "Kanst du dich nur ersparen, / so hastu satt an dir" (ll. 30–31). This recalls the neo-Stoic belief in the virtuous inner self as the greatest good and a man's only essential possession. The self, however, which Fleming portrays as having appeared sufficient to him when he was a youth, is not the virtuous inner self of the Stoics, but rather his physical existence: "das schlug ich Alles aus für diese Handvoll Blut, / die mir doch hier verdirbt" (ll. 28–29). But it is corporeal existence and all other things external to the mind to which the Stoic taught himself to be indifferent, for he knew he had little or no power to oppose what might befall them. Seneca, in *De tranquillitate animi*, illustrated the Stoic attitude with a tale of the philosopher Theodorus.[37] Threatened with death and improper burial, the philosopher conceded to the tyrant his "hemina sanguinis," the "Handvoll Blut" which was his body, to do with as he wished, for what happened to his body was something over which he had no control and about which he was wisely indifferent.[38]

In lines 37–52 Fleming describes precisely the things that make him fearful of returning home and which, by torturing his thoughts, weaken his constitution and lessen the likelihood of his surviving long enough to set foot again on native soil. It is, of course, the war itself, still raging, that is the ostensible cause of his worry, but this passage again treats of Fleming's journey, this time of the ill consequences it has had for those he left behind, and ultimately, for himself. "Angst" has destroyed his inheritance; the meaning of this is not entirely clear, but the same power has "die Mutter umgebracht"; presumably he refers to her anxiety over him caused by his absence (his stepmother, Ursula Zehler, died in December 1633, shortly after his departure). His father, he suspects, has also suffered from worry, and Fleming anticipates the worst, namely that he, Fleming, will die, denying his father his only remaining consolation. (When read in conjunction with line 48, "nun aber ist mit mir ihm aller Trost darvon," it seems probable that "Verlust" in line 44 means Fleming's death, rather than simply his absence on the journey.) Additionally, Fleming notes that his long absence from home will have caused his friends to forget him: much good will it do him to have earned a reputation as a traveler if his dearest friends no longer remember him. The consequences of the journey seem to be all ill, and there is a strong note of self-reproach in these lines.

In the last section of the poem, which commences with line 53, Fleming shifts his gaze from the dismal scene awaiting him at home back to his immediate situation and mood. He paints these in antithetical terms: he lives "in so viel Toden" and alternates between "Furcht und Lust in Trost' und Zweifel." In the chiastic structure of this phrase, the negative emotions enclose the positive ones and have, as it were, the last word; indeed, Fleming says grimly that his situation and mood are hurrying him to the grave. This gloomy passage is, however, merely preliminary to the adversative "doch gleichwol" which opens line 56 and initiates the transformation from despair to hope, from the *lamentatio* to the *consolatio* that constitutes the final statement of the poem.

Fleming's consolation has its source in his conviction that despite death, he too will share in the sacramental and communal joy that awaits Arpenbek on his return home, and that through his poetry, he will live beyond his death. Despite his prophecy that his own old friends will have forgotten him, Fleming himself makes a commitment to friendship by writing a poem, "diß kurze Liedlein," for his friend Arpenbek's wedding. In the final poignant image of the poem—Fleming's spirit hovering in the wings and gladdened to hear his own epithalamium read aloud at the wedding feast—Fleming derives comfort from his ability as a poet to perpetuate not only the memory of others, but also his own.

Characteristics of Fleming's Poetic Epistles

The biblical scholar G. A. Deissmann made an often helpful distinction, since carried over into classical studies, between what he calls *Brief* and *Epistel*: the former is a purely private communication, the latter a literary product intended for the literary public, despite its ostensibly single addressee.[39] According to this understanding, most of the letters preserved from the Renaissance are *Episteln*; a very few, like Lipsius's private letters, which, contrary to his wish, were not destroyed, and which convey a far less flattering portrait of him than do those he intended for publication, are private *Briefe*. Georg Luck, who found the distinction useful in the explication of classical texts, points out that the writer of an *Epistel*, Ovid for example, often includes background information already known to the ostensible addressee, but without which the public would not be able to understand what was being communicated.[40] A rather extreme example of this can be found in Lotichius's elegy to his friend Christoph Hardesheim (Elegy I.10). A large portion of the poem is devoted to describing to Hardesheim what had befallen him (Hardesheim) on a journey. The narration of an episode known firsthand to the addressee serves mainly to inform the literary public. Interestingly, there does exist a short poem by Lotichius that seems to be a *Brief* rather than an *Epistel*: it is to Carolus Clusius, and in it Lotichius, rather than giving the background to the situation that occasioned it, merely alludes to the situation in a manner comprehensible only to Clusius.[41] Similarly, Ernst Hatch Wilkins's study of Petrarch's *Epistola metrica* III.7 to Pietro Alighieri suggests that for analogous reasons it may also be considered a *Brief*.[42] These examples indicate that verse composition does not always preclude a letter's being private, although it makes sense that by and large a writer would not go to the trouble of casting his thoughts in verse unless he expected to make it a public literary work.

Much of the second part of *An Herrn Olearien vor Astrachan* (P.W.IV.44) possesses the trait that Luck noted as characteristic of private communications, the trait of incomprehensibility to anyone but the addressee. Similarly, *Nach seinem Traume* (P.W.IV.50), which is constructed entirely around a dilemma never explained, would, in accordance with Luck's distinction, fall into the category of private epistle. Both *An einen seiner vertrautesten Freunde* (P.W.IV.49) and *An Herrn Hansen Arpenbeken* (P.W.IV.51) would be classified as public, since in both poems the poet fills in enough background for the reader somewhat familiar with the men and the journey to grasp what is being talked about. And yet the distinction between *Brief* and *Epistel* does not seem entirely adequate to Fleming's poetic epistles. Of the four poems, *An Herrn Olearien vor Astrachan* and *Nach seinem Traume*—the "private," partially incomprehensible ones—seem paradoxically the most literary. They make use of the more ornamental style appropriate to the demonstrative genre, a style more likely to be used to impress a larger literary public. More important, as far as it is possible to tell both were intended for publication. Olearius included the enigmatic *An Herrn Olearien vor Astrachan* in the *Prodromus*, the first provisional sampling of Fleming's poems, printed in 1641. Both *An Herrn Olearien vor Astrachan* and *Nach seinem Traume* appear in the complete *Teütsche Poemata*, and this implies that Fleming himself had included both in the manuscript of poems that he was preparing for publication when he died. It appears, then, that Fleming intended both poems to be public and that he regarded their obscure references to personal problems as no hindrance to this. Possibly the whole manner of dealing with these poems and their obscure passages had to do with tact. If the problem that Fleming felt compelled to bring up in each poem had to do, for example, with Brüggemann's actions, it could only hurt the image of the expedition to acquaint the general public with it. That such a sense of decorum informed documents relating to the expedition intended for the public is confirmed by some passages of Olearius's *Reisebeschreibung*. Olearius not infrequently hints at problems created by Brüggemann, and sometimes the references are rather opaque. Thus, he tells us at one point that the pleasure felt by members of the expedition on entering Persia was spoiled "so wegen einer principal Person Eigensinnigkeit . . . darvon lieber zu schweigen/ als mit mehren zu gedencken/ höfflicher" (p. 415). Olearius, like Fleming, only hints at trouble here and does not name names: he makes it clear that this reticence is deliberate and preferable. Perhaps, then, in the case of *An Herrn Olearien vor Astrachan* and *Nach seinem Traume*, Fleming deliberately made his references to trouble obscure to a wide public (although they would be clear to a select few) so that the poems could be published for their representational and artistic merits without damaging the reputation of persons connected with the embassy.

The other two poems, *An einen seiner vertrautesten Freunde* and *An Herrn Hansen Arpenbeken*, though technically public in Deissmann and Luck's sense, seem more intimate and personal than *An Herrn Olearien vor Astrachan* and *Nach seinem Traume*. They are stylistically somewhat less expansive, both tending to convey information briefly, rather than using much amplification for epideictic effect. Furthermore, the fact that readers other than the addressee have no trouble following what is being said in *An Herrn Hansen Arpenbeken* is less the result of Fleming's conscientiously explaining the situation—as was the case with Lotichius's letter to Hardesheim—than of his need to convey information to Arpenbek himself. As already noted, *An Herrn Hansen Arpenbeken* is unlike *An einen seiner vertrautesten Freunde* (or, for that matter, any other poetic epistle discussed here) in that it actually fulfills the real epistolary function of informing. In one sense, then, of all the poems, *An Herrn Hansen Arpenbeken* most closely resembles an actual private letter addressed to an individual, as opposed to being only ostensibly a private letter while in reality constituting a literary piece intended for a wider audience. Nonetheless it, like Fleming's other poetic epistles and like Opitz's poems to Zincgref and Seußius, was published in accordance with the author's wishes; one must conclude that all four of Fleming's poems are, like Opitz's epistles, "public" according to Deissmann and Luck's definition.

But there is a difference between the two poems by Opitz and the four by Fleming that involves something not entirely unrelated to the distinction between public and private letters; it has to do with the types of subject matter the two poets chose to include in their poems. I noted in my discussion of Opitz's poetic epistles that although he includes some autobiographical detail, such as is appropriate to the familiar epistle, he includes less than did some other writers of poetic epistles. Moreover, what he does include serves essentially to set the scene preparatory to the "real" subject matter of his letter, his exposition of neo-Stoic philosophy or a discussion of the current state of literature. Opitz's central subject matter is not so much personal as civic-minded. This is quite evident in the poem to Zincgref; in the poem to Seußius, Opitz is ostensibly concerned with finding a way out of a personal dilemma, but the choice between women, cards, drink, and poetry that he portrays himself as confronting is clearly fabricated and serves mainly to make Opitz's foregone choice of poetry stand out as an exemplary public-spirited decision. Fleming's subject matter, on the other hand, in *An einen seiner vertrautesten Freunde*, *Nach seinem Traume*, and *An Herrn Hansen Arpenbeken*, and to some extent in *An Herrn Olearien vor Astrachan*, is himself. He concentrates on describing an apparently real problem he is facing and on achieving some kind of resolution.

Not only do Opitz's and Fleming's poems differ with respect to subject matter; they also differ in purpose. Opitz's purpose in his poem to Seußius is to choose a course of action and then to encourage himself in the pursuit of that course; in his letter to Zincgref, the course of action—continuing in efforts on behalf of Germany and German literature—is already clear, and the purpose of the poem is simply to encourage Zincgref in that course. Fleming's main rhetorical aim in his poems is not so much to decide on a course of action as to help restore his tranquillity and immunity to the assaults of the affects after these have momentarily been lost.

Literary works that aim to restore a person's *tranquillitas animi* in the wake of misfortune are consolatory; Fleming's poetic epistles thus seem to be closely linked to the genre of the *consolatio*, which Scaliger defined for his late-Renaissance contemporaries as an "oratio reducens moerentes ad tranquillitatem."[43] Indeed, three of Fleming's poetic epistles have two-part structures reminiscent of the *consolatio* as discussed in chapter 1. In *An einen seiner vertrautesten Freunde*, *Nach seinem Traume*, and *An Herrn Hansen Arpenbeken* Fleming develops at length the theme of his own unhappiness—a *lamentatio*—and then in a complementary section he finds reason for consolation. *An einen seiner vertrautesten Freunde*, with its symbolic corresponding landscapes, is perhaps the most brilliant realization of this structure. The second part of *An Herrn Olearien vor Astrachan* bears within it this structure too, and given how different in subject matter and tone its two parts are, the poem as a whole can be regarded as consisting of a nearly autonomous panegyric, followed by a two-part *consolatio* (although the consolatory portion is unusually brief), rather than as a single three-part poem.

In chapter 1 I referred to Krummacher's suggestion that Fleming's modification of the normal three-part epicedium structure in the direction of the two-part *consolatio*, a genre which is quintessentially Stoic, reveals Fleming's openness to neo-Stoicism (at least from late 1633 or 1634 on) in a manner perhaps even more telling than his simple use of Stoic themes. The same argument can, I believe, be made with reference to Fleming's poetic epistles. They contain ample explicit traces of neo-Stoic thought and values, and additionally, they, like the later epicedia, are structured after the manner of the Stoic *consolatio*.

Fleming's tendency to mold genres to the form of the *consolatio* may go beyond the epicedium and the poetic epistle. Pyritz noted that many of Fleming's poems in the tradition of the Petrarchan love complaint have optimistic endings and interpreted this as Fleming's individual metamorphosis of the Petrarchan motif system and as peculiarly expressive of Fleming's own personality (pp. 265–69). Alewyn stressed what Pyritz noted in passing, that the optimistic motifs actually belong to the neo-Stoic motif complex, and pointed out that they thus in their own way participate in one of the "überpersönliche Gebilde" of baroque thought and literature, rather than being Fleming's personal contribution. The example of the poetic epistles and their two-part structure suggests that a similar structure, present in some of Fleming's love poetry (e.g., *An die baltischen Sirenen*, O.V.25, and *An Anemonen, nachdem er von ihr gereiset war*, O.V.40), may point yet again, even more convincingly than Alewyn's recognition of neo-Stoic motifs, to the importance of neo-Stoic thought in Fleming's later poetry. His peculiar optimism in the love poems may thus be not so much a manifestation of what Pyritz (p. 266) calls an "Annäherung an die realen psychischen Vorgänge" (in contrast to the "irreal" ones of Petrarchism) as of a neo-Stoic habit of mind that involved continual reference to the topoi of consolation as counteragents to any turn of fortune, to any force (e.g., love, or the unhappiness of separation) which disturbed the equanimity of the mind. It is thus not necessarily so much Fleming's personal experience of love with Elsabe and Anna Niehus that caused him to "overcome" Petrarchism; rather his neo-Stoicism, once wholeheartedly adopted probably sometime in late 1633 or 1634, motivated him to oppose the literary depiction of Petrarchan distress with the neo-Stoic arguments that lead the mind back to tranquillity.

To return to the poetic epistles themselves: I have noted that Fleming's poems differ from Opitz's with regard to subject matter and purpose. There is one further important manner in which they differ, the degree of intimacy portrayed in the relationship between poet and addressee. The relationship between Opitz and his correspondents is rather formal and stiff. He does call Zincgref "liebster Freund," but there is very little sense of any intimacy between them in *An Herrn Zincgrefen*; Opitz gives the impression of discussing professional matters with a fellow professional. The distance between poet and addressee in the poem to Seußius is quite pronounced. Opitz never actually addresses Seußius directly, referring to him instead in the third person; he speaks of him as a model of the poet-scholar, not as someone to whom he, Opitz, is particularly close. The case is quite different with Fleming's poems. Fleming could conceivably have written the poetic epistles to himself, since his purpose is to restore his own equanimity, but he turns instead to trusted friends and in essence confesses to them his troubles—involving them in his efforts to restore tranquillity. There is an intimacy of shared personal experience in these poems that is lacking in Opitz's. The intimacy of the relationship between poet and addressee in Fleming's poems is reflected in their conversational quality. Fleming repeatedly turns to his addressee to say "du weißt, um was ich traure" or the like, giving the impression of a closeness and a capacity for interchange that we do not sense in Opitz's more reticent poems. That letters should be like conversations is one of the oldest maxims of epistolary theory, and Fleming may have been deliberately striving for this effect. In a sense, he succeeds so well at times that he undermines the very epistolarity of the poems. For epistles are predicated upon a distance between writer and recipient that cannot be bridged by speech, but in P.W.IV.49 Fleming gives us the distinct impression that Olearius is there with him: "Hier gehn wir oft und schauen mit Erblassen / dein Rasen an, du schaumichter Hirkan!"; "Komm, laß uns itzt . . . spaziren gehn!" And in fact we have no reason to believe that Fleming was separated geographically from his correspondents as Opitz clearly was from Zincgref and presumably was from Seußius. But without the evidence of an autograph, it is impossible to tell whether Fleming actually sent his poetic epistles to his friends, or simply wrote poems in accordance with epistolary conventions to persons present. In either case, he endowed the poems with a tone of intimacy and familiarity that contrasts with the rather formal and professional distance maintained by Opitz.

To sum up the differences between the poems by Opitz and those by Fleming, one might say that Opitz's poems look forward to the seventeenth-century cultivation of occasional poetry. Rather than offering us intimate glimpses of himself or his relationship with his addressee, Opitz chooses a topic, vernacular poetry or the neo-Stoic ideal, and expounds on it according to the promptings of rhetoric. Fleming's focus on himself in his poetic epistles, his self-revelation, and the sense he conveys of intimacy with the addressee, indicate the greater closeness of these poems to the Renaissance traditions of the familiar letter and the poetic epistle.

Epilogue

Fleming's foreboding of his own death in his poetic epistle to Arpenbek proved only slightly premature. He was able to complete the return journey from Persia to Moscow and Reval, despite a constitution weakened by hardship and illness, and he doubtless attended Arpenbek's wedding in Reval on May 13, 1639, as well as the weddings of other members of the expedition. Still a welcome guest at the home of Heinrich Niehus, he became engaged at the end of this, his second stay in Reval, to the youngest daughter, Anna. It was understood that he would complete his medical studies and then return to Reval to marry and take up a post as city physician. Three days after his engagement, on July 11, 1639, he departed for Travemünde. He never returned to Saxony, and thus did not see his father and sister again, but instead set out via Gottorp and Hamburg for Leiden, where the University had already attracted many German students whose native universities had been disrupted by the war. The medical faculty at Leiden had not yet become greatly renowned, and Fleming was perhaps a generation too early to benefit from the quality of medical teaching soon associated with the school. Of the two faculty members there at the time, Otto van Heurne and Ewald Screvelius, he chose the more obscure, Screvelius, as his sponsor. On January 23, 1640, after about four months in Leiden, he received his medical degree, having completed a dissertation on venereal disease.[1] In March Fleming undertook the first stage of the return journey to Reval, but arrived in Hamburg mortally ill. He had already, perhaps in Leiden, organized his poems for publication and now, evidently still in full command of his faculties, he added to his poems the famous "Grabschrift" (So.II.14), three days before his death on April 2, 1640. Although he never saw the Niehus family again, he was buried in their family crypt in Hamburg, the city of their residence until 1633.

The brevity of Fleming's life—he was thirty when he died—wraps his poetic career in an aura of precocity. The developmental model explicitly or implicitly present in much interpretation of his work suggests that had Fleming lived longer, his poetry would have become more and more uncannily modern in its sentiment and expression. The preceding studies suggest otherwise. Throughout his career Fleming emulated the literary models of his predecessors and contemporaries. Sometimes the models are obvious, as with the epithalamium for Brokmann, sometimes they are more obscure; the case of the *Arae Schönburgicae* suggests that there is still fruitful work to be done in seeking Fleming's sources. Fleming was too good a poet to offer flat imitations of his models, but it is also notable that his modification of them was respectful, not radical. Some of what strikes us as particularly modern in Fleming's verse has been shown to have its sources in Renaissance traditions that have come together under a fortunate constellation of circumstances in Fleming's life and poetry. Thus it can be seen that the poetry celebrating reciprocal fidelity between lovers has sources in Renaissance friendship poetry and theory, in a certain epithalamial tradition, and in German *Gesellschaftslieder* about separation, and that these came together during Fleming's separation from his fiancées. The discursive quality of Fleming's poetic epistles, which makes them appear so much more attractive and modern in comparison to Opitz's rather stilted efforts, can be attributed to his approximating more closely the humanist ideal of the friendly epistle, rather than the occasional poem. Much of what we appreciate in Fleming also originates in his having possessed a sense for sound—for rhythm and euphony—and a capacity for creating these in the German language of the early seventeenth century without sacrificing sense. Had Opitz not lived, Fleming would probably have been a now obscure poet of neo-Latin. But as it was, he was able to take the still slightly rough language of the new poetry and refashion it into lines that were smoother, more concise, and more pleasing, and into poems often more coherent and unified. The rhythm of Fleming's verse, his flexible style, and his thematic coherence contribute to his still being appreciated today. But it should not be forgotten that this poetry, at times so modern in appearance, has firm roots in its own time.

Notes

Sources are usually cited in notes only by author and (short) title. Complete bibliographic information can be found in the list of works cited. Once a source has been cited within a given chapter, page references are often given in the text.

Introduction

1. Georg Philipp Harsdörffer and Johann Klaj name both Opitz and Fleming when they place their *Pegnesisches Schaefergedicht* (1644) in its generic context (p. 4). Johann Rist, in his *Neüer Himlischer Lieder Sonderbahres Buch* (1651), praises Fleming's chaste love songs and various poems along with those of Opitz and others (fols. A4r and A5v). Philipp von Zesen preferred Fleming to Opitz in some matters: "Opitz/ welcher in seinen Gedichten etwas flüssiger und färtiger als Flämming/ wiewohl dieses geist durchdringender/ und dichterischer/ ja gleichsam himmelsflammender ist" (*Hochdeutsche Helikonische Hechel* [1668], p. 66; p. 349 in Zesen, *Sämtliche Werke*). See also p. 120 (p. 394, *Sämtliche Werke*) of the same work, as well as Zesen's sonnet *An die Stadt Leypzig*, in his *Deutsches Helicons Erster und Ander Theil* (1641), Ander Theil, p. 4; *Sämtliche Werke*, pp. 271–72.

2. Morhof, *Unterricht Von Der Teutschen Sprache und Poesie*, p. 426.

3. Eckermann, *Gespräche mit Goethe*, p. 183 (conversation of January 4, 1827).

4. Gervinus on Opitz: *Geschichte der poetischen National-Literatur der Deutschen*, pt. 3, p. 206ff.; his remark about Fleming appears on p. 238. Hoffmann von Fallersleben on Opitz: *Politische Gedichte aus der deutschen Vorzeit*, pp. 211–42.

5. Alewyn, "Hans Pyritz: Paul Flemings deutsche Liebeslyrik," p. 440.

6. Among the important biographies are an early one by Karl August Varnhagen von Ense in his *Biographische Denkmale* and Walter Schlesinger's in *Sächsische Lebensbilder*. The other biographies, many written with a regional or religious focus, are too numerous to list here; many can be found in Siegfried Scheer's bibliography of works on Fleming, "Paul Fleming 1609–1640." The (deliberately) fictional accounts reach back at least to the first half of the nineteenth century, with Franz Theodor Wangenheim's vast *Paul Flemming, oder Die Gesandtschaftsreise nach Persien* from 1842, and continue down to this day. Recent additions are *In allen meinen Taten* by Werner Legère and Uwe Berger's *Das Verhängnis oder Die Liebe des Paul Fleming*.

7. Maync, "Paul Fleming," p. 67. For the remarks of Gervinus, Goedeke, and Pyritz see chapter 4, and the first note to that chapter.

8. Fleming, *Deutsche Gedichte*, pp. 855, 885.

9. In 1931 Pyritz submitted the first part of his work on Fleming as a dissertation, *Paul Flemings "Suavia."* The remaining sections appeared within a year: "Der Liebeslyriker Paul Fleming in seinen Übersetzungen" and *Paul Flemings deutsche Liebeslyrik*. These scattered essays finally appeared as the single unified work they were intended to be when they were reprinted three decades later under the title *Paul Flemings Liebeslyrik: Zur Geschichte des Petrarkismus*. My references will be to this volume.

10. Conrady, *Lateinische Dichtungstradition und deutsche Lyrik des 17. Jahrhunderts*; Dyck, *Ticht-Kunst*; Barner, *Barockrhetorik*; and Segebrecht, *Das Gelegenheitsgedicht*.

11. Fechner's "Paul Fleming" is a thoughtful treatment of Fleming's life and works. Like Alewyn, he cautions against the temptation to turn Fleming's life and poetry into legend. Since it deserves to become a standard reference work, a few minor errors should be corrected. The expedition traveled along the shores of the Caspian, not the Black Sea (p. 370) to reach Persia. Elsabe Niehus married Salomon Matthiä, who became a professor of Oriental and Greek languages at the University of Dorpat, not in Reval (p. 371). Fleming's extant Latin poetry begins not with works for the Schönburgs (p. 373), but in 1624 with an epicedium for the wife of Johann Hermann Schein. For Joseph Scaliger at the top of p. 374, read Julius Caesar. The argument, p. 368, (also made by others) that Fleming attained his doctorate in Leiden so quickly because he was very well prepared (or extremely gifted, as is sometimes maintained) cannot be endorsed without closer attention to degree-granting practices at that university at that time; quickly bestowed degrees were no exception in the seventeenth century. My disagreement with Fechner and others regarding Schein's importance is treated in chapter 3. An important and original study of Fleming appeared in 1987 after the present work was essentially complete, Peter Krahé's "Persönlicher Ausdruck in der literarischen Konvention." Krahé demonstrates the difficulty, or indeed, he argues, the impossibility, of locating sincere personal expression in Fleming's work when one ceases to rely on individual passages for evidence. He points to Fleming's repeated use, in varying situations, of the same or same types of phrases, which, when read individually and in isolation, seem individually chosen to express personal conviction. Krahé also offers cogent arguments against the Fleming legend, the "so zerrissenes und spannungsvolles Bild des Dichters, . . . für das seine Biographie keine rechten Anhaltspunkte liefert" (p. 510). A 1984 article by Dietmar Schubert, " 'Man wird mich nennen hören,' " begins promisingly but ultimately endorses Pyritz's theses. I have not been able to examine the same author's dissertation, *Paul Fleming: Monographische Studie unter besonderer Berücksichtigung der Wirkungsgeschichte nach 1945*.

12. Wiedemann, [Review], p. 590.

13. Albertus Bornemann, *Die Überlieferung der deutschen Gedichte Flemings*. For the sake of brevity, I refer to D. *Paul Flemings POetischer Gedichten So nach seinem Tode haben sollen herauβgegeben werden/ Prodromus* simply as *Prodromus*.

On the dating of Fleming's *Teütsche Poemata*, see Lappenberg's discussion on p. 847 of the *Deutsche Gedichte*. More recently, Christian Wagenknecht ("Paul Flemings Teutsche Poemata") has reiterated Lappenberg's sound but often overlooked argumentation.

14. Friedrich Neumann's *Geschichte des neuhochdeutschen Reimes von Opitz bis Wieland* deals extensively with Fleming's language, as does Eugen Hartmuth Mueller's *Die Sprache Paul Flemings*. Virgil Moser's "Deutsche Orthographiereformen des 17. Jahrhunderts," has a substantial section (pp. 216–34) devoted to the orthography of the early Fleming editions.

15. Dünnhaupt, *Bibliographisches Handbuch der Barockliteratur*; the imprint for Major is no. 12A. Neither Dünnhaupt nor I realized that Lappenberg knew and printed the poems that Dünnhaupt lists as nos. 26 and 28 and that I published on pp. 7–8 of "Gedichte von Paul Fleming in der Stolbergschen Leichenpredigten-Sammlung"; they are Lappenberg's M.III.18 (*Super Funere Cujusdam*) and P.W.II.3 (*Über eine Leiche*). The texts taken from the funeral sermons offer significant variants; the funeral-sermon text of P.W.II.3, for example, makes reference in its last lines to the fact that two deaths, not just one, are being commemorated. Lappenberg was unable to identify the deceased or to determine the dates of their death, information provided by the funeral sermons. My error suggests that a first-line index, in addition to Lappenberg's indices of proper names and of unusual words and locutions, would be helpful.

16. In "Paul Fleming," I have attempted to present an overview of the material that has come to light since Lappenberg's edition. To this can now be added the finds described by Klaus Garber in "Paul Fleming in Riga."

Chapter 1

1. Fleming, *Deutsche Gedichte*, p. 859. It is distressing that this, like many of Lappenberg's cautiously phrased speculative statements, comes to be taken as fact without the adduction of further evidence. For example, in the introduction to his "Paul Fleming's Latin Religious Lyrics," Jim Warren Krout not only treats the destruction as indubitable but extends it also to the early Latin poetry: "[H]e destroyed all his previously [prior to meeting Opitz in September 1630] written German poetry and his Latin poetry except for poems addressed to Rubella" (p. 5). In "Paul Fleming und seine Rußlandreise" Hans Rodenberg asserts that "Die Wirkung des Büchleins [*Das Buch von der Deutschen Poeterey*] auf Fleming zeigte sich äußerlich darin, daß er alles, was er bis dahin gedichtet hatte, verbrannte" (p. 233); he cites nothing to support this.

2. Fleming, *Lateinische Gedichte*, p. 478.

3. Lappenberg, in keeping with his general principle of separating Latin and German poems into two different volumes, prints the Latin poems of the *Arae Schönburgicae* as Sy.IX.1 (1–15, 19–21) and the German poems as P.W.II.1(a–e); this makes it difficult to visualize the cycle as a whole. Heinz

Entner kindly helped me obtain a microfilm of the unique copy of the original imprint. I have (re)assigned numbers to the poems strictly in accordance with the order of this imprint; the reader may find it helpful to refer to the right-hand column of the parallel listing provided.

4. Fleming, *Deutsche Gedichte*, p. 852, n. 3, and Conrad Müller, "Paul Fleming und das Haus Schönburg," p. 27, agree on a date of late 1629, although neither points to unequivocal evidence. M.VII.2 for Maria Juliane as printed in Olearius's 1649 edition of Fleming's epigrams (*Nova Epigrammata*) has the notation "Obiit in arce Hartensteinia patria MDCXXIX," and it may have been upon this rather late witness that Lappenberg was relying. Müller (ibid.) suggests that the date of death that is sometimes given, February 14, 1630, was the date of the *Totenfeier* ("welche fast ständig nicht unerheblich später fällt"). Two of the poems in the *Arae Schönburgicae* seem, however, to support the later February date as the death date. In *Ad Hyemem*, the bridegroom reproaches winter for taking Maria Juliane with him as he departs and makes way for spring: "Ver venit, fugiens fugis. / Heus! senex male, quid mihi / ver meum rapis?" (ll. 17–19). Similarly, P.W.II.1(c), *Epigramma* opens "Die . . . / ist mit der Frülingszeit . . . / von uns gerissen hin." I have not been able to locate a funeral sermon—to which a biography would normally be appended—for Maria Juliane.

5. It is puzzling that O.IV.2—a sprightly song for two cousins of the Maria Juliane of the *Arae Schönburgicae*, to one of whom, Johann Heinrich, she had been betrothed—makes no mention either of the engagement or of her death. The text is, however, missing some lines, and it is possible that these made reference to one or both of those topics.

6. On Fleming's grandfather, see Conrad Müller, "Paul Fleming und das Haus Schönburg," p. 6.

7. Information on the House of Schönburg is taken from Walter Schlesinger's *Die Landesherrschaft der Herren von Schönburg* and Ernst Eckardt's *Chronik von Glauchau*.

8. Josef Nadler, for different reasons, speculates on the Flemings' possible Low Country origins; see *Literaturgeschichte der deutschen Stämme und Landschaften*, vol. 2, p. 325. See also Fechner, "Paul Fleming," p. 367.

9. See Erler, *Die Immatrikulationen*, p. 111. It is curious that the brief biography of Abraham Fleming in a church *Visitationsprotokoll* from September 18, 1617 mentions study, but not in Leipzig. The *Protokoll*, preserved at least into the early years of this century in the state archive in Dresden, is the subject of an article by Franz Blanckmeister, "Aus Paul Flemings Vaterhaus," and provides an unusual glimpse of Fleming's surroundings when he was very young.

10. Fleming, *Deutsche Gedichte*, pp. 852, 854.

11. Ibid., p. 852.

12. Or 1606. Lappenberg gives 1606 on p. 524 of the *Lateinische Gedichte*, but 1600 on p. 853 of the *Deutsche Gedichte*. Conrad Müller, in "Paul Fleming und das Haus Schönburg," p. 10, gives 1600. The second strophe of Sy.IX.1.1 suggests she was posthumous to her father, Hugo II (d. 1606). It

seems clear, however, from the *curriculum vitae* appended to Johann Zechendörffer's funeral sermon for Hugo von Schönburg, fols. O1v–S3v, that she was not posthumous, and one can infer from it with reasonable certainty that her birth date was 1600.

13. *Martini Opicii Teutsche Pöemata vnd Aristarchus . . . Sampt einem Anhang Mehr auserleßener geticht anderer Teutscher Poeten*. Opitz's poems from this anthology were edited and republished by Georg Witkowski under the title *Teutsche Poemata*. The poems not by Opitz were republished as *Auserlesene Gedichte Deutscher Poeten*, edited by Zincgref. I will cite from these more recent editions, calling them (Opitz's) 1624 *Poemata* and (Zincgref's) 1624 *Anhang*, respectively.

14. Pyritz, *Paul Flemings "Suavia"*.

15. Another important work on the sixteenth- and seventeenth-century epicedium is G. W. Pigman's *Grief and English Renaissance Elegy* from 1985. Whereas Krummacher focuses on the classical and Renaissance literary sources and on the topical and structural constants of the epicedium, Pigman examines how religious and social attitudes to mourning evolved during the sixteenth and seventeenth centuries in England and how this evolution was reflected in the tone and arguments of epicedia. It would be well worth approaching the German epicedium from Pigman's perspective, with its diachronic and intellectual-historical dimensions.

16. Fracastoro is known to literary historians as well as historians of medicine for his epic *Syphilis sive de morbo gallico* (Verona, 1530); Fleming makes reference to it in the introduction to his doctoral thesis on syphilis. Scaliger's tribute to him is printed on pp. 239–53 of his *Poemata omnia*. Fleming wrote an epigram (E.VII.12) for Fracastoro; he probably had the *Arae Fracastoreae* in mind when he speaks of Scaliger in line 5.

17. For example, Fleming's and Scaliger's poems to the graces both open by asking "who will give me song(s)"; Scaliger's *Ad Famam* opens "Diva fraenatrix," Fleming's *Idem ad Hyemem* opens "Dive fraeniger"; the *Epicedia* by Scaliger and Fleming include, respectively, the lines: "Terram terra premit, tellus tellure gravatur" and "tellus tellurem, terrea terra premit."

18. Georg Ellinger, on p. 193 of vol. 3.1 of his *Geschichte der neulateinischen Literatur Deutschlands im sechzehnten Jahrhundert*, says of the *Manes Lipsiani*: "[A]uch mischt sich wenig glücklich ein spielerischer Ton ein: so ergeht an die Bienen die Aufforderung, aus Lipsius' Grabe Honig zu saugen." Barbara Becker-Cantarino, *Daniel Heinsius*, p. 89, remarks: "After five rather undistinguished epigrams a 'Playful Poem to the Little Bees' strikes an entirely different chord." Harry Schnur included the poem on pp. 186–89 of his anthology *Lateinische Gedichte deutscher Humanisten* and in his notes identifies the meters used.

19. Stephan Tropsch notes on p. 133 of his *Flemings Verhältnis zur römischen Dichtung* the numerous forms used by Fleming that he does not find in the standard classical authors. It may be that Fleming borrowed these new forms from other neo-Latin poets. In his *Companion to Neo-Latin Studies*, Jozef IJsewijn mentions the need for studies of neo-Latin versification (p. 259).

20. The connection is noted by Barbara Becker-Cantarino in *Daniel Heinsius*, p. 92, where "Julius Caesar" should be read for "Justus." Heinsius also used the name "Thaumantis."

21. Opitz, *Buch von der Deutschen Poeterey*, chapter 3 (in *Gesammelte Werke*, vol. 2, pt. 1, p. 353).

22. The dedicatory poem to Dousa's sons precedes the cycle along with the *Ad Manes* in the editions of Heinsius's *Poemata* of 1606, 1610, and 1613. It is placed at the end of the cycle in the original imprint of 1605 and in the 1617 and later editions of Heinsius's *Poemata*. In the parallel listing I follow the order of Heinsius's *Poematvm editio tertia* from 1610, in which for the first time the three cycles of epicedia, all of which Fleming evidently knew, were printed together. The 1605 imprint includes additionally an *Elegia Ex iiii libro nondum edito elegiarum Danielis Heinsii, in obitum Iani Dousae*; it is deleted from printings of the cycle in Heinsius's collected poems, taking its place instead among his elegies.

23. Becker-Cantarino, *Daniel Heinsius*, p. 66, commenting on a collection of Greek verse published by Heinsius in 1613, notes that "their importance lies in the display of his extraordinary gift for language, as only a very few humanists succeeded in writing flawless verses in classical Greek."

24. In 1618 Opitz had combined Latin and German in his *Hipponax ad Asterien*, which consists of a long poem in Latin followed by five short poems of various types in German; see Opitz, *Gesammelte Werke*, vol. 1, pp. 98–113. Marian Szyrocki, *Martin Opitz*, p. 29, suggests that the German poems were offered as evidence of the suitability of the German language for poetry. I have not found evidence that Fleming was aware of these love poems or was influenced by their bilingual example. Fleming's undertaking, being longer, was more ambitious, and his cycle was written for a more serious occasion. I have found no other similarly bilingual (German and Latin) precedent for Fleming's cycle. Joseph Dallett, in a private communication, suggested that Heinsius's cycle for Scaliger, which is especially remarkable for its inclusion of a poem in the Doric dialect among its Greek poems, may also have played a role in Fleming's choosing to embed German poems within the Latin cycle.

25. The significance of the *puellus* or *verna* is not entirely clear, but the reference is presumably to a German boy (*verna* can mean a native). The *viator* is exhorted to seek him; "if he will not speak" ("si non loquetur"), "let him prattle/croon this" ("lallet hoc"). The words that follow ("Hac sub scrobe / conduntur pietas, venus, lepores") may be regarded as the exact wording of the tomb inscription, which the boy clumsily attempts to quote—and which would do the passerby not conversant with Latin little good—or they may provide a paraphrase of the boy's inelegant German description of what lies beneath the marker. Joseph Dallett (see preceding note) noted that Heinsius's Doric poem in the *Manes Scaligeri* and the Greek poem, *Aliud, ex persona mortui*, that follows it may have suggested aspects of Fleming's linguistic strategy and of *Ad viatorem*.

26. Erich Trunz, in "Die Entwicklung des barocken Langverses," p. 445, notes that Silesia, in contrast to the rest of Germany, had a tradition dating

back to the sixteenth century of adding a few German poems to collections of Latin celebratory poems. The many young Silesians who came to study in Leipzig, particularly in the aftermath of the religious persecutions in Silesia, were probably responsible for introducing this custom to Leipzig simultaneously with the Opitzian verse reform. In 1629 one finds, for example, several German poems included among the epicedia appended to Johannes Höpnerus's funeral sermon for the learned bookseller, Zacharias Schürer. Georg Witkowski, in his *Geschichte des literarischen Lebens in Leipzig*, pp. 107 and 111, implies that 1631 was the year when Opitzian verse, especially the alexandrine, first became widely used in Leipzig, and my own inspection of occasional poetry from that city supports his view. Trunz, p. 462, is too conservative when he says the alexandrine gained dominance in middle-class Leipzig circles around 1640. The remarkable rapidity with which Opitzian verse came to be accepted after its first introduction into Leipzig in 1629 and 1630 has been noted by Leonard Forster, who argues that the ear of the German public had been made ready for the new style by German alexandrines on broadsheets of Dutch provenance; further sheets of this type found by John Roger Paas may support Forster's case. See Forster, "German Alexandrines on Dutch Broadsheets before Opitz" and Paas, "The Seventeenth-century Verse Broadsheet," pp. 35–44.

27. Elisabeth Lang ("Das illustrierte Flugblatt des Dreißigjährigen Krieges") has studied the types of verse on the broadsheets produced in the years 1620–21 and 1631–32, when, in contrast to the intervening period, production was high. Noting the prevalence of Opitzian alexandrines in the later period, she suggests that after German alexandrines on Dutch broadsheets had helped the line achieve quick acceptance among German poets like Fleming (Forster's argument; see preceding note), the poetry of such forward-looking writers in turn prepared the ground for the extensive use of the alexandrine on the numerous Leipzig sheets commemorating events in 1631 and 1632.

28. The distinction between song and ode is not well defined in this period. For simplicity's sake, I generally use Fleming's own term, ode, for his strophic poems.

29. Kirchner's cycle is on pp. 24–27 of Zincgref's 1624 *Anhang*.

30. The latter, of course, is in part a consequence of the change in genre from epithalamium to epicedium, but it is also consonant with the general decorousness of the new poetry. When Fleming is salacious in an epithalamium, as in *Auf Herrn Garlef Lüders und Jungfrau Margarethen Brauns Hochzeit in Moßkow* (P.W.III.5), the references are more intellectual and witty than in Kirchner's poems.

31. From 1631: P.W.IV.1, P.W.V.1 and 2; from 1636: P.W.IV.48 and P.W.V.17; P.W.IV.49 from 1636 employs cross rhyme in *vers communs*.

32. Beissner, *Geschichte der deutschen Elegie*, p. 54ff.

33. Ulrich Bornemann, *Anlehnung und Abgrenzung*, p. 59, notes Fleming's limited attention to Heinsius's *Nederduytsche Poemata* in comparison with Opitz. Beissner errs when he says on p. 58 of his *Geschichte der deutschen Ele-*

gie that most neo-Latin epicedia employed heroic hexameter; in general, his chapter on the baroque elegy shows an awareness of too restricted a corpus of neo-Latin poetry, conditioned no doubt in part by the difficulty of gaining access to source material, but probably also by Beissner's particular understanding of the elegy.

34. Olearius, *Dialogus*, fol. A2r. Perhaps the imperfections here result from an acquaintance with Opitz's *Aristarchus* (1617) and 1624 *Poemata*, with their metrical uncertainties, and an ignorance of or imperfect knowledge of the 1624 *Buch von der Deutschen Poeterey* and the revised edition of his poems, the *Acht Bücher, Deutscher Poematum*, published in 1625, in which nearly all problems of prosody had been worked out.

35. The poem by the Silesian Martin Christenius (on fols. B4r–C1r of the *Epicedia In Beatissimam*), unlike Olearius's for Hütten, consistently achieves regular, natural iambs, but occasionally suppresses unstressed vowels. A poem sent from Wittenberg by an "A.B." (August Buchner?; . . . *Epicedia Quae ad*, fols. B1v–B2r) achieves regular iambs through slightly less forgivable means; adjective endings are suppressed, and "seim" is used for "seinem." A further Wittenberg contribution (. . . *Epicedia Quae ad*, B3r–B3v) includes the unspeakable line "Nicht lengr genossen sein müssn so gschwind beraubet werdn!" A poem by "Casparus Brandes Halberstad. LL. Stud." (*Epicedia In Beatissimam*, fols. B2v–B3v), on the other hand, exhibits sufficient control of the medium to allow this unknown to use alliteration and rather complex but perspicuous sentence construction with few problems of pronunciation or sense.

36. This is from a translation of Petrus Lotichius Secundus's Elegy II.4, which circulated widely after Tilly's sack of Magdeburg in 1631. See my "Did Opitz Translate Lotichius' Elegy on Magdeburg?"

37. See Georg Baesecke, *Die Sprache der Opitzischen Gedichtsammlungen von 1624 und 1625*, sec. 66 ("Betonung"), on Opitz's prosodic practice. Particularly in the 1624 *Poemata* there occur instances of reversed feet in the first position in a line. Also interesting is August Buchner's observation that the first two syllables in an iambic line can form a spondee; see his *Anleitung Zur Deutschen Poeterey*, p. 117.

38. And even this may simply be an instance where the modern ear demands too much. In the late eighteenth century there was still controversy over the stress of the second syllable of "endlos." See passages from the correspondence of Friedrich Schiller and Wilhelm von Humboldt cited by Alfred Kelletat, "Zum Problem der antiken Metren im Deutschen," pp. 66–67, where Schiller decides to treat the word as a spondee rather than as a trochee or part of a dactyl.

39. The sixth line of the *Elegie an das traurige Hartenstein* includes the apocopated form "ohn" before a consonant; this might seem a violation of Opitz's stricture in chapter 7 of the *Buch von der Deutschen Poeterey* against deleting the letter *e* at the ends of words. The shortened "ohn" was, however, commonly used in prose in this period.

40. On Opitz, see Baesecke, *Die Sprache der Opitzischen Gedichtsammlungen*,

sec. 51; on Fleming, see Neumann, *Geschichte des neuhochdeutschen Reimes*, p. 107, and Mueller, *Die Sprache Paul Flemings*, secs. 57 and 58. Lappenberg discusses Fleming's rhymes briefly on pp. 897–98 of the *Deutsche Gedichte*, and Eva Dürrenfeld seems to base her discussion in "Paul Fleming und Johann Christian Günther" p. 102, on Lappenberg. Both suggest that some of Fleming's "impure" rhymes cannot be ascribed to dialect but, by implication, to carelessness. Neumann studies the question more extensively and nowhere notes rhymes whose presence is not explicable on the basis of Fleming's own Saxon dialect or his imitation of Opitz's Silesian. Whether the apparently impure rhymes are in fact more prevalent in earlier poems than later ones, as Lappenberg suggests (p. 898), needs further investigation. The imprints discovered since Lappenberg published his edition need to be taken into account, as do the additions and changes made to his chronology of the poems.

41. Opitz explicitly rejects "han" at the beginning of chapter 6 of the *Buch von der Deutschen Poeterey*. The pronunciation "verkahrt" is traceable to Fleming's Saxon dialect (Neumann, *Geschichte des neuhochdeutschen Reimes*, p. 132 and Mueller, *Die Sprache Paul Flemings*, p. 25) and contrasts with the usual seventeenth-century pronunciation (Grimms' *Deutsches Wörterbuch* under "verkehren"). Neumann implies that these problematic rhymes could account for Fleming's failure to republish the *Arae Schönburgicae*. Familiarity with the dialects of seventeenth-century poets is necessary in order, among other things, to recognize that apparently impure rhymes may not have been perceived as such even by strict Opitzian poets. Opitz's injunction to use High German could not and did not banish all regional differences. One cannot, as Volker Klotz ("Spiegel und Echo, Konvention und Individualität im Barock," p. 117) attempts to do, corroborate an interpretation of Fleming's *An Anna, die spröde* (O.V.38) by pointing to "die einzige Stelle eines auffällig unreinen Reims," that is, to "gesinnet" and "gönnet" in the third strophe. The rhyme was neither impure nor remarkable in Fleming's dialect—or Opitz's. Both permitted the rhyme $i : \ddot{o}$, and both poets would have said what we would represent as "gesinnet" : "ginnet" (see Neumann, *Geschichte des neuhochdeutschen Reimes*, pp. 123–26). Similarly, Alfred Behrmann, in his analysis of O.V.7 (*Madrigal*) in his *Einführung in die Analyse von Verstexten*, pp. 38–39, describes the rhymes "streubet" : "umleibet" and "Kummer" : "Sommer," as well as "kömmt" : "nimmt" as "unrein" and proffers this as evidence that Fleming deliberately weakened the tendency to strophic form in this madrigal. But see Neumann, pp. 107 and 121. Finally, see A. G. De Capua's discussion of O.V.42 (*An Anna aus der Ferne*) on p. 55 of his *German Baroque Poetry*, in which he describes the rhyme "Wink : "ging" as "uncouth"; Neumann, p. 296: "Die beste Technik läßt also diese Reime [rhymes in *-ng : -nk*] zu."

42. Heinrich Welti, in his *Geschichte des Sonettes in der deutschen Dichtung*, p. 76, and Friedrich Wilhelm Schmitz, in his *Metrische Untersuchungen zu Paul Flemings deutschen Gedichten*, p. 101, point out that Opitz did not explicitly call for a clear break in syntax and thought between the quatrains and the

tercets of a sonnet and that he did not consistently observe such in his own writing. Fleming's sonnets, by comparison, include a notably higher number with a break than do Opitz's. Nonetheless, Welti remarks the following: "Die stilwidrige Verknüpfung der Quartette und Terzette ist zwar bei Fleming, insbesondere bei den Sonetten seiner reiferen Jahre, ziemlich selten, der Mangel an bestimmter innerer Gliederung aber doch so oft bemerklich, daß wir wohl berechtigt sind, daran zu zweifeln, daß unserem Dichter die Zweiteiligkeit als wesentliches Merkmal der Form erschienen sei" (p. 89). Many of the sonnets in which the octet and the sestet are run together cannot be dated, and some (So.III.22, 44, 58) probably date from the latter part of Fleming's career, so that Welti's implied conclusion that Fleming gradually came closer to the ideal sonnet form in the course of his career cannot be substantiated.

43. I have not been able to find a precedent for this particular comparison. It seems almost a logical extension of the frequent comparisons between love and war and between love and death; one might expect an exhaustive exploration of the relations among the three *artes*. Beissner, attempting to rescue Fleming for his elegy tradition, remarks of this poem: "Tatsächlich aber ist der Tod des edlen Fräuleins nur der Anlaß zu einer nachdenklichen, elegisch gedämpften Gegenüberstellung der Kriegsnot, . . . und des . . . Todesgeschicks" (*Geschichte der deutschen Elegie*, p. 70). This is nonsense.

44. Eckardt, *Chronik von Glauchau*, pp. 466–67.

45. On Opitz's early stylistic development, see Janis Little Gellinek's *Die weltliche Lyrik des Martin Opitz*, esp. chapter 2.

46. On the identity of the deceased in O.II.2 (Elisabeth, not Agnes), see Geyer's "Zur Bibliographie Flemings," pp. 167–68, or my "Neues zu Paul Fleming," p. 182.

47. Anthony Harper notes that in the poetry of Martin Christenius, friend and fellow student of Fleming, one encounters the theme of war to a greater extent than one might expect even in this age. When the Leipzig poets are more extensively studied, it may be found that this is one of their salient characteristics. See Harper's *Schriften zur Lyrik Leipzigs 1620–1670*, pp. 97–100. Schubert has recently remarked that the theme of war and peace seems to be more pervasive in Fleming's poetry than in that of his contemporaries (" 'Man wird mich nennen hören,' " p. 1690).

48. Nelson, *Baroque Lyric Poetry*, p. 36.

49. Not in Lappenberg's edition. Hermann Oesterley found the text and printed it in "Zu Paul Fleming."

50. This ode was unknown to Lappenberg. It is reprinted on pp. 4–5 of my "Gedichte von Paul Fleming in der Stolbergschen Leichenpredigten-Sammlung" and below.

51. Ernst Robert Curtius noted that this device of rapid recapitulation was common in Spanish literature of the Golden Age and traced its use back to late antiquity (*European Literature and the Latin Middle Ages*, pp. 287–91). Adelheid Beckmann mentions its use in French and German in *Motive und Formen der deutschen Lyrik*, pp. 114–16. Adolf Beck has written a longer study of the

form, with particular attention to poems by Weckherlin and to Fleming's *Alloquutio*, although he does not mention the *Epigramma* or Fleming's sonnets; see his "Über einen Formtypus der barocken Lyrik in Deutschland und die Frage nach seiner Herkunft." One of Fleming's poems in P.W.III.6 (ll. 440–53) as well as So.III.22 are modeled after Opitz's *Ihr/ Himmel/ lufft vnnd wind/ jhr hügel voll von schatten* from chapter 7 of the *Buch von der Deutschen Poeterey*; like the *Epigramma* and unlike Opitz's poem, both disguise the fact that elements are being listed, so that the recapitulation comes as a surprise in the final lines of the poem.

52. See the articles on "Fenster" and "brechen" in the Grimms' *Deutsches Wörterbuch*. Martin Opitz's phrase "Die Fenster brechen mir" in a translation from Ronsard conveys in context more of the etymological sense (loss of sight of the dying or dead) than does Fleming's; in Simon Dach's *Letzte Rede Einer vormals stoltzen vnd gleich jetzt sterbenden Jungfrawen* the figurative sense of "dying" predominates when he writes "die Augen sind gebrochen." See Opitz's *Trostschrifft: An Herrn David Müllern* in the *Weltliche Poëmata: Der Ander Theil*, p. 175; Dach's poem is reprinted on p. 67 of vol. 3 of his *Gedichte*.

53. For a biography of Caspar Kirchner, "Opitz' Landsmann, Gönner und Vetter," see George Schulz-Behrend's introductory remarks to Opitz's epithalamium for Kirchner on pp. 133–35 of vol. 1 of Opitz's *Gesammelte Werke*.

54. See nos. 7, 9, 47, 71, and 109 of *Den Bloem-Hof van de Nederlantsche leught*. Heinsius's "Pastorael" is on pp. 26–33 of the *Nederduytsche Poemata*. On the form and the themes often associated with it, see Th. Weevers's "The Influence of Heinsius on Two Genres of the German Baroque."

55. Lappenberg, impressed by the intensity with which Fleming studied the 1624 collection, remarks that "diese [Sammlung] ihn veranlaßte, manche in derselben enthaltenen Gedichte nicht so sehr nachzuahmen, als mit ihnen zu wetteifern" (*Deutsche Gedichte*, p. 898).

56. In 1595 a translation into German by "F. C. V. B." of the first book appeared; the later books were translated in 1616 and 1617, apparently by a different translator, "I. [J.] B. B. B." A second edition appeared (starting?) in 1615. The *Bibliotheca Societatis Teutonicae Saeculi XVI–XVIII* offers fairly detailed bibliographic entries (under Montreux) for the first edition and the first volume of the second; the information on volumes two through five is sketchy and does not give dates. No. 796 in Curt von Faber du Faur's *German Baroque Literature* is apparently the second edition of the first book: *Die Schäffereyen Von der schönen Juliana* (1615). Faber du Faur tentatively resolves the initials "F. C. V. B." as "F. C. von Borstel." Hilkert Weddige, in *Die "Historien vom Amadis auß Franckreich"*, pp. 81–87, offers evidence that the translator of the first book was actually Fridrich Castalio von Basel. The entire multivolume work appears to exist in the United States only in the original French edition, published 1592–98: *Le premier [-cinquième] livre des bergeries de Juliette*. On p. 353 of his *Der locus amoenus und der locus terribilis*, Klaus Garber indicates that the Herzog August Bibliothek, Wolfenbüttel, possesses copies of books 2–5 and also that a digest, or *Schatzkammer*, of the enormous work was published in 1617. The translation was known to Opitz, whose *Echo oder Wi-*

derschall (no. 11 in the 1624 *Poemata*) is modeled on Arcas's lament over Magdalis's hard-heartedness in the opening pages of the first volume; Garber, ibid., p. 226ff., discusses this. I am grateful to an anonymous reader for the University of North Carolina Studies in the Germanic Languages and Literatures for bringing to my attention information about the editions and authorship of the translation.

57. It is no wonder that Lappenberg, in Fleming, *Deutsche Gedichte*, p. 687, was puzzled by this poem, since he naturally assumed that the Juliana of the third strophe was the bride.

58. See Baesecke's *Die Sprache der Opitzischen Gedichtsammlungen von 1624 und 1625*, sec. 66 ("Betonung").

59. Nearly eighty years ago, Georg Wenderoth, in his skeptical assessment of the extent to which Fleming's involvement with the Niehus sisters found direct expression in his love poetry, remarked that what truly characterizes Fleming's verse is not sincerity of expression, but rather "die Glätte seiner Sprache, die Gewandtheit in Rhythmik und Reim" ("Paul Fleming als Petrarkist," p. 124).

60. Becker-Cantarino notes that the traditional *laudatio*, *lamentatio*, and *consolatio* can be discerned distributed among the poems of Heinsius's cycles for Scaliger and Dousa (*Daniel Heinsius*, pp. 88, 90, and 93). The *consolatio* in the *Manes Dousici* is, however, oblique rather than explicit; lamentation and praise dominate.

61. This poem was not known to Lappenberg. It was printed by Martin Bircher in "Paul Fleming."

62. I understand "Nechst" in line 38 to mean "recently." Alfred Götze's *Frühneuhochdeutsches Glossar* gives "letzthin" for adverbial "nechst." Compare the only other instance where Fleming uses "nächst" adverbially, So.III.43, l. 2. Biographical information is taken from the *curriculum vitae* appended to Polycarpus Leyser's funeral sermon for Thomas, *LeichPredigt . . . Beym Begräbnis des . . . Michael Thomae*, fols. C3v–D2v. Fleming was not the only major seventeenth-century artist to commemorate an event in Michael Thomas's life. A jurist, Thomas was particularly friendly with Georg and Benjamin Schütz, who shared his profession; their brother, Heinrich Schütz, composed one of his earliest preserved works, a "Concert mit 11 Stimmen" (SWV 21) on the occasion of Thomas's marriage on June 15, 1618. See the article on Schütz by Joshua Rifkin et al. in *The New Grove Dictionary of Music and Musicians*, pp. 2, 6, and 24.

63. On the dating of the epicedia for Hans von Löser, see my "Neues zu Paul Fleming," pp. 180–81.

64. Gellinek notes, in contrast, traces of Opitz's neo-Stoicism as early as 1617, in the *Aristarchus* (*Die weltliche Lyrik des Martin Opitz*, p. 30).

65. This poem was unknown to Lappenberg. See my "Gedichte von Paul Fleming in der Stolbergschen Leichenpredigten-Sammlung," pp. 3–4.

66. It is above all by these instances where Fleming brings his private grief into poems for others or other purposes that one can really measure the magnitude of his sorrow, although the German epicedium for Gloger

(P.W.II.7) certainly dramatizes the grief. The poems for Michael Thomas, Gedeon Hanemann, and the Swedish queen were not included in the manuscripts Fleming had prepared for publication. This could be the result of chance, or it might be that, at some distance from Gloger's death, Fleming felt that the highly charged references to his own grief were not appropriate and did not enhance the poems.

67. Krummacher, "Das barocke Epicedium," p. 122, n. 69, cites J. A. Fabricius to this effect.

68. The last strophe may be a conscious contrafactum of the last strophe of an ode Opitz wrote to his publisher, David Müller, on the death of his wife (printed in the *Weltliche Poëmata: Der Ander Theil*, pp. 157–59). Opitz's poem consists almost exclusively of neo-Stoic consolatory arguments and closes on a relentlessly optimistic note:

> Nach rawer Lufft vnd Regen/
> Nach Plitz' vnd Donnerschlägen
> Kömpt heller Sonnenschein.
> Der Winter ist verjaget/
> Deß Mertzens Wärme saget
> Jetzt werde Früling seyn.

I am unsure how to interpret Fleming's reference to the seasons in his final strophe; possibly he intends them simply to describe Leipzig in that awful year, but perhaps he means the reader to connect winter with death for those Frau Kuchen has left behind, and thus salvation and reunion with her. This would be an oddly laconic and unremittingly grim formulation of the common consolatory argument that the bereaved will eventually be reunited with the deceased.

69. See my "Gedichte von Paul Fleming in der Stolbergschen Leichenpredigten-Sammlung," p. 6, for information on the deceased contained in the funeral sermon to which this poem and others were appended.

70. Pyritz, *Paul Flemings Liebeslyrik*, p. 265. Lohmeier discusses *In Groß-Neugart der Reußen* (P.W.IV.20) extensively in "Paul Flemings poetische Bekenntnisse" and suggests (p. 356) that Fleming's stay in Novgorod in 1634 represented a significant turning point in his adoption of neo-Stoic ideas: "[W]enn man die häufige Wiederkehr stoischer Begriffe und Vorstellungen in seinen späteren Gedichten bedenkt, kann man den Eindruck gewinnen, als habe Fleming während seines Aufenthalts in Nowgorod tatsächlich eine Einsicht gewonnen oder sich eine zuvor nur angelernte Einsicht wirklich zu eigen gemacht, die ihn dann nicht mehr verlassen sollte."

71. Various dates are given for the wedding celebrated by this cycle, that of Agnes von Schönburg-Waldenburg and Christian von Schönburg-Wechselburg. Lappenberg apparently realized that his sometimes unreliable source, Hübner's *Tabellen*, erred in giving 1629; Conrad Müller, also sometimes shaky on dates, gives 1633 ("Paul Fleming und das Haus Schönburg," p. 14). It seems there is a real reason for some confusion, for while the wedding was apparently planned for May 1631 (and Fleming's cycle of epithalamia is

dated 1631 and clearly designates the season as spring), it was for some reason (illness seems most likely) delayed until 1632. See Schön, "Eine Schönburgische Hochzeitsfeier im Jahre 1632," p. 38. I am grateful to Heinz Entner for his assistance in clearing this up.

72. Lappenberg notes that Abraham Fleming received "unter dem 8. Mai 1615 die vom Consistorium zu Leipzig am 15. d. M. bestätigte Berufung an die Pfarre zu Topseiffersdorf" (Fleming, *Deutsche Gedichte*, p. 854). Franz Blanckmeister ("Aus Paul Flemings Vaterhaus") reports of the *Visitation* in 1617 that the visitor was Johannes Scheubner, pastor of Penig—an area subject, as far as I have been able to determine, to Saxon, not Schönburg, ecclesiastical sovereignty.

73. The Schönburg family still exists and continues to evoke eloquent recollection. Marie Vassiltchikov, in her *Berlin Diaries: 1940–1945* (London: Chatto & Windus, 1985), recalls Princess Eleanore-Marie Schönburg-Hartenstein, who, along with Vassiltchikov, was an active observer of the July 20th plot on Hitler's life. Vassiltchikov also has occasion to mention the scion, Count Franz-Felix von Schaffgotsch, of another house important to early seventeenth-century poets.

Chapter 2

1. Lappenberg reproduces the Latin version as Sy.IX.7, the German as P.W.IV.1. Citations will be taken from Lappenberg's editions.

2. "Assyria" is mentioned in the Latin version of the poem, "Syrien" in the German. "Syria" is already used in place of "Assyria" in classical texts.

3. My translation. The passage from *De Germania* is in chapter 33 of that work.

4. Dörrie, *Der heroische Brief*, pp. 469–70. The following discussion of the development of the genre is based on Dörrie's chapter "Mahn- und Sendschreiben" (pp. 431–82).

5. Rodenberg, "Paul Fleming und seine Rußlandreise," p. 236.

6. Varnhagen von Ense, "Paul Flemming," pp. 16 and 17.

7. Schlesinger, "Paul Fleming," p. 140.

8. For a survey of various types of seventeenth-century political poetry by both learned poets and broadsheet versifiers, with attention to the possible effects of censorship on airing partisan views, see Volker Meid's "Im Zeitalter des Barock."

9. Szyrocki, *Die deutsche Literatur des Barock*, p. 93.

10. See, for example, Georg Winter's *Geschichte des Dreißigjährigen Krieges*, p. 353ff. On propaganda during the war, see Diethelm Böttcher's "Propaganda und öffentliche Meinung im protestantischen Deutschland 1628-1636," esp. p. 333ff., on public opinion and propaganda relating to the Protestant response to the Edict of Restitution. See Harms et al., *Die Sammlung der Herzog August Bibliothek in Wolfenbüttel*, vol. 2, nos. 224, 225, and 259, for critical responses in broadsheets to the conference and Johann Georg's neutrality.

(References to sheets in this volume will hereafter follow its editors' practice of giving the volume number in roman followed by the arabic number assigned to the sheet, e.g., II: 224.)

11. Rudolf Alexander Schröder, another biographer of Fleming, similarly bemoans Fleming's having to witness the conference: "[E]r mußte das Jahr danach [1631] in Leipzig jenen kläglichen Fürstenkonvent erleben, der durch Lauheit und Untreue, an denen sein eigener Landesherr einen großen Teil der Mitschuld trug, den Fall des unglücklichen Magdeburg herbeiführen half und auf den es daher mit Recht Spottverse hagelte" ("Paul Fleming," p. 609). Schubert, who discusses the poem at some length, notes that the poem arose in connection with the conference but does not examine the implications of this fact (" 'Man wird mich nennen hören,' " p. 1690).

12. My account is based largely on C. V. Wedgwood's *The Thirty Years' War* and on the documents cited.

13. Böttcher, "Propaganda und öffentliche Meinung," p. 327. See also Harms et al., II: 214, a broadsheet printed for the occasion of the centenary. In it Elector Johann of Saxony is depicted presenting the text of the Confession of Augsburg to an eagle, representing the emperor, which hovers protectively over Luther.

14. *Copia vnd Abschrifft/ Des Churfürsten zu Sachsen Ausschreibens*, fol. A3r.

15. *Copia der Evangelischen Chur-Fürsten vnd Stände . . . Schreiben*, fols. B1v–B2r.

16. See Nischan, "Reformed Irenicism and the Leipzig Colloquy of 1631."

17. The Latin text (l. 90) speaks of foreigners in the plural and thus may refer to all three powers. Lappenberg, in his notes to the poem, says that the German text must refer to France; it is unclear to me why he thinks this to be the case.

18. The wordplay, "dolphin" for "[Gustav] Adolf," would seem an obvious one, but I have not encountered it in contemporary texts; the periphrastic names for the Swedish king generally draw upon the lion of his coat of arms and the northerly situation of his lands. In his only other reference to a dolphin in his German poems, in *An Herrn Johan Klipstein* (P.W.IV.15), Fleming mentions the fable of the poet Arion who, traveling by ship, was thrown overboard but rescued by a dolphin attracted to him by his singing. It may be this supposed characteristic of kindness in dolphins that prompted Fleming to make it, the "Menschenfreund," Germania's companion.

19. Pyritz (*Paul Flemings Liebeslyrik*, p. 61, n. 59) appears to be the only scholar to take explicit note of the irenic strain in Fleming's poetry, when he remarks in passing on Fleming's translation (Ü.30) of an epigram by the Polish Catholic neo-Latin poet Matthias Casimir Sarbievius, which Pyritz finds "für die auch sonst hervortretende irenische Haltung des Protestanten bezeichnend."

20. See the *Bibliographie der Sächsischen Geschichte*, ed. Rudolf Bemmann, vol. 1, half vol. 1, pp. 265–70. A selection of the writings composed for the occasion of the conference is found in the chapter "Der Konvent zu Leipzig. Die Zerstörung Magdeburgs" in the anthology *Der dreißigjährige Krieg:*

Eine Sammlung von historischen Gedichten und Prosadarstellungen, ed. Julius Opel and Adolf Cohn (pp. 192–236).

21. The poem for Johann Georg was unknown to Lappenberg. Wendelin von Maltzahn discovered an imprint of it and printed the text in his "Ein Gedicht von Paul Fleming." See also John Roger Paas, "Ergänzende Einzelheiten zu Paul Flemings deutschen Einblattdrucken."

22. The broadsheet is reproduced with commentary as II: 223 in Harms et al., *Die Sammlung der Herzog August Bibliothek in Wolfenbüttel*.

23. On Andreas Bretschneider III, see the article by A. Kurzwelly in the *Allgemeines Lexikon der bildenden Künstler*, ed. Ulrich Thieme and Felix Becker. On p. 159 of my "Ein Vorspiel zum Westfälischen Frieden," I incorrectly identified the artist as Daniel Brettschneider.

24. Karl August Müller, *Kurfürst Johann Georg der Erste, seine Familie und sein Hof*, p. 185. Rudel signs a poem appended (fol. H5v) to Hoe von Hoenegg's funeral sermon for Paul Laurentius "Elias Rüdelius, P. aulicus"; on p. 621 of the second volume of the *Katalog der fürstlich Stolberg-Stolberg'schen Leichenpredigten-Sammlung*, the abbreviation is resolved, perhaps erroneously, as "Hofprediger." There is a further version of Rudel's poem that, like Fleming's, includes the text in both Latin and German, without illustration; its title also recalls Fleming's: *Querela Europae, Ad diversos Imperii Germ. Proceres, Ordines, Status, de accepto membrorum suorum Vulnere & clade diffamata*.

25. See Harms et al., *Die Sammlung der Herzog August Bibliothek in Wolfenbüttel*, p. 392, on the iconography of Europa in this sheet. On the posture associated with the melancholic, see Panofsky, *Albrecht Dürer*, vol. 1, pp. 162–63 and vol. 2, figs. 210–14.

26. Wendelin von Maltzahn, "Ein Gedicht von Paul Fleming," p. 449, suggests that Fleming's own poem must have circulated as an illustrated broadsheet. This is, however, probably an error arising from the numbers that appear with this poem in the older editions. Maltzahn assumed they refer to numbered objects in a lost illustration, when in fact they signal Fleming's own notes to his text.

27. Krapf and Wagenknecht, *Stuttgarter Hoffeste*, vol. 2, illus. 42. The broadsheet, *Hertzliches Seufftzen vnnd Wehklagen* is reproduced with commentary as II:165 in Harms et al., *Die Sammlung der Herzog August Bibliothek in Wolfenbüttel*.

28. Rist's poem is reprinted on pp. 232–35 of Herbert Cysarz's *Vor- und Frühbarock*. Schottel's poem, *Lamentatio Germaniae Exspirantis: Der nunmehr hinsterbenden Nymphen Germaniae elendeste Todesklage*, was reprinted by Ernst Voss at the beginning of this century.

29. An example is the heroic epistle *Germania ad Caesarem Ferdinandum* by Georg Sabinus, in which, apparently for the first time, Germany appears as a speaker in a heroic epistle. See Dörrie, *Der heroische Brief*, p. 456.

30. Fleming's portrait of Germania resembles that of the Psalmist in lines 21–29 of his translation, also from 1631, of the sixth Psalm (P.W.I.1), suggesting either borrowing or simply a certain standard repertory in the portrayal of humans in extreme circumstances.

31. My account relies on Edgar Marsch's *Biblische Prophetie und chronographische Dichtung* and Werner Goeze's *Translatio Imperii*.
32. Lohenstein, *Afrikanische Trauerspiele*, p. 353.
33. Lappenberg dated Sy.II.1 "um 1630." Such an early date would make Stölten's argument more persuasive, as drawing attention to atrocities committed by the Imperials while Johann Georg was still bent on loyalty to the empire might call for courage grounded in conviction. However, an autograph copy of the poem in the Ratsschulbibliothek in Zwickau is dated August 2, 1631. I am preparing an edition of the manuscript.
34. Albert Bornemann, "Paul Fleming"; Jones, "The Mulde's 'Half-Prodigal Son.'"
35. Kroker, "Leipzig in Liedern und Gedichten des dreißigjährigen Krieges," p. 89.
36. Christenius(?), *Ernewerte Hirten-Lust*. The imprint is undated, but other epithalamia for the same couple give the date of 1634.
37. Joshua Rifkin et al., "Heinrich Schütz," pp. 7–8.

Chapter 3

1. There is some dispute over how best to designate this genre; see Maché, "Opitz's *Schäfferey*," pp. 36–37, n. 9. It seems simplest for my purposes to retain Opitz's own term.
2. Beling, *Verdeutschete Waldlieder*. On this work and its inspiration, see Erich Trunz's afterword to Opitz's *Weltliche Poëmata: Der Ander Theil*, p. 103*.
3. Olearius(?), *Angenemer Widerwille*. This poem for Bachmann (also called Rivinus), professor of poetry in Leipzig from 1635 to 1636, does not appear in the standard Olearius bibliographies. Hugo Hayn, in his *Bibliotheca Germanorum Nuptialis*, notes an epithalamium (no. 283) published in 1635 under a similar name ("Laurino d'Oliva") and indicates that he does not think it a pseudonym for Olearius. On "Corydon-Lieder," see Weevers, "The Influence of Heinsius," pp. 527–32; Ulrich Bornemann, *Anlehnung und Abgrenzung*, p. 89; and Waldberg, *Die deutsche Renaissance-Lyrik*, pp. 115–20. Heinsius's *Pastorael* (*Corydon die weyde schaepen*), mentioned in chapter 1 in connection with the form of Fleming's *Der klagende Bräutigam. II*, is the prototype of many German Corydon-Lieder; Opitz adapted it freely for his *Galathee* (*Coridon, der gieng betrübet*), the first poem in the "Oden oder Gesänge" of the 1625 edition of his poems (*Acht Bücher, Deutscher Poematum*). The *Angenemer Widerwille* retains the conventional opening description of a shepherd and a river, albeit in this case the Castalian Spring, and wordplays on the couple's names (*Berg*erin and *Bach*mann) replace the usual references to real rivers and specific locales. The epithalamium also retains the direct speech common in Corydon-Lieder, although normally the male voice is recognizable as that of the poet, whereas here it is the voice of the groom; the most interesting aspect of many Corydon-Lieder, the autobiographical, is thus absent.

4. Further information on these two imprints can be found in my "Leipzig Pastoral."

5. See Harper's "Ein neu aufgefundenes Frühwerk von Gottfried Finckelthaus?" and "Zur Opitz-Rezeption in Leipzig."

6. Garber places the novel in the context of the developing pastoral and discusses the question of authorship on p. 592 ff. of his "Martin Opitz' Schäfferey von der Nimfen Hercinie."

7. The main source of information about the journey is the *Vermehrte Newe Beschreibung Der Muscowitischen vnd Persisichen Reyse* of Adam Olearius, hereafter cited as *Reisebeschreibung*. Dieter Lohmeier, on pp. 9*-28* of his afterword to the 1971 reprint of the 1656 edition, offers a concise account of the journey. In the introduction to his translation of the parts of Olearius's work relevant to Russia, Samuel H. Baron also describes the expedition, with particular attention to Russia, but also to economics and the place the expedition occupied among the many European attempts to open the East to trade (*The Travels of Olearius in Seventeenth-Century Russia*). An account focused on Fleming's role in the expedition is offered by Lappenberg in Fleming, *Deutsche Gedichte*, p. 865ff.

8. On the history of Reval, see vol. 1 of Nottbeck and Neumann's *Geschichte und Kunstdenkmäler der Stadt Reval*.

9. There is a birthday or nameday poem for Fleming from a Katharina Temme and two other women; Katharina may be Dorothea's sister. See B.III.10.

10. See the entry for Brokmann in Recke and Napiersky's *Allgemeines Schriftsteller- und Gelehrten-Lexikon der Provinzen Livland, Esthland und Kurland*.

11. Brokmann wrote a *Carmen Alexandrinum Esthonicum ad leges Opitij poëticas compositum* for the wedding of Hans von Hövel and Margaretha Stahl in 1637.

12. Meyer, *Der deutsche Schäferroman*, pp. 23–24; Schaumann, *Zur Geschichte der erzählenden Schäferdichtung in Deutschland*, p. 20; Carnap, *Das Schäferwesen*, p. 22. Karl Otto, in his discussion of *Schäfereien* after *Hercinie*, mentions Fleming's briefly; see his introduction to Opitz's *Die Schäfferey von der Nimfen Hercinie*, pp. 28*-29*. Maché, "Opitz' Schäfferey," passes Fleming over in silence.

13. Maché, "Opitz' Schäfferey," p. 36, noted this tendency of Opitz's imitators to dispense with displays of encyclopedic learning.

14. Opitz, *Die Schäfferey von der Nimfen Hercinie*, p. 9. Citations from *Hercinie* are taken from Peter Rusterholz's edition.

15. Numbers refer to Lappenberg's continuous line numbering of all the verse in the work.

16. Maché, "Opitz' Schäfferey," p. 37, noted that imitators of Opitz's *Hercinie* consistently strove for greater thematic unity, but he overlooks Fleming when he says that Dorothea Eleonore von Rosenthal in her *Poetische Gedancken* of 1641 was the first to do this.

17. Included in the 1625, 1629, and 1644 editions of Opitz's works. See pp. 571–74 (pt. 2) of vol. 2 of Opitz, *Gesammelte Werke*.

18. Gellinek, *Die weltliche Lyrik des Martin Opitz*, p. 190.

19. Becker-Cantarino prints the letter and poem on pp. 196–97 of "Drei Briefautographen von Paul Fleming."
20. Garber, "Martin Opitz' *Schäfferey*," p. 551, discusses Opitz's use of a pastoral genre to celebrate a member of the nobility. With *Hercinie*, he says "wurde nun . . . die Brücke der Pastorale zum Hochadel geschlagen"; Fleming reverses the process.
21. Although the concept of realism is complex, my use of it here it does not necessitate arcane theoretical definitions; I simply mean what common sense tells us realism means. The portrayal of living men is realistic, that of nymphs is not.
22. Garber, "Martin Opitz' *Schäfferey*," p. 572, indicates, if I understand him correctly, that Nüßler and Venator are fellow Silesians. But this is mistaken, for while Nüßler was, like Opitz, Silesian, Venator was born and spent most of his life in the Palatinate. On Venator, see Volkmann's *Balthasar Venator*.
23. Although I have not been able to verify it, I would guess that a meeting of Opitz, Venator, Buchner, and Nüßler would have been similarly impossible. Perhaps Fleming was aware of this and playing upon it. In Opitz's work the characters seem so little individualized and too many passages of the work fantastic for the reader to entertain seriously the notion that the meeting might really have happened. In contrast, the pervading verisimilitude in P.W.III.6 permits Fleming to play with one of the few aspects of it which, for a hidden reason, renders the entirety impossible.
24. Maché, "Opitz' *Schäfferey*," p. 36, draws attention to the term "unerwartete Begebenheit." See p. 23 of Harsdörffer and Klaj's *Pegnesisches Schaefergedicht* (1644), where the phrase appears as "unverwartete Begebenheit"; Maché, p. 36, no. 7, indicates that Birken changed it to "unerwartete" in a revised edition.
25. Olearius's poetic interests have already been touched upon. In Fleming, *Deutsche Gedichte*, p. 869, Lappenberg reports that Pöhmer wrote in Olearius's *Stammbuch* in Moscow on October 29, 1634, and that he quoted a few verses from Opitz's *Vielgut* and assured Olearius that he loved "te et omnes vere Opitianos."
26. Olearius's and Pöhmer's interest in poetry has been mentioned. Polus was a poet laureate, and an ode by him for Fleming is preserved (B.III.20).
27. Garber, *Der locus amoenus*, p. 114.
28. Garber, "Martin Opitz' *Schäfferey*," p. 570, points out that the praise of "die einfache, ständisch niedrig gestellte, aber tugendhafte Geliebte" is common in seventeenth-century pastoral. Opitz's contemporaries, however, found his insistence upon his beloved's simplicity worth remarking on, even making fun of; Finckelthaus's parody is discussed below. Fleming, as will be shown, did not feel constrained by the pastoral genre to depict a woman from a lower class. The fact that the genre did not absolutely require a lower-class woman, the insistently apologetic tone of Opitz's assertions relating to her, and the fact that the beloved's class was irrelevant to the lengthy discussion of Platonic love suggest that an extraliterary factor was involved in Opitz's choosing to portray such a woman, namely, that the woman actually

existed. Garber opposes the introduction of this biographical dimension and twice asserts that Opitz's beloved was fictional (see pp. 567 and 577). While there is good reason to be cautious about interpretations involving the interplay of highly conventionalized literature and little-known historical figures, it is worth noting a certain lack of consistency in the exercise of this caution. Garber does not hesitate to make statements about *Hercinie* based on the biography of Opitz's patron, while denying the very existence of the beloved. There is a male bias built into the documentation of figures in this period—men were more likely to leave records than women. The documentary bias is compounded when a critic privileges absolutely reference to the lives of the well-documented, that is, men, while denying all validity to reference to those whose very existence can at times only be surmised from nondocumentary sources.

29. Lappenberg, following the Leipzig imprint of this work, prints "der rechte Liebe Lohn" in the *Deutsche Gedichte*, while the Reval imprint, which he did not know, has "der rechten Liebe Lohn." On the Reval imprint see pp. 177–79 of my "Neues zu Paul Fleming."

30. Anthony Harper kindly supplied me with a microfilm of the Wrocław University Library copy of *Floridans Lob- vnd LiebesGedichte* and in a letter pointed out another copy in the library of the University of North Carolina at Chapel Hill.

31. Harper, in introducing this newfound *Schäferei*, quite rightly pointed to its derivation from Opitz's *Hercinie* and points to several of the parodies, in the technical sense, of Opitzian poems ("Ein neu aufgefundenes Frühwerk von Gottfried Finckelthaus," pp. 116–18). In the brief space available to him, he did not discuss their humorous side. Harper also suggests that Finckelthaus may have known Fleming's *Schäferei* for Brokmann, as similar phrases appear in the two works. This may, however, merely reflect their common model, *Hercinie*. The phrases "das Dorf gieng auf das Feld" (Fleming) and "das Dorff war in dem Feld" (Finckelthaus) probably derive from the poem towards the end of *Hercinie* in which Opitz's three friends alternately speak; Buchner says "Das dorff geht auff das feldt." That Finckelthaus could have known Fleming's work is not in dispute; P.W.III.6 appeared initially in Reval in 1635 but was reprinted the same year in Leipzig. The references to it in Martin Rinckart's *Die Müllerin-Stimme* from that year (B.I. in Fleming's *Deutsche Gedichte*) and in a hitherto overlooked *Schäferei* from 1636, *Auff den NahmensTag . . . H. Johann Kostens/ Vnd H. Johann Schäffers* by Johannes Bohemus (which borrows from both Opitz and Fleming), suggest it was widely and well received. Perhaps Fleming's friend Hartmann Grahmann took a copy of the Reval printing with him when he returned to Germany in May 1635 and had it reprinted for circulation in Saxony.

32. No. 116 in the 1624 *Poemata*. It also appeared in the later editions of Opitz's poems, where, after 1625, the refrain is altered slightly. Finckelthaus evidently knew the poem in its earlier form. Waldberg, *Die deutsche Renaissance-Lyrik*, p. 120ff., discusses the many poems written in imitation of this one.

33. See also Berent, *Die Auffassung der Liebe bei Opitz und Weckherlin und ihre geschichtlichen Vorstufen.* Summarizing his examination of Opitz's poetry against the background of what is known of his life, Berent writes that Opitz sees "in der Liebe letztlich eine zerstörerische Macht" (p. 159).

34. In thus projecting his own fears onto the female sex, Opitz participated, wittingly or otherwise, in a traditional understanding of women, witches, and witchcraft descending in part from the *Malleus Maleficarum*, the work, published in 1487 by Henricus Institoris and Jacobus Sprenger at the instigation of Pope Innocent VIII, that launched the witch-hunting craze in Europe. Although ostensibly directed against persons of either sex in league with the devil, most of the tract (as foreshadowed in the title) focuses on women and is obsessed with asserting (or reasserting, as the authors view the situation) male control over all aspects of procreation. The many passages in which the authors attribute to women nearly unlimited ability to control the male sex organs make explicit the origins of the paranoia that reappears in a more generalized form in Opitz. These passages would be laughable, had they not actually been given credence and acted upon. Whether Opitz himself actually believed in witches is less important than his attitude towards women, which shows the lingering influence of the beliefs codified by Institoris and Sprenger.

35. See Huebner, *Das erste deutsche Schäferidyll*, pp. 86–96, on Opitz's sources for this scene.

36. Most discussions of *Hercinie* are in any case small parts of larger works on the pastoral or on Opitz and are generally descriptive rather than interpretive. Even given these restrictions, it is remarkable how little attention is paid to the significance of the encounter with the witch. Carnap, in his discussion of *Hercinie* on pp. 18–21 of *Das Schäferwesen*, makes no reference at all to it, while Meyer refers to it only briefly for its borrowing from Theocritus (*Der deutsche Schäferroman*, p. 22). Schaumann mentions it simply to illustrate the fact that "zu den Requisiten der Gattung gehören Geistererscheinungen" (*Zur Geschichte der erzählenden Schäferdichtung*, p. 14). Huebner's initial synopsis of the plot of *Hercinie* (*Das erste deutsche Schäferidyll*, p. 17) ignores the witch, and he does not include the encounter with her among the *Hauptmomente* of the work (p. 20). Beyond seeking its sources—no small task, and admirably done—he is interested in the episode only in relation to the question of whether a person of Opitz's education in that age would have believed in witches. Bernhard Ulmer, in *Martin Opitz*, similarly examines the episode only for the light it sheds, or does not shed, on Opitz's belief in witches (pp. 135–37). Gellinek (*Die weltliche Lyrik des Martin Opitz*, p. 170) notes only that the scene upsets the equilibrium Opitz had achieved with the song "Ist mein Hertze gleich verliebet." Otto does not discuss it in his introduction to the reprint. The brief evaluations of the episode offered by Rusterholz in his afterword to his edition of the work and by Garber in "Martin Opitz' *Schäfferey*" are discussed below.

37. Garber, "Martin Opitz' *Schäfferey*," p. 572.

38. The Reval imprint has "deiner recht geniessen" in the second to last

line; Lappenberg's sources, the Leipzig imprint and the *Teütsche Poemata*, have "dich allein besitzen."

39. Garber, "Martin Opitz' *Schäfferey*," p. 572.

40. For example, Floridan: "Denn mir bewust/ daß sie nicht allein öffters jhre Wangen/ sondern auch die Worte also anzustreichen wissen/ daß sie den/ so jhres Sinnes nicht recht kündig/ durch jhre eusserliche Wörterschönheiten leichtlich herumb führen können" (*Floridans Lob- vnd LiebesGedichte*, fol. E3r). Compare Venator: "So bist du in aller zeiten historien vndt exempeln dermaßen durchtrieben/ daß du wol weißest/ wie das frawenzimmer nicht allein offtmals die wangen/ sondern auch die worte zue färben pfleget/ vndt daß kein waßer geschwinder eintrucknet als weiberthrenen" (*Hercinie*, p. 24). Floridan: "Wilstu aber so recht bey jhnen antreffen/ so mustu die Vernunfft zu Geferten haben" (fol. E3v). Venator: "Wilt du sehen was schönheit ist/ so mußt du die augen der vernunfft zue rhate nemen" (p. 16).

41. Finckelthaus does not indicate the source of the tale, but it seems unlikely that it originated with him.

42. In "Imitations Petrarch: Opitz, Fleming," Stephen Zon offers a detailed and sensitive analysis of how Opitz's and Fleming's sonnets differ from Petrarch's and from one another's. A minor problem arises in Zon's interpretation of the closing lines of Fleming's poems due to his neglect of the context provided by P.W.III.6 and a misprint ("neuer" for "neue") in his text of Fleming's poem. Fleming is, indeed, challenging Opitz's poem, but he is not "issuing in turn still another challenge to *any* 'neuer Freier' " (p. 510, my emphasis), but rather precisely to the bridal couple ("neue Freier") whose wedding P.W.III.6 celebrates. The emphasis is less on Polus's/Fleming's failure to define love and defiant challenge to others to do better, than on the implication that only those whose emotions (and not just their intellects) are engaged will be able to offer any approximation of an answer.

43. Günther Müller, *Geschichte des deutschen Liedes*, p. 74.

44. Pyritz, *Paul Flemings Liebeslyrik*, p. 278. Subsequent page references to Pyritz given in the text will be to this work.

45. This passage, which Alewyn cites on p. 442 of "Hans Pyritz," can be found on p. 287 of Pyritz, *Paul Flemings Liebeslyrik*.

46. Fechner, "Paul Fleming," p. 380.

47. See, for example, two major postwar literary histories, the respective volumes on the baroque from the West and East German *Geschichten der deutschen Literatur von den Anfängen bis zur Gegenwart*, which follow Pyritz in asserting that Fleming overcame (Petrarchan) tradition in his love poetry and arrived at a new form of natural or personal poetry: Newald, *Die deutsche Literatur vom Späthumanismus zur Empfindsamkeit 1570–1750*, p. 188, and Joachim G. Boeckh et al., *Geschichte der deutschen Literatur 1600 bis 1700*, p. 213. The latter, curiously, chose to illustrate this overcoming of tradition and assertion of "naturhaft volkstümliche Töne" with a passage from O.V.11 that is unmistakably Petrarchan. Most students of seventeenth-century literature today, in the wake of the studies by Dyck, Barner, and others, agree that Pyritz's portrayal of Fleming's development is flawed, but besides Fechner's recent study there has been little in the way of explicit revision in the rather

sparse Fleming literature. Ferdinand Ambacher also sought to show the limitations of Pyritz's view in his not widely received dissertation, "Paul Fleming and 'Erlebnisdichtung' "; the study suffers from being overly formalistic. See also Krahé's study, "Persönlicher Ausdruck in der literarischen Konvention."

48. Schlesinger, "Paul Fleming," p. 136.

49. Some or all of the epicedia may have been paid for. There is little concrete evidence indicating whether Fleming was remunerated for his poems. Fechner suggests ("Paul Fleming," p. 368) that Fleming's father's funeral sermons provided occasions for Fleming to earn money by writing epicedia, which seems not unlikely. However, there are no records that prove it unequivocally. In any case, only a single funeral sermon by Abraham Fleming is known; see my "Neues zu Paul Fleming," pp. 173–74. Only a single known imprint with a poem by Fleming makes reference to the source of financing; this is one containing Sy.V.1, an epicedium for King Gustav Adolf. The imprint, *Threnologiae Super obitum . . . Dn. Gustavi Adolphi*, which was unknown to Lappenberg, has on its title page the phrase "Excusae Lipsiae Impensis Eliae Rehefeldii"; Elias Rehefeld's was one of the major Leipzig presses.

50. The following description of the Thomasschule in this period is based on Otto Kaemmel's *Geschichte des Leipziger Schulwesens* and vol. 1 of Rudolf Wustmann's *Musikgeschichte Leipzigs*.

51. Wustmann, *Musikgeschichte Leipzigs*, p. 98.

52. Günther Müller, *Geschichte des deutschen Liedes*, p. 73. Gerald Gillespie, *German Baroque Poetry*, p. 68, points to a chorus (end of act II) of *Il Pastor fido* as the source of the subject matter of this poem. In *Die Lyrik des Andreas Gryphius*, Victor Manheimer notes, p. 130, that Johannes Plavius's epithalamium *Der blinde Cupido* may have suggested Fleming's phrasing and rhythm; his *Auff hn. Jochim Flato vnd fraw Marien Linderhausen hochzeit* might similarly have served as a model. These appear on pp. 73–74 and 62, respectively, of Heinz Kindermann's *Danziger Barockdichtung*. Kindermann notes, p. 24, that Plavius was, like Fleming, from Vogtland. The connection between Fleming and the neglected Plavius or their common sources might be of interest. In *Poetry and Song in the German Baroque*, R. Hinton Thomas, like Müller, states in passing (p. 21) in his chapter on Schein that the musicality of some of Fleming's verse derived from contact with Schein. Thomas also makes the reverse of the usual argument about the Fleming-Schein connection, suggesting that Fleming "may have deepened Schein's knowledge of poetry" (ibid.). This is possible, but as Fleming probably did not seriously take up German poetry until he came into contact with university students after he had left the Thomasschule (1628), and thus quite late in Schein's career, it seems unlikely that Fleming would have been a major influence, at least on Schein's German verse.

53. Brauer, "Jakob Regnart, Johann Hermann Schein und die Anfänge der deutschen Barocklyrik," p. 401.

54. There are two possible exceptions: Fleming's amphibrachic O.V.3, *Auf die Italiänische Weise: O fronte serena*, resembles formally Schein's *Mit Freuden, mit Scherzen* (*Musica boscareccia*, pt. 3, no. 10), although Fleming retains amphibrachs in the fifth and tenth lines where Schein changes to iambs.

Fleming's title suggests an Italian source, possibly common to both songs. Supersaxo, *Die Sonnette Paul Flemings*, p. 121, notes that So.IV.1 uses the same verse lines as a poem by Schein, *O Amarilli zart* (printed on p. 99 of vol. 1 of Cysarz, *Barocklyrik*; originally a separate imprint, it became no. 12 of the *Diletti pastorali*); the overall forms, however, are different (sonnet and madrigal).

55. Part 2 of Unger, *Studien über Paul Flemings Lyrik* (pp. 30–47). A potentially important formal difference between the poems of Fleming and those of Schein is immediately apparent: Fleming uses trochaic forms in about two-thirds of his odes; his iambic ones tend to be stiff; Schein consistently used an iambic line.

56. Texts and music are printed in the *Sämtliche Werke*, edited by Arthur Prüfer, and the *Neue Ausgabe sämtlicher Werke*, edited by Adam Adrio. Unfortunately, neither offers a critical edition of the texts; this remains a *desideratum* of German literary scholarship. I cite Schein's poems from Prüfer's edition.

57. Opitz's poem is no. 8 in the 1624 *Poemata*. A comparison of these three poems by Schein, Opitz, and Fleming is instructive. Although the subject matter is death of unrequited love, Schein's poem nonetheless has playful overtones, with imploring, sometimes almost blackmailing entreaties of Corydon for a "Schmätzelein" from Filli's "Lippelein." Schein interrupts Corydon's plaint by introducing a brief response from Filli in the final strophe. Despite the fact that she tells Corydon she cares not if he dies, her introduction undermines the emotional intensity of the preceding lament by reminding one that it is but a play being acted out. A less than deadly serious element is also present in the slyly suggested hope that Filli will finally be brought to kiss the lips of Corydon when he is dead—and that even then not all hope (for him) will be lost. Opitz's poem—an early one—is unsatisfactory because it is wordy and repetitive. But it is not artless immaturity that makes the humanist poet describe the consequences of death at the beloved's hands well before the end of the poem. By introducing this topic two-thirds of the way through, he is able to talk at length of having ensured his everlasting fame before his death through his poems carved on trees and his grave inscription. Fleming's poem is much more tightly constructed than Opitz's; he avoids *insistierende Nennung* and instead skillfully employs rhetorical devices such as gradatio and anaphora. By concentrating on the persona's precisely and vividly expressed complaint, rather than using dialogue or digressing to the topic of fame, Fleming endows his lover with a greater sense of urgency and single-mindedness; any playfulness is that of highly intellectual wit, not the arcadian whimsy and naïveté of Schein.

58. See, for example, nos. 69, 75, 82, 102 in Hoffmann von Fallersleben's *Die deutschen Gesellschaftslieder*.

59. Käte Lorenzen's apparently similar conclusion in her article on Paul Fleming in *Musik in Geschichte und Gegenwart* has had little resonance in Fleming scholarship: "Seltsamerweise wurde [Fleming] nicht von seinem verehrten Lehrer, . . . Schein . . . , in seiner Dichtweise bestimmt, sondern

sah Opitz als Vater der deutschen Dichtung überhaupt wie auch der eigenen an" (col. 306). The brevity of Lorenzen's discussion and her focus on the indisputable greater importance of Opitz for Fleming makes it difficult to assess how entirely she rejects Schein's influence.

60. The presence of minor *Gesellschaftslied* motifs in Fleming's poetry argue for his indebtedness to the tradition. *Basilene* (O.V.24) begins "Eine hab' ich mir erwälet"; in *An Elsabe* (O.V.31) he says "Mein Herze, das sich itzt so quält, / hat dich und keine sonst erwält" (ll. 23–24); in *Anemone* (O.V.37) he calls Anna Niehus "Auserwählte nach der einen" (l. 1). Similar phrases are frequent in *Gesellschaftslieder*; see nos. 23, 60, 106, and 112 in Hoffmann von Fallersleben, *Die deutschen Gesellschaftslieder*.

61. Dürrenfeld, "Paul Fleming und Johann Christian Günther," p. 52; Unger, *Studien über Paul Flemings Lyrik*, p. 9.

62. Grunaeus's poem is printed with a translation in Schnur, *Lateinische Gedichte deutscher Humanisten*, pp. 182–83.

63. The passage is from chapter 18 of Cicero's *De amicitia*; text and translation are here cited from pp. 174–75 of *De senectute, De amicitia, De divinatione*.

64. Heinz Wilms, "Das Thema der Freundschaft in der deutschen Barocklyrik und seine Herkunft aus der neulateinischen Dichtung des 16. Jahrhunderts"; see esp. p. 62ff. and pp. 101–5.

65. This is one of the epigrams Opitz offers as a model in the *Aristarchus*. See p. 70 of vol. 1 of Opitz, *Gesammelte Werke*.

66. Lappenberg dated this ode and its dedicatory epigram (E.X.3) 1632, but an imprint listed by Ernst Kroker in the *Bibliotheca Societatis Teutonicae* bears the date 1633, as do several other works written for this occasion. One of these, the *Continuation der jüngst beschehenen . . . Hirten-Lust* by Martin Christenius(?), mentioned at the beginning of this chapter, includes a brief biography of the groom.

67. Another epithalamium for Steyer by "Mauritius Schinstern" (probably Martin Christenius) listed by Hayn in his *Bibliotheca Germanorum Nuptialis* indicates that Steyer had become "Der Kirchen zu S. Salvator in Breßlaw Pfarrer."

68. First reprinted on pp. 113–17 of my "Paul Fleming." In two instances (strophes 1 and 16) I have added apostrophes which, due to the quality of the microfilm, I was unsure of when preparing the text for the *Michigan Germanic Studies* article; the period at the end of strophe 17 is correct.

69. The belief that love need not be bound by geography probably goes back to Renaissance ideas of friendship, perhaps as influenced by neo-Stoicism, with its insistence that the properly tranquil mind is everywhere at home. There is a passage in *Hercinie* in which Venator expresses this sentiment; the difficulty of determining whether he is actually speaking of male friendship, as much of the phrasing implies, or love between man and woman, as the context would call for, points once again to the frequent transfer from one sphere to the other: "Wie nun freylich ein freundt ein lebendiger schatz ist/ der lange gesucht/ kaum gefunden/ vndt schwerlich verwahret wirdt: so ist doch die vngefärbte liebe an keinen ort gebunden/ vndt jhre ab-

wesenheit wirdt zum theil durch das gedächtniß voriger gesellschafft/ zum theil durch schreiben/ welches die rechten fußstapffen vndt kennezeichen trewer gemüter sindt/ nicht wenig erträglicher gemacht" (p. 23). It is characteristic of the two poets that Opitz (or Venator) gives practical advice about maintaining a friendship over distance, while Fleming invokes reciprocated love as the sign of one's true home and the exchange of selves as that which maintains troth during separation.

70. Joseph Leighton ("The Poet's Voices in Occasional Baroque Poetry") and Barton W. Browning ("The Poet Addresses Himself") explore, inter alia, a related topic: the reasons why the speaker in Fleming's poems so often strikes the modern reader as individualized and realistic, and thus exceptional in seventeenth-century German poetry. Both Leighton and Browning presented strong arguments that this particular impression, when examined closely within the context of seventeenth-century literary conventions, proves to be grounded more in the expectations of the modern reader than in Fleming's poetry itself.

Chapter 4

1. Gervinus, *Geschichte der poetischen National-Literatur*, pt. 3, p. 238: "Diese Reise . . . nahm ihm den Gelehrtendünkel"; Goedeke, *Elf Bücher Deutscher Dichtung*, vol. 1, p. 292: "Sein Vaterland liebte vielleicht kein Dichter jener Zeit inniger als Fleming, trotz der Flucht aus demselben, die ihn vor der Erstarrung in der Schulweisheit der Zeitgenossen glücklich bewahrte."

2. Ambacher, "Paul Fleming and 'Erlebnisdichtung,' " pp. 159–61, explicitly disagrees with Pyritz's contention. See also Krahé, "Persönlicher Ausdruck in der literarischen Konvention," pp. 486–93, on the journey and on how literary critics have understood the importance of the journey. On p. 491 he concludes: "Der Gewinn für Flemings Dichtung dürfte vielmehr in dem Zuwachs an Themen liegen, den der Verlauf des Unternehmens allein äußerlich bot, und in der formalen Konzentration und Erfüllung literarischer Ideale der Zeit . . . als in einer Steigerung des individuellen Ausdrucks."

3. Beller, "Thema, Konvention und Sprache der mythologischen Ausdrucksformen in Paul Flemings Gedichten," p. 177. Beller speculates that Fleming may actually have felt it incumbent upon him in the small world constituted by the embassy to play the role of representative humanist poet even more intensively than he would have in Europe.

4. Boeckh et al., *Geschichte der deutschen Literatur 1600 bis 1700*, p. 208, seem to have overlooked this aspect of the expedition: "Die Lösung aus den heimatlichen gesellschaftlichen Bedingungen enthob ihn frühzeitig davon, sich mit den feudalen Verhältnissen in Deutschland auseinanderzusetzen; als Angehöriger der Reisegesellschaft und als Gast im Ausland lebte er unter anderen Bedingungen."

5. Compare *Hofordnungen* for other German courts of the period in Kern, *Deutsche Hofordnungen*.

6. Boeckh et al., *Geschichte der deutschen Literatur 1600–1700*, p. 207, say "Die Aufgaben, die Fleming im Dienste der Reisegesellschaft zu erfüllen hatte, waren von geringer Bedeutung." If the reference is to nonceremonial duties, these scholars overlook Fleming's leadership of the Novgorod contingent of the expedition in 1634, while at the same time implying more knowledge of Fleming's other nonceremonial duties in general than actually exists. If the reference is to the ceremonial duties outlined in the *Hofordnung*, it is incorrect: these were an essential part of court etiquette. That Fleming waited at table and carved has been taken as proof of his "ziemlich untergeordnete Stellung" (Rost, "Paul Fleming," p. 166). This betrays the modern perspective, for to be given these duties at court in the Middle Ages or the baroque era was a mark of distinction. One need only read the listing, by rank, of members of the expedition in Olearius's *Reisebeschreibung*, pp. 56–59, to see that Fleming's position was just beneath the officers of highest rank.

7. The problems involved in determining which of Opitz's and Fleming's poems are poetic epistles are discussed below.

8. Wilms, "Das Thema der Freundschaft," p. 167.

9. Du Bellay, *La Deffence et Illustration de la Langue Françoyse*, p. 116.

10. For a detailed discussion of these sources see part 1 of my "Opitz, Fleming, and the German Poetic Epistle."

11. Sebillet, for example, says "Prens donc l'élégie pour epistre Amoureuse" (*L'Art poétique françoys*, p. 155).

12. Ibid., p. 154.

13. Petrarch, *Rerum familiarum libri*, pp. 10–11.

14. Conrady, *Lateinische Dichtungstradition*, p. 183.

15. See pp. 74–89 of my "Martin Opitz, Paul Fleming, and the German Poetic Epistle" and pp. 527–31 of my "Martin Opitz and the Tradition of the Renaissance Poetic Epistle."

16. The two poems are printed on pp. 32–36 of Opitz's *Weltliche Poëmata: Der Ander Theil*. *An Nüßlern*, which was included in the fourth book of *Wälder*, "Darinnen Liebesgedicht der Ersten Jugendt begriffen sind," in the *Weltliche Poëmata: Der Ander Theil*, is also very epistlelike insofar as it contains extended, ostensibly autobiographical, musings. These turn out, however, to be less spontaneous than they initially appear, as they are prompted by and provide a contrast to Opitz's description of Nüßler's future wedded life; parts of the poem were explicitly offered as an epithalamium for Nüßler and his bride. See pp. 325–26 (pt. 1) and pp. 646–52 (pt. 2) of vol. 2 of Opitz, *Gesammelte Werke*.

17. For a more extended discussion of these poems, see pp. 90–135 of my "Martin Opitz, Paul Fleming, and the German Poetic Epistle" and my "Martin Opitz and the Tradition of the Renaissance Poetic Epistle."

18. Determining which of Fleming's poems he and his contemporaries would have regarded as poetic epistles involves essentially the same process as that entailed in defining the corpus of Opitz's efforts in this genre: that is, it requires seeking longer nonoccasional poems written in alexandrines or *vers communs* to another person of approximately the same social class as

Fleming himself. This eliminates such poems as P.W.IV.45 which, though charming for its informality and seeming spontaneity, is one in which the occasion (Hieronymus Imhof's nameday) places definite limits on the range of topics that can be treated in it and the extent to which Fleming can speak of himself. P.W.IV.53, written to Hartmann Grahmann, would have been recognizable to Fleming's contemporaries as belonging to a very special class of occasional poem, the hodoeporicon, or travel-description poem. P.W.IV.2, 52, and 54 are written to members of the high nobility and thus lack the informality of the friendly letter; P.W.IV.15, 21, and 31, though written to persons closer to Fleming's own social class, are essentially panegyrics and have little of Fleming himself in them. P.W.IV.20 and 48, while discursive and reflexive, lack addressees.

19. Fleming, *Deutsche Gedichte*, pp. 715, 883, and 888.

20. Wilms, "Das Thema der Freundschaft," p. 161; Lohmeier, afterword to Olearius, *Reisebeschreibung*, p. 6*; Supersaxo, *Die Sonette Paul Flemings*, p. 116.

21. See pp. 169–83 of my "Martin Opitz, Paul Fleming, and the German Poetic Epistle" for detailed consideration of this question.

22. Lipsius, *Von der Bestendigkeit*, fols. 11v–12r.

23. Lines 19–32 are striking enough to have been anthologized as though a single poem. See Demetz and Jackson, *An Anthology of German Literature*, p. 263.

24. Cicero, *De amicitia*, p. 188 (21.80). See Wilms, "Das Thema der Freundschaft," esp. 101–8, on the classical and Renaissance theory of friendship.

25. See the bibliography for Olearius in Dünnhaupt's *Bibliographisches Handbuch*, nos. 14, 18, and 30, and Lohmeier's bibliography of Olearius appended to Olearius, *Reisebeschreibung*, independent publications nos. 11 and 24.

26. Brüggemann figures in Olearius's and Lappenberg's accounts, and thus in most later secondary literature, as the villain of the expedition. Even in a brief account of the journey in his "absonderlich Hirten Gespräch" appended to Oswald Beling's *Verdeutschete Waldlieder* (mentioned at the beginning of chapter 3), Olearius takes the opportunity to allude to what he clearly felt to have been the justified prosecution of Brüggemann in Duke Friedrich's courts: "Als nach 6. Erndten Zeit ich bin nach Hauß gekommen/ | Hat mich der fromme Herr in seinen Schutz genommen/ | Vnd meinen Feind erlegt/" (ll. 77–79). Paul Johansen ("Der Dichter Paul Fleming und der Osten," p. 42) and Dieter Lohmeier (afterword to Olearius, *Reisebeschreibung*, p. 27*) point out that the sources of information for Brüggemann's character and actions are one-sided. Baron offers a more judicious account than most and draws upon extensive source material.

27. Dürrenfeld, "Paul Fleming und Johann Christian Günther," p. 171.

28. Plutarch, *Table-Talk*, 9.14.746. Cited by Comes, *Mythologie*, p. 787.

29. Quintilian, *Institutio oratoria*, pp. 470–71 (3.7.15).

30. See Tropsch, *Flemings Verhältnis zur römischen Dichtung*, p. 104.

31. Vives, *De conscribendis epistolis* (1536), vol. 2, p. 291; Cicero as quoted by Lipsius in his *Epistolica Institutio*, p. 9; see also Cicero's *Ad Quintum Fratrem*, p. 68 (2.9).

32. Alewyn, *Vorbarocker Klassizismus und griechische Tragödie*, p. 43.

33. "Maisan": Moriz Heyne in his article on "Meisan" in Grimms' *Deutsches Wörterbuch*, for which this passage and P.W.IV.46, l. 48 ("so must' auch der Meisan von Grund' aus mitte fort") supply the sole witnesses, gives the definition "vordersegel eines schiffes." I believe he has been misled by his reliance on the earlier article "Focke," which cites Fleming, So.III.41, l. 1 ("Mach nun die Focke voll und schwängre den Meisan"), and which adduces the evidence of the French cognate "misaine." The *Oxford English Dictionary* points out the divergent usages of the cognate terms in Italian, English, and French, noting that the agreement of Italian and English usage (aftermost mast or its sail) suggests that the French (foresail or foremast) is not the original. Fleming seems to have used the word in the sense "foresail" in So.III.41, but in the English sense of "mizzen" in the other two places. The *Reisebeschreibung* supplies confirmation: on p. 72, Olearius, describing the first shipwreck (to which Fleming is referring in P.W.IV.46, l. 48), says that "ehe wir es uns versahen/ zerbrach mit erschrecklichen Krachen der grosse Mast sampt der Maisan"; p. 77 supplies an illustration with the ship, originally a three-master, now possessed of only the foremast and half of the main. On p. 402 there is a similar passage about the second shipwreck (which Fleming is describing in P.W.IV.49); Olearius exclaims at the passengers' good fortune at not being injured when the mainmast broke in three pieces and went overboard with the "Maysan," for most of them were at the time huddled about the "Maysan." One can discern in the illustration of this moment (on the same page) a group of figures grouped around the aftmost mast.

34. Lines 11–14 of *Auff Herrn Johann Mayers vnd Jungfraw Margarethen Gierlachin Hochzeit*, which was included in the 1625, 1629, and 1644 editions of Opitz's works. See p. 585 (pt. 2) of vol. 2 of Opitz, *Gesammelte Werke*.

35. See Curtius, *European Literature and the Latin Middle Ages*, p. 95; see also pp. 192–93 and 195–200 on the *locus amoenus*.

36. On Olearius's landscape description, see p. 51* of Lohmeier's afterword to Olearius, *Reisebeschreibung*.

37. Recounted in Chapter 14 of Seneca's *De tranquillitate animi*, p. 232.

38. Jones, examining Fleming's attitude to his decision to leave Germany, says that in this poem Fleming "transcends the conventional attitude of the stoic and speaks directly of his own feelings. . . . Fleming expresses profound doubts, not only about the value of travelling and his decision to leave Germany, but also about his own stoicism" ("The Mulde's 'Half-Prodigal Son,' " p. 133). Jones cites lines 19–44 as illustration. Such a reading fails to perceive that lines 29–33 ("ich dachte: Laß es fahren, / gib alles hin für dich! Kanst du dich nur ersparen, / so hastu satt an dir"), projected as interior dialogue, do not represent neo-Stoic thoughts endorsed by a younger self that later proved of dubious value, but rather the older man's portrait of his failure when younger to grasp the true sense of the neo-Stoic belief in the self. In the passage Jones cites, Fleming portrays himself as a sort of object lesson without making the moral explicit, for this was unnecessary. Just as the contemporary reader of his seascape description in *An einen seiner vertrautesten*

Freunde (P.W.IV.49) would perceive from the Petrarchan imagery in that passage that the seascape had some metaphorical relationship to Fleming's romantic problems, so would that same reader perceive the ironic difference between the young Fleming's concept of self and the Stoic's and would also recognize the travel motif and relate it to what thinkers like Lipsius had said on that subject. Far from expressing skepticism about neo-Stoic values in P.W.IV.51, Fleming suggests that it was precisely his failure to heed them that brought him to this pass.

39. Deissmann, "Prolegomena zu den biblischen Briefen und Episteln," pp. 187–252.

40. Luck, "Brief und Epistel in der Antike."

41. See Bernhard Coppel, "Marginalien zu dichterischen Berührungspunkten zwischen Petrus Lotichius Secundus und C. Valerius Catullus."

42. Wilkins, "Petrarch's *Epistola Metrica* to Pietro Alighieri."

43. Scaliger, *Poetices libri septem*, p. 168.

Epilogue

1. On the thesis, see my "Paul Fleming's Inaugural Disputation in Medicine."

Works Cited

Primary Literature

Abschied/ Deß zu Leipzig/ von den Evangelischen Protestirenten Chur-Fürsten/ Ständten vnd Herrn Abgesandten/ gehaltenen/ vnd den 2. Aprilis dieses 1631. Jahrs/ geschlossenen Convent-Tags. N.p.: n.p., [1631]. (Herzog August Bibliothek, Wolfenbüttel: 50.9 Pol [30].)

Bebel, Heinrich. *Commentaria epistolarum conficiendarum.* 1503. (University Library, Münster: Coll. Erh. 406.)

Beling, Oswald. *Verdeutschete Waldlieder/ Oder 10. Hirten Gespräche Des allerfürtrefflichsten Lateinisch: Poeten Virg. Marons/ . . . .* Edited by Adam Olearius. Hamburg: Johann Naumann, 1649. (Faber du Faur no. 341.)

Den Bloem-Hof van de Nederlantsche Ieught. 1608 and 1610. Edited by L. M. Van Dis and Jac. Smit. Amsterdam and Antwerp: Wereld-Bibliotheek, 1955.

Bohemus, Johannes. *Auff den NahmensTag Der WolEhrenvesten/ Großachtbarn/ Hochgelahrten vnd Hochweisen/ H. Johann Kostens/ Vnd H. Johann Schäffers/ Beyder Rathsmeister/ etc. in Hall. Vberschicket dieses AnbindGedichte/ zu sonderlichen Ehren M. Johann. Bohemus/ den 24. Junij 1636.* Halle: Peter Schmid, [1636]. (Herzog August Bibliothek, Wolfenbüttel: Yv 148 Helmst. [87].)

Brokmann, Reiner. "Carmen Alexandrinum Esthonicum ad leges Opitij poëticas compositum." [In a collection of epithalamia for Hans von Hövel and Margaretha Stahl, married November 20, 1637], fols.):(3v –):(4v. Reval: In Reusners nachgelassener Witwe Drückerey. (Ratsschulbibliothek, Zwickau: 6.5.19 [24].)

Buchner, August. *Anleitung Zur Deutschen Poeterey.* Wittenberg, 1665. Reprint edited by Marian Szyrocki. Deutsche Neudrucke/Reihe Barock, 5. Tübingen: Max Niemeyer, 1966.

[Christenius, Martin?]. *Continuation Der jüngst beschehenen/ vnd noch darauff erfolgeten Hirten-Lust: Auff die/ Deß Ehrenvesten/ Fürnehmen vnd Kunstreichen Herrn Martin Schörckels/ Apotheckers zu Leipzig/ Vnd der Viel Ehr-vnd Tugendreichen Jungfrawen Margarethen Putscherin/ heut angestellte hochzeitliche Ehren-Frewde/ Ferner beschrieben Von Mauritius Schinstern.* Jm Jahr 1633. N.p.: n.p., 1633. (Herzog August Bibliothek, Wolfenbüttel: 68.17 Poet [10].)

[Christenius, Martin?]. *Ernewerte Hirten-Lust/ Auff die/ des Edlen/ Vest-vnd Mannhafften Herrn Friederich Kühleweins/ Jhr Excell. Herrn Generall Leutenants von Arnheimb &c. wolverordneten hohen Officirers. So dann der Erbaren/ Viel-Ehrentugendreichen Jungfrawen Rosinen/ gebornen Vetzerin/ &c. Hochzeitlichen Ehrenfrewden/ vnter dem Namen Lindamors vnd der schönen Galatheen Vffgesetzt vnd beschrieben/ Von Amando Jägern/ J.S.* N.p.: n.p., [1634]. (Herzog August Bibliothek, Wolfenbüttel: 68.17 Poet [14].)

Cicero, Marcus Tullius. *Ad Quintum Fratrem; ad M. Brutum; Fragmenta epistularum*. Edited by W. S. Watt. Vol. 3 of *Epistulae*. Oxford: Clarendon, 1958.

———. *De senectute, De amicitia, De divinatione*. With English translation by William Armistead Falconer. Loeb Classical Library. London: William Heinemann; New York: G. P. Putnam's Son, 1923.

———. *Letters to Atticus*. 3 vols. With English translation by E. O Winstedt. Loeb Classical Library. Cambridge, Mass.: Harvard University Press, 1912–18.

———. *The Letters to his Friends*. 3 vols. With English translation by W. Glynn Williams. Loeb Classical Library. London: William Heinemann; Cambridge, Mass.: Harvard University Press, 1943–54.

Comes, Natalis. *Mythologie*. 2 vols., single pagination. Translation of *Mythologiae* (Venice, 1551) by J. de Montlyard, revised and edited by J. Baudouin. Paris, 1627. Reprint. The Renaissance and the Gods, 26. New York and London: Garland Publishing, 1976.

Copia Der Evangelischen Chur-Fürsten vnd Stände/ wie auch sämptlicher Protestirenden Graffen/ Herrn vnd Bevollmechtigter zu Leiptzig gewesenen Abgesandten Schreiben/ An Die Röm: Käyserl: Mayest: die Auffkündigung fernerer Contribution, Einquartirung für die Käyserl. Armada vnd andere Reichs Gravamina mehr betreffend/ sub dato Leiptzig/ den 18. Martij, Anno 1631. Leipzig: n.p., 1631. (Herzog August Bibliothek, Wolfenbüttel: 287.16 Qu [21].)

Copia vnd Abschrifft/ Des Churfürsten zu Sachsen Ausschreibens/ An alle vnd jede Evangelische Churfürsten/ Fürsten vnd Stände/ auff den 6. Februari. bestimbten Fürsten-Tag naher Leipzig zukommen. N.p.: n.p., 1631. (Herzog August Bibliothek, Wolfenbüttel: 50.9 Pol [32].)

Dach, Simon. *Gedichte*. 4 vols. Edited by Walther Ziesemer. Schriften der Königsberger Gelehrten Gesellschaft, Sonderreihe, 4–7. Halle: Max Niemeyer Verlag, 1936–38.

Du Bellay, Joachim. *La Deffence et Illustration de la Langue Françoyse*. 1549. 3d ed. Edited by Henri Chamard. Paris: Librairie Marcel Didier, 1966.

Epicedia In Beatissimam . . . in caelestem patriam . . . emigrationem, . . . Dn. Zachariae Schureri . . . scripta . . . à Fautoribus, Cognatis & Amicis. Leipzig: Gregorius Ritsch, 1629. Appended to: Johannes Höpnerus. *Christliche LeichPredigt/ . . . Bey angestelltem Christlichen Begräbnis Des . . . Zachariae Schürers. . . .* [Leipzig]: Gregorius Ritsch, 1629. (Herzog August Bibliothek, Wolfenbüttel: Stolberg-Leichenpredigt 20638.)

. . . Epicedia, Quae Ad . . . [Zachariae Schüreri] viduam . . . in Academia Witterbergensi conscripta & transmissa sunt à Cognatis, Fautoribus & Amicis. Leipzig: Gregorius Ritsch, [1629]. Appended to: Johannes Höpnerus. *Christliche LeichPredigt/ . . . Bey angestelltem Christlichen Begräbnis Des . . . Zachariae Schürers. . . .* [Leipzig]: Gregorius Ritsch, 1629. (Herzog August Bibliothek, Wolfenbüttel: Stolberg-Leichenpredigt 20638.)

Erasmus, Desiderius. *De conscribendis epistolis*. 1522. Edited by Jean-Claude Margolin. In pt. 1, vol. 2 of *Opera Omnia*, edited by J. H. Waszink et al. Amsterdam: North-Holland Publishing Company, 1977.

[Finckelthaus, Gottfried]. *Floridans Lob- vnd LiebesGedichte/ Bey Besprächung*

Seiner beyden Wolbekanten Am Ersten/ Tag gesungen/ Vnd nachmals zu Pappir gebracht. Leipzig: Henning Grosse, 1635. (University Library, Wrocław: 8oV 1122 (3); University of North Carolina at Chapel Hill: PT 1709 .B5 [minor orthographic variation in title page].)

Fleming, Paul. *Arae Schönburgicae Exstructae à Paulo Flämmig/ Harttenstein.* Leipzig: Janson, 1630. (Staatsbibliothek, Berlin, GDR.)

———. *D. Paul Flemings POetischer Gedichten So nach seinem Tode haben sollen herauβgegeben werden/ Prodromus.* Hamburg: Tobias Gunderman, 1642. Reprint. Hildesheim: Georg Olms, 1969. [Cited as *Prodromus.*]

———. *Deutsche Gedichte.* Edited by J[ohannes] M[artin] Lappenberg. BLVS, 82 and 83. Stuttgart: BLVS, 1865.

———. *Gedichte Auff des Ehrnvesten vnd Wolgelahrten Herrn Reineri Brockmans/ . . . Vnd der . . . Jungfrawen Dorotheen Temme/ Hochzeit.* Leipzig: Gregorius Ritsch, 1635. (Faber du Faur no. 316.)

———. *Gedichte Auff des Ehrnvesten vnd Wolgelarten Herrn Reineri Brocmans/ . . . Vnd der . . . Jungfrawen Dorotheen Temme/ Hochzeit.* Reval: Chr. Reusner, 1635. (Library of the Academy of Sciences, Tallinn, Estonia, USSR: XII–947/28.)

———. *Germaniae exsulis ad suos filios sive proceres regni epistola.* Colophon: Leipzig: Friedrich Lanckischs Erben, 1631. (Herzog August Bibliothek, Wolfenbüttel: 48.6 Poet.[39].)

———. *Lateinische Gedichte.* Edited by J[ohannes] M[artin] Lappenberg. BLVS, 73. Stuttgart: BLVS, 1863.

———. *Nova Epigrammata Pauli Flemingi D.* Edited by Adam Olearius. Amsterdam: Johann Blaeu, 1649. (Herzog August Bibliothek, Wolfenbüttel: 1471b Helmst. 8o.)

———. *Ode auff Herrn M. Salomon Steyers vnd Jungfrawen Annen Junghansinn Hochzeit.* Leipzig: n.p., 1632. (University Library, Wrocław: 549679.)

———. *Teütsche Poemata.* Lübeck, [1646]. Reprint. Hildesheim: Georg Olms, 1969.

Harsdörffer, Georg Philipp. *Frauenzimmer Gesprächspiele.* 8 vols. 1644–49. Reprint edited by Irmgard Böttcher. Deutsche Neudrucke/Reihe Barock, 13–20. Tübingen: Max Niemeyer, 1968–69.

Harsdörffer, Georg Philipp, and Johann Klaj. *Pegnesisches Schaefergedicht.* Nuremberg, 1644. Reprinted in *Pegnesisches Schäfergedicht 1644–1645*, edited by Klaus Garber. Deutsche Neudrucke/Reihe Barock, 8. Tübingen: Max Niemeyer, 1966.

Heinsius, Daniel. *Lavdatio Nobilissimi . . . Viri Jani Dousae, . . . Accedunt ejusdem Manes Dousici, Elegia item Funebris Josephi Scaligeri, & aliorum quaedam.* Leiden: Officina Ioannis Patii, 1605. (Folger Shakespeare Library, Washington D.C.: Bx 9419 B4 F3 1606 Cage.)

———. *Nederduytsche Poemata.* Amsterdam, 1616. Reprint edited by Barbara Becker-Cantarino. Nachdrucke deutscher Literatur des 17. Jahrhunderts, 31. Bern and Frankfurt a. M., 1983.

———. *Poemata avctiora.* Edited by Nicolaas Heinsius. Leiden: Francis. Hegerus, 1640. (University Library, Münster: X2373.)

214   Works Cited

———. *Poemata emendata.* . . . *Editio quarta.* Leiden: J. Orlers & Johannes Maire, 1613. (University of Chicago: PA 8525.H3A17 1613 RB.)
———. *Poemata, emendata.* . . . *Editio sexta.* Leiden: Johannes Maire, 1617. (Newberry Library, Chicago: Y 682 .H362.)
———. *Poematum Editio nova.* Leiden: Elzevier & J. Maire, 1621. (University Library, Münster: X2372.)
———. *Poematvm editio tertia.* Leiden: Johannes Maire, 1610. (Folger Shakespeare Library, Washington, D.C.: Acquisition no. 197259).
———. *Poematvm nova editio.* . . . Leiden: Johannes Maire, 1606. (University of Chicago: PA 8525.H3A17 1606 Rare book.)
Hoe von Hoenegg, Matthias. [Funeral sermon for Paul Laurentius.] Dresden: Gabriel Stuempffeldt, 1624. (Herzog August Bibliothek, Wolfenbüttel: Stolberg-Leichenpredigt 14872.)
Höpnerus, Johannes. See *Epicedia In Beatissimam* and . . . *Epicedia, Quae ad.*
Institoris, Henricus and Jacobus Sprenger. *Malleus maleficarum.* Strassburg, 1487. Translated by Montague Summers, London, 1928. Reprint. New York: Benjamin Blom, 1970.
Jägern, Amandus. See Christenius, Martin.
Leyser (Leiser), Polycarpus. [*Curriculum vitae* appended to] *LeichPredigt . . . Beym Begräbnis des . . . Michael Thomae. . .* , fols. C3v–D2v. Leipzig: Johann-Albrecht Mintzel, [1631]. (Herzog August Bibliothek, Wolfenbüttel: Stolberg-Leichenpredigt 22116.)
Lipsius, Justus. *Epistolica Institutio.* 1591. Antwerp, 1605.
———. *Von der Bestendigkeit.* Translation of *De Constantia* (Leiden, 1584) by Andreas Viritius. 2d ed. Leipzig, 1601. Reprint edited by Leonard Forster. Sammlung Metzler; Realienbücher für Germanisten. Abt. G: Dokumentationen, Reihe b: Zu Unrecht vergessene Texte, M45. Stuttgart: Metzler, 1965.
Lohenstein, Daniel Caspar von. *Afrikanische Trauerspiele: Cleopatra, Sophonisbe.* Edited by Klaus Günther Just. BLVS, 294. Stuttgart: Anton Hiersemann, 1957.
Lotichius Secundus, Petrus. *Poëmata omnia.* Edited by Petrus Burmannus Secundus. 2 vols. Amsterdam, 1754.
Montreux, Nicolas de. *Le premier [-cinquième] livre des bergeries de Juliette.* 5 vols. Tours: G. Drobet, 1592–98. (Library of Congress, Washington, D.C.: PQ1647.M5A63.)
———. *Die Schäffereyen Von der schönen Juliana.* . . . Translated by F[ridrich] C[astalio] V[on] B[asel]. Frankfurt a. M.: Jonas Rosa, 1615. (Faber du Faur no. 796.)
Morhof, Daniel Georg. *Unterricht Von Der Teutschen Sprache und Poesie, deren Uhrsprung, Fortgang und Lehrsätzen.* . . . Kiel: Joachim Reumann, 1682. (Faber du Faur no. 1516.)
Münster, Sebastian. *Cosmographia, das ist: beschreibung der gantzen welt.* . . . Basel: Bey den Henricpetrinischen, 1628. (Herzog August Bibliothek, Wolfenbüttel: 12.4 Hist. 2o).
[Olearius, Adam?] *Angenemer Widerwille Der Liebreichen Silvien gegen den in*

Lieb entbrandten Coridon eröffnet/ Bey dem HochzeitFest Herrn M. Andreß Bachman von Halle/ Keyserlichen belorberten Poeten/ &c Vnd Jungf. Catharina-Jsabella Bergerin von Scheuditz. [Signed] Andinum d'Orliens. Leipzig: Abraham Lambergs Erben, 1633. (Herzog August Bibliothek, Wolfenbüttel: 68.17 Poet [3].)

Olearius, Adam. *Dialogus Oder Gespräch Der seligen Vaters-Seelen mit den Kindern/ Des Ehrnvesten vnd Wolgeachten Herrn Herman Hüttens/ Vornehmen Bürgers vnd Handelsmann in Leipzig. . . . Durch M. Adamum Olearium.* Leipzig: Gregorius Ritsch, 1629. (Ratsschulbibliothek, Zwickau: 6.6.32 [26].)

―――. *Sieges- vnd Triumffs-Fahne Gustavi Adolfi Magni. . . . Durch Ascanium Olivarium* [pseud.]. Leipzig: Abraham Lambergs Erben, 1633. (Herzog August Bibliothek, Wolfenbüttel: 65.6 Poet [21].)

―――. *Vermehrte Newe Beschreibung Der Muscowitischen vnd Persischen Reyse.* Schleswig, 1656. Reprint edited by Dieter Lohmeier. Deutsche Neudrucke/ Reihe Barock, 21. Tübingen: Max Niemeyer, 1971. [Cited as *Reisebeschreibung.*]

Opitz, Martin. *Acht Bücher, Deutscher Poematum.* Breslau, 1625. In vol. 2, pt. 2 of Opitz, *Gesammelte Werke.*

―――. *Aristarchus sive de contemptu linguae teutonicae.* Beuthen, [1617]. In vol. 1 of Opitz, *Gesammelte Werke.*

―――. *Buch von der Deutschen Poeterey.* Breslau, 1624. In vol. 2, pt. 1 of Opitz, *Gesammelte Werke.*

―――. *Gesammelte Werke: Kritische Ausgabe.* 5 vols. to date. Edited by George Schulz-Behrend. Stuttgart: Anton Hiersemann, 1968–. Vol. 1, *Die Werke von 1614 bis 1621.* BLVS, 295. 1968. Vol. 2, pts. 1 and 2, *Die Werke von 1621 bis 1626.* BLVS, 300, 301. 1978–79.

―――. *Hipponax ad Asterien.* Görlitz, [1618]. In vol. 1 of Opitz, *Gesammelte Werke.*

―――. *Martini Opicii Teutsche Pöemata vnd Aristarchus . . . Sampt einem anhang Mehr auserleßener geticht anderer Teutscher Poeten. . . .* Edited by Wilhelm Zincgref. Strassburg, 1624. See Opitz, *Teutsche Poemata,* and Zincgref, *Auserlesene Gedichte Deutscher Poeten.* Also in vol. 2, pt. 1 of Opitz, *Gesammelte Werke.*

―――. *Die Schäfferey von der Nimfen Hercinie.* Breslau, 1630. Reprint edited by Karl F. Otto, Jr. Nachdrucke deutscher Literaturwerke des 17. Jahrhunderts, 8. Bern and Frankfurt a. M.: Herbert Lang, 1976.

―――. *Die Schäfferey von der Nimfen Hercinie.* 1630. Edited by Peter Rusterholz. Reclam Universal-Bibliothek, 8594. Stuttgart: Reclam, 1969.

―――. *Sylvarum libri tres. . . .* Frankfurt a. M., 1631. (Jantz no. 1923.)

―――. *Teutsche Poemata.* 1624. Edited by Georg Witkowski. Neudrucke deutscher Litteraturwerke des XVI. und XVII. Jahrhunderts, 189–92. Halle: Max Niemeyer, 1902. [Cited as "1624 *Poemata.*"]

―――. *Weltliche Poëmata: Der Ander Theil.* Frankfurt a. M., 1644. Reprint edited by Erich Trunz. Deutsche Neudrucke/Reihe Barock, 3. Tübingen: Max Niemeyer Verlag, 1975.

Ovid. *Tristia. Ex Ponto.* Vol. 6 of *Ovid in Six Volumes.* With English translation by Arthur Leslie Wheeler. 1924. Loeb Classical Library. Reprint. Cambridge, Mass.: Harvard University Press; London: William Heinemann, 1975.

Petrarch, Francesco. *[Canzoniere.] [Epistolae Metricae.]* In *Rime, trionfi, e poesie latine,* edited by F. Neri et al. La letteratura italiana: Storia e testi, 6. Milan: R. Ricciardi, 1951.

———. *Rerum familiarum libri I–VIII.* Translated by Aldo S. Bernardo. Albany: State University of New York Press, 1975.

Plutarch. *Table-Talk.* Vol. 8 and 9 of his *Moralia.* With English translation. Loeb Classical Library. London: William Heinemann; Cambridge, Mass.: Harvard University Press. 1961, 1969.

Pontanus, Jacobus. *Poeticarum institutionum libri tres.* Ingolstadt, 1594. (University of Wisconsin, Madison, microfilm of copy at Duke University.)

Quintilian. *Institutio oratoria.* 4 vols. With English translation by H. E. Butler. Loeb Classical Library. New York: G. P. Putnam's Sons; London: William Heinemann, 1921–22.

Rist, Johann. *Das Friedewünschende Teütschland.* Hamburg: Heinrich Wärners Seel. Witwe, 1649. (University Library, Mannheim: H.B. M 17.)

———. *Neüer Himlischer Lieder Sonderbahres Buch.* Lüneburg: Bei Johann und Heinrich Sternen, 1651. (Faber du Faur no. 393.)

Rudel, Elias. *Querela Europae, Ad diversos Imperii Germ. Proceres, Ordines, Status, de accepto membrorum suorum Vulnere & clade diffamata.* Leipzig: Gregorius Ritsch, [1631]. (Ratsschulbibliothek, Zwickau: 6.8.7 [44].)

Sabinus, Georg. *Germania ad Caesarem Ferdinandum.* In his *Poemata,* fols. B1v–B3v. Colophon: Strassburg: Crato Mylius, 1544. (Herzog August Bibliothek, Wolfenbüttel, P1551.80 Helmst.)

Sannazaro, Jacopo. *Arcadia & Piscatorial Eclogues.* Translated by Ralph Nash. Detroit: Wayne State University Press, 1966.

Scaliger, Julius Caesar. *Poemata omnia in duas partes divisa.* In Bibliopolio Commeliniano, 1600. (Milton S. Eisenhower Library, Baltimore: PC2635 .S54P8.)

———. *Poetices libri septem.* Lyon, 1561. Reprint edited by August Buck. Stuttgart: F. Fromann, 1964.

Schein, Johann Hermann. *Diletti pastorali.* 1624. In vol. 3 of Schein, *Sämtliche Werke.*

———. *Musica boscareccia.* Pt. 1, 1621. Pt. 2, 1626. Pt. 3, 1628. In vol. 2 of Schein, *Sämtliche Werke.*

———. *Neue Ausgabe sämtlicher Werke.* Edited by Adam Adrio. Kassel: Bärenreiter, 1963–.

———. *Sämtliche Werke.* 7 vols. in 4. Edited by Arthur Prüfer. Leipzig: Breitkopf & Härtel, 1901–23.

———. *Studenten-Schmauss.* 1626. In vol. 3 of Schein, *Sämtliche Werke.*

———. *Venus Kräntzlein.* 1609. In vol. 1 of Schein, *Sämtliche Werke.*

Schindschersitzky [pseud.]. *Jüngst-erbawete Schäfferey/ Oder Keusche Liebes-Beschreibung/ Von der Verliebten Nimfen Amoena, Vnd dem Lobwürdigen Schäffer*

Amandus. . . . Leipzig: Rehefeld, 1632. In *Schäferromane des Barock,* edited by Klaus Kaczerowsky, pp. 7–96. Reinbek bei Hamburg: Rowolt, 1970.

Schinstern, Mauritius. *See* Christenius, Martin.

Schottel, Justus Georg. *Lamentatio Germaniae Exspirantis: Der nunmehr hinsterbenden Nymphen Germaniae elendeste Todesklage.* 1640. Edited by Ernst Voss. *Journal of English and Germanic Philology* 7 (1907–8): 1–31.

Sebillet, Thomas. *L'Art poétique françoys.* 1548. Edited by Félix Gaiffe. Société des textes français modernes, 13. Paris: Société nouvelle de librairie et d'édition, 1910.

Secundus, Joannes Nicolai. *Epistolarum Liber Primus; Secundus.* In his *Opera Omnia,* edited by Petrus Burmannus Secundus, reedited by Petrus Bosscha, 2:25–96. Leiden: S. et J. Luchtmans. 1821. (Oberlin College.)

Seneca, L. Annaeus. *De tranquillitate animi.* In *L. Annaei Senecae dialogorum libri dvodecim,* edited by L. D. Reynolds, pp. 207–38. Oxford: Clarendon Press, 1977.

Theocritus. [Idylls.] In *The Greek Bucolic Poets,* with English translation by J. M. Edmonds. Loeb Classical Library. Cambridge, Mass.: Harvard University Press; London: William Heinemann, 1912; revised reprint, 1977.

Threnologiae Super obitum improvisum qvidem, ac immaturum: pium tamen ac beatissimum . . . Dn. Gustavi Adolphi . . . In proelio Lützensi . . . animam exhalantis. . . . Leipzig: Elias Rehefeld, [1632]. (Ratsschulbibliothek, Zwickau: 9.5.6 [85].)

Ursinus Velius, Caspar. *Epistolarum Liber.* In his *Poematum libri quinque.* Basel: Joannes Froben, 1522. (Herzog August Bibliothek, Wolfenbüttel: 36.13 Poet.)

Velius. *See* Ursinus.

Virgil. *Eclogues, Georgics, Aeneid, 1–6.* Vol. 1 of *Virgil in Two Volumes.* With English translation by H. Rushton Fairclough. Loeb Classical Library. Revised reprint. Cambridge, Mass.: Harvard University Press; London: William Heinemann, 1978.

Vives, Joannes Ludovicus. *De conscribendis epistolis.* 1536. In his *Opera Omnia,* 2:263–314. Valencia, 1782. Reprint. London: The Gregg Press, 1964.

Zechendörffer, Johann. [*Curriculum vitae* appended to his] *Die Andere Leichpredigt/ . . . Bey der Begräbnüs/ deß . . . Herrn Hugen/ Freyherrn von Schönburg. . . ,* fols. O1v–S3v. Gera: Martin Spieß, 1607. (Herzog August Bibliothek, Wolfenbüttel: Stolberg-Leichenpredigt 20406.)

Zesen, Philipp von. *Deutsches Helicons Erster und Ander Theil/ Oder Unterricht/ wie ein Deutscher Vers und Getichte auf mancherley Art ohne fehler recht zierlich zu schreiben.* . . . Wittenberg, 1641. In vol. 9 of Zesen, *Sämtliche Werke.*

———. *Hochdeutsche Helikonische Hechel/ oder des Rosenmohndes zweite woche: darinnen von der Hochdeutschen reinen Dichtkunst/ und derselben fehlern . . . gehandelt wird.* Hamburg, 1668. In vol. 11 of Zesen, *Sämtliche Werke.*

———. *Sämtliche Werke.* Edited by Ferdinand van Ingen. Berlin and New York: Walter de Gruyter, 1970–. Vol. 9, *Deutscher Helicon,* edited by Ulrich Maché. 1971. Vol. 11, *Spraach-Übung, Rosen-Mand, Helikonische Hechel, Sendeschreiben an den Kreutztragenden,* edited by Ulrich Maché. 1974.

Zincgref, Julius Wilhelm, ed. *Auserlesene Gedichte Deutscher Poeten.* 1624. Neudrucke deutscher Litteraturwerke des XVI. und XVII. Jahrhunderts, 15. Halle: Max Niemeyer, 1879. [Cited as "1624 *Anhang.*"]

Secondary Literature

Alewyn, Richard. "Hans Pyritz: Paul Flemings deutsche Liebeslyrik." In *Deutsche Barockforschung,* edited by Richard Alewyn, pp. 437–43. Cologne and Berlin: Kiepenheuer & Witsch, 1965. Originally published in the *Deutsche Literaturzeitung* 54 (1933): cols. 924–32.

———. *Vorbarocker Klassizismus und griechische Tragödie: Analyse der "Antigone"-Übersetzung des Martin Opitz.* Heidelberg: Verlag von G. Köster, 1926.

Ambacher, Ferdinand. "Paul Fleming and 'Erlebnisdichtung.'" Diss., Rutgers University, 1972.

Baesecke, Georg. *Die Sprache der Opitzischen Gedichtsammlungen von 1624 und 1625.* Diss., Göttingen. Braunschweig: Krampe, 1899.

Barner, Wilfried. *Barockrhetorik: Untersuchungen zu ihren geschichtlichen Grundlagen.* Tübingen: Max Niemeyer, 1970.

Baron, Samuel H., ed. and tr. Introduction to *The Travels of Olearius in Seventeenth-Century Russia.* Stanford: Stanford University Press, 1967.

Beck, Adolf. "Über einen Formtypus der barocken Lyrik in Deutschland und die Frage seiner Herkunft: Mit Exkurs: Über einen möglichen Ursprungsort der asyndetischen Worthäufung im Barock." *Jahrbuch des freien deutschen Hochstifts* (1965): 1–48.

Becker-Cantarino, Barbara. *Daniel Heinsius.* Twayne's World Author Series, 477. Boston: Twayne, 1978.

———. "Drei Briefautographen von Paul Fleming." *Wolfenbütteler Beiträge: Aus den Schätzen der Herzog August Bibliothek* 4 (1981): 191–204.

Beckmann, Adelheid. *Motive und Formen der deutschen Lyrik des 17. Jahrhunderts und ihre Entsprechungen in der französischen Lyrik seit Ronsard: Ein Beitrag zur vergleichenden Literaturgeschichte.* Hermaea: Germanistische Forschungen, n.s., 5. Tübingen: Max Niemeyer Verlag, 1960.

Behrmann, Alfred. *Einführung in die Analyse von Verstexten.* Sammlung Metzler, 89. Realienbücher für Germanisten. Abt. B: Literaturwissenschaftliche Methodenlehre. Stuttgart: Metzler, 1970.

Beissner, Friedrich. *Geschichte der deutschen Elegie.* Grundriss der germanischen Philologie, 14. Berlin: Walter de Gruyter, 1941.

Beller, Manfred. "Thema, Konvention und Sprache der mythologischen Ausdrucksformen in Paul Flemings Gedichten." *Euphorion* 67 (1973): 157–89.

Bemmann, Rudolf, ed. *Bibliographie der Sächsischen Geschichte.* Vol. 1, *Landesgeschichte.* Half vol. 1. Schriften der [Königlich] sächsischen Kommission für Geschichte, 23.1. Leipzig and Berlin: B. G. Teubner, 1918.

Berent, Eberhard. *Die Auffassung der Liebe bei Opitz und Weckherlin und ihre geschichtlichen Vorstufen.* Studies in German Literature, 15. The Hague and Paris: Mouton, 1970.

Berger, Uwe. *Das Verhängnis oder Die Liebe des Paul Fleming*. Berlin and Weimar: Aufbau-Verlag, 1983.

Bibliotheca Societatis Teutonicae Saeculi XVI–XVIII: Katalog der Büchersammlung der Deutschen Gesellschaft in Leipzig. Nach dem von Ernst Kroker bearbeiteten handschriftlichen Bestandsverzeichnis der Universitätsbibliothek Leipzig. 2 vols. Leipzig: Zentralantiquariat der DDR, 1971.

B[ircher], M[artin]. "Paul Fleming: Zwei unbekannte Gedichte auf Martha Elisabeth Aeschel, geb. Herold (1631)." *Wolfenbütteler Barock-Nachrichten* 11 (1984): 10–14.

Blanckmeister, Franz. "Aus Paul Flemings Vaterhaus." *Das Pfarr-Haus* 25 (1909): 163–65.

Boeckh, Joachim G. et al. *Geschichte der deutschen Literatur 1600 bis 1700*. Vol. 5 of *Geschichte der deutschen Literatur von den Anfängen bis zur Gegenwart*, edited by Klaus Gysi et al. Berlin, GDR: Volk und Wissen, 1963.

Bornemann, Albert. "Paul Fleming: Veranlassung zu seiner Reise; Seine Gelegenheits-Dichtung." In the 30th Programm (Ostern 1899) of the Stadtgymnasium ehemaliges Rats-Lyceum zu Stettin, pp. 3–22. Stettin: Herrcke & Lebeling, 1899.

Bornemann, Albertus. *Die Überlieferung der deutschen Gedichte Flemmings*. Diss., Greifswald. Stettin: Hessenland, 1882.

Bornemann, Ulrich. *Anlehnung und Abgrenzung: Untersuchungen zur Rezeption der niederländischen Literatur in der deutschen Dichtungsreform des siebzehnten Jahrhunderts*. Respublica Literaria Neerlandica, 1. Assen/Amsterdam: Van Gorcum, 1976.

Böttcher, Diethelm. "Propaganda und öffentliche Meinung im protestantischen Deutschland 1628–1636." In *Der Dreißigjährige Krieg: Perspektiven und Strukturen*, edited by Hans Ulrich Rudolf, pp. 325–67. Darmstadt: Wissenschaftliche Buchgesellschaft, 1977. Originally published in the *Archiv für Reformationsgeschichte* 44 (1953): 181–203 and 45 (1954): 83–98.

Brauer, Walter. "Jakob Regnart, Johann Hermann Schein und die Anfänge der deutschen Barocklyrik." *Deutsche Vierteljahrsschrift für Literaturwissenschaft und Geistesgeschichte* 17 (1939): 371–404.

Browning, Barton W. "The Poet Addresses Himself: An Authorial Posture in 17th-Century Poetry." Paper presented at conference, Literary Culture in the Holy Roman Empire 1555–1720, at Yale University, March 26–28, 1987.

Carnap, Ernst Günter. *Das Schäferwesen in der deutschen Literatur des 17. Jahrhunderts und die Hirtendichtung Europas*. Diss., Frankfurt a. M. Würzburg: Richard Mayr, 1939.

Conrady, Karl Otto. *Lateinische Dichtungstradition und deutsche Lyrik des 17. Jahrhunderts*. Bonner Arbeiten zur deutschen Literatur, 4. Bonn: Bouvier, 1962.

Coppel, Bernhard. "Marginalien zu dichterischen Berührungspunkten zwischen Petrus Lotichius Secundus und C. Valerius Catullus." In *Acta Conventus Neo-Latini Lovaniensis*, edited by Jozef IJsewijn and E. Keßler, pp. 159–70. [Louvain]: Leuven University Press; Munich: Wilhelm Fink Verlag, 1973.

Curtius, Ernst Robert. *European Literature and the Latin Middle Ages*. Translated by Willard Trask, 1953. Bollingen Series, 36. Reprint. Princeton: Princeton University Press, 1973.

Cysarz, Herbert, ed. *Vor- und Frühbarock*. Vol. 1 of *Barocklyrik*. Deutsche Literatur: Sammlung literarischer Kunst- und Kulturdenkmäler in Entwicklungsreihen: Reihe 13 Barock, Barocklyrik, 1. Leipzig: Reclam, 1937.

De Capua, A. G. *German Baroque Poetry: Interpretive Readings*. Albany: State University of New York Press, 1973.

Deissmann, G. Adolf. "Prolegomena zu den biblischen Briefen und Episteln." In his *Bibelstudien*, pp. 187–252. Marburg: N. G. Elwert'sche Verlagsbuchhandlung, 1895.

Demetz, Peter, and W. T. H. Jackson, eds. *An Anthology of German Literature 800–1750*. Englewood Cliffs, N.J.: Prentice Hall, 1968.

Dörrie, Heinrich. *Der heroische Brief: Bestandsaufnahme, Geschichte, Kritik einer humanistisch-barocken Literaturgattung*. Berlin: Walter de Gruyter, 1968.

Dünnhaupt, Gerhard. *Bibliographisches Handbuch der Barockliteratur: Hundert Personalbibliographien deutscher Autoren des siebzehnten Jahrhunderts*. 3 vols. Hiersemanns bibliographische Handbücher, 2.1–3. Stuttgart: Anton Hiersemann, 1980–81.

Dürrenfeld, Eva. "Paul Fleming und Johann Christian Günther: Motive, Themen, Formen." Diss., Tübingen, [1963].

Dyck, Joachim. *Ticht-Kunst: Deutsche Barockpoetik und rhetorische Tradition*. Bad Homburg v.d.H, Berlin, and Zürich: Verlag Dr. Max Gehlen, 1966.

Eckardt, Ernst. *Chronik von Glauchau: Eine historische Beschreibung der Stadt, verbunden mit einem Jahrbuche über die wichtigsten Ereignisse und einer Geschichte des Hauses Schönburg*. Glauchau: Verlag von Arno Peschke, 1882.

Eckermann, Johann Peter. *Gespräche mit Goethe in den letzten Jahren seines Lebens*. 1836–48. Wiesbaden: Insel-Verlag, 1955.

Ellinger, Georg. *Geschichte der neulateinischen Literatur Deutschlands im sechzehnten Jahrhundert*. Vols. 1–3.1 (all that appeared). Berlin and Leipzig: Walter de Gruyter, 1929–33.

Erler, Georg, ed. *Die Immatrikulationen vom Wintersemester 1559 bis zum Sommersemester 1634*. Vol. 1 of *Die Jüngere Matrikel der Universität Leipzig 1559–1809*. Leipzig: Giesecke & Devrient, 1909.

Faber du Faur, Curt von. *German Baroque Literature: A Catalogue of the Collection in the Yale University Library*. New Haven: Yale University Press, 1958.

Fechner, Jörg-Ulrich. "Paul Fleming." In *Deutsche Dichter des 17. Jahrhunderts: Ihr Leben und Werk*, edited by Harald Steinhagen and Benno von Wiese, pp. 365–84. Berlin: Erich Schmidt Verlag, 1984.

Forster, Leonard. "German Alexandrines on Dutch Broadsheets before Opitz." In *The German Baroque*, edited by George Schulz-Behrend, pp. 11–64. Austin and London: The University of Texas Press, 1972.

Garber, Klaus. *Der locus amoenus und der locus terribilis: Bild und Funktion der Natur in der deutschen Schäfer- und Landlebendichtung des 17. Jahrhunderts*. Literatur und Leben, n.s., 16. Cologne and Vienna: Böhlau, 1974.

———. "Martin Opitz' *Schäfferey von der Nimfen Hercinie* als Ursprung der Prosaekloge und des Schäferromans in Deutschland." *Daphnis* 11 (1982): 547–603.

_____. "Paul Fleming in Riga: Die wiederentdeckten Gedichte aus der Sammlung Gadebusch." In *Daß eine Nation die ander verstehen möge: Festschrift für Marian Szyrocki zu seinem 60. Geburtstag*, edited by Norbert Honsza and Hans-Gert Roloff, pp. 255–308. Chloe (Beihefte zum *Daphnis*), 7. Amsterdam: Rodopi, 1988.
Gellinek, Janis Little. *Die weltliche Lyrik des Martin Opitz*. Bern and Munich: Francke Verlag, 1973.
Gervinus, Georg Gottfried. *Geschichte der poetischen National-Literatur der Deutschen*. Part 3, *Vom Ende der Reformation bis zu Gottscheds Zeiten*. 2d ed. Leipzig: Verlag von Wilhelm Engelmann, 1842.
Geyer, [no first name given]. "Zur Bibliographie Flemings." *Schönburgische Geschichtsblätter* 2 (1895–96): 165–69. (Staatsbibliothek Preußischer Kulturbesitz [Berlin].)
Gillespie, Gerald. *German Baroque Poetry*. Twayne's World Authors Series, 103. New York: Twayne, 1971.
Goedeke, Karl, ed. *Elf Bücher Deutscher Dichtung: Von Sebastian Brant (1500) bis auf die Gegenwart: Aus den Quellen*. 2 vols. Leipzig: Hahn'sche Verlagsbuchhandlung, 1849.
Goeze, Werner. *Translatio Imperii: Ein Beitrag zur Geschichte des Geschichtsdenkens und der politischen Theorien im Mittelalter und in der frühen Neuzeit*. Tübingen: J. C. B. Mohr, 1958.
Götze, Alfred. *Frühneuhochdeutsches Glossar*. Kleine Texte für Vorlesungen und Übungen, 101. Bonn, 1912. 7th ed. Berlin: Walter de Gruyter, 1967.
Grimm, Jacob, and Wilhelm Grimm. *Deutsches Wörterbuch*. 16 vols. in 32. Leipzig: Verlag von S. Hirzel, 1854–1971.
Harms, Wolfgang, Michael Schilling, and Andreas Wang, eds. *Die Sammlung der Herzog August Bibliothek in Wolfenbüttel: Kommentierte Ausgabe*. Vol. 2, *Historica. Deutsche illustrierte Flugblätter des 16. und 17. Jahrhunderts*, 2. Munich: Kraus International Publishers, 1980.
Harper, Anthony. "Ein neu aufgefundenes Frühwerk von Gottfried Finckelthaus?" *Daphnis* 7 (1978): 689–96. Reprinted in Harper, *Schriften*, pp. 115–22.
_____. *Schriften zur Lyrik Leipzigs 1620–1670*. Stuttgarter Arbeiten zur Germanistik, 131. Stuttgart: Akademischer Verlag, 1985.
_____. "Zur Opitz-Rezeption in Leipzig: Eine frühe Leipziger Schäferei in der Nachfolge der *Schäfferey von der Nimfen Hercinie*." *Daphnis* 11 (1982): 605–12. Reprinted in Harper, *Schriften*, pp. 123–30.
Hayn, Hugo. *Bibliotheca Germanorum Nuptialis: Verzeichniss von Einzeldrucken deutscher Hochzeitgedichte und Hochzeitscherze in Prosa von Mitte des XVI. Jahrhunderts bis zur Neuzeit*. Cologne: Verlag von Franz Teubner, 1890.
Hoffmann von Fallersleben, August Heinrich, ed. *Die deutschen Gesellschaftslieder des 16. und 17. Jahrhunderts*. 1844. 2d ed. Leipzig: Verlag von Wilhelm Engelmann, 1860.
_____. *Politische Gedichte aus der deutschen Vorzeit*. Leipzig: Engelmann, 1843.
Huebner, Alfred. *Das erste deutsche Schäferidyll und seine Quellen*. Diss., Königsberg. Königsberg: Hartungsche Buchdruckerei, 1910.
IJsewijn, Jozef. *Companion to Neo-Latin Studies*. Amsterdam, New York, and

Oxford: North-Holland Publishing Company, 1977.

Jantz, Harold. *German Baroque Literature: A Descriptive Catalogue of the Collection of Harold Jantz and a Guide to the Collection on Microfilm.* 2 vols. New Haven: Research Publications, 1974.

Johansen, Paul. "Der Dichter Paul Fleming und der Osten." *Hamburger Mittel- und Ostdeutsche Forschungen* 2 (1960): 9–46.

Jones, G. L. "The Mulde's 'Half-Prodigal Son': Paul Fleming, Germany and the Thirty Years War." *German Life and Letters* 26 (1972–73): 125–36.

Kaemmel, Otto. *Geschichte des Leipziger Schulwesens vom Anfange des 13. bis gegen die Mitte des 19. Jahrhunderts (1214–1846).* Schriften der Königlich sächsischen Kommission für Geschichte, 16. Leipzig and Berlin: B. G. Teubner, 1909.

Katalog der fürstlich Stolberg-Stolberg'schen Leichenpredigten-Sammlung. 4 vols. Foreword by Werner Konstantin von Arnswaldt. Leipzig: Degener, 1927–35.

Kelletat, Alfred. "Zum Problem der antiken Metren im Deutschen." *Der Deutschunterricht* 16.6 (1964): 50–85.

Kern, Arthur, ed. *Deutsche Hofordnungen des 16. und 17. Jahrhunderts.* 2 vols. Denkmäler der deutschen Kulturgeschichte, 2. Abt.: Ordnungen, 1 & 2. Berlin: Weidmannsche Buchhandlung, 1905–7.

Kindermann, Heinz. *Danziger Barockdichtung.* Deutsche Literatur; Sammlung literarischer Kunst- und Kulturdenkmäler in Entwicklungsreihen. Reihe 13, 2 Barock, Ergänzungsband. Leipzig: Reclam, 1939.

Klotz, Volker. "Spiegel und Echo, Konvention und Individualität im Barock. Zum Beispiel: Paul Flemings Gedicht 'An Anna, die spröde'." In *Rezeption und Produktion zwischen 1570 und 1730: Festschrift für Günther Weydt zum 65. Geburtstag*, edited by Wolfdietrich Rasch, Hans Geulen, and Klaus Haberkamm, pp. 93–119. Bern and Munich: Francke Verlag, 1972.

Krahé, Peter. "Persönlicher Ausdruck in der literarischen Konvention: Paul Fleming als Wegbereiter der Erlebnislyrik?" *Zeitschrift für deutsche Philologie* 106 (1987): 481–513.

Krapf, Ludwig and Christian Wagenknecht, eds. *Stuttgarter Hoffeste: Texte und Materialien zur höfischen Repräsentation im frühen 17. Jahrhundert.* 2 vols. Neudrucke deutscher Literaturwerke, n.s., 26 and 27. Tübingen: Max Niemeyer, 1979.

Kroker, Ernst. "Leipzig in Liedern und Gedichten des dreißigjährigen Krieges." *Schriften des Vereins für Geschichte Leipzigs,* 5 (1896): 31–99.

Krout, Jim Warren. "Paul Fleming's Latin Religious Lyrics: Translations into the English." Diss., Purdue University, 1975.

Krummacher, Hans-Henrik. "Das barocke Epicedium: Rhetorische Tradition und deutsche Gelegenheitsdichtung im 17. Jahrhundert." *Jahrbuch der deutschen Schillergesellschaft* 18 (1974): 89–147.

Kurzwelly, A. "Andreas Bretschneider." In *Allgemeines Lexikon der bildenden Künstler von der Antike bis zur Gegenwart*, edited by Ulrich Thieme and Felix Becker. 37 vols. Leipzig: Wilhelm Engelmann, 1907–50.

Lang, Elisabeth. "Das illustrierte Flugblatt des Dreißigjährigen Krieges: Ein

Gradmesser für die Verbreitung der Opitzischen Versreform?" *Daphnis* 9 (1980): 65–87 and 670–75.
Legère, Werner. *In allen meinen Taten: Ein Paul-Fleming-Roman*. Berlin, GDR: Union Verlag, 1982.
Leighton, Joseph. "The Poet's Voices in Occasional Baroque Poetry." Paper presented at conference, Literary Culture in the Holy Roman Empire 1555–1720, at Yale University, March 26–28, 1987.
Lohmeier, Dieter. "Paul Flemings poetische Bekenntnisse zu Moskau und Rußland." In *Russen und Rußland aus deutscher Sicht 9.–17. Jahrhundert*, edited by Mechthild Keller, pp. 341–70. West-Östliche Spiegelungen, series A, vol. 1. Munich: Wilhelm Fink Verlag, 1985.
Lorenzen, Käte. "Paul Fleming." In *Die Musik in Geschichte und Gegenwart*, edited by Friedrich Blume, 4: cols. 305–7. Kassel: Bärenreiter Verlag, 1955.
Luck, Georg. "Brief und Epistel in der Antike." *Das Altertum* 7 (1961): 77–84.
Maché, Ulrich. "Opitz' *Schäfferey von der Nimfen Hercinie* in Seventeenth-Century German Literature." In *Essays on German Literature in Honor of G. Joyce Hallamore*, edited by Michael Batts and Marketa Goetz Stankiewicz, pp. 34–40. [Toronto]: University of Toronto Press, 1968.
Maltzahn, Wendelin von. "Ein Gedicht von Paul Fleming." *Archiv für die Geschichte deutscher Sprache und Dichtung* 1 (1874): 448–51.
Manheimer, Victor. *Die Lyrik des Andreas Gryphius: Studien und Materialien*. Berlin: Weidmannsche Buchhandlung, 1904.
Marsch, Edgar. *Biblische Prophetie und chronographische Dichtung: Stoff- und Wirkungsgeschichte der Vision des Propheten Daniel nach Dan. VII*. Philologische Studien und Quellen, 65. Berlin: E. Schmidt, 1972.
Maync, Harry. "Paul Fleming (1609–1640): Zu seinem dreihundertsten Geburtstage." *Deutsche Rundschau* 141 (Oct.-Dec. 1909): 56–70.
Meid, Volker. "Im Zeitalter des Barock." In *Geschichte der politischen Lyrik in Deutschland*, edited by Walter Hinderer, pp. 90–113. Stuttgart: Reclam, 1978.
Meyer, Heinrich. *Der deutsche Schäferroman des 17. Jahrhunderts*. Diss., Freiburg i. Br. Dorpat: C. Mattiesen, 1928.
Moser, Virgil. "Deutsche Orthographiereformen des 17. Jahrhunderts." *Beiträge zur Geschichte der deutschen Sprache und Literatur* 60 (1936): 193–258.
Mueller, Eugen Hartmuth. *Die Sprache Paul Flemings: Untersuchung des Laut- und Formenstandes*. Diss., University of Minnesota, 1937. Heidelberg: Winter, 1938.
Müller, Conrad. "Paul Fleming und das Haus Schönburg." *Mitteilungen des fürstlich Schönburg-Waldenburgschen Familienvereins Schloß Waldenburg* 6 (1939): 5–30.
Müller, Günther. *Geschichte des deutschen Liedes vom Zeitalter des Barock bis zur Gegenwart*. Geschichte der deutschen Literatur nach Gattungen, 3. Munich: Drei Masken Verlag, 1925.
Müller, Karl August. *Kurfürst Johann Georg der Erste, seine Familie und sein Hof nach handschriftlichen Quellen des Königlich Sächsischen Haupt-Staats-Archivs dargestellt*. Dresden and Leipzig: G. Fleischer, 1838.

Nadler, Josef. *Literaturgeschichte der deutschen Stämme und Landschaften*. 4 vols. 1912–18. 2d ed. Regensburg: Josef Habbel, 1923–28.
Nelson, Lowry. *Baroque Lyric Poetry*. New Haven: Yale University Press, 1961.
Neumann, Friedrich. *Geschichte des neuhochdeutschen Reimes von Opitz bis Wieland*. Berlin: Wiedmannsche Buchhandlung, 1920.
Newald, Richard. *Die deutsche Literatur vom Späthumanismus zur Empfindsamkeit 1570–1750*. Vol. 5 of *Geschichte der deutschen Literatur von den Anfängen bis zur Gegenwart*, edited by Helmut de Boor and Richard Newald. 1951. Reprint of 6th (1967) revised edition. Munich: Beck, 1975.
Nischan, Bodo. "Reformed Irenicism and the Leipzig Colloquy of 1631." *Central European History* 9 (1976): 3–26.
Nottbeck, Eugen von, and Wilh[elm] Neumann. *Geschichte und Kunstdenkmäler der Stadt Reval*. 2 vols. Reval: Franz Kluge's Verlag, 1904.
Oesterley, Hermann. "Zu Paul Fleming." *Archiv für Litteratur-Geschichte* 14 (1886): 41–47.
Opel, Julius, and Adolf Cohn, eds. *Der Dreißigjährige Krieg: Eine Sammlung von historischen Gedichten und Prosadarstellungen*. Halle: Buchhandlung des Waisenhauses, 1862.
Oxford English Dictionary, The Compact Edition of the. 1933. Oxford: Oxford University Press, 1982.
Paas, John Roger. "Ergänzende Einzelheiten zu Paul Flemings deutschen Einblattdrucken." *Wolfenbütteler Barock-Nachrichten* 11 (1984): 14–15.
―――. "The Seventeenth-century Verse Broadsheet." Diss., Bryn Mawr College, 1973.
Panofsky, Erwin. *Albrecht Dürer*. 2 vols. Princeton: Princeton University Press, 1943.
Pigman, G. W. *Grief and English Renaissance Elegy*. Cambridge and New York: Cambridge University Press, 1985.
Pyritz, Hans. "Der Liebeslyriker Paul Fleming in seinen Übersetzungen." *Zeitschrift für deutsche Philologie* 56 (1931): 410–36. Reprinted in Pyritz, *Paul Flemings Liebeslyrik*, pp. 86–111.
―――. *Paul Flemings deutsche Liebeslyrik*. Palaestra, 180. Leipzig: Mayer & Müller, 1932. Reprinted in Pyritz, *Paul Flemings Liebeslyrik*, pp. 9–11 and 113–327.
―――. *Paul Flemings Liebeslyrik: Zur Geschichte des Petrarkismus*. Palaestra, 234. Göttingen: Vandenhoeck & Ruprecht, 1963. [References are to this volume unless otherwise noted.]
―――. *Paul Flemings "Suavia."* Diss., Berlin, 1931. Munich: Kastner & Callwey, 1931. Reprinted in *Münchener Museum für Philologie des Mittelalters und der Renaissance* 5 (1931): 251–321 and in Pyritz, *Paul Flemings Liebeslyrik*, pp. 15–85.
Recke, Johann Friedrich von, and Karl Eduard Napiersky. *Allgemeines Schriftsteller- und Gelehrten-Lexikon der Provinzen Livland, Esthland und Kurland*. 4 vols. Mitau: 1827–32. Reprint. Berlin: Haude & Spenersche Verlagsbuchhandlung, 1966.
Rifkin, Joshua, et al. "Heinrich Schütz." In *The New Grove Dictionary of Music*

and Musicians, edited by Stanley Sadie, 17:1–37. London: Macmillan, 1980.
Rodenberg, Hans. "Paul Fleming und seine Rußlandreise." *Sinn und Form* 5 (1953): 232–54. First published in *Internationale Literatur* 11 (1941).
Rost, Bernhard. "Paul Fleming: Darstellung seines Lebensganges." In *Aus vergangenen Tage unserer Heimat*, edited by Richard Oertel, pp. 157–88. Hartenstein: Matthes, 1926.
Schaumann, Ursula. *Zur Geschichte der erzählenden Schäferdichtung in Deutschland*. Diss., Heidelberg. Duderstadt i. Hann.: E. C. Kohlus, 1930.
Scheer, Siegfried. "Paul Fleming 1609–1640: Seine literarhistorischen Nachwirkungen in drei Jahrhunderten." *Imprimatur* 9 (1939): 16 separately paginated pages after p. 176.
Schlesinger, Walter. *Die Landesherrschaft der Herren von Schönburg: Eine Studie zur Geschichte des Staates in Deutschland*. Quellen und Studien, 9.1. Münster and Cologne: Böhlau-Verlag, 1954.
———. "Paul Fleming." In *Sächsische Lebensbilder*, edited by Sächsische Kommission für Geschichte, 2:133–48. Leipzig: Oskar Leiner Verlag, 1938.
Schmitz, Friedrich Wilhelm. *Metrische Untersuchungen zu Paul Flemings deutschen Gedichten*. Quellen und Forschungen zur Sprach- und Culturgeschichte der germanischen Völker, 111. Strassburg: Karl J. Trübner, 1910.
Schnur, Harry, ed. and tr. *Lateinische Gedichte deutscher Humanisten*. Reclam Universal-Bibliothek, 8739/45. Stuttgart: Reclam, 1966.
Schön, Theodor. "Eine Schönburgische Hochzeitsfeier im Jahre 1632." *Schönburgische Geschichtsblätter* 4 (1897–98): 23–38.
Schröder, Rudolf Alexander. "Paul Fleming." 1935. In *Gesammelte Werke*, 3:598–651. Berlin and Frankfurt a. M.: Suhrkamp, 1952.
Schubert, Dietmar. " 'Man wird mich nennen hören . . . ': Zum poetischen Vermächtnis Paul Flemings." *Weimarer Beiträge* 30 (1984): 1687–1706.
———. *Paul Fleming: Monographische Studie unter besonderer Berücksichtigung der Wirkungsgeschichte nach 1945*. Diss., [Berlin, GDR?]. Potsdam, 1984. [Not seen.]
Segebrecht, Wulf. *Das Gelegenheitsgedicht: Ein Beitrag zur Geschichte und Poetik der deutschen Lyrik*. Stuttgart: Metzler, 1977.
Sperberg-McQueen, M. R. "Did Opitz Translate Lotichius' Elegy on Magdeburg?" *MLN* 96 (1981): 604–12.
———. "Gedichte von Paul Fleming in der Stolbergschen Leichenpredigten-Sammlung." *Jahrbuch der deutschen Schillergesellschaft* 26 (1982): 1–8.
———. "Leipzig Pastoral: Two Epithalamia by Martin Christenius, With a Note on Paul Fleming." Forthcoming in a Festschrift for George Schulz-Behrend, edited by Barbara Becker-Cantarino and Jörg-Ulrich Fechner. Chloe (Beihefte zum *Daphnis*). Amsterdam: Rodopi.
———. "Martin Opitz and the Tradition of the Renaissance Poetic Epistle." *Daphnis* 11 (1982): 519–46.
———. "Neues zu Paul Fleming: Bio-bibliographische Miszellen." *Simpliciana* 6/7 (1985): 173–83.
———. "Opitz, Fleming, and the German Poetic Epistle." Diss., Stanford University, 1981.

———. "Paul Fleming: A Report on a Newly-Found Poem and Imprints in Zwickau and Wrocław." *Michigan Germanic Studies* 12 (1986): 105–32.

———. "Paul Fleming's Inaugural Disputation in Medicine: A 'Lost' Work Found." *Wolfenbütteler Barock-Nachrichten* 11 (1984): 6–9.

———. "Ein Vorspiel zum Westfälischen Frieden: Paul Flemings 'Schreiben vertriebener Frau Germanien' und sein politischer Hintergrund." *Simpliciana* 6/7 (1985): 151–72.

Stölten, [Hermann]. "Gustav Adolf und seine Zeit in Paul Fleming's Gedichten." *Deutsch-evangelische Blätter* 21 (1896): 401–14.

Supersaxo, Liselotte. *Die Sonette Paul Flemings: Chronologie und Entwicklung.* Diss., Zürich. Singen (Hohentwiel): Steinhauser, 1956.

Szyrocki, Marian. *Die deutsche Literatur des Barock: Eine Einführung.* Rowohlts deutsche Enzyklopädie, 300/301. Sachgebiet Literaturwissenschaft. Reinbek bei Hamburg: Rowohlt, 1968.

———. *Martin Opitz.* 1956. 2d rev. ed. Munich: Beck, 1974.

Thomas, R. Hinton. *Poetry and Song in the German Baroque: A Study of the Continuo Lied.* Oxford: Clarendon Press, 1963.

Tropsch, Stephan. *Flemings Verhältnis zur römischen Dichtung.* Grazer Studien zur deutschen Philologie, 3. Graz: K. K. Universitäts-Buchdruckerei und Verlags-Buchhandlung 'Styria,' 1895.

Trunz, Erich. "Die Entwicklung des barocken Langverses." *Dichtung und Volkstum [Euphorion]* 39 (1938): 427–68.

Ulmer, Bernhard. *Martin Opitz.* Twayne's World Authors Series, 140. New York: Twayne, 1971.

Unger, Konrad. *Studien über Paul Flemings Lyrik.* Diss., Greifswald. Greifswald: F. W. Kunike, 1907.

Varnhagen von Ense, Karl August. "Paul Flemming." In his *Biographische Denkmale.* Vienna, 1825–26. 3d expanded edition, pt. 4 (Vol. 10 of *Ausgewählte Schriften von K. A. Varnhagen von Ense*), pp. 1–115. Leipzig: F. A. Brockhaus, 1872.

Volkmann, Erich. *Balthasar Venator.* Diss., Berlin. Berlin: Triltsch & Huther, 1936.

Wagenknecht, Christian. "Paul Flemings Teutsche Poemata." *Wolfenbütteler Barock-Nachrichten* 6 (1979): 378.

Waldberg, Max von. *Die deutsche Renaissance-Lyrik.* Berlin: Verlag von Wilhelm Hertz, 1888.

Wangenheim, Franz Theodor. *Paul Flemming, oder Die Gesandtschaftsreise nach Persien: Historischer Roman.* 3 vols. Leipzig: Reinhold Beyer, 1842.

Weddige, Hilkert. *Die "Historien vom Amadis auss Frankreich": Dokumentarische Grundlegung zur Entstehung und Rezeption.* Beiträge zur Literatur des XV. bis XVIII. Jahrhunderts, 2. Wiesbaden: Franz Steiner Verlag, 1975.

Wedgwood, C[icely] V[eronica]. *The Thirty Years' War.* New Haven: Yale University Press, 1939.

Weevers, Th. "The Influence of Heinsius on Two Genres of the German Baroque." *The Journal of English and Germanic Philology* 37 (1938): 524–32.

Welti, Heinrich. *Geschichte des Sonettes in der deutschen Dichtung: Mit einer Ein-*

leitung über Heimat, Entstehung und Wesen der Sonettform. Leipzig: Verlag von Veit, 1884.

Wenderoth, Georg. "Paul Fleming als Petrarkist." *Archiv für das Studium der neueren Sprachen und Literaturen* 124 (1910): 109–24.

Wiedemann, Conrad. [Review of reprint of Paul Fleming's *Deutsche Gedichte*, edited by Lappenberg]. *Germanistik* 8 (1967): 589–90.

Wilkins, Ernest Hatch. "Petrarch's *Epistola Metrica* to Pietro Alighieri." In his *Studies in the Life and Works of Petrarch*, 33–47. Cambridge, Mass.: The Mediaeval Academy of America, 1955.

Wilms, Heinz. "Das Thema der Freundschaft in der deutschen Barocklyrik und seine Herkunft aus der neulateinischen Dichtung des 16. Jahrhunderts." Diss., Kiel, 1962.

Winter, Georg. *Geschichte des Dreißigjährigen Krieges*. Allgemeine Geschichte in Einzeldarstellungen, III.3.2. Berlin: G. Grote'sche Verlagsbuchhandlung, 1893.

Witkowski, Georg. *Geschichte des literarischen Lebens in Leipzig*. Schriften der Königlich sächsischen Kommission für Geschichte, 17. Leipzig and Berlin: B. G. Teubner, 1909.

Wustmann, Rudolf. *Musikgeschichte Leipzigs in drei Bänden*. Vol. 1: *Bis zur Mitte des 17. Jahrhunderts*. Schriften der Königlich sächsischen Kommission für Geschichte, 18. Leipzig and Berlin: Teubner, 1909.

Zon, Stephen. "Imitations Petrarch: Opitz, Fleming." *Daphnis* 7 (1978): 497–512.

Index

Acken, Brigitta van, 166, 167
Ad Auroram sponsus (Sy.IX.1.6), 14, 15, 32
Ad Charitas (Sy.IX.1.1), 13, 184 (n. 12), 185 (n. 17)
Ad Dn. Johan. Hermannum Schein, . . . Obitum praematurum, Sui Filioli . . . Hieronymi, lugentem, 111
Ad Georgium Glogerum, Amicum unum, (Sy.II.3), 141–42
Ad Joannem Georgium Electorem Saxonicum (Sy.III.3), 63
Ad Lunam (Sy.IX.1.8), 15
Ad Mortam (Sy.IX.1.5), 13
Ad Reginam Opt. Max. (Sy.IX.11), 46, 193 (n. 66)
Ad Reinerum Brocmanum S. (Sy.IV.1), 142
Ad Solem. See *Idem ad Solem*
Ad Timotheum Swirseum (Sy.II.10), 142, 143, 145, 148
Ad viatorem (Sy.IX.1.20), 20
Aeschel, Martha Elisabeth Heroldin, Fleming's epicedium for, 41–42
Alcuin, 135
Alewyn, Richard, 1, 3, 4, 110, 111, 120, 131, 159, 176
Alexandrine line, 21, 22, 23, 24, 26, 27, 69, 79, 82, 108, 137, 139, 140, 158–59, 187 (n. 26 & 27). See also Elegiac alexandrines; Heroic alexandrines
Alloquutio (Sy.IX.1.15), 14, 31, 191 (n. 51)
Als Einer von seiner Liebsten verreisete (O.IV.35), 130
Als etliche seiner Freunde von ihm zogen (O.IV.7), 79, 121, 132
Als H. Görg Wilhelm Pöhmer von ihm aus Moskaw nach Deutschland verreisete (P.W.IV.23), 30
Als H. M. Elias Major Poëta Laureatus worden (P.W.IV.7), 8
Als Herr Görge Ernst Kademan Magister wurde (O.IV.18), 114
Als ihn einer seiner vertrautesten Freunde angebunden hatte an denselben (So.III.3), 151
Als sie im Schnee sich erlustirete (from P.W.III.6), 104–5
Amor (O.V.12), 114
An Ambrosien (So.IV.1), 113, 114, 203 (n. 54)
An Anemonen, die Liebste (O.V.41), 130
An Anemonen, nachdem er von ihr gereiset war (O.V.40), 126, 176
An Anna aus der Ferne (O.V.42), 189 (n. 41)
An Anna, die spröde (O.V.38), 189 (n. 41)
An Basilenen, nachdem er von ihr gereiset war (O.V.27), 121, 126, 130, 131
An den Durchlauchtigsten, Hochgebohrnen Fürsten . . . Johann Georgen, 64, 74
An denselben Fürstl. Holsteinischen Rat und Gesandten (So.III.22), 32, 190 (n. 42), 191 (n. 51)
An die baltischen Sirenen (O.V.25), 176
An die Stolze (O.V.20), 114, 115
An die Wolge zu Niesen (So.III.32), 165
An die Wolgebornen Herrn Hans Heinrichen und Herrn Christianen, Herren von Schönburg (O.IV.2), 11
An einen seiner vertrautesten Freunde (P.W.IV.49), 134, 135, 142–43, 158–66; oath to Elsabe Niehus, 143; formal characteristics, 158–59, 187 (n. 37); style, 158–59, 174; structure, 159, 175; Petrarchan elements in, 161–63; neo-Stoic thought in, 164; landscape in, 164–66; compared to other poetic epistles, 167, 175; as *Brief* or *Epistel,* 173, 174; epistolarity of, 177
An Elsabe (O.V.31), 50, 113, 114, 205 (n. 60)
An Herrn Hansen Arpenbeken (P.W.IV.51), 134, 135, 142–43, 166–72, 179; war as topic in, 28–29; compared to other poetic epistles, 167, 175; structure, 168, 175; neo-Stoic thought, 170–71; friendship as theme in, 172; style, 174
An Herrn Hartman Grahman, Fürstl. Holstein. Gesandten Leibarzt, geschrieben in Astrachan (P.W.IV.53), 154, 162, 165, 170, 208 (n. 18)
An Herrn Heinrich Nienborgen . . . in Groß-

229

Naugarod (P.W.IV.21), 73, 208 (n. 18)
An Herrn Heinrich Schützen (O.IV.15), 74–75
An Herrn Johan Klipstein (P.W.IV.15), 112, 195 (n. 18), 208 (n. 18)
An Herrn M. Christof Buhlen, von seiner Charitillen (O.IV.14), 28, 76, 126
An Herrn Magnus Schuwarten, Churfürstl. Durchlaucht zu Sachsen u.s.w. Rent-Secretarien (O.IV.1), 11, 74
An Herrn Martin Christenien über Ableben dessen Vatern, Mutter und Schwester (O.II.12), 41
An Herrn Olearien vor Astrachan der Reußen in Nagaien (P.W.IV.44), 134, 135, 142, 150–57; reference to Dohna in, 72–73; neo-Stoic thought in 145, 155, 156; obscurity of, 150, 155, 156; structure of, 151, 157, 175; excursus on German poetry, 152; style, 157, 159; compared to other poetic epistles, 168, 175; as *Brief* or *Epistel*, 173–74;
An Herzogen Friederichs zu Schleswig-Holstein Fürstl. Durchleuchtigkeit (P.W.IV.52), 208 (n. 18)
An Maria Moller und Lic. Crusius (O.V.35), 114
An sich (So.III.26), 7, 145, 155
Anagramm (P.W.II.6), 111
Anemone (O.V.37), 125, 205 (n. 60)
Anthologia Latina, 84
Arae Schönburgicae (P.W.II.1 & Sy.IX.1), 4, 87, 180; among Fleming's earliest poems, 10–11; models for, 12–21; and Scaliger's *Arae Fracastoreae*, 13–14; as epicedia, 13, 40; formal characteristics, 15, 21–24; and Heinius's *Manes Dousici*, 15–19; as amatory poetry, 16–17; printing history of, 17, 189 (n. 41); use of vernacular in, 19–21, 40; and Kirchner's epithalamial cycle, 22. See also titles of individual poems
Arcas, 36
Arpenbek, Johan, 167, 179; P.W.IV.51 for 156, 160, 166–72, 179; O.III.21 for, 167; P.W.IV.42 for, 167
Auf Ableben des Woledlen Hansen von Löser, des Jüngern (P.W.II.12), 42
Auf Abscheiden zweier Vertrauten (O.IV.36), 114

Auf das verlorne Kleinot (So.III.44), 190 (n. 42)
Auf den Jungferberg in Nagaien der Reußen (So.III.38), 165
Auf der Durchläuchtigsten Frauen, Frauen Marien Eleonoren, . . . Ankunft in Leipzig (O.IV.3), 46
Auf der edlen Marien Möllers Namenstag (O.IV.37), 114
Auf der Liebsten Demant (from P.W.III.6), 104-@5
Auf der Tugendreichen dreien Jungfrauen Annen, Magdalenen und Juden . . . von Wirths . . . Töchter . . . Absterben (O.II.5), 41, 46
Auf des Edlen Georg Seidels von Breßlau Leichbestattung (P.W.II.10), 49
Auf des Edlen und Hochgelahrten Herrn Philipp Krusens, . . . geliebten Hausfrauen Ableben (P.W.II.14), 45, 50
Auf des ehrenfesten und hochgelahrten Herrn Hartman Grahmans . . . Hochzeit (O.III.22), 151
Auf des ehrnvesten und wolgelahrten Herrn Reineri Brockmans . . . Hochzeit (P.W.III.6), 5, 82–109, 169, 180; scholars' neglect of, 83; and Opitz's *Hercinie*, 83–109; structure of, 84–88, 97, 107; unity and coherence of, 87–88, 95–96; reception of, 92; realism of, 92–95, 96; as critique of Opitz's depiction of love, 96–109; theme of love in, 96–97, 99–100, 104–5, 106–9, 111, 131; Petrarchan love in, 104–5, 108, 109; theme of *Treue*, 120–21. See also under first lines of individual poems
Auf des Fürstl. Holstein. Rats . . . Philippi Krusii, . . . Eheverlöbnüß (O.IV.32), 114
Auf des Hochedlen Herrn Peter Krußbiorn, . . . seines erstgebornen Söhnleins Absterben (O.II.13), 41, 80
Auf des Hochgelehrten Herrn Oleariens . . . Rede (P.W.IV.46), 162
Auf des Wohledlen Herrn Hieronymus Imhofs . . . Namenstag (P.W.IV.45), 156, 168, 208 (n. 18)
Auf des Wolgebornen Fräuleins, Fräulein Agnesen [sc. Elisabeth] *von Schönburg u.s.w. Beisetzung* (O.II.2), 27, 50, 190 (n. 46)

Index 231

Auf des Wolgebornen Herrn, Herrn August Siegfrieds, Herrn von Schönburg . . . Ableben (O.II.1), 27, 49, 50, 51
Auf die Italiänische Weise: O fronte serena (O.V.3), 115, 203 (n. 54)
Auf eben selbiges unter eines Andern Namen (P.W.II.8), 41
Auf eine Hochzeit in Leipzig (O.III.9), 125
Auf eine Hochzeit zu Dresden (O.III.4), 29–30
Auf einer Jungfrauen Absterben (P.W.II.4), 41
Auf eines guten Freundes Geburtstag (O.IV.4), 79, 121–22, 132
Auf Eines seinen Namenstag, in Astrachan geschrieben (So.III.58), 190 (n. 42)
Auf Eines seiner besten Freunde Geburtstag (O.IV.10), 79, 132
Auf eines von Grünental Leichbestattung (P.W.II.2), 48
Auf Frau Elisabeth Paulsens in Revel Ableben (O.II.16), 41
Auf Frau Helenen Ilgens, Herrn Peter Kuchens seligen Ehegattens, Ableben (O.II.7), 41, 47, 48
Auf Godfried Wilhelms seinen Namenstag (O.IV.13), 114
Auf H. Georg Glogers Med. Cand. seliges Ableben (P.W.II.7), 49, 149, 192 (n. 66)
Auf H. Johann Arpenbeks . . . Namenstag (P.W.IV.42), 167
Auf Herren D. Polykarpus Leysers . . . seliges Ableben (O.II.11), 8, 42, 45
Auf Herren Timothei Poli neugebornen Töchterleins Christinen ihr Absterben (O.II.14), 71
Auf Herrn Christof Schürers, . . . Leichbegängnüß (O.II.10), 29
Auf Herrn D. Daniel Dörings und Jungfrau Rosinen Schwendendörfers Hochzeit (O.III.1), 124
Auf Herrn Garlef Lüders und Jungfrau Margarethen Brauns Hochzeit in Moßkow (P.W.III.5), 187 (n. 30)
Auf Herrn Ilgens Leichbestattung (P.W.II.11), 41
Auf Herrn Johan Michels sein Doctorat (P.W.IV.8), 28
Auf Herrn Johann Casimir, Herzoge zu Sachsen, Namenstag (P.W.IV.2), 64, 208 (n. 18)

Auf Herrn Martin Münsterbergers seines geliebten Söhnleins sein Absterben (O.II.17), 30, 41
Auf Herrn Martin Rinkarts sein Tier im Rore (So.III.1), 11
Auf Herrn Martin Schörkels und Jungfrau Margarethen Putschers Hochzeit (O.III.2), 124
Auf Herrn Peter Kuchens Ableben (O.II.6), 41, 46, 47
Auf Herzogen Friedrichs zu Schleswig-Holstein . . . Namenstag (P.W.IV.54), 208 (n. 18)
Auf Jungfrau Beaten Marien Möstels Begräbnüß (O.II.8), 41, 46
Auf Jungfrau Magdalena Weinmans Ableben (O.II.4), 48–49
Auf Jungfrau Marien Schürers Begräbnüß (O.II.3), 49
Auf M. Heinrich Lütgens, revlischen Musikantens, Namenstag (O.IV.28), 114
Auf Verreisen Eines seiner guten Freunde (O.IV.19), 79, 114, 132
Auff Absterben der Edlen vnd vieltugentsamen Frawen Marthen-Elisabethen/ geborne Heroldin, 41
Aus dem Italiänischen (O.V.2), 115
Aus dem Pastor Fido (O.V.1), 115, 162
Aus H. Kaspar Barthen seinem Lateinischen Liebesscherze (P.W.V.1), 187 (n. 31)
Aus Sarbievs seinem Lateine (Ü.30), 195 (n. 19)
Auserwählte nach der einen (O.V.37), 125, 205 (n. 60)
Ausonius, 82

Bachmann, Andreas, 78
Barner, Wilfried, 3
Basilene (O.V.24), 205 (n. 60)
Bebel, Heinrich, 137
Becker-Cantarino, Barbara, 89–90
Beissner, Friedrich, 55
Beling, Oswald, 78
Beller, Manfred, 133
Bergerin, Catharina-Isabella, 78
Bloem-Hof van de Nederlantsche leught, 34
Bohemus, Johannes, 200 (n. 31)
Bornemann, Albert(us), 7, 8, 75–76
Brandes, Casparus, 188 (n. 35)
Brauer, Walter, 113–14

Brautlied (O.III.21), 114, 167
Bretschneider, Andreas, 64, 65, 66–67
Brief, 172–74
Brigittae van Acken, Arpenbecii amoribus (E.III.48), 167
Brokmann, Reiner, 82–95 passim, 131, 169, 180; Stammbucheintragung for, 87, 90–91; character in P.W.III.6, 104, 105, 106, 121; Sy.IV.1 for, 142
Brüggemann, Otto, 80, 82, 91; poems in P.W.III.6 for, 87, 88–90; conduct and reputation of, 89, 143, 148, 150, 173
Buchner, August, 91, 94, 95, 98, 188 (n. 35)
Buhle, Christoph, 28, 76

Carnap, Ernst Günter, 83
Catullus, 84, 135
Chor der Hirten (P.W.IV.25), 89–90
Christenius, Martin, 76, 78–79, 109 (n. 47), 188 (n. 35), 205 (n. 66)
Cicero, 122, 138, 148, 149, 157
Conrady, Karl Otto, 3, 138
Consolatio, 6, 41, 46, 47, 175–76
Crell, Sebastian, 113
Cross rhyme, 22. See also Elegiac alexandrines
Crusbiorn, Peter, 80

D. Ferdinandi II . . . excessus inter Mauros nunciatus (E.V.50), 73
Dach, Simon, 191 (n. 51)
Daniel, Book of, 70–71
Das getreue Elsgen (O.V.29), 113, 114
Davids des hebreischen Königs und Propheten Bußpsalme (P.W.I.1-8), 50
Deissmann, G. A., 172
Denaisius, Petrus, 123–24, 125, 131
Der klagende Bräutigam. I (P.W.II.1.d), 31, 32–33
Der klagende Bräutigam. II (P.W.II.1.e), 4, 31, 33–40, 96, 114
Der VI. Psalm (P.W.I.1), 196 (n. 30)
Des Amyntas Charitille (O.V.5), 115
Die warme Frühlingsluft macht ihren Himmel klar (from P.W.III.6), 108, 191 (n. 51)
Dohna, Karl Hannibal Burggraf von, 72–73, 154
Döring, Daniel, 124
Dörrie, Heinrich, 55, 56, 57, 67

Dousa, Janus, 14, 16, 17, 18, 19
Dünnhaupt, Gerhard, 8
Dürer, Albrecht, 65
Dürrenfeld, Eva, 4, 121, 150, 157, 162
Dutch poetry, 22, 34, 78, 136
Dyck, Joachim, 3

Edict of Restitution, 58–59, 60, 63
Ein getreues Herze wissen (O.V.30), 7, 113, 114, 115, 122, 124, 125
Eine hab' ich mir erwählet (O.V.24), 205 (n. 60)
Elegiac alexandrines, 22, 69
Elegie an das traurige Hartenstein (P.W.II.1.b), 19, 20, 22, 23, 25–27, 29, 31, 69, 132, 158, 188 (n. 39)
Elegie an sein Vaterland (P.W.IV.48), 187 (n. 31), 208 (n. 18)
Elegy, 22, 136–37
Elsgens treues Herz (O.V.30), 7, 113, 114, 115, 122, 124, 125
Epicedion in Jo. He. Scheinium (Sy.III.1), 11, 111
Epicedium: Fleming's epicedia, 5, 40–50, 111, 139; genre, 13, 40, 176; meters used in, 17
Epicedium (Sy.IX.1.19), 185 (n. 17)
Epigram, 32
Epigramma (P.W.II.1.c), 31–32, 191 (n. 51)
Epistel, 172–74
Epistle. See *Brief*; *Epistel*; Poetic epistle; Prose epistle
Epithalamium: and theme of *Treue*, 123–31, 148, 180
Erasmus, Desiderius, 137
Erlebnisdichtung, 3, 138
Es ist umsonst das Klagen (O.V.31), 50, 113, 114, 205 (n. 60)
Es ist unverwant mein Herze (O.V.29), 113, 114

Famae Ac Perennitati Nobilis et Ingeniosiss. Viri Joannis Hermanni Scheinii, . . . (M.VII.5), 111
Fechner, Jörg-Ulrich, 4, 110–11
Ferdinand II, Emperor, 58, 59, 73
Ferdinand III, Emperor, 73
Ferdinando III (E.IV.26), 73
Finckelthaus, Gottfried, 79, 80, 100–101, 106–7

Fleming, Abraham, 11–12, 51–52, 171, 179, 203 (n. 49)
Fleming, Dorothea, 12
Fleming family, 11–12, 50–52
Fleming, Paul (grandfather of poet), 11, 12
Fleming, Paul: amatory poetry and, 16–17, 24; biographies of, 2; characteristic closings of poems by, 29–31; dating of works by, 7, 11, 143–44, 183 (n. 13), 190 (n. 42), 193 (n. 71), 197 (n. 33); doctoral dissertation, 179, 185 (n. 16); earliest poems by, 10; early poems, putative destruction of, 10; epicedia by, 5, 40–50, 111, 139; epigrams of, 32; epithalamia by, 124–25, 126–31; irenicism, 64–67; meter in odes by, 204 (n. 55); pastoral tradition and, 79–80; pastoral odes by, 79; patronage, 6, 73, 75, 77, 154, 157; personal and autobiographical in poetry of, 29–31, 132, 153–54, 155–56, 168–71, 175; poetic epistles by, 134–35, 141–43, 172–78, 180; political views of, 72; position and duties of during journey, 134; posthumous reputation of, 1, 2; prosody in poetry of, 27, 38–40; reasons for leaving Germany, 6, 75, 170; remuneration for poems by, 203 (n. 49); in Reval, 80–83; style in poetry of, 24–27, 33, 35–38, 40, 68–69, 88–89, 144, 146, 157, 158–59, 165, 169, 173, 180; verse forms used by, 21–22, 185, (n. 19); war as topic in poetry of, 27–29. *See also under titles of individual poems*
Fleming, Ursula Zehler, 171
Fracastorius, Hieronymus, 13
Friedrich III, Duke of Holstein, 80, 81, 91, 134
Friendship: poetry of, 121–22, 123, 135, 180; theory of, 122, 148–49, 180; theme in Fleming's poetry, 144, 148–49, 157, 172
Früelings-Hochzeitgedichte (P.W.III.2), 50

Garber, Klaus, 96, 104, 106
Geburtstags-Gedichte (P.W.V.17), 187 (n. 31)
Gellinek, Janis, 40, 88, 89, 98–99, 102
Georgio Glogero meo (Sy.II.1), 72, 197 (n. 33)
German language: in Leipzig poetry, 20–21; in the *Arae Schönburgicae*, 19–21
German poetry. *See* Opitzian poetry
Germania: iconography of, 64–67
Gervinus, Georg Gottfried, 1, 133
Gesellschaftslied, 110, 111, 113, 120, 123, 125, 130, 131, 180
Gillespie, Gerald, 114, 115
Gloger, Georg, 30, 44, 45–46, 56, 72–73, 76, 121, 126; P.W.II.7 for, 49, 149, 192 (n. 66); Sy.II.1 for, 72, Sy.II.3 for, 141–42
Goedeke, Karl, 133
Goethe, Johann Wolfgang von, 1
Götze, Katharine Schürerin: Fleming's epicedium for, 29
Grahmann, Hartmann, 133, 143, 154, 165, 200 (n. 31), 208 (n. 18)
Grunaeus, Simon, 121
Grünthal, Julius von: P.W.II.2 for, 48
Guarini, Giovanni Battista, 117
Günther, Johann Christian, 1
Gustav Adolf (king of Sweden), 5, 44, 55, 57, 58, 59, 64, 203 (n. 49)
Gymnasium Revaliense (Sy.VII), 82

H. Dan. Heinsius sein Lateinischer Liebesscherz (P.W.V.2), 187 (n. 31)
Hanemann, Gedeon: Fleming's epicedium for, 45, 193 (n. 66)
Harper, Anthony, 79
Harsdörffer, Georg Philipp, 66, 94. *See also* Nuremberg poets
Heimliches Einverständniß (O.V.28), 113, 114, 121
Heinsius, Daniel: funerary cycles by, 12; *Lusus ad Apiculas*, 14; *Manes Lipsiani*, 14, 15; *Manes Scaligeri*, 14, 15; *Manes Dousici*, 14–@21, 22, 87, 192 (n. 60); *Ad Sidera*, 15; *Ad Solem*, 15; and Dousa, 16; Greek verse by, 19, 21; and Kirchner, 34; *Nederduytsche Poemata*, 34; *Pastorael*, 34, 197 (n. 3)
Heinsius, Nicolaas, 17
Helding, Michael, 55
Heroic alexandrines, 22
Heroic epistle, 55, 67
Heroldin, Martha Elisabeth. *See* Aeschel
Herr, wer er auch wird sein (from P.W.III.6), 87, 88–89
Herrn Fürstl. Holsteinischen Rate und Ge-

sandten u.s.w. (Philipp Kruse) . . . übersendet (So.III.12), 151
Herrn Pauli Flemingi der Med. Doct. Grabschrift (So.II.14), 7, 155, 179
Hessus, Helius Eobanus, 55, 135, 141
Heurne, Otto van, 179
Heus, hospes! (M.VII.19), 66
Hirtenlied auf eines Freundes in der Moskow gehaltener Hochzeit (O.III.17), 79
Hoe von Hoenegg, Matthias von, 60–61
Hoffmann von Fallersleben, August Heinrich, 1, 123
Höpnerus, Johannes, 23, 187 (n. 26)
Horace, 135, 151, 152
Hortulan und Lilie (O.III.10), 77
Hütten, Herman, 23
Hutten, Ulrich von, 55

Idem ad Hyemem (Sy.IX.1.3), 185 (n. 17)
Idem ad Solem (Sy.IX.1.7), 14, 15, 32
Ilgen, Helene. See Kuchen, Helene Ilgen
Imhof, Hieronymus, 133, 156, 168, 208 (n. 18)
In allen meinen Taten (O.I.4), 7, 155
In ein Stambuch, zu Niesoway in Schirvan am Kaspischen Strande, (So.III.51), 162
In Groß-Neugart der Reußen (P.W.IV.20), 28, 50, 170, 193 (n. 70), 208 (n. 18)
Institoris, Henricus, 201 (n. 34)
Irenicism, 64–67, 72
Ist er itzo schon von hinnen (from P.W.III.6), 87, 89–90

Ja, Leben, ich bin angezündet (from P.W.III.6), 105
Jägern, Amandus. See Christenius
Joanni Samueli Scheinio (E.V.3), 111
Johann Casimir, Duke of Saxony, 64
Johann Georg I, Elector of Saxony, 56, 58, 60–64, 67, 72, 73, 74, 77; Fleming's German panegyric for, 64, 74
Johann Sigismund, Elector of Brandenburg, 59
Jones, G. L., 75, 76
Junghansinn, Anna: Fleming's epithalamium for, 126–31, 132

Kirchner, Caspar, 22, 33–40
Klagegedichte über das unschuldigste Leiden und Tod unsers Erlösers Jesu Christi (P.W.I.9), 46
Klaj, Johann, 66, 94. See also Nuremberg poets
Kom, schöner Tag (from P.W.III.6), 87, 89
Kroker, Ernst, 76
Krummacher, Hans-Henrik, 13, 40, 41, 44, 45, 50, 176
Kruse, Barbara, 45, 50
Kruse, Philipp, 32, 80, 87, 89, 91
Kuchen, Helene Ilgen, 47, 48
Kuchen, Peter, 46, 48
Kühlewein, Friederich, 79

Landscape, 96, 164–66
Lang, Elisabeth, 23
Lansius, Thomas, 54
Lappenberg, J. M.: on Fleming, 2, 4, 10, 75, 111; on Fleming's poems, 31, 33, 122, 130, 143, 144, 147, 152; edition of Fleming by, 7–9, 151, 168
Laß dich nur Nichts nicht tauren (O.I.9), 155
Laß es sein, mein Sinn, und schweige (from P.W.III.6), 97, 99, 120
Laudes Gustavi Adolphi Magni, Sueonum Regis (Sy.III.4), 59
Leipzig Conference, 57–58, 59, 60, 62, 64–67
Letter. See Brief; Epistel; Poetic epistle; Prose epistle
Leyser, Polycarpus, 8, 45
Libri Manium Glogerianorum, 45, 149
Liefländische Schneegräfin (P.W.III.7), 111–12, 113
Life as dream, motif of, 147
Lipsius, Justus, 14, 137, 145–46, 170, 172
Literae Basilenae S. (E.III.45), 143
Locus amoenus, 164, 165, 166
Lohenstein, Daniel Caspar von, 71
Lohmeier, Dieter, 143
Lotichius Secundus, Petrus, 135, 136, 140, 141, 172–73, 174, 188 (n. 36)
Love, theme of, in Fleming's poetry. See under Auf des ehrnvesten und wolgelahrten Herrn Reineri Brockmans . . . Hochzeit; Petrarchan love and love poetry
Luck, Georg, 172
Lusus ad apiculas (Sy.IX.1.12), 14

M. Adamo Oleario, Legationis Secretario (Sy.II.14), 142
M. Steyero Propempticum (M.V.21), 45–46, 126
Madrigal (O.V.7), 114, 115, 189 (n. 41)
Madrigals, 117
Major, Elias, 8
Mandelsloh, Albrecht von, 149
Marie Eleonor (queen of Sweden), 46
Marot, Clément, 136
Matthiä, Salomon, 143, 182 (n. 11)
MDCXXXII (O.IV.5), 79, 132
Mein Unglück ist zu groß (O.V.32), 113, 114, 130
Merck, Johann, 113
Meyer, Heinrich, 83
Michael, Tobias, 112, 113
Micyllus, Jacob, 135
Misogyny: in Opitz's Hercinie, 102–4, 106–7, 109; in Finckelthaus's Floridan, 106–7
Moscow, 81, 90
Moller family, 82, 158
Moller, Johann, 82
Moller, Katharine, 158
Montreux, Nicolas de, 36–37
Morhof, Daniel Georg, 1
Möstel, Beata Maria, 46
Müller, Günther, 109, 113, 116
Münster, Sebastian, 66
Münsterberger, Martin, 81
Muß sie gleich sich itzund stellen (O.V.28), 113, 114, 121
Myth of the four empires, 70–71

Nach des VI. Psalmens Weise (O.I.4), 7, 155
Nach seinem Traume an seinen vertrautesten Freund (P.W.IV.50), 75, 134, 135, 142, 143–50, 151, 160, 161, 163, 164; compared to other poems, 68, 150, 168, 175; dating of, 143–44; obscurity of, 143, 144, 145, 149–50, 151, 155, 159; structure of, 144–45, 175; friendship in, 144, 148–49; neo-Stoic thought in, 145–46, 147; style in, 159; as Brief or Epistel, 173–74
Nauwach, Johann, 112
Nelson, Lowry, 29
Nemesis, 163

Neo-Latin poetry: influence of on Fleming, 12–16, 22
Neo-Stoic thought, 145–56, 147; and Fleming's epicedia, 5, 45–50, 176; in Fleming's love poetry, 99, 132, 176; and Opitz, 46, 99, 141, 192 (n. 63); in Fleming's poetic epistles, 145–46, 147, 155, 156, 164, 170–71, 176
Newald, Richard, 4
Niehus, Anna, 2, 122, 176, 179; O.V.40 to, 126; poems for, 3, 109, 111, 113, 114, 116, 120, 121, 122, 131
Niehus, Elsabe, 2, 122, 126, 167, 176, 182 (n. 11); poems for, 3, 109, 111, 113, 114, 116, 120, 121, 122, 131; and P.W.IV.50, 143, 147; and P.W.IV.49, 143
Niehus family, 179
Niehus, Heinrich, 179
Nienborg, Heinrich, 73
Nuremberg poets, 83
Nüßler, Bernhard Wilhelm, 91, 94, 95, 98

Occasional poetry, 138–39, 140, 167, 177
Olearius, Adam, 78, 80, 81, 94, 133, 134, 149, 150, 167; Sy.II.12 for, 8; 1629 epicedium by, 23; Hirten-Gespräch, 78, 208 (n. 26); P.W.IV.44 for, 72, 150–57; character in P.W.III.6, 91, 92, 93, 95; Sy.II.14 for, 142; and P.W.IV.50, 143, 144; and Brüggemann, 148, 150, 173; Sieges- vnd Triumffs-Fahne, 152; P.W.IV.49 for, 158–66;
Opitz, Martin, 1, 6, 33, 55, 111, 112, 136; ACh Liebste laß vns eilen, 108; ALhier in dieser wüsten Heydt, 115; Als er auß Siebenbürgen sich zurück anheim begab, 140; amatory poetry, view of, 16–17; An eine Hochfürstliche Person, 88–89; An H. David Müllern/ vber seiner Haußfrawen Marien Renischin absterben, 193 (n. 68); An Herrn Johann Seußius, 140–41, 142, 177; An Herrn Zincgrefen, 140–41, 142, 177; An Nüßlern, 207 (n. 16); Antwort auff Herrn Balthasar Venators teutsches Carmen, 140; Aristarchus, 46; Auff Herrn Johann Mayers vnd Jungfraw Margarethen Gierlachin Hochzeit, 162; Begräbnuß Gedichte. Auff den tödtlichen abgang Jhr Fürstl. Gn. Hertzog Jörg Rudolffs . . .

Ehegemahlin, 31; *Brich an/ du schöner tag*, 87, 90–91; *Buch von der Deutschen Poeterey*, 40, 108, 136, 158; *COridon sprach mit Verlangen*, 34; Dohna and, 72–73, 154; *Es ist gewagt*, 97, 98; friendship, theme in poetry of, 122, 123; *Galathee*, 197 (n. 3); *Hipponax ad Asterien*, 186 (n. 24); *Ihr/ Himmel/ lufft vnnd wind*, 108, 191 (n. 51); *Ist mein hertze gleich verliebet*, 97, 98, 100–101, 106; *JSt Liebe lauter nichts*, 108, 162; *Meine Frewde die mich bindet*, 105–6; misogyny of, 102–4, 106–7; pastoral tradition and, 78–79; personal in poetry of, 31, 141, 174–75; poetic epistles by, 139–41, 150, 167, 174–75, 176–78, 180; politics of, 5; prosody in poetry of, 27, 38; rhyme in poetry of, 24; *Schäfferey von der Nimfen Hercinie*, See *Schäfferey . . .*; *Sechstine*, 105; *Sonnet über die augen der Astree*, 105; style in poetry of, 27, 88–89; *Sylvarum libri tres*, 141; *Trostlied*, 40; *Weil mein Verhengniß wil*, 97–98, 146; *WOl dem der weit von hohen dingen*, 101

Opitzian metrics: in Leipzig poetry, 23; and Fleming's poetry, 22, 23, 40

Opitzian poetry: in Leipzig, 20–21, 107, 187 (n. 26 & 27); Brokmann and, 82; theme in P.W.IV.44, 151, 152; and Schein, 112, 120; G. W. Pöhmer and 199 (n. 25)

Orliens, Andinum d' (pseud. for Olearius?), 78

Ovid, 55, 135, 152, 162, 172

Pastoral tradition in Renaissance and in Germany, 78–79

Persia, expedition to, 1, 80–81, 133–35; effects of, on Fleming's poetry, 2, 6, 133–35; and Fleming's neo-Stoicism, 45; Fleming's reasons for joining, 75; organization of, 134; Fleming's attitude to, 142, 143–44; hardships of, 150, 154–55, 168, 169, 179; effects of, on Fleming, 170

Petrarch, Francesco, 55, 108, 135, 138, 139

Petrarchan love and love poetry: and Fleming's love poetry, 3, 99–100, 109–10, 125, 131, 176; and *Hercinie*, 97, 98, 99–100, 108–9; and P.W.III.6, 99–100, 104–5, 108, 109; and friendship poetry, 121; contrasted to epithalamia, 124; and P.W.IV.49, 161–63; motifs in Opitz's poetry, 162

Petro Crusbiornio, . . . Odae germanicae dedicatio (E.VI.18), 80

Petrus, Salomon, 142

Philyrena (O.V.10), 97, 99, 120

Plavius, Johannes, 203 (n. 52)

Pléiade, 136

Plutarch, 151

Poetic epistle, 6; in neo-Latin, 22, 135–36, 139, 141–42; history of, 135–36; arrangement of topics in, 136, 139, 141; theory of, 136–38; subjects appropriate to, 136, 137–39, 141; relationship to prose epistle, 137–38; verse form of, 137, 139; and occasional poetry, 167; *Brief* or *Epistel?*, 172–74. See also under titles of Fleming's poetic epistles

Pöhmer, Georg Pius, 133

Pöhmer, Georg Wilhelm, 80, 94, 133; P.W.IV.23 for, 30; character in P.W.III.6, 91, 92, 93, 94, 95

Polus, Timotheus: O.II.14 for daughter of, 71; character in P.W.III.6, 91, 92, 94, 95, 104; Sy.IV.2 for, 142; Sy.II.22 for, 142, 143–44, 156, 161

Pontanus, Jacobus, 136

Propempticum Cl. Oleario scriptum (Sy.II.12), 8

Prose epistle, 137–38, 141

Prüfer, Arthur, 118

Putscher, Margarethe, 79, 124–25

P.W.III.6. See *Auf des ehrnvesten und wolgelahrten Herrn Reineri Brockmans . . . Hochzeit*

Pyritz, Hans: on Fleming's life and poetic development, 2, 4, 111, 133; assessed by Alewyn, 3; influence of, 4, 111; on *Treue* in Fleming's poetry, 5–6, 109–10, 131; on Lappenberg's edition, 7, 8; on Fleming's *Suavia*, 12; on Fleming's optimism, 50, 176; on Schein and Fleming, 113; on *Gesellschaftslied* and Fleming, 113, 120; on Fleming's and Opitz's poetry of friendship, 122–24

Quintilian, 152

R. Brockman an seine Dorothea (O.V.14), 105
Recapitulation scheme, 31, 32, 108
Regnart, Jakob, 110, 111, 120
Rhyme, 23–24, 189 (n. 41). See also Cross rhyme
Rinckart, Martin, 11, 200 (n. 31)
Rist, Johann, 22, 66, 71
Rodenberg, Hans, 56, 57
Ronsard, Pierre, 108, 158
Rosenthal, Dorotha Eleonore von, 198 (n. 16)
Rudel, Elias, 64, 65, 66, 73
Rusterholz, Peter, 105–6

S. Augustinus sein (So.I.19), 162
Sabinus, Georg, 55, 135, 196 (n. 29)
Salomoni Petraeo, Legationis Persicae Sacerdoti, (Sy.IV.6), 142
Sannazaro, Jacopo, 103
Scaliger, Joseph Justus, 14
Scaliger, Julius Caesar, 12, 13–14, 15, 136, 175
Schäferei, genre, 78, 83
Schäfferey von der Nimfen Hercinie, by Martin Opitz, 5, 78, 79, 82; compared to P.W.III.6, 83–88; structure of, 84–88, 97, 103, 107; characters in, compared to those in P.W.III.6, 91–92; realism and, 92–95, 96; lack of unity in, compared to P.W.III.6, 95–96; love as theme in, 96–109; parodied by Finckelthaus, 100–101; female figures in, 102–4; witch episode in, 102–4; misogyny in, 102–4, 106–7, 109; Opitz's sources for, 103; in secondary literature, 103. See also under first lines of poems under Opitz
Schaffgotsch family, 86, 92, 152
Schaffgotsch, Hans Ulrich, 86
Schaumann, Ursula, 83
Schein, Hieronymus (son of Johann Hermann), Fleming's epicedium for, 111
Schein, Johann Hermann: Sy.III.1 for, 11; putative influence on Fleming's poetry, 110–11, 113–20; Fleming's epicedia for, 111; Fleming's references to, 111–12; Fleming's personal relationship to, 112–13; Studenten-Schmauss, 112, 113; Musica boscareccia, 112, 113, 114–17; Diletti pastorali, 114–15, 117; Venus-Kräntzlein, 114, 117–20; Filli deine lieb Euglein klar, 115; Sieh da, mein lieber Coridon, 115–16; O Scheiden, o bitter Scheiden, 116; Aurora schön mit ihrem Haar, 117; and Gesellschaftslied, 120; and Opitzian poetry, 112, 120; Mit Freuden, mit Scherzen, 203 (n. 54); O Amarilli zart, 204 (n. 54)
Schindschersitzky, 79
Schinstern, Mauritius. See Christenius
Schirmer, David, 64
Schlesinger, Walter, 56, 75, 111
Schmuck, Vincentius, 42
Schönburg family, 6, 11–12, 50–52
Schönburg, August Siegfried von, 27, 49, 50, 51
Schönburg, Elisabeth von, 27, 50
Schönburg, Hugo II von, 12
Schönburg, Katharina von, 12, 50
Schönburg-Penig, Wolf III von, 12
Schönburg-Remse, Johann Heinrich von, 12, 37, 51
Schönburg-Waldenburg, Maria Juliane von, 10, 12, 16, 20, 25, 37, 50
Schörkel, Martin, 79, 124–25
Schottel, Justus Georg, 66
Schreiben vertriebener Frau Germanien (P.W.IV.1), 5, 53–54, 67–71, 169, 187 (n. 31); in secondary literature, 54–57; as heroic epistle, 55; dating of, 57; historical background to, 57–60; politics reflected in, 60–64, 72–73; style and structure of, 68–70; epistolary traits in, 69; myth of four empires in, 70–71; and Saxon patronage, 73–74
Schröder, Rudolf Alexander, 75
Schürer, Christoph, 29
Schürer, Maria, 49
Schürer, Zacharias, 23, 187 (n. 26)
Schürerin, Katharine. See Götze
Schütz, Heinrich, 74–75, 77, 78, 112, 192 (n. 62)
Schuwart, Magnus, 74
Schwendendörffer, Rosine, 124
Screvelius, Ewald, 179
Sebillet, Thomas, 136
Secundus, Janus, 17, 136
Segebrecht, Wulf, 3
Seidel, Georg, 49
Seneca, 171

Seußius, Johann, 11, 140, 141, 142, 177
Si c'est pour mon pucellage (anonymous), 34
Sidney, Sir Philip, 78
Sidoniae conjugi Scheinianae (E.V.1), 10
So viel Athen und Rom (from P.W.III.6), 87, 90–91
Sonnet. *An das hochedle Haus Schönburg* (P.W.II.1.a), 19, 20, 23, 24–25, 27, 29
Sonnet: genre and form, 22, 24, 32, 189 (n. 42)
Sprenger, Jacobus, 201 (n. 34)
Steyer, Salomon, 45–46, 126; Fleming's epithalamium for, 126–31, 132
Stigel, Johannes, 55
Stölten, Hermann, 55–56, 57, 58, 61, 72
Stuttgart court festivals, 66
Suavia (Sy.VIII), 12, 16, 17
Super Funere Cujusdam (M.III.18), 183 (n. 15)
Super nebula miranda in triumfali obitu Gustavi Magni (Sy.V.1), 203 (n. 49)
Supersaxo, Liselotte, 4, 7, 8, 113, 147
Swirsen, Timotheus, 142, 143, 145, 148
Sylvius (name for Fleming), 77
Szyrocki, Marian, 57

Taedae Schönburgicae (P.W.III.1 & 2; P.W.V.1 & 2; & Sy.IX.3), 50, 193 (n. 71)
Tasso, Torquato, 117
Temme, Dorothea, 82
Teütsche Poemata: dating of, 183 (n. 13)
Thalia, 151
Thaumantis, 15, 16
Theater metaphor, 147, 164
Theocritus, 78, 103
Thirty Years' War: effects of, 25, 58, 76, 152–53, 169
Thomas, Michael, 44; Fleming's epicedium for, 30, 31, 42–44, 76, 132, 193 (n. 66)
Thomasschule, 110, 112–13
Tilly, Johann Tserklaes von, 44, 57
Timotheo Polo S. (Sy.IV.2), 142
Timotheo Polo Suo S. D. (Sy.II.22), 142, 143–44, 156, 161
Treue, theme of: in Fleming's poetry, 5, 107, 109–11, 113, 114, 120–32, 180
Treue Pflicht (O.V.32), 113, 114, 130

Tropsch, Stephan, 133

Über den ungewöhnlichen Sturm (So.III.43), 192 (n. 62)
Über den Zusammenfluß der Wolgen und Kamen (So.III.36), 165
Über eine Leiche (P.W.II.3), 41, 183 (n. 15)
Über Herrn Johan von Wangersheim erstgebornen Söhnleins Kunradens Absterben an die Freundschaft (O.II.15), 41
Überschriften, 32
Unger, Konrad, 114, 121, 123
Ursinus Velius, Caspar, 136

Varnhagen von Ense, Karl August, 56, 75, 143
Velius. *See* Ursinus
Venator, Balthasar, 91, 94, 95; character in *Hercinie*, disquisition on love by, 98, 102, 104, 105, 106
Vers communs, 22, 89, 137, 139, 140, 158, 159
Verse epistle. *See* Poetic epistle
Vetzerin, Rosine, 79
Virgil, 78, 103
Vives, Joannes Ludovicus, 137, 157

War, theme of: in Fleming's poems, 27–29
Was tun doch wir, daß wir die süßen Jahre (in P.W.III.6), 107–8
Weckherlin, Georg Rodolph, 31
Wedgwood, C. V., 58
Weinmann, Magdalena, 48–49
Wie er wolle geküsset sein (O.V.15), 104, 113, 114
Wie? Ist die Liebe Nichts? Was liebt man denn im Lieben? (from P.W.III.6): 108–9
Wiedemann, Conrad, 4
Wilkins, Ernst Hatch, 173
Wilms, Heinz, 122, 135, 143, 157
Wirth, Anna, Magdalene, & Judith, 46

Zehler Fleming, Ursula. *See* Fleming, Ursula Zehler
Zincgref, Julius Wilhelm: 1624 *Anhang*, 12, 22, 31, 33, 123; Opitz's poetic epistle for, 140, 142, 177
Zur Wechselburg (O.IV.6), 79, 132

www.ingramcontent.com/pod-product-compliance
Lightning Source LLC
Chambersburg PA
CBHW020751160426
43192CB00006B/302